Liquid Light

Liquid Light

Ayahuasca Spirituality

and the

Santo Daime Tradition

G. William Barnard

Columbia University Press

New York

Columbia University Press
Publishers Since 1893
New York   Chichester, West Sussex
cup.columbia.edu

Library of Congress Cataloging-in-Publication Data
Names: Barnard, G. William (George William), 1955– author.
Title: Liquid light : Ayahuasca spirituality and the Santo Daime tradition/
G. William Barnard.
Description: New York : Columbia University Press, 2022. |
Includes bibliographical references and index.
Identifiers: LCCN 2021043554 (print) | LCCN 2021043555 (ebook) |
ISBN 9780231186605 (cloth) | ISBN 9780231186612 (trade paperback) |
ISBN 9780231546720 (ebook)
Subjects: LCSH: Santo Daime (Cult)—Case studies. |
Ayahuasca ceremony—Brazil—Case studies. | Hallucinogenic drugs
and religious experience—Case studies.
Classification: LCC BL2592.S25 B37 2022 (print) | LCC BL2592.S25 (ebook) |
DDC 299/.93—dc23/eng/20211116
LC record available at https://lccn.loc.gov/2021043554
LC ebook record available at https://lccn.loc.gov/2021043555

Cover design: Noah Arlow
Cover image: Mandala image on the cover by the gifted artist and daimista J.C.

Contents

Acknowledgments

Writing *Liquid Light* has been a multiyear, multi-individual, and (dare I say) multidimensional process. Not surprisingly, therefore, I'm grateful for the opportunity to thank everyone who helped to make this book possible.

First and foremost, I want to thank my beloved wife Sandra for her steady and ever-present love over the years. It can be challenging when your husband disappears into the rain forest for several months at a pop, but throughout it all she was unfailingly supportive. I especially want to thank her for the enormous time and energy that she selflessly offered while reading a later draft of this text. Her keen and insightful editorial suggestions came right when I needed them most.

Thanks as well to Jonathan Goldman who, along with his wife Jane Seligson, introduced me to the Santo Daime and nurtured my development during the early days of my involvement with this path. Here's hoping that my depiction of our first retreat together is at least somewhat close to how they remember it.

I am also grateful to Taran Rosenthal for his ongoing and heartwarming friendship. His encouraging words after reading an early draft of *Liquid Light* meant the world to me.

This book was radically transformed, for the better, as a result of the loving yet insightful editorial suggestions offered by C.C., one of my dearest friends in the Santo Daime. Few people (if any) gave the book more time than he did. Only he knows how much he helped me through that one really rough patch. He (and his wife S.C.) truly light up my life.

Aurah has also always had my back during many of the years I spent research-ing and writing *Liquid Light*. And the website simply wouldn't have happened without her. Thank you so much, Aurah. Your selfless dedication and hard work have been a priceless gift to me. And thank you as well to all of the people of Céu da Luz do Amor Divino—you all have a special place in my heart.

I also want to thank Marc Blainey, a fellow scholar of the Santo Daime, for his insightful editorial comments. Marc embodies engaged, careful, and tuned-in scholarship at its best.

And Jeff Kripal, dear friend and gifted scholar of the humanities, was willing to give me a careful, arriving just at the right-moment, reading of a later version of this text, even in the middle of his crazy-busy schedule. His detailed and helpful comments were invaluable.

And thanks as well to Jeff for introducing me to Mike Murphy and Esalen. Those week-long seminars with smart people talking about intriguing topics in that beautiful place were a true godsend and offered a context for me to think through some of the central topics of this text. Thanks, Mike—you are an ongoing inspiration to me.

And Rachel Harris, God bless her, read a really early (and really long!) draft of *Liquid Light* and was always so positive and supportive in her feedback. Her heartfelt words of encouragement meant so much to me.

And Bill Richards's words of wisdom came true, even if I never believed that I could do it (amazingly, I actually was able to cut one-third of the book). Thanks so much, Bill, for being the shining person you are.

And thanks as well to that Santo Daime scholar par excellence, Edward MacRae, not only for welcoming me so warmly into his home in Salvador and for sharing with me some hard-to-locate books in Portuguese, but also for supporting my dogged attempts to get funding for the research that undergirds this text.

I am also deeply grateful for the encouraging words and courageous example of Chris Bache. He has blazed a path that I follow with profound appreciation.

And I am thankful for the time given by the collection of daimistas who graciously volunteered to read a draft of *Liquid Light*. Thanks so much to N.S. who shepherded this process with good-natured grace; to D.L.D. for his astute editorial suggestions; to P.S. for his legal insights; to J.M. for letting me know how much he loved the book; and finally to J.B. for the gift of his supportive encouragement.

And *Liquid Light* would never have been published if not for the kindly yet dogged persistence of my editor at Columbia University Press, Wendy Lochner. Thanks so much for believing in me, Wendy (and for all of your patience with me as well!). And thanks also to Lowell Frye, an associate editor at Columbia University Press, for all his help in the production phase of the book.

I was also blessed to have the deeply attuned and deeply skilled assistance of the brother/sister dynamic duo, R.C. and J.C. They are both astonishingly gifted human beings. R.C. played and produced all of the music for the recordings of my hymns, and J.C. received, and then artistically expressed, the mandala that is featured on the cover of *Liquid Light* and on the book's website.

And this book could never have been written without the sparkly eyed, down-to-earth, flat-out fun conversations that I have had (for over ten years!) with Cristina B., my gift from God Portuguese tutor. Thank you so much, Cristina, for sharing the delights of this beautiful language with me.

Cristina's congenial and hardworking daughter, Caroline B. was also a big help to me—she transcribed and helped to translate a series of recorded interviews I had made during my first visit to Brazil.

Thanks as well to Southern Methodist University for providing the research funds that made that transcription/translation possible. And a special thanks to my colleagues in the Religious Studies Department for fondly putting up with their more or less mystical colleague.

And I am grateful to the American Academy of Religion for the individual research grant that was so generously given to me in 2011—those funds helped make an early three-week trip to Brazil possible.

I was also blessed to have received the disciplined and good-natured hard work of a number of research assistants: Marne Erasmus, Meghan Beddingfield, and Gabriel Garza somehow managed to appear just when I needed them. Their hours spent typing up journals from my fieldwork and organizing hundreds of pages of notes about the historical development of the Santo Daime into a coherent whole helped make this book (and the website) possible.

My heartfelt thanks as well to all of the daimistas in all of the Santo Daime centers that I visited in Brazil who welcomed this North American researcher with open arms. My thanks as well to Luciano and Maurén M., who made me feel so at home in their apartment in Rio after my stint in Céu do Mapiá (and then a couple of years later accompanied me to a Daime-bioenergetic retreat in the mountains outside Rio).

I also want to express my profound gratitude to Mestre Irineu and all of the elders of the Santo Daime who have served as beacons of the Light of the Santo Daime. And my heartfelt prayer of thanks as well to all the divine Beings who have guided and continue to guide me on this magical path of spiritual awakening and transformation.

And finally, this book is dedicated to all of the courageous and dedicated people who have led and continue to lead Santo Daime churches throughout the world, especially T.H. and his wife H.H. who have been and continue to be an inspiration to me with their love, humility, and steadfast commitment to this wondrous, if at times challenging, spiritual path.

Liquid Light

Introduction

A lot has been written recently about the therapeutic potential of psychedelics.[1] But very little has been written about what it's like when an entire religion forms around a psychedelic substance. It is my hope that *Liquid Light* will begin to address this lacuna by offering an in-depth immersion into the complex and fascinating world of the Santo Daime—a relatively new religion that emerged out of the Amazon rainforest region of Brazil in the middle of the twentieth century and now has churches throughout the world. It is a religion based on the sacramental use of *ayahuasca*, a psychedelic brew that, in the Santo Daime, is only consumed within a tightly structured liturgical format. The Santo Daime is a "hybridic" religion that weaves together folk Catholicism, West African religions, the Kardecist Spiritist tradition, neoesoteric modes of discourse, and indigenous/*vegetalista* practices and assumptions into its own utterly unique and inherently congruent tapestry of religious beliefs and rituals.[2]

In *Liquid Light*, I hope to serve as your proxy—to let you, as it were, see through my eyes (and hear through my ears, etc.) how I entered into this intriguing world for the first time and then, slowly, step by step, began to make sense of what was taking place both within and around me. This book is my attempt to describe, in a way that is as highly personal and vivid as possible, some of what I have encountered during the more than fifteen years that I've been drinking *Daime*, the name given by the Santo Daime tradition to ayahuasca. (During this time, I would guess that I participated in well over four hundred ceremonies.) In *Liquid Light*, I focus primarily on my two-and-a-half-month stay (from June to August in 2010) in Céu do Mapiá, the intentional community created in the early 1980s in the middle of the Brazilian Amazon rainforest that is the epicenter of the most prominent "line" of the Santo Daime.

> To be consistent in my terminology, when I write about the "Daime," I'm always referring to the sacramental brew, whereas the term "Santo Daime" refers to the religious tradition. I mention this because daimistas (practitioners of the Santo Daime tradition) are not always quite so consistent, often saying, "I've been in the Daime now for five years," when referring to the religion, and saying, "We're going to have another serving of the Santo Daime," when referring to the sacramental brew. In addition, all of the names of people in this text are pseudonyms, except for individuals who are well-known, public figures within the Santo Daime tradition, as well as a few friends who have given me explicit permission to use their actual names.

In *Liquid Light*, I reflect on the beauty, richness, and complexity of the Santo Daime religious tradition, underscoring the crucial difference between taking psychedelics as part of a committed, disciplined, ongoing, spiritual path and taking psychedelics in a recreational or even therapeutic way. However, I make no claims here to represent "the" Santo Daime—this entheogenic tradition (i.e., a tradition in which psychedelics are used with an explicitly spiritual intention) is much too complex, changeable, and multifaceted for any one "voice" to somehow "capture" it. I also make no claims that reading this book is, in any way, a substitute for just plunging in and drinking Daime and singing hymns for hours within one of the ritual structures that the Santo Daime tradition provides. But *Liquid Light* can at least offer its readers a glimpse into just how magical and mysterious the universe is when we peer beneath the surface, and how dramatically most of us have underestimated our inner capacity to connect with, and learn about, previously hidden strata of our own consciousness. It is my hope that after reading this book, readers will come away with the understanding that, at least in the case of the Santo Daime, psychedelics can be used reverently, as genuine sacraments, and that this religion with roots in the Amazon rainforest is, at least for many people, a powerfully transformative and profoundly illuminative spiritual path. (I also hope that the name *Liquid Light* itself will evoke not only the Light-infused liquid of the Daime but also the shimmering light of spiritual insight that it can catalyze.)

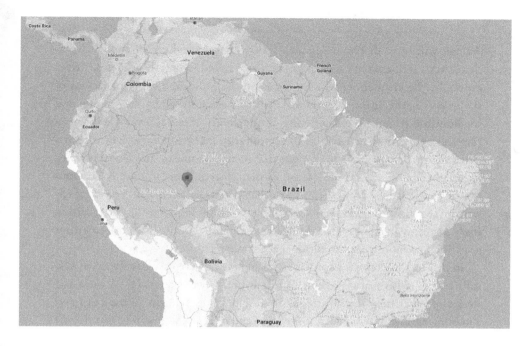

FIGURE INT.1 Map of Céu do Mapiá

NOT YOUR TYPICAL ACADEMIC TEXT

As you will soon discover, *Liquid Light* is by no means your standard academic text. It does contain chapters that are crafted in overtly academic prose, especially the chapters in which I focus on the philosophical implications of *mirações* (i.e., the visionary/mystical experiences catalyzed by the Daime) and mediumship (the conscious offering of one's body/mind as a vehicle for nonphysical beings and/or energies to temporarily manifest themselves within a ritual context), as well as the chapters that focus on some of the central psychological, sociological, and ethical issues that emerge from an overtly religious use of psychedelics. Nonetheless, at other times, I switch the "voice" of my writing to reflect the perspective of someone who is immersed in the tradition itself, resulting in chapters that look and sound much more like a travelogue or a spiritual memoir than a traditional academic text.

In this text, therefore, I consciously attempt to write in a way that is as pluralistic and multivocal as possible. While at times I will express myself as an academic, at other times I will write as an initiate of the religion. What can I say? I'm both. Insider and outsider, as well as something else, something that doesn't fit well within any neatly defined category.

I have to confess that I've actually enjoyed this sort of rhetorical balancing act, although I'll admit that it can at times be rather daunting. While writing this book, I've often felt a bit like I've been (as they say in Portuguese) *equilibrando os pratos* (literally, "balancing the plates"), in that I've felt something like a juggler who is working extremely hard, albeit with as much ease as possible, to keep several plates simultaneously spinning in the air. I've actually enjoyed the challenge of writing in a way that my academic colleagues can respect, while also writing a book that is accessible to a wider, educated audience intrigued by psychedelic spirituality, and at the same time simultaneously speaking to, and accurately reflecting, the experiential reality of *daimistas*—knowing that each of these three audiences possesses radically different standards for what counts as "good writing."

This is therefore *not* going to be one of those books written about the Santo Daime tradition, and I've read many of them, that gives you the impression that the author has never even taken the tiniest sip of this potent liquid. While the vast majority of scholarly accounts of the Santo Daime do a wonderful job of describing the ritual behavior and central beliefs of daimistas, at times it can appear as though these accounts are so concerned with uncovering the economic, political, and cultural underpinnings of the Santo Daime tradition (which is what academics are, of course, trained to do!) in a way that is "objective" or "neutral," that any sense of the awe-inspiring magic that frequently emerges within a Santo Daime "work" (i.e., ritual) can be hard to find.[3]

It is my hope that at least some of the patina of that magic will shine in and through *Liquid Light*, especially during the first-person, immersive, depictions of what it feels like, from within, to be a daimista. Hopefully in and through this text you will discover not only what it's like to be right in the middle of Santo Daime ceremonies, but also, perhaps more importantly, you will get glimpse into what it feels like to be within the mind and body (and subtle body—more on that later) of a daimista—what it feels like to be someone who is a regular and deeply committed practitioner of this relatively new religious tradition.

On the website for this book, you will find a glossary (www.liquidlightbook. com/glossary) that lists the major technical terms found in this text, terms that are italicized the first time that they appear. You will also discover two appendixes: (1) "Psychedelics 101"—a straight-to-the-point introductory depiction of the bedrock basics of what anyone interested in psychedelics should know about these transformative substances (www.liquidlightbook. com/psychedelics); and (2) "Santo Daime 101"—a highly compressed account of the key beliefs and practices of the Santo Daime tradition (www .liquidlightbook.com/santodaime). On this same website, you will also find two documents that, taken together, offer a compressed outline of the historical unfolding of the Santo Daime tradition. The first, "The Historical Development of the Santo Daime: Section One—The Life and Work of Mestre Irineu," focuses on the almost-seven-foot-tall black man in Brazil who was the founder of the Santo Daime tradition (www.liquidlightbook.com /mestre). The second document, "The Historical Development of the Santo Daime: Section Two—The Life and Work of Padrinho Sebastião," focuses on the charismatic, white-bearded, prophetic figure who began what is currently the largest lineage of the Santo Daime (www.liquidlightbook.com /padrinho). On the website you can also find "Supplemental Materials," a placeholder for an assortment of other material related to the Santo Daime tradition that simply could not be contained within this already voluminous text (www.liquidlightbook.com/supplemental).

While *Liquid Light* is at times rigorously academic, you won't find any colorful pictures of brain scans of people who have taken psychedelics in this text. (Not that there's anything wrong with those sorts of images, as long as we remain keenly aware of the severe limitations of what those pictures can actually tell us about the complexities of human consciousness.) Instead, this text allows me to explore something that is every bit as valuable as these scientific studies, that is, what psychedelics reveal about the depths of what it means to be human; what they uncover about the multidimensional nature of reality; and what they have to say about who we are and what we have the potential to become. I'm a religious studies scholar. I get to talk about these sorts of issues.

And yet, I'm also not a typical religious studies scholar, in that, at least primarily, I do not focus my attention on many of the issues that concern many religious studies scholars: gender, race, indigenous rights, colonization. I'm keenly aware of the crucial importance of these issues but exploring them is the job of others—not mine. My job is different. My job is to draw upon the cumulative knowledge and richness of my life as a religious studies scholar—someone with several decades of study in and books about the psychological and philosophical implications of nonordinary states of consciousness *and* someone who is an initiate in the Santo Daime religion—to create the most thoughtful and clearly expressed depiction possible of the complex layers of the Santo Daime religious tradition. My job is to infuse *Liquid Light* with the sum total of my decades of ongoing attempts to look deeply into the nature of mystical experience, consciousness, and a multitude of nonordinary experiences and events (i.e., trance, possession, shamanic journeys, visionary episodes, miraculous healings, psi phenomena). My job is to draw upon the philosophical perspective of two brilliant thinkers whose work I know well and have written books about—William James and Henri Bergson—to better understand the underlying dynamics of the visionary/mystical experiences (mirações) that I began to have while drinking the Daime. My job is to attempt, quasi-mediumistically, to give you, the reader, the inner "feel" of what it's like to be a daimista—what it's like to have your consciousness open and flower under the impact of drinking Daime; what it's like to incorporate, in the spontaneous movements of your own body, within a highly charged ritual setting, the energies and consciousnesses of a vast range of nonphysical beings. My job is to attempt to give you a "taste" of the lived experience and richness of what it's like to be a daimista, albeit one highly idiosyncratic daimista—me.

I'm currently a sixty-six-year-old full professor of religious studies. If I can't speak freely, creatively, and from my heart; if I can't say what really matters, in a way that is as enlivened, juicy, multi-perspectival, intellectually rich, and heartfelt as I know how, then who in God's name will? If tenure is not for this, then what is it for?

Therefore, my intention with *Liquid Light* is to imbue what I write, as I am writing, with "something more," something elusive but also very real—a vibratory "radioactivity" (of Light and Love and Presence) that will hopefully linger in what I've written, shining in and through the words. In many ways, therefore, the process of writing *Liquid Light* has been, in and of itself, a sacramental activity, in that my underlying intention has been to offer up each moment of the process for the highest good of all; to connect my heart, moment to moment, to that deepest Source within me; to ask for that divine Presence within me to write in and through my *aparelho* (literally, "apparatus" or "instrument," used in this case to refer to the body/mind/spirit of an individual).

In addition, given the fact that there is a fairly specific vibratory quality to the experience of drinking ayahuasca, it only makes sense that people who, like me, are involved—intimately, repeatedly—in the world of ayahuasca spirituality, might well begin to express themselves in a certain specific and congruent aesthetic style. So, for instance, when I attempt to express in words what it feels like to be a daimista, the words that I use to express myself might often, for someone who is unfamiliar with ayahuasca spirituality, sound as if they are filled with hyperbole; there might well be lots of Capitalization (it all feels divine, so why not, for example, write about the Sacred Bicycle Pump); the language might at times seem somewhat exaggerated or "too big." But you can at least rest assured that I am consciously, and at times a bit playfully, using this style of language, because (in my humble opinion), it at least partially reflects the "hugeness" of the state of consciousness and the sheer impact of the Energy that you can frequently experience as a daimista or as someone using entheogens more generally. This specific style of writing is, to my mind at least, much more aligned with the reality disclosed by ayahuasca than the more normal, restrained language of most academics. So, although I'm quite aware that this way of using language can be like nails on a chalkboard for some readers, I'm fine with using it as one, shall we say, shade of color in my palette.

I am also acutely aware that certain scholars may feel a bit ill at ease, not just in response to the rather unusual rhetorical style of *Liquid Light* but also because I have explicitly written about my own experiences.[4] There might well be certain readers who will shake their heads sadly, convinced that I've become some sort of unthinking convert or, worse, an advocate for some (doubtless nefarious) cause, simply because I'm open about my ongoing participation in the Santo Daime tradition. But I would hope that any educated and thoughtful reader would concede that everyone possesses some, often tacit, set of assumptions about how everything hangs together; about what really matters; about who we are underneath it all; about the purpose, if any, of life. We all move through life pro-pelled and guided, more or less, by this rough-edged, ever-mutating, rarely con-scious, overarching set of presuppositions, attitudes, and values. Given that we all have these assumptive worlds, I have decided that I might as well attempt to be as self-reflexive and transparent as possible about the different vantage points from which I have written *Liquid Light*. Hopefully, doing so will increasingly enable me to acknowledge and appreciate the limitations *and* the advantages that come from the highly idiosyncratic perspective that I possess—a perspective that inevitably colors the way that I have written this book.

DO YOUR BEST, THEN LET IT GO

As I mentioned, much has been written recently on the important research that is taking place, for instance, at Johns Hopkins, New York University, and the University of California, Los Angeles, on the therapeutic potential of psyche-delics.[5] While it is refreshing to see this flurry of articles on the therapeutic pos-sibilities of these mind-altering substances, fairly little has been written recently on the spiritual and/or specifically religious use of psychedelics, with the notable exception of a handful of several well-received texts.[6] Therefore, I was delighted when Wendy Lochner, an editor from Columbia University Press, contacted me to inquire whether I might consider writing a book on psychedelics, specifically, a Jamesian analysis of psychedelic states of consciousness. I told her that I would be happy to write a book that examined psychedelics from a Jamesian point of view, given the fact that my own research on William James and the comparative study of mysticism, combined with my years of research on the Santo Daime, prepared me to take on, almost exactly, this specific task.[7]

As I began to write the book, I attempted to imbue the creative process with an underlying intention that is perhaps best expressed in the Sanskrit term *niṣkāmakarma* (action without desire). Niṣkāmakarma is the spiritual attitude that is most clearly expressed in the Bhagavad Gītā, one of the key scriptures of the modern Hindu tradition.[8] Niṣkāmakarma is when you do the absolute best that you know how to do in the task that is yours to do and then, when you are done, you give up any/all attachments to the outcome; you let go of whether it goes well or not; you don't worry what others think about what you've done, since you've offered it all to God and you've asked God to work in and through you. Therefore, in that spirit, I offer this text, from my heart, to anyone who is interested in learning more about the fertile intersection between psychedelics and spirituality, knowing that I've done the very best that I know how to do and that part of doing my best is my heartfelt and ongoing attempt to offer it all to that Highest Source, to let "That," as much as possible, write in and through me.

NAVIGATING A MINEFIELD

I have to admit, however, that as a practicing daimista, letting go of what others think of what I've written here in *Liquid Light* has not always come easily. More than twelve years ago, after I made the explicit decision to consciously begin to research the Santo Daime, I would periodically take part in ritual "works" with various Brazilian elders of the tradition. At some point, usually after the work had ended, I would approach the elder who had led the ceremony. After informing him (or less often, her) of my intention to write a book that focused on the Santo Daime, I would ask for his or her blessings. Inevitably, the elder would smile, perhaps ask a brief question or two, and then happily bestow his or her blessings. However, at some point fairly late in this "asking-for-blessings-from-elders" process, I participated in a work led by a woman named Baixinha, a crucially important elder in the Santo Daime tradition.

Baixinha at that time was around seventy-three years old, tiny (less than five feet tall), plump, and cross-eyed, with long gray hair. She was something like a mixture of a twinkly eyed child and a regal queen. When I approached her at the end of the work and told her about my intention to write a book on the Santo Daime, she paused for a while, seemingly lost in thought, and then said, "Are you sure?" (Gulp!) She then proceeded to speak with me for the next twenty to thirty minutes about just how difficult this task would be. The highlights of what she said went something like this: *I've been working with the Daime now for over twenty years and I don't know if I am ready to write a book on it. You don't want to just write about the externals of the Santo Daime, do you? But writing about what it really means to be a daimista—that's not easy. But if you're determined to do it, you're going to have to be aware that there are lots of different factions in the Santo Daime, lots of people with lots of different agendas, and lots of competing ideas about what the Santo Daime is and who should be in charge. So, as you're researching, you need to know that you're stepping into a minefield—and you'll need to know how to make your way through that minefield without getting yourself blown up. You'll need to know when to stay quiet and just listen, and when to speak up, and ask questions. But if you keep attuned with the Divine Mother, you'll be OK. Your heart seems sincere, so if you really feel called to do this, you have my blessings.*

It ends up that everything that Baixinha told me was, not surprisingly, true. Therefore, I wasn't completely caught off guard when, during the process of sharing early drafts of this book, I encountered a few ruffled feathers. And this is because, and it is important to know, even though I'm a *fardado*, my goal is not to promote the Santo Daime. (A "fardado" is an initiate in the Santo Daime tradition; it literally means "a person who wears a uniform.") I am not an evangelist. Therefore, at times in this text I openly discuss certain parts of the Santo Daime tradition that have been problematic for me, for a wide variety of reasons. I have deeply valued my time within this beautiful tradition, but I honestly don't think that presenting a "Hallmark card" portrayal of the Santo Daime is a good idea. I don't think that this sort of "wearing its Sunday best" depiction of the Santo Daime actually serves anyone. Instead, it is crucial, to my mind, to represent this tradition with as much factual accuracy and kindness and heart as possible.

After I had received some initial feedback from readers of earlier versions of *Liquid Light*, I shared a more polished and nuanced version with some North American "elders" in the tradition. (I put the word "elders" in quotes, because many of these individuals were—and are—not chronologically elderly. But in every other respect they function like elders, in that they all possess a subtle and profound knowledge of the Santo Daime tradition.) I was happy to share this draft with them, not only as a gesture of respect for the long years and hard, heartfelt work that they have given to the Santo Daime, but also because I knew that *Liquid Light* would benefit greatly from their years of immersion within this tradition. And I have to say that their insights helped—immeasurably. The text you are reading benefited immensely from the clarity and (dare I say it?) wisdom of the suggestions and questions that they offered, typically with enormous tact and kindness. And even if, after a series of discussions with these elders, I chose to refrain from writing about certain sensitive topics that had the potential to create unnecessary problems for the tradition, I never felt pressured or censored in any way.[9] In the end, I always felt that the choices that I made were my own and emerged from my own attempts to discuss the tradition in a way that is as accurate as possible while writing in a way that respected the understandable desire of these elders to protect their tradition. (I should also point out that *Liquid Light* benefited profoundly from the incisive and heart-felt contributions of numerous non-Daime friends, both academic and not.

Each of them, in a unique way, dedicated enormous time and energy to reading various versions of this text and offered critically important suggestions on how to improve it.)

My hope is that most readers will eventually come to see that I have worked hard to do justice to two ethical stances that are frequently in tension with each other: (1) My academic sense of integrity—my desire to examine the history, beliefs, practices, and social structures of the Santo Daime in a way that is thorough, open, honest, and probing. (2) My deep love for the Santo Daime religion and the people in it—my profound gratitude for what I've received, and continue to receive, from this wondrous tradition. These two ethical imperatives, which are in effect simply another version of what William James calls the "toughminded" and "tenderhearted" perspectives on life, are not always easy to reconcile, but I can at least say that I have made every attempt to adjudicate between these often quite different points of view with as much skill, heart, and attunement as humanly possible.

PORTUGUESE STUDIES

As soon as I recognized, and acknowledged, that writing this book was the next stage of my research agenda, a recognition that took about two years to finally emerge, I emailed Andrew Dawson, one of the few scholars I was aware of at the time who was writing about the Santo Daime in English.[10] In that email, I asked him if he had any advice for me. His response was clear and straightforward: if you're going to study the Santo Daime, you need to learn Portuguese.

I took that suggestion to heart. Almost immediately, I made a vow to myself that I was going to stop listening to music while driving my car and instead listen only to Portuguese. After a few months, during which I basically wore holes in my ninety-hour set of Pimsleur Portuguese CDs, I had the profound good fortune to find Cristina, a highly skilled Portuguese tutor in the Dallas area, a woman who was also, amazingly, a *conselheira*, the highest rank that a woman can have within the União do Vegetal, another Brazilian, and now international, ayahuasca religion. (Cristina is extremely modest about her role in the UDV, but let's just say that given that she is someone who has been immersed in that tradition for over four decades, she has an enormously helpful and open-minded perspective on ayahuasca religions to share with me.)

More than a decade later, I continue to study Portuguese with Cristina—not only chatting informally but also translating various texts in Portuguese about the

Santo Daime, as well as texts on the life of Mestre Irineu and Padrinho Sebastião. Cristina has also worked with me to translate the hymns I started to receive in English into Portuguese, and she even helped me to fine-tune the handful of hymns that I have received in Portuguese. Bottom line: this book simply could not have been written without her.

I

First Encounter with the Daime

PLUNGING RIGHT IN

I first heard of the Santo Daime when I was participating in a spiritual retreat run by my wife Sandra for her students at the Seven Oaks retreat center in Virginia. (My wife Sandra is a gifted spiritual teacher who runs the Full Spectrum Center for Spiritual Awakening in Meadville, Pennsylvania.)[1] During one of the breaks, I was browsing around in the lovely quiet bookstore at the center and one book in particular caught my eye: *Forest of Visions*, by Alex Polari (currently a revered elder, or *padrinho*, in the Santo Daime). Later retitled *The Religion of Ayahuasca*, this book was at that time the only book in English that had been written on the Santo Daime religion.[2] As a religious studies scholar trained in the anthropology of religion, I was already aware, albeit not in any great detail, of the existence of shamanic and neoshamanic ceremonies in South America that revolved around drinking ayahuasca. But I also knew that some of the shamans who led these ceremonies would at times use that potent brew not just for healings and divination and to deepen their awareness of the spiritual strata of reality but also for curses and love spells or to gain power over others—and I simply didn't want to get involved in those activities, on any level.[3] It was clear to me that ayahuasca was a powerful substance, and (speaking personally) I only wanted to drink it as a way to deepen my spiritual awareness. So, having settled down in a chair to look over *Forest of Visions*, I was delighted to learn that the Santo Daime was a tradition in which ayahuasca was taken as a sacrament; during elaborate, heartfelt ceremonies; and with the conscious intention that each participant would become an increasingly translucent conduit of divine Light, Love, and healing in this world. I thought to myself: now that's a context in which I could see myself taking ayahuasca.

After buying *Forest of Visions*, I spent the next few days diving into the text, which was filled with wonderful stories about Alex Polari's initial exposure to the Santo Daime; numerous evocative pictures of the early days of Céu do Mapiá (again: a centrally important Santo Daime community in the heart of the Amazon rain forest); along with some fairly obscure esoteric discussions as well as numerous citations of, to me at least, rather off-putting Santo Daime hymns. (I was pretty certain that the book was originally written for other daimistas.) *Forest of Visions* was intriguing, but as a newcomer to this entheogenic world, at times I had to buckle down and wade through some fairly formidable linguistic hurtles.

One of the clearest, and to me most helpful, sections of the book was the preface. And, with a pleasing synchronicity, soon after reading *Forest of Visions*, two close friends of mine told me that they had recently taken part in a healing workshop led by the person who had written that preface, Jonathan Goldman. When I questioned them further, they emphasized that they had really respected the skill with which Jonathan had run the weekend. I completely trusted the assessment of these two women (they were both teachers in the energy healing school that my wife and I had graduated from a few years before), so I asked them if they could give me his contact information. A few days later, I called Jonathan, and we had a short but fruitful conversation. After introducing myself, I jumped right in and asked: "How can I get to Céu do Mapiá?" (I figured that if I wanted to be exposed to the Santo Daime tradition, I might as well go to the source.) Jonathan laughed a bit, and then said, "Well, sure, I can help you get to Mapiá if you really want to go there, but it might be better if you took a few baby steps first. We're going to be having a five-day retreat with the Daime in a few weeks in North Carolina. If you're interested, I can give you some information about that."

For some odd reason, it had never even occurred to me that the Santo Daime religion might exist outside of Brazil. But I quickly found out, to my surprise and delight, that there was a nascent, albeit increasingly robust, Santo Daime presence in the United States as well.[4]

Importantly: I am not in a position to share with anyone the location of Santo Daime centers in the United States. For a variety of legal reasons, please don't ask me for this information.

As I continued talking to Jonathan, everything within me said "yes." Not surprisingly, I signed up for the retreat not long afterward.

It wasn't until a few months after the retreat that I discovered that my initial exposure to the Santo Daime, albeit deeply beautiful and powerful, was also, shall we say, somewhat less than traditional. Nonetheless—acting as your proxy—I'm going to just dive right into my experience of that retreat. Rest assured, however, that later in this text I will give plenty of attention to the more orthodox ritual forms of the Santo Daime.

THE RETREAT BEGINS

A few weeks after my conversation with Jonathan, I was picked up at the baggage claims area of a North Carolina airport by Arthur, a short, wiry, highly abstracted, "barely on this planet" man in his late sixties with a scruffy white beard. I soon found myself in the front seat of his rather beat-up, dull-green Ford F-150. I was seated by the window, while Pamela, a petite, well-kept woman in her forties with long blonde hair, was squeezed between Arthur and me on the springy front seat of the truck. Not long after we started down the highway, I was delighted to discover that Pamela had, like me, spent years in Siddha Yoga—we had both been part of the "Meditation Revolution" brought to the United States in the 1970s from India by a charismatic yogi named Swami Muktananda.[5] (I had not met Pamela before, although she had spent time at the residential meditation center that Muktananda had established in upstate New York. She was more of a frequent visitor, whereas I had been a hardcore, full-time, live-in participant there.) Neither Arthur nor Pamela had been involved with the Santo Daime for very long, but because I was a complete neophyte, I listened, fascinated, as they both talked animatedly about what had prompted them to drink ayahuasca and why they had chosen to plunge into this five-day Santo Daime retreat in the middle of a state park in North Carolina.

It took us almost two hours to finally arrive, late in the afternoon, at the spartan, low-slung, concrete-block welcome center of the park. The park, while rather small, was quite beautiful—its sandy soil was filled with scrunched-up scrub oaks and towering pines; a placid river flowed behind the grouping of tiny rustic cabins; and a small wooden viewing platform overlooked a marsh. A few others were already at the welcome center, and during the next couple of hours, I had a chance to get to know, at least briefly, most of the twenty or so people who would be taking part in the retreat as we checked in at the welcome center and were told where we would be staying. (I was with a group of about five other men—including Jonathan—in an extremely no-frills cabin with only one small hand-cranked window and three bunk beds.) Anyone I didn't get a chance to meet during the check-in process I became acquainted with soon afterward when we were all milling around in the dining room for supper (your basic institutional it-couldn't-possibly-be-any-blander food).

I have to say that I was immediately impressed with Jonathan. He was over six feet tall; probably in his late fifties; and seemed to glow from the inside out—he was a warm, welcoming, and articulate person. His wife Jane was earthy and matter of fact—a no-nonsense, but congenial, and clearly intelligent woman.

I soon found out that Jonathan and Jane would be assisted during the retreat by two people: Taran, a compact, muscular man in his late thirties with probing and inquisitive eyes who had been involved in the Santo Daime for six years, having made several trips to Brazil with Jonathan and Jane after several years of studying Tibetan Buddhism at the Naropa Institute in Boulder, Colorado; and Bonnie, a tall, large-framed woman in her midthirties who radiated a force field of presence and had been part of Jonathan's "crew" for several years now.

The next morning, I scrambled out of my top bunk, and after walking over to the men's bathroom area and taking a shower, I met up with Leo, a soft-spoken man in his forties from Montreal (another student of Tibetan Buddhism) for a session of Tai Chi in a grassy area outside our bungalow. (Earlier I had been delighted to discover that Leo knew one of the three Tai Chi forms that I had been practicing for several years and was planning to practice it every morning before our "work" with the Daime.) Afterward, the two of us made our way to the dining room. After getting to know more of the retreat participants over breakfast, I then slowly walked back to my cabin and changed into my "whites" (we had all been asked to wear white clothes during the rituals with the Daime)—white cotton long pants; a white cotton T-shirt; a soft, white long-sleeved cotton pullover; and a white cotton sweatshirt. It was mid-February, and even though the sun was shining, I could occasionally see my breath, so I appreciated each and every layer.

The retreat itself formally began around ten that morning. After having left our shoes piled up outside the door, we made our way into the ramshackle, low-ceilinged, wooden-walled, concrete-floored, exceedingly small (at most twenty-five by twenty feet) shack/cabin that would act as the "container" for the spiritual energies that would be catalyzed by the Daime. We had been instructed to set up our own little "nest"—our highly circumscribed personal space—that typically consisted of some combination of backjacks—(a type of portable back support made from a metal frame covered with rugged cotton cloth), yoga mats, blankets, pillows, water bottles, and if you weren't a newcomer like me, a cloth bag or small backpack stuffed to the brim with spiral-bound locally printed books (*hinários/hymnals*), each containing the Portuguese lyrics and English translations of hundreds of Santo Daime hymns that had been "received" (channeled) by various elders in the tradition.

These nests (or as I began to think of them later, "launching pads") were where each of us stayed throughout the retreat; we either laid down when we were strongly "in the Force" or sat up, usually cross-legged, if we were feeling somewhat more capable of dealing with everyday reality and perhaps could even sing along with the more experienced psychonauts who would blend their voices with Jonathan, Jane, Bonnie (and Taran playing the guitar)—that is, the crew who were responsible for leading the work, and who sat together against the back wall of the cabin, slightly separated from the rest of us, clearly establishing a type of hierarchal orientation in the space.

All of our warm and fuzzy and semi-chaotic little nests were arranged in a loose-limbed, circle. In the center of the circle was a very small, low to the ground, wooden table that was covered with pictures of figures who are crucial to the Santo Daime: Mestre Irineu (the almost seven-foot-tall black man who was the founder of the tradition); Padrinho Sebastião (the originator of the largest lineage, or line, of the Santo Daime); Padrinho Alfredo (Padrinho Sebastião's son and the current head of this line); Baixinha (a woman who had been a *Mãe de Santo*—a female leader of the Brazilian mediumistic tradition of Umbanda—for decades before becoming a revered elder within the Santo Daime tradition); the Virgin Mary; and Jesus. The table was also decked out with three white taper candles; a vase of flowers; a bowl of water; and in the very center of the altar, a double-barred cross. (I was later told that the top, smaller bar of the cross symbolized the second coming of the Christ Consciousness in all of those who drink the Daime.)

Jonathan began the retreat by asking each of us to take some time to think about why we had come to this retreat; specifically, what we wanted to offer up for healing and what positive qualities we wanted to call forth within our lives. Then, one by one, in our own time, we would walk slowly and reverently up to the altar, each of us bundled up in various configurations of white jackets, white sweats, and white scarves. We'd then kneel on the square cushion placed in front of the altar and state out loud our prayers and intentions for the retreat. (I asked—firmly, with as much sincerity and heart as I could muster—to release the anger and judgment that I often felt stewing inside of me. I also asked to be filled with God's love, wisdom, power.)

FIGURE 1.1 Padrinho Sebastião painting. Courtesy of the Goldman collection.

After this, we all stood and recited some prayers (including a slightly tweaked version of the Our Father, and the Hail Mary—each said three times, aloud, collectively, along with another prayer that I had never heard before). Jonathan then walked over to a hip-high, rough wooden table that had been set up close

FIGURE 1.2   Mestre Irineu painting.

to the front door to the cabin, where he proceeded to pour the Daime from a couple of liter-sized mason jars into a simple yet elegant glass pouring dispenser, something like a smaller version of what you might use to pour iced tea on a hot summer day. We then lined up in a rather haphazard and casual way, and as each

FIGURE 1.3 Jonathan Goldman and Baixinha

of us came up, Jonathan would pour our allotted dose of Daime into a shot glass, apparently discerning within himself via some type of mysterious guidance how much to give to each person.

When I swallowed my first dose of Daime (about three-quarters of a shot glass of the rather thick and somewhat viscous dark brown liquid), I was actually somewhat surprised—while it had an extremely unusual taste, it didn't taste anywhere near as awful as I had been led to expect. In fact, it was actually a little sweet. After I reverently gulped down my Daime, with just a tinge of anxiety, I then made my way back to my cozy spot, where I fussed a bit with the white wool yoga mat that I had from my time with Muktananda, placing it over a cloth-covered foam rubber wedge that I used to tilt my pelvis forward a bit so that it was less stressful to sit upright for long periods of time, and placed all of these in turn on top of the cushion that was sewn into the backjack. I then draped the upright section of the backjack itself with an intricately woven deep blue shawl, so that the shawl formed a sort of regal, and padded, backdrop for my yogic "throne." Having finally arranged my "nest" to my satisfaction, I sat upright, comfortably cross-legged, took a few deep breaths, shut my eyes, and waited for the fireworks to begin.

It wasn't long before I discovered that my "Here I go! I'm ready!" meditative posture was a bit premature, because after Jonathan finished serving the Daime, pouring himself the final serving, and after the shot glasses had been washed and put back on the table (Jonathan was assisted throughout this process by Taran and another daimista, both of whom were clearly "in the know" about what to do), we were instructed to fold up our mats so that we'd have plenty of firm footing and lots of unimpeded space to stand in as Jonathan led us through a series of guided bodily movements/visualizations.

Jonathan, like me, in another coincidence that I thought was rather striking, had been trained in bioenergetics, a later development of the Reichian therapeutic modality.[6] From the perspective of bioenergetics, the cosmic life force, understood in ways that are similar if not identical to the qi in Chinese Taoism and the $pr\bar{a}na$ in Yoga and Tantra, should ideally circulate freely in-and-through each of our physical bodies. Unfortunately, each of us, due to a series of early childhood challenges/traumas, has built up a variety of "defense structures"; that is, each of us has in a specific way capped or fragmented or armored against that life force—an unconscious and ultimately self-destructive "strategy" that generates a corresponding set of psychological and physiological problems, if not flat-out disease. In bioenergetics, healers help their clients move their bodies in specific ways; guide them so they breathe more consciously and often forcefully; or prompt them to make loud, expulsive sounds—all of this, and more, in order to free up stagnant or blocked or fragmented energy so that it can, eventually, flow through the body/mind in a way that is increasingly harmonious and health giving.

I was, from the get-go, deeply impressed with Jonathan's skill. He immediately let us know that although participating in these sorts of bioenergetic exercises was not a typical feature of Santo Daime rituals, over the years he had come to realize that by moving and breathing and making sounds in these ways we could, as he put it, "help the Daime" so that it would not have so much "junk" to clear out before beginning its deeper work.

We began by standing with our feet shoulder-width apart, with our knees bent, as if we were sitting on the edge of a stool, focusing our attention on the energy that was coming up from the earth and circulating in a cone-shaped vortex, into the base of the spine/the first chakra (literally, "circle" or "wheel") while also coursing through our legs. (According to yogic philosophy, chakras are subtle energy juncture points that correspond to specific locations in the physical body.) We were then asked to stand with our right feet forward, with our knees still slightly bent, our weight primarily on our right feet. We were invited to direct our attention to the "kidney point" located in the ball of the right foot. (Jonathan was also trained in acupuncture and therefore brought that background into his bioenergetic work as well.) We were then asked to sense our energetic connection to the rivers and lakes that are located deep under the earth, the sources of pure water that could be invited, spiritually, to bubble up into our bodies through the "spring" that is located in the balls of the feet. We then connected to, and freed up, other acupuncture points in the foot, typically by leaning into them rather forcefully, and then switched to the left foot and repeated the pattern.

This sort of work continued for the next fifteen minutes or so. For example: we were asked to strongly press our fingers into the tightness we could discover at the base of the neck, all the while letting groans emerge, in order to free up the energetic "tube" or "chimney" that was located there so that Light could flow down more freely from the Astral into our bodies/minds. (In the Santo Daime, the Astral is seen as a powerful spiritual realm.) We also interlaced our hands behind our backs and breathed in and out several times, deeply, so that the chest would open up more freely and therefore allow love and trust to more fully manifest within us. It all felt wonderful—I gave myself to each process as fully as possible, while in the back of my mind also taking notes so that I could remember some of these exercises to share with my wife's students when I next traveled up to her energy-healing school for a long-weekend workshop.

After the bioenergetic exercises were complete, we all were invited to either sit down in our assigned spots and meditate or to stretch out on our mats, with our eyes closed, turning our attention within—all of this as soft, New Age ambient music began to play in the background. Because I was beginning to feel a sort of underlying burble of unusual but forcefully insistent energy starting to thrum in my body, I chose to lay down on my back, with my head supported by a small pillow that was decorated with a lavender counted cross-stitch design that was sewn by my mother years before; I covered myself with the blue woolen shawl; I consciously released any tension that I discovered within myself via a methodical body scan; and I began to repeat the mantra that has been one of the key practices in my spiritual life (*So'ham*—in Sanskrit, "I am That," that is, I am One with the Divine Source of All), all the while aligning the mantra with my breath ("So" on the exhalation, and "ham" [pronounced "hum"] on the inhalation, focusing intently as well on the space between the inhalation and the exhalation—the space between thought to be the entryway into divine Presence).

For quite a while, nothing major seemed to be happening, except for the growing awareness of a subtle shift in the underlying "tone" of my experience—it was almost as if there were a tacit background bass drum reverberating just below the surface; a type of subterranean stirring; a viscerally felt energetic vibratory pulsation that wanted to emerge, experienced most directly as type of underlying physical tension, a sort of preconscious bracing against what increasingly seemed to want to surge up from within.

Then, with my eyes closed, in a way that began so subtly and naturally that I almost didn't notice, I began to see a series of brilliant jewel-like colored points of light flickering in a variety of dancing patterns—lights that, more and more, began to feel like flickering windows into a shimmering divine world of colors; colors that seemed to me to be more intrinsically pure than color we normally see in different objects in the physical world, perhaps better described as "upgrades" of color. Soon, to my amazement, I also began to see these colored lights with my eyes open as well. As I gazed at this jewel-like twinkling display, I increasingly felt my heart opening in gratitude and wonder as I watched the scintillating points of (primarily) blue and gold light begin to descend in evanescent showers throughout the room, superimposing themselves, delicately, gently, upon the more mundane and less vibrant colors of our physical space—all of this while I was also beginning to notice soft stirrings of energy in my third eye and crown chakras (upper-level energy centers). It felt as if the energetic streamings that corresponded to the space between my eyebrows and the top half of the sphere of my skull were expanding and relaxing; as if these energetic portals/vortices of energy within me were being gently opened—and those openings in turn were linked, increasingly, to an inner embrace of a Light-filled divine Presence, along with a relaxed and joyous recognition of and settling into my own True Nature.

And all of this was just the prelude to the hours that came next, hours during which I was, as it were, thrown into a rushing current within, as I began to be tossed and turned in an extremely powerful and turbulent inner river of Force and Light that sent me forward through a series of nonordinary temporal moments and spaces that were punctuated with Power-filled visionary perceptions that would almost force themselves into my conscious awareness, coming with an insistence that was impregnated with Meaning and Beauty (here We Are, Revealing Ourselves) or carrying with them an aching nostalgia brought on by glimpses of otherworldly architecture; and so on and so on.

It just went on and on, with "me" (because who "I" was in all of this had a quite different energetic configuration than my pre-Daime "I") watching from within as the rather stunned recipient of sheer creative spontaneity, coping as well as I could with the ceaselessly unfurling abundance of divine fecundity that was taking place within the "screen" of my awareness.

And it kept coming. Most of it I have no way of remembering—while it was happening it was more real than normal reality, but I simply had no internal categories to make sense of most of it, no cognitive "slots" for these experiences—experiences that were like scraps of a dream that kept scattering like birds whenever I would reach out to hold onto them. Or put differently, it was as if each "world" that I entered into (or that entered into me) was tuned to a different key than my ordinary world—each world had its own inherently unique vibratory signature, and therefore any of the ways in which memory is normally accessed, via an underlying set of tacit linguistic assumptions, simply didn't function in that quite rarified reality.

This was my first taste, at least since my two LSD experiences when I was nineteen, of a full-bore psychedelic flux of experience, of what it's like to find myself so utterly immersed in the extremely rich, poignant, breathtakingly beautiful flow of what's happening, both inside and outside, that there's simply no place for some detached, sit-back-and-watch witness to calmly remember it all.

It was also the case that for much of the time during that first day I was working with how to cope with the extremely challenging and demandingly insistent presence of nausea. When the nausea was really strong, I'd attempt to become as aware as possible of where I might be resisting and tightening against the seemingly ever-increasing "voltage" of the energetic surges that would rush in-and-through me, and then I would consciously try to relax. Time and time again, I would, with intention, work to open up, to breathe deeply and fully. Thankfully, the nausea would often subside, only to re-emerge down the line, especially when I would, once again, viscerally brace myself against the newest volcanic eruption of Power that seemed to want to surge into, and through, my subtle body.

Amazingly, at least to me, I never threw up. Even when Jonathan offered a second serving. And then later, a third.

"GETTING WELL"

The phenomenon of purging (or "getting well" as many daimistas like to say) has been a fascinating study for me. Here are a few initial observations. First, I've noticed that I do not have to purge nearly as often as I used to. That's because I finally figured out that if I was feeling nauseous during a Santo Daime work, my nausea was often simply the physical counterpart of a sudden, knee-jerk, almost cellular resistance to the Force that would seize me, causing me to subconsciously brace against the onslaught of the Force—and that bracing itself would often manifest, physically, as a type of belly tightness, a sort of physical and energetic constriction that in turn would often manifest as nausea.

Thankfully, at some point in my journey in the Santo Daime I finally "got" that when I'm struggling with nausea in a work, I need to relax that area of my body—consciously, intentionally, repeatedly; I need to give myself permission to sway in the Current rather than to tighten up against it. And when I do that, when I breath into my belly (attentively, tenderly), when I invite softness, comfort, and ease, the nausea will often diminish and/or disappear.

I've also noticed that at this point, when I *do* purge, it tends to happen in a simple, no-fuss, no-muss way—the Daime forcefully expels whatever needs to come out from within my physical and subtle body, and then, after a sort of "breathing-the-present-in" time period, followed by a moment or two of energetically "shaking it off," I'll simply return to my work in the *salão* feeling cleaned out and alert. (In Portuguese "salão" just means "large room," but within the Santo Daime tradition, the salão is the ritual space in which the spiritual works take place.)

Second, I've come to realize that a strong purging in a work can be a profound gift from God/the Divine Mother. We don't always have to work to get rid of nausea—we can also simply (especially if the Daime is forcefully urging this to occur) let that purging erupt from our depths; we can give ourselves fully to that sensation. Purging in this way is extremely primordial; it's an ancient, deeply visceral release of toxicities; and it is often the automatic, utterly natural, bodily response to an influx of seemingly limitless divine Force and Splendor into our physical and energetic bodies. So, if you're in a Santo Daime work and you feel nauseous, usually I'd say just go ahead and purge. Feel good about it. Feel grateful for it—it's not at all like vomiting when you're drunk—purging prompted by the Daime feels liberative, healing, cleansing. (Nonetheless, I also have to mention that there are definitely times in a work, especially if you're a guardian—more on that later—when you'll be tempted to purge; to give in to the nausea, but because there's so much you need to attend to in the salão, you simply can't—and part of developing "firmness" as a daimista is this ability to skillfully work with the nausea that the Daime can at times bring.)

Third, purging is not just limited to vomiting. I would suggest, for example, that the torrents of tears that can erupt during some works are also often a purging of the heart, a powerfully healing and cathartic release of previously bound up feelings. Similarly, and importantly, the cleansing release of purging can also occur via sudden and sometimes distressingly urgent bowel movements. And these bowel movements themselves can, at least at times, transmute into something more: occasions in which the celestial gates can fly wide open. There are times, for example, when the Daime is gurgling in my abdomen like a time-activated depth charge and *** *We are here with you, flowing sheets of rainbow Light* *** and I'll have to be very, very careful when passing the Daime-created gas that distends my belly *** *The Queen of the Forest reaches out Her Hand out to you, oh so* *tenderly**** and then, having made my way to the bathroom to sit on the toilet, I'll be feeling the slightly painful movement of the gas itself as it presses and pushes through my intestines *** *Let torrents of Blessings flow down on you from all divine Beings, may Light descend upon you from the radiant heights* *** followed by the gurgling and shifting intestinal sensations that take place within me as I'm having a bowel movement *** *Hail, Hail, the Most High, the Sun Arrives.* ***

Talk about an alchemical fusion of high and low! At least for me, I can't help but be amused by all of this almost laughable earthiness infused with such powerful visionary unfoldings of astral wonder. A bathroom that is transformed into a gleaming celestial temple. Truly.

Fourth, God only knows what is being released when we purge. For example, a few years into my immersion in the world of the Santo Daime, I was participating in a powerful mediumship work. We were outside, in a *terreiro* (an outdoor ritual area)—under the trees, next to a field of corn—and the leader of the work was energetically interacting with a suffering spirit within me (much more about suffering spirits later on), and suddenly a geyser of vomit emerged from my mouth—it quite literally felt as if a firehose of gushing vomit was erupting from within me—I swear it felt like gallons of liquid spewed out from me. But then, when that process was complete, after feeling somewhat shaken by the force of what had happened, but at the same time deeply cleansed, I rejoined the work, and started singing the hymns once again—feeling very clear, very open and transparent—and that receptive spaciousness appeared to have created an opening for what came next in the work: an enormous influx of Light and Redemptive Power that surged into my consciousness, giving me the gift of the mystical knowledge of the Christ, full stop. I was swept up in love, feeling such awe at the Power of this utterly Radiant and Beautiful Being of Light and Love, surging with Joy and effortless Power who (I just knew) had (has!) descended into this realm to free, to save, to liberate, to awaken, to transform—everyone, everywhere, throughout all time and for all time.

Purging is also not always simply a matter of clearing out an individual's energetic "stuff." I have spoken with several people who help to facilitate Santo Daime works, and they have shared with me how at times they can feel the energy in the ritual space suddenly become extremely intense, and the forceful purging that is then catalyzed within them helps to shift the collective energetic "stuckness" that was taking place during that moment in the ritual. Simply by purging, not for themselves alone, but instead as a type of vicarious representative of the collective energies of everyone in the room, they, as it were, "comb out" the energetic entanglement that was previously present, enabling the energies that before were so bound up to flow with increasing freedom and harmony, a process that is often followed by the infusion of a deep sense of sacred stillness in the salão.

MY FIRST DAY: CONTINUED

Meanwhile, back to my North Carolina retreat experience. From my rather dazed perspective, even to sit up from the mat when the Force was really strong was an almost heroic achievement. But then I would slowly begin to hear, from somewhere far away, as if it were happening miles in the distance, the sound of glasses tinkling. And equally slowly, it would dawn upon me that those sounds meant that Jonathan and his assistants were getting ready to serve yet more Daime. At those times, it would feel like it was an almost impossible task to get up; but somehow, amazingly, I would slowly, carefully, winch myself up from my quasi-paralyzed horizontal position on my camp mat. I would eventually find myself woozily balancing on my knees, and as my eyes opened, I would slowly begin to process the onrush of visual perceptions that flooded into me.

During these times, it was as if I couldn't even imagine drinking more Daime, since I felt utterly saturated with the energy and the transfigured state of consciousness that it was bringing. But I always said *yes*—I really wanted to go for it, to not hold back. But it was hard, since even smelling the Daime during the second (and third) serving felt like it was almost more than I could bear. Unlike the first serving, and Jonathan actually served a little less the last two times, the Daime at that point tasted absolutely revolting. It was as if each cell in my body was clenching, instinctively repulsed by the utter otherworldliness of the Daime. It was clear to me, even then, that the Daime was working really hard within my energetic matrix to reconfigure it so that it could vibrate at a higher, more refined frequency—a frequency that also, however, seemed to possess this eerie and alien quality, and my subtle and physical body wasn't at all happy about this transfiguration process—it was as if I had stepped onto some sort of energetic Star Trek transporter pad, and while part of me was enthusiastically saying "Beam me up, Scotty," another part of me, the more visceral level, was yelling "Hell no, we won't go!," struggling tooth and nail against that reconfiguration, fighting against being wrenched out of the very familiar and comfortable, vibratory level of everyday reality that I was, unconsciously, so used to inhabiting.

And then there were all of the hymns that were being sung. Not by me: I couldn't even begin to imagine how it was possible for anyone who had drank Daime to sit up, much less sing hymns in Portuguese. But Jonathan, Jane, Bonnie, and Taran, as well as some of the "old hands" among us (with Taran accompanying the hymns with very skillful guitar work) sang hymn after hymn, with the hymns seemingly propelled by, or riding on, the sharply rhythmic, raspy insistence of the maracás that Jonathan, Jane, and Bonnie were playing.

And each hymn seemed to bring with it its own unique intensity and energetic note; each hymn carried and catalyzed a type of vibratory pressure, so that more and more Force was pumped into me, in-and-through the ever-changing melody, words, and rhythms of each hymn. As the hymns kept coming, it felt like the Force was gripping me, shaking my body repeatedly as though I was a rag doll in the mouth of a benevolent pit bull, and all I could do was to breathe into what was happening. And then there'd be another wave rolling through and I'd ride it, let it thrash me around some, and then take more deep, conscious breaths, as yet another hymn began.

I will admit that there were times within myself when I noticed that I was actually feeling good about how I was handling everything. (I wasn't, after all, weeping like some of my fellow participants, and on some deep level I was actually managing to stay calm and to remain in my heart.) Still, the intensity kept building and shifting, and more and more visionary events were unfolding, and the Portuguese was sounding really strange, even as I was, at the same time, in awe of the melodic beauty and subtlety of the hymns (and thank God for the periodic translations into English that Jonathan would offer, out loud, so that I had occasional glimpses into the profound messages that these hymns transmitted).

I never said, "It's too much," but it was really, really close.

And then Jonathan, Taran, and Bonnie started to walk around the room, energetically working with various people. They were apparently channeling different types of disincarnate beings—and mercy: the beings that were "coming through" were just so weird. Jonathan and Taran would both occasionally make these unearthly sounds (one that really stood out to me was sort of like a whale call—starting deep and then rising in pitch—as if the being was breaching, with little burbles of curiosity and pleasure, from some unknown depths into this world). They'd move from person to person in a type of shuffling, "what in the world is this physical body I'm inhabiting?" sort of way—their physical movements not quite fitting into the normal postures, gestures, and cadences of our world, all the while making occasional forceful invocations to various Christian saints and exotically named spirits as they stood over the prone or seated bodies of the participants. And then they would perhaps brush down the body of the person they were working with, exhaling a force-ful "whoosh" of breath as their hands swept downward through the person's energy field; or their hands would whirl really fast in various complex geomet-ric configurations in-and-through the energy fields surrounding each person, as if they were working to clean those fields from various patterns of invisible debris. And much of the time their fingers were clicking and their tongues were whistling, and I just wanted to go fetal and close my eyes and cover my ears. It was just so much, and again and again I would release these deep sighs, or these un-premeditated, almost primordial groans would emerge out of me as if I was giving birth to something that was somehow simultaneously completely for-eign and yet (oddly) also brought with it the heartfelt, albeit inchoate, knowl-edge that "this is home."

But mercy, that home had definitely been forgotten for quite some time, and I just needed a moment or two to adjust.

And what the heck were those invisible, nonphysical, but viscerally felt, and deeply alien, beings doing who, all of the sudden, out of nowhere, seemed to be huddled around my prostrate physical form? It sure seemed like they were examining me, probing in-and-around my energy field with what appeared to be long spindly fingers, and doing all of this with a curious yet detached atti-tude, all the while making these tremendously fast and intricately patterned clicking sounds.

And then they were gone.

And all the time the Daime was coursing through my body, and the Force was just pressing and pressing, rushing in, pushing through the cellular, energetic resistance that I consciously, repeatedly, asked to release. Unbelievably, I kept asking, silently within myself, for more, even as I'd at times find myself hanging on to memories of my wife, my cats, my house, my office—that formerly familiar world that seemed so far away, but nonetheless was deeply valued and missed. I was feeling so much love and appreciation for my wife and I'd repeatedly send love to her, hoping that on some level it was getting through.

And for hours, starting fairly early on in the day, helicopters flew over our cabin, literally shaking the walls with the thundering force and almost deafen-ing bass throbbing of their rotors, followed by the roar and creak and invasive whine and scrape of bulldozers that seemed to pass by within yards of our door.

I kept having to fight against paranoia, saying to myself, "Oh my God, what is happening? Is this the prelude to a massive police bust?" I was telling myself to be calm, there's got to be a reason for this. (It ended up that the park rangers just happened to have training exercises in the area right outside our door that very day—exercises that appeared to be, as it were, physical accompaniments to or echoes of the massive, forceful, invasive, penetrative power of the Daime that was working its way in-and-through all of us.)

And there was something that was much more subtle, much more difficult to articulate, something that was present, on and off again, throughout the three days that we drank Daime: this indescribable "otherworldly" presence/energy/ vibratory frequency; this almost stilted, surreal, slightly not of this earth atmosphere, like a superimposition of another dimension (dimensions!) onto this one, accompanied at times by this rather spooky sense of spiritual wings that were fluttering just outside of the grasp of physical ears.

And all of this was combined with a really odd upwelling of what felt like nostalgia for an archetypal realm that was just out of reach; a realm that resonated, mysteriously, within me as having some sort of elusive link to Narnia, the mythical realm described by C. S. Lewis in his books for children. Narnia—a world that coexists with our world. Narnia—the world of tree spirits and dwarves and talking animals, including (crucially) Aslan, the Christ who appeared in that world in the form of a radiant, all-wise, all-powerful lion. Narnia—the world into which young children from our world would at times accidentally stumble (or be drawn into by Providence—take your pick) and then undergo dramatic and spiritually essential tests and journeys and battles, only to eventually mature into kings and queens who would rule this mythical realm of primordial beauty and majesty, having themselves been anointed by the King: Aslan (kings and queens who would, years later, be drawn back into our world, only to then, mysteriously, become transformed back into children, as if the years and years of experience that they had undergone in Narnia had somehow immediately evaporated.)

There was just something about Narnia and Aslan during this day's work (and not just because Eleanor, this exceedingly sweet, kind-hearted, gray-haired woman from the Santo Daime church in Maryland was wearing an Aslan T-shirt—although that almost certainly helped).

And all of this that I have attempted to describe is just the barest fraction of what happened during that day.

I do remember, however, as that first day wore to a close (we finished around 6:00 p.m. every day), that Taran was hovering over me as I was flat on my back on my camping pad. He then crouched down and finally knelt beside me for quite some time. He seemed to be incorporating some sort of Native American spirit, and he put his hand on my heart, and his deep warm voice was saying something to me, something soothing, loving, comforting, and he was giving me a message from this spirit. (I later realized, to my dismay, that I remembered none of it.)

I do remember, however, closing the day. We all had somehow managed to bring ourselves to a standing position on our mats and we sang several more hymns and then recited the Our Father and Hail Mary again, three times each. The whole time I felt so haggard and worn out that I could barely remain standing, so much so that at times I had to lean over, my head and torso dropping forward and down as I supported my weight on my knees, and I just breathed in and out, asking for a little more strength so that I could make it through. And then, almost miraculously, something shifted and I found that I actually could lift myself up again, all the while releasing this huge sigh.

Then we were all standing in a circle, with the altar in the center, and Jonathan was leading us in a Circle of Healing, where we were asked to call to mind those people we loved, people who were struggling or people to whom we simply wanted to send our love and blessings. We were asked to say their names out loud, standing there with our right hands raised, sending each name into the center, to the *cruzeiro*, the double-barred cross. And I said my wife's name, Sandra, then the names of my parents and my siblings and their children, and various others, all of this as everyone around me was firmly, for the most part, also contributing names into the center, which increasingly seemed to be this whirling complex nexus of energetic strands. Finally, everything quieted down. And then Jonathan said out loud, forcefully, a prayer for healing that we repeated, also forcefully, phrase by phrase after him.

Then, after a moment of reverent silence, Jonathan formally spoke in the name of key members of the Santo Daime pantheon, reciting the prayer that officially closes every Santo Daime work ("In the name of God, Father, All Powerful; of the Virgin Sovereign Mother; of our Lord Jesus Christ; of the Patriarch St. Joseph; and of all the Divine Beings of the Celestial Court, under the order of our Master Empire Juramidam, our Work is closed, my brothers and my sisters. Praise be to God in the heights! May our Mother, the most Holy Mary, be forever praised above all humanity.") I then attempted to mimic the hand motions of everyone, as they made these mysterious small signs of the cross with their right thumb, first over the forehead, then the mouth, then the heart, and then they all made a larger sign of the cross, moving the right middle finger from the forehead, to the heart, to the left shoulder, to the right shoulder, and finally ending with the lips lightly kissing the fingertips of the right hand.

And then, at long last, we were officially done, which was followed by lots of clapping, smiles, hugging, greeting each other, and chatting. But I was really out of it, and I guess both Jonathan and Taran noticed, because they very kindly and gently led me to the showers and spent a lot of time with me, making sure that I was able to navigate the quite daunting task of undressing and showering—even going so far as to fill up a pitcher with hot water and herbs and pouring it over my head at the end of the process—I'm guessing as some sort of final cleansing.

After the shower I made my way back to my bunk bed and crashed for a while. Finally, after lying there, exhausted, my nerves still sizzling and raw, I managed, moving extremely slowly, to find my way to the floor when I heard another roommate stirring, and went with him, arm in arm through the dark, so grateful that he was there to find the correct trail. We finally, almost miraculously, made it to the dining room.

After managing to only eat a few bites for dinner (the idea of eating seemed almost incomprehensible) and mumbling a few words with a somewhat shaky smile to the people nearby, I ultimately ended up back at our group's ritually charged cabin, where there was a lengthy sharing session, in which we all had the opportunity, if we wished, to talk about our experience and to ask questions to Jonathan, who responded, often quite eloquently, to what people offered into the collective space.

While I don't remember much about the specifics of what others shared, I do remember thinking to myself: these are really special people. Even the ones who pushed my buttons clearly possessed "something"—a radiance, an inner glow, a loving heart. I was especially touched by how present and generously attentive everyone was when I shared, trying my best to be as open as I could, about how challenging my day had been. I told them (and what follows in italics is my accurate as possible paraphrase of that conversation): *You know, there's part of me that simply can't imagine why in the world I would do two more days of this.* Pretty much everyone laughed, and then continued to chuckle when I confessed, *After the work was over, I was (I swear!) thinking to myself: "How in the heck do I get out of here?" I kept finding some part of me plotting my exit strategy: "I wonder how I could call a taxi? I don't have a car, and this workshop is basically miles in the boonies . . ."*

However, everyone became quietly attentive when I went on to tell them that I finally decided: *Heck, I'm just going to go for it.* Jonathan nodded appreciatively when I said that, and then he asked me, *Did you ever ask for help from the Beings or from the Daime? Did you ever ask them to lay off you for a bit?* I said, *No—but I came close. What I tried to do, instead, was to allow myself to be taken right to the edge. Then I'd just hang out in that intensity with as much awareness as possible; it seemed important to really let myself feel into all of that newness and strangeness.* Jonathan then said, *Your willingness to go for it with such heart shows just how ready you are for this work—and the Daime was responding to that readiness by giving you a lot. The Daime's willingness to meet you so fully means that it respects you quite a bit. But you should know that if it ever does become too much to handle, you can always ask the Daime to turn it down a notch—there's nothing wrong with that.* He then went on to say, *I want to tell you this: I heard, very clearly, from the Daime, from within, that the Divine Beings are very pleased that you've come here. They told me that there is a program, a plan for you.* Hearing him say that, really clearly, with his whole heart, with everyone listening, sort of threw me for a loop (and probably fed into whatever infantile narcissistic sense of specialness that lingered, under the surface, within me). I tried my best to rally and finally said, with a smile, *Well, now I understand why, somewhere in the middle of it all, I said to myself: "I've worked all my life for this."*

Nonetheless, I also admitted, right then and there, that I was having a lot of trouble with all of the Christian language in the hymns and prayers. I said: *My spiritual life is about yoga and meditation and Eastern mysticism, so whenever I'd hear the hymns talk about sin and punishment I was really, to be honest, turned off. I mean, I tried to be respectful, but I just couldn't bring myself to say the Our Father and Hail Mary out loud. I just couldn't relate. And sometimes just hearing the word "Jesus" makes me wince inside.* Jonathan listened with a tiny smile on his face and then said, *I completely understand. I mean, come on, I'm Jewish. I was a lot like that at first myself. But now look at me! So, genuinely, thank you for sharing that—I really appreciate your clarity and courage.*

As he said that, I could almost hear within myself the words from a hymn that Jonathan had received a few weeks before and that had been sung that day. "There is no one outside of yourself who can tell you what you should believe." When I heard this hymn, it really touched something in me—it seemed in some mysterious and deeply powerful way to carry, via the words and music, the heart, the quintessence of that expanded/altered time and place. That verse was a type of touchstone for me, in that I could tell myself, *So what that there's all of this weird stuff in the Santo Daime. At least they're not trying to convert me; at least they're not telling me what I should believe. If that's really true, then there might actually be a way that I could be part of something like this.*

But oh my God (I thought to myself): there really is some truly weird stuff going on in this tradition—especially all of that mediumistic strangeness . . .

Jonathan made sure to address the issue of mediumship right up front in the sharing session (he couldn't have avoided it if he had tried, since everyone seemed to have questions about it).

He said something pretty close to what I've put in italics below in my paraphrase:

During this type of work, there's often a lot of mediumship. One level of mediumship is when we consciously invoke Beings of Light, these really powerful Beings who want to help everyone to spiritually evolve. We can learn how to work with these Beings really quickly, really deeply, when we take the Daime. When we drink Daime we are taught, by the Daime, how to attune ourselves to this level, how to let them work in-and-through us. But, that's not the only type of mediumship that happens in the Santo Daime tradition. Some daimistas, not everybody, just those people who are called to this type of spiritual work, are willing to voluntarily open themselves up to what in the Santo Daime we call "suffering spirits." These are spirits of people who have died, but for a number of reasons are still sticking around—they haven't moved on yet to the next world. They're sort of stuck here. Many of them died suddenly, or violently, or they were deeply addicted to drugs, or sex, or alcohol, or to the adrenaline rush of picking fights. Many of them don't even know that they're dead—and yet, because they don't have a physical body, they'll find themselves attracted to someone in this physical reality with similar tendencies and they'll sort of sidle up to them and get intertwined in that person's energy field, almost like energetic parasites, and in a sense feed off of the person's fears, or anger, or misery. They might even amplify those feelings in the person, sort of egging them on. In fact, there are a lot of people who are dealing with suffering spirits in this world, even if they don't know it. They're often drug addicts, or alcoholics, or people who are really struggling in different ways, and these people are, at least in part, that way because they're unconsciously sensitive to spiritual energies; they just sort of automatically take on this really heavy, difficult energy that comes into almost everyone just from living, especially in urban environments, or their energy field becomes infested with all of these suffering spirits that are glomming on—it's like this dark cloud of suffering spirits has become intertwined with that person's energetic system. So lots of the people who are really suffering—they're really not just feeling their own suffering. They're also taking on the suffering of other beings, either incarnate or disincarnate—and in some way, that's sort of beautiful, in that at least unconsciously, those people are offering themselves as a way for that suffering to be worked through. But most of these people don't have very many tools to help them to work with that suffering in an effective way, so they just sort of stew in it. Hopefully, over time, and with God's grace, some of it manages to get transformed, but if it does, it's a really slow process.

But, thank God, there's a much better way to be a medium than that sort of unconscious mediumship. We can also learn how to work with those energies consciously, with the Daime to help us. There are some daimista mediums who consciously, willingly, open themselves to these suffering spirits; these spirits are actually welcomed into their bodies and minds. And that's no joke. It's not easy to feel all of that pain, that hatred, that fear; to really feel it.

He then turned to Pamela and said, *When you were wailing, Pamela, you were really feeling that suffering, weren't you? But I'd be willing to bet that, on another level, you weren't identifying with that level of suffering either—that you were, on a deeper level of your being, staying really calm, really quiet inside, right? As a medium, you can allow these spirits to express themselves in-and-through you, you can let them cry and wail, and you can feel their pain, but on a deeper level, I bet there's a part of you, a really deep part of you, where you stay centered, quiet, calm, in your heart and in the Light—that's what gives these suffering spirits a chance to let go, to go to the Light, to be transformed.*

It's a real honor to work with these suffering spirits in the Santo Daime, because even they are, on some level, attracted to the Light of the Daime. They might enter this sacred space and they're filled with doubts, and they're saying no, and they're resisting with all their might, but even with all of that, they still, on the deepest level, want to be free. On some level they long for what they know that the Daime is offering to them. So, to incorporate them is our way of offering charity; it's our way to be vehicles for the Light of the Christ. In this way, the spirit of the Christ, in-and-as the Daime and in-and-through us to the extent that we say yes *to it, wants to transform these dense, dark, twisted-up energies; the Christ within us seeks to redeem these suffering spirits, to radiate Forgiveness and Unconditional Love into their field so that they can experience the explosion of joy that erupts when they come to know, directly, with amazement and thankfulness, what they really are: pure Light.*

Sort of bodhisattva-like, I thought to myself. (From the perspective of Mahāyāna Buddhism, bodhisattvas are enlightened beings who, out of compassion, are willing to be reborn again and again, and hence take on suffering, in order to help others reach enlightenment.)

DAY TWO: "I WENT UP, I WENT UP, I WENT UP."

I woke up the next morning (Friday) on the upper bunk in my cramped cabin, having had a vivid dream of my former spiritual teacher, Swami Muktananda. (I spent over seven years with this powerful and ambiguous spiritual teacher.) In the dream, Muktananda was in something like a hotel ballroom, and he was teaching four of us how to surf. All that we could do, however, was to pretend to move as if we were actually in the ocean on a surfboard. But then, all of the sudden, he gave each of us a shove and whoosh!—we were in this very real, very wet, swiftly flowing river. I quickly discovered that I couldn't swim against the current, so instead I headed for the shore, swimming really hard. Once I climbed up onto the bank, I used my cell phone (that miraculously had emerging unscathed) to call home for someone to pick me up.

I thought that the dream was fairly auspicious.

I started that morning with a strong, focused intention: to really go for it. I told myself: Don't get stuck in any fascination with all of that spirit incorporation. Don't get caught up in all of that spooky shit. You've got yourself a golden opportunity here. You know that the Daime is really powerful; it's the real deal. So, why not take advantage of that and link up with it as much as you can allow and really go for it: go far, go deep. Go for God, for pure love, for divine wisdom, for divine power. Go full bore for union with God, for complete enlightenment. As I said this to myself, I could even picture myself with a wand in my hand, pointing it at all of the wild, weird, and wonderful phenomena that the Daime might manifest while strutting its stuff on the astral stage, and then "zapping" each of these manifestations, in essence saying again and again: Nope. I'm not satisfied. That's all lovely, that's all very well and good, but I want more. I want God.

Of course, any and every moment, whether "normal" or psychedelic, is—at least to my ontologically nondualistic vision of reality—a manifestation of God. (And to be fair to myself, I even realized this in that very instant.) God is right here and right now; our own conscious experience is nothing but a divine manifestation, morphing into infinite forms. So there's really no need for the big bang of enlightenment (whatever *that* is). And there's no need to reject or rebuff the flashy astral stuff that the Daime can reveal, because that too is God revealing one of God's own infinite forms—a form that is especially tailormade, just for us; a form that is given as a gift so that we can come to know and to enjoy some of the wonders of this miraculous universe that are typically hidden from our sight; a form that is given to us so that we can realize, in just that specific way, a flash of that creative Matrix who is experiencing and creating life in-and-through each one of us. It's wonderful to have a profound yearning for deeper levels of truth, love, and power. It's beautiful to have genuine and profoundly transformative experiences of our typically hidden but always present divine nature. Nonetheless, the gift of our genuine, heartfelt longing for spiritual awakening has, at least in some ways, been given to us by previous experiences such as these, by these gifts of grace.

After breakfast, there was the now somewhat familiar pattern of everyone rustling around setting up their spots; followed by standing and reciting the prayers;
then lining up—very informally—to drink Daime; then some bioenergetic exercises; then lying down, listening to some soft gentle music, as the Daime slowly
began to kick in.

Looking back at my notes from that day, I can tell that I had difficulty
remembering many specifics from the first part of that day's work—that is, from
the time when the Daime had been switched on within me, when I was just
plunged into what seemed to be an endless ocean of visionary experiences and
was pushed to my limits, and often beyond. What I mainly remember, even
now, was the underlying "vibe" of that morning—it was so otherworldly; there
was this tacit, but visceral, knowing, somehow, that different dimensions were
suddenly "dialing into" our space/time (or alternatively, that we were being
"beamed up" into those alternative worlds), so that everything shone from
within with this overlay of dramatically "alien" or "mythical" energies and presences. And that haunting sense of "weirdness" (not altogether off-putting, often
quite poignant) was clearly magnified by the times when Jonathan and Taran
walked around the room, incorporating various unknown but definitely spooky
spirits, walking really slowly, and looking at their bodies as if they were hovering
a few feet above them, fascinated and intrigued at how these bodies of flesh
and blood and bone moved, their bodies shuffling about rather oddly, as if the
beings within them weren't quite used to driving around in this particular type
of car. And then, of course, they would at times, out of the blue, once again start
making those really eerie sounds that would rise up from some way-out-there
place within them.

Throughout the day I grew to really appreciate Jonathan and the crew. In their
own way, they all seemed to be really at ease in themselves and very real—fully
there, grounded, alive, firm, and strong, yet also, at least at times, genuinely play-
ful and seeming to enjoy each moment. I'm not saying that each of them couldn't
at times also get rather intense. But I often felt utter awe at how they were able to
drink all of that Daime and yet, for hours and hours, somehow managed to stay
so alert, so deeply tuned into what people were going through, and then seemed
to know exactly what was needed in each situation; how they could be sitting
there for hours, just solidly holding the space for everyone; or how they could
open themselves up so easily and fully to this whole variety of spiritual beings
that they would channel at different points during the work; or how they just
seemed so attuned, in a really relaxed way, to the flow of the work—how they
knew which hymns to sing; or when it was the right time to encourage everyone in the room to silently turn their attention within; or when they needed to

lovingly help different people who were, each in a unique way, going through often very charged and demanding processes. How was it possible for them to be there so fully and lovingly with everyone, seemingly tirelessly, for hour upon hour of high-voltage Santo Daime work, when they too had drunk quite sizable quantities of Daime?

As for me, I often couldn't imagine how it would be possible to even sit up, much less sing hymns or play the maracá or guitar, or remain so firm, and open, and loving. Most of the time I just wanted to lie down; to dive in; and to let the Daime sweep me away, but with me firmly at the tiller, navigating through the inner tumult, with my longing for only the Highest guiding me.

And at some point, somewhat near the end of the work, I was really opening myself up, being taken deep within by the Daime. And I was also, oddly, being taken up: at some point, it felt like I was transported "upward" (whatever that means in these nonspatial levels of consciousness—nonetheless, there really was a sense of up). Then, it felt just as one of the hymns of Mestre Irineu describes: "I went up, I went up, I went up, it was with joy." And in this case, when I "arrived," when I "woke up" in that exalted level of reality, I discovered that I had finally become, but somehow, astonishingly, had also always been an integral part of and a participant in a council of sacred elders, a holy communion of saints. We were all radiant divine beings—a fellowship of those who had succeeded in manifesting, with almost complete transparency, God's love, freedom, power, joy—all of the divine qualities. And having woken up to that radiant and magnified level of reality, I realized that all of this is always happening "above" my normal, egoic awareness in a way that is typically unseen, and this archetypal realm is infusing and enlivening my earthly existence. During that altered time/space, I was totally "there" as a monadic (ocean-in-the-drop) condensation of this joyful, dancing, overlapping, utterly fulfilled, utterly radiant, God-connected, many-in-Oneness. Nonetheless, and simultaneously, at least in some distant level of my awareness, I was also connected to my physical form as it was lying there, prostrate on the thin camp mattress, and I was dimly aware of the "ordinary" world around me as well.

And as a crucial subset of that awareness, I was listening to voices of my fellow participants in the cabin singing with such heart and feeling those hymns of glorious beauty and complexity—each word, each melodic phrase helping to sing God into creation; we were God infusing God with Life, in-and-through the celestial Light that was pouring through the words and music of those hymns (and the guitar). It truly felt to me as if that higher dimension that I was currently inhabiting/contributing to was somehow pouring through into ordinary reality, transfiguring everything, as if all of us in that tiny rustic cabin were becoming increasingly transparent, in-and-as the quirky, completely individual, and irreplaceable people we were.

I kept saying to myself, with such awe, such gratitude: this can't be real—can it? But it is. Oh my God. Thank you. Thank you. Thank you. It felt as if I had somehow managed to shrug off the mud and grit from the lower realms in which I, as a human being, typically moved. And interfused with that moment was this vivid image of the convicts in the film *Raising Arizona*, erupting upward from the earth outside the prison that had previously held them captive; emerging through the tunnel of their own making; clawing their way through the final barrier of blinding earthen ooze. The primary difference was that, in my case, I was surfacing into this new yet deeply familiar world of wonder and grace; I was a prodigal son, enriched with experience, being welcomed back—back home, back to where I am fully who I am. And there I was: rocking and reeling in waves of profound love; transfixed with sheer awe at what I was witnessing, at times with my eyes closed, at times while seated with my eyes open, looking around me at each person in the room, each one dressed in white, seeing each one as a sacred, utterly unique, highly precious, and completely beautiful form of God; shaking my head in wonder and periodically murmuring to myself, while holding my hands reverently on my chest, "Oh my God! Oh my God."

Everything was transfigured. And I just knew. We're all in this together, it's an open secret. We're all in a cosmic boat together, traveling in that realm (this realm!) of divine Power and Beauty and Presence and Light that is also this specific ongoing moment on this shimmering earth. And there in that cabin, God's glory was shining in-and-through us, as though we were in a wind tunnel of majesty; it was pouring through and illuminating us as we were singing in that tiny cabin (or seen another way, that crystalline paradise). All of us were praising God; we were all impregnated with divinity; we were all saturated with it; we were all charged with the mission of incarnating God's Love and Presence on this earth in-and-through our bodies and minds; we were all singing those hymns together—hymns of power; hymns that opened portals to the higher dimensions; hymns that opened the way; hymns that offered us a highly specific vibratory link to God's Presence and Light. And we were all swaying in God, as God. And then something momentous shifted and Christ was fully there; Christ was among us—in-and-as Jonathan? Me? Everyone? Yes, Yes, Yes. And more, much more, than I could possibly imagine.

I was simply awestruck. I was ecstatic to finally be back, joyfully welcomed to where I belonged, to who I truly was and am. I just knew: I am a Being of Light in the fellowship of other Beings of Light, each of us, in his or her utterly unique way, manifesting divinity. I felt almost exactly as if I was living in the final pages of C. S. Lewis's final book in the Narnia series, *The Last Battle*, in which, at the very end of everything (or said differently, at the very *beginning* of everything), God's Daughters and Sons joyously entered a transfigured Edenic world, a world that was the "higher octave" of their previous world. Nonetheless, these Sons and Daughters (joyously) felt compelled to keep going higher, deeper, farther into the very edges of that world until they entered, astonishingly, into an even more transfigured and radiant version of their previous world. And they kept going, drinking in God's presence. And there was no end to what they discovered while they were, themselves, becoming increasingly joyous, free, alive, and fulfilled. And there was more, and more, each world more potent, more real, more joyous, more complete than the one before.

I swear it was just like that, all of us becoming more and more ourselves, and more and more fully divine, capable of holding and radiating more Light, more Love, more Presence than we had ever imagined was possible. It was the great culmination; it was/is what we're heading for—the Always and the Not Yet— sheer divinity always Present, and yet there's always More.

Amazingly, that spiritual culmination coincided, seamlessly, with the ending of the work, because soon, all of us were standing in a somewhat bleary and dazed circle, and I was still in the Power, glowing. I was standing there in my place, dancing, swaying, as the closing hymns were sung—feeling so loose, so free, and so alive. Everything felt magical. And then, after all the closing hymns and prayers, after the circle of healing, after the work was officially over, Jonathan and Taran both came over, and each of them, in their own way, gave me this strong loving embrace. And then Jonathan said, "You did wonderful work today," and I felt so joyous. After they left, I stood there on my mat, so lit up, and I reached out to hug Leo (whose place was to my right), and he was also lit up, and we just embraced each other, so fervently, so filled with excitement, and we babbled to each other in our joy at what we had experienced. It was then that I discovered, to my astonishment, that he too had felt that sense of divinity pouring into the room; he too had received that knowledge that each of us is connected; that each of us was awakening and doing the work of the Christ here on this earth; he too felt that all of us were plugged into Light and that we were increasingly learning how to let our true natures shine forth. Leo hugged me again and practically shouted in my ear: "Remember this! Remember this!"

Afterward, I went around hugging people—they all seemed so scrumptious, so lovable. At one point, spotting Pamela, I ran over to where she was, enthusiastically joining in the close-knit gathering of women, many of whom were sprawled around the floor, casually talking and laughing together. At one point, Pamela was kneeling in from of me, glowing, radiant, saying how she felt this really strong connection to me; that it was more than our shared Siddha Yoga background; that she just knew that I was her spiritual brother. And I felt it too—it really did feel like she was my sister. So sweet. . . . And then I was huddling with Clemence (the gentle earth-mother logistical facilitator for the retreat), and she was telling me how important it was to write down as much as I could remember of what had happened during the work; how during the work itself, it's like we all have downloaded several gigabytes of data that will automatically be stored in our subconscious, but that it's a really good exercise to bring that spiritual information, as much as possible, to the surface of consciousness.

I don't have too many notes from that night's sharing session, just that Jonathan was at ease, funny, eloquent, and tuned-in, as usual. At one point he responded to one woman who shared how much she longed for God by telling her that although longing for God is crucial, and a strong prayer genuinely establishes a link to the Astral, nonetheless, at times we can hijack legitimate longing with our neediness, with our demands, and we can start to broadcast a "pushing out energy" or forcing current—and at some point, it's really important to learn how to switch our spiritual attitude to one of opening up, of acceptance, of receiving with gratitude whatever is given, moment to moment. He also spoke about how when we are able to do this, we are opening up our capacity to see what's really happening, underneath it all. (The whole time I was sitting there, cheering him on inside.)

And then I shared, filled with exhilaration, the wondrous experience that I had undergone that afternoon—my voice at times shaky, feeling so deeply filled with such gratitude and awe. And afterward Jonathan praised the depth of my intention, pointing out how my heartfelt longing for enlightenment helped to co-create my experience with the Daime, emphasizing how the Daime responds to what we ask for—even if, at least at times, in unexpected ways.

DAY THREE: RELEASING

Saturday began with the same ritual process as the previous two days. I entered into that ramshackle cabin and saw that the raggedy circle (with all of its backjacks and pillows and pads and blankets) was still holding firm. People dressed in white were ambling in after breakfast, and then it all gradually began: standing for prayers, then drinking Daime, then more bioenergetic exercises, then lying down and listening to soothing music while feeling the Force approach.

This time I went into our work with a sense of longing that was at least somewhat toned down from Friday's overall intentionality (which had been, in essence: I insist that you, God, give me nothing less than enlightenment). Instead, I lay down on my mat and just opened up and relaxed. And gradually, almost without noticing it, I began to find myself bathing in golden Light and Power. I felt so deeply plugged in: it was as if I was charging my cells, letting them become increasingly infused with more and more Love, Energy, and Presence. I was also strongly feeling my crown and third eye energy centers opening, as well as a subtle internal sensation that was like an ongoing unfurling of rustling feathers, all of this while also seeing, with my eyes closed, the mostly blue and gold Light that poured down into me and washed through me. Throughout this whole time I was also feeling the otherworldly uncanniness of the atmosphere— that unique, known only through direct experience "note" or vibratory "tone" of the Daime. The room was filled, as it were, with muted clicking sounds vibrating in the background of awareness and with a whispering that was barely heard, like hummingbird wings, fluttering on the edges of perception. All of this was taking place within me while, in a way that was not at all incongruent, Jonathan, Jane, Taran, and Bonnie kept up an easy, joking, sort of "just between us" knowing laughter and banter as they almost casually, with a lot of calm and grounded easiness, nudged the work forward.

By this time, I was really beginning to appreciate the open-ended but strongly held "container" that was the structure of the Self-Transformation works. I loved all of the space and time to really go deep within, knowing that someone (Jonathan and the crew) would be there tending, so tenderly, to those people who were struggling (thrashing, weeping). At other times, various people in the cabin would come up to Jonathan as he was sitting there on his backjack, apparently embodying some sort of Spiritual Presence and he would help to open up the mediumship of these people, holding out his arm with his hand raised in blessing and at times making a loud ejaculatory whoop. At other times, Jonathan would announce, clearly, firmly, which hymns we were going to sing and then he and the crew would proceed to sing them with such clarity, heart, and attunement, accompanied by the rhythmic hiss of the maracás and the strumming beauty of the guitar. And the whole time, I would just lie there on my mat, in awe at the sweetness, complexity, and beauty of the hymns—just letting them wash over me; letting them carry me forward; letting them orient me back to my heart; letting them remind me, with their celestial overtones, of my divine heritage.

But I'll admit, this work was also rough at times. By this time, simply the smell of the Daime, to say nothing of its taste, would provoke an intense visceral reaction within me—almost of dread, and certainly of repulsion. After drinking it, and as the workshop progressed, it sure felt like the concentration level of the Daime was getting more potent. My body would at times begin to sweat strongly, or after drinking my serving of Daime with a grimace on my face, I'd quickly leave the serving line and hurriedly exit the cabin to go outside, my body hunched over and quivering, my head bowed, as I'd shake my arms out by my sides, all while spontaneously emitting these forcefully explosive expulsive sounds as I attempted to simply cope with the powerful, almost invasive potency of the Daime penetrating my digestive system—feeling strongly the divine Pressure building within as the Daime started to work to reconfigure my subtle body so that it would be able to vibrate in alignment with the deeper/higher dimensions of Reality that it was attempting to introduce me to. This was happening, but not without my body/mind instinctively recoiling, resisting, tensing up against the onslaught—leading at times to me once again having to battle with the concurrent waves of nausea that would arise, only to then (thank God) finally subside.

There was one time when I was almost pinned to my mat; swept away in the current of the Force of the Daime; feeling filled to overflowing with the energy of the Daime, as if it was saturating my cells; and then I heard, as if from very far away, Jonathan at the front of the cabin starting to offer more Daime, with the concurrent periodic clink of shot glasses and the glass serving pitcher. My initial response was, I don't know if I *can*, but then, surprisingly, something within me shifted and I managed to make my way up to my knees, enough for Jonathan to spot me and come to me to offer another serving. Each time, even though it was extremely difficult, I always decided to go for it, to dive into what was being offered, both physically and spiritually, as much as possible, without holding back. And in the end, those moments themselves, (on my knees in front of the Daime!) would often feel exceedingly reverent and sacramental, almost bordering on sacrificial—as I offered myself, with all of my resistances, for healing, for the highest possible transformation.

Toward the end of the work I was lying there, deeply immersed, feeling simultaneously swept away and flattened by the Daime, when suddenly I felt, again as if from far away, this powerful release in my bowels. At first I thought it was simply gas, but then I realized, with a gradual welling up of embarrassment and chagrin, that much more than gas had been released. It took me a few moments to adjust to my changed situation. I lay there attempting to consciously shift gears from *far away/deep in the Force of the Daime* to *OK, I can't just lie here.* I've got to get up and do something. So, rallying myself, I got up from my mat and awkwardly but as quickly as possible (white pants!), still reeling in the Force, I shuffled hurriedly out of the cabin, and then, in my dazed and deeply in the Force state, I somehow managed to make it back to my cabin; locate a change of clothes; trudge down the trail to the cinderblock institutional bathroom; strip off my soiled clothes; take a shower; get re-dressed; shuffle back to my cabin to drop off my embarrassingly stained pants/underpants; and then, still reeling in the Force, I made my way back to where it all started, back to the work with the Daime.

Stepping inside, Taran greeted me, saying, with a lot of kindness, "Welcome back, brother. I was just about ready to go and look for you, to check and see if you were alright. How are you doing?" I hugged him and then quickly and quietly told him the highlights of my adventure. He barely even looked surprised. Instead, he reassuringly whispered, with a knowing half-smile, "I've been there before, brother. Let me help you back to your place."

Then, as I was slowly making my way back to my mat, with Taran's firm arm supporting me, I saw that Jonathan was lifting himself up from a horizontal position on his own mattress (a very rare sight indeed—he almost never laid down). He then leaned over and softly began to sing something to Taran, who by that time had settled back down beside Jonathan up front. Taran then picked up his guitar, and quickly working out the correct melody, started to accompany Jonathan as he sang what I later learned was a hymn that Jonathan had received just moments earlier: "New Life."

> Sing, Sing, Sing Little Bird
> To welcome the new day
> Sing, sing, sing little bird
> The Master's on his way
>
> Ring, ring, ring little bell
> To waken the new heart
> Call the angels down to earth
> To bless your brand-new start

Right after Jonathan finished singing the hymn he announced that he was offering it to a longtime friend, but I knew then, and I know now, that this hymn was also, at least in my mind, strongly linked to *my* new life, *my* brand-new start on the Santo Daime path.

That evening after the sharing session, sitting around in the tiny cabin with a few of the other men, I told Jonathan about the diarrhea, and he just laughed and then went on to describe, in exquisite detail, how one time in Brazil he had to gone to the toilet fourteen times, and as he put it, not all of that shit made it to the toilet. He told me, almost offhandedly: "Yeah, the Daime clears out the liver; it causes it to shoot out bile—this yellow liquid."

That night I lay there in my bunk, almost paralyzed with exhaustion and yet still buzzing underneath it all with the lingering presence of the Daime in my system, and in that "wired but tired" state it was as if, on some barely perceptible level of consciousness, I was still continuing the work. Scraps of memories from all three of the works were rising and subsiding of their own accord, in a fairly constant and energized way, for hours and hours that night. And then fairly early the next morning, just before waking up in my top bunk that Sunday for our final gathering, I had a dream. In the dream I was lying on my back, right where I was (in "real" life): in the cabin, on the top bunk. And in the dream, Taran walked over from his bunk. He stood beside me, right by my head/shoulder, and he tapped me gently on my left shoulder to wake me up. I looked up at him and smiled and he smiled back and said, "Bill, I already love you so much." That's when I "really" woke up. And a few hours later, after the morning session was done, after having returned to the cabin and while getting my belongings all packed for the journey home, I told this dream to Taran (and Jonathan). Taran laughed when he heard it, and said, "It's true, man, it's so true." (By the way, Taran later became, and remains, a very dear friend and brother on the spiritual path.)

DAY FOUR: BREATHING

Amazingly, at least to me, I got up from that almost sleepless night feeling wonderful, very bright and energized—really clear, my *nādīs* (the yogic term for pathways of the subtle energy that flows in-and-through the body/mind) all cleaned out, sparkly, and new—albeit perhaps a bit raw and tender. However, my stomach was an exception to all of that physical well-being: it felt as if a huge snake was crawling through my belly for most of Saturday night and through much of Sunday as well, the energetic counterpart of the (thank God not smelly) gas that was rumbling through my system along with God knows what other physiological processes.

Thankfully, however, that grumbling stomach of mine was almost never a factor during the final, non-Daime session we did together as a group for the retreat: a purificatory process of prolonged, repetitive, conscious, deep breathing—accompanied by the (essential!) rhythmic pulsations of music coming from the compilation CD in the boom box sitting on the floor.

Jonathan had told us, ahead of time, that he and his crew had discovered that working with our breath in this way at the end of our retreat would really help to smooth off the edges of what had been unearthed through the work with the Daime during the past three days.

We also had been told earlier that at some point in the process it was common to "cross the bridge" and that when that inner event happened, "something else" would take over, and we'd find ourselves "breathed" rather than "trying to breathe." That switch seemed to have turned on a heck of a lot sooner for others than for me, since within a few minutes, the cabin was filled with wailing people. But I just kept dutifully chugging away with my breath, beginning to wonder if anything would ever happen, until finally, probably after forty minutes (at least), something shifted, and my body began to rapidly and forcefully undulate up and down, moving in sync with the powerful fluxes of subtle energy that I felt rushing through me, wave after wave, rippling up my body. At times my butt would rise up and then forcefully crash down onto the mat; or I'd watch from within, almost bemused, as my torso would arch up while my eyes would roll back and up into my skull, and my arms would float above my head, or would create these elaborate "designs" in extremely fast motions above my torso, all while my body/mind was swaying in rhythm to the now rather forceful music—everything moving spontaneously, of its own accord, with no preplanning. I felt as if I was floating on my back in this warm, boundlessly expansive, Light-filled place within myself, just watching everything that was happening with a sense of delight and appreciation. And then I began to feel more waves coursing through me and from me, waves of gratitude and love—I felt almost flooded with how amazing it was that I was able to be there. I felt deeply moved by the depths of grace that had been shown me—how I had been led there just when I thought a new stage in my spiritual life was needed—and soon I began to laugh loudly, fully, freely. Tears were pouring down my cheeks, so much so that they even began to flow into my ears. I felt so deeply grateful for what I had been given. Then I remembered the first day, and all of my fears of the police barging in (and the other fears that went with that image) and suddenly, from this place of feeling so much gratitude and love, I just knew that if I was feeling this depth of divine Love that it would be possible to take in all that suffering, all of that injustice, and be able to transform it into Light. And as this Knowing was radiating within my heart, I was imbued with a visceral and powerfully convincing sense of Christ standing in front of me and within me, and I was shown that it *is* possible to manifest that Christ consciousness, to say *yes* to that within ourselves more and more fully, and in so doing, we could become vehicles for that divine Power to take on the suffering of the world and redeem it, in-and-through each one of us.

We wrapped up that morning with a final, rather more-brisk-than-usual sharing session. After the sharing, Jonathan led us in a guided contemplation as a way to examine our initial prayers, having us ask ourselves: "In what ways were our prayers answered by the Daime?" He then asked us to ask ourselves: "What is my homework?" As soon as he asked the question, I had an immediate, albeit somewhat fleeting, image of wings opening behind and above me, all while hearing from within a song fragment "I'm going to spread my wings and fly."

After all of the hugs goodbye, and the group photos, and the exchange of email addresses, I loaded all my stuff into the back of Arthur's truck and we drove to the airport, where I caught my flight back to my home Dallas, and was picked up at the DFW airport by my wife. And that night I had dream after dream of working more with the Daime—each dream seeming to unfold and unpack some of the Power and the Light that I had experienced during the retreat. All of this as I kept waking up and hearing, over and over again, excerpts from the hymns. And again, on Wednesday and Thursday night, there were more hours of dreaming about the Daime—with the dreams at times so lucid, so vivid, so lifelike that I was sure that I was actually "there" (in one case, "there" was a hospital where we were consciously working to integrate the use of the Daime with more standard medical procedures)—all while I was also conscious, on some level, of lying there in my bed, "plugged in" to the Power, Light, and high vibration of the Daime.

WHAT I DID NOT YET KNOW ABOUT THE SANTO DAIME

You might have thought that after that wildly powerful first Santo Daime retreat that I'd become an instant convert to the Santo Daime path. But honestly, almost the opposite happened. There was just *so* much about the Santo Daime that I felt deeply uncomfortable with, particularly the Christian focus, especially as it was expressed in the sometimes rather intense lyrics of some of the hymns.

I also continued to think about mediumship. Why in the world would I ever want to mess around with low astral spirits?

And I was having an almost allergic reaction to learning about uniforms, hearing that instead of wearing "whites," daimistas wore actual uniforms to works and sometimes danced back and forth in regimented lines while singing the hymns.

I want to emphasize that when I went on that five-day retreat in February of 2005, I had actually only been exposed to a very small and rather unorthodox slice of the Santo Daime tradition (at least in the formal, institutional sense).

Jonathan and Jane's Self-Transformation way of working with the Daime, I later discovered, was actually rather controversial from the perspective of some fairly high-ranking people in certain "wings" of the Santo Daime religious tradition. (I still remember one Self-Transformation work that I attended a couple of years later where this highly opinionated "hyperorthodox" daimista kept openly grumbling about the nontraditional nature of what Jonathan and Jane were doing.)

Most churches, for example, don't have men and women lying down next to each other while drinking the Daime. (Now, to be fair, Jonathan and Jane shifted this aspect of the Self-Transformation works not too long after this retreat, so that during later Self-Transformation works, even if we still had our "horizontal launching pads," the men were now on their "side" and the women were on their "side.")

Most churches also don't do bioenergetic exercises before starting a work.

Most churches also don't end works with a session of spiritualized breathwork. (By the way, I'm not sure to what extent Jonathan and Jane were overtly influenced by or were trying to replicate the holotropic breathwork process that was started by Christina and Stan Grof, but the two are rather similar).[7] But again, at some point, Jonathan and Jane stopped including the breathing exercises as part of their Self-Transformation works. I'm not sure when or why they stopped doing this.

And in most Santo Daime churches, the only people wearing white are those who haven't chosen to become fardados, or initiates into the tradition. Fardados are individuals who wear *fardas*, or uniforms. (In Portuguese the word is typically only used when referring to a military or police uniform—a distinction that is itself significant, given the military bent of the Santo Daime—more on this facet of the Santo Daime later.) Fardados are people who have decided that the Santo Daime is their spiritual path and therefore want to commit to it. When you become a fardado you shift, as one prominent *padrinho* (Brazilian elder) would often say, from being a "passenger on the boat" to someone who wants "to help row the boat"—a fardado is someone who wants to serve, to help. So when I left the initial retreat in North Carolina, I had not yet seen any women wearing crisp white blouses with a six-pointed star stitched on the front left pocket, along with a navy-blue bow tie, and a pleated navy-blue skirt (well past the knees, please). And I hadn't yet seen men wearing their Sunday-best, starched, white, long-sleeved shirts adorned with plain navy-blue ties and well-pressed navy slacks, with a brass six-pointed star pinned to their chests. (For more information about the historical development of the farda and the use of the star, see "The Historical Development of the Santo Daime: Section One—The Life and Work of Mestre Irineu" at www.liquidlightbook.com/mestre.)

And that's just the uniform for what are called the "blue works," so n̶ because both the women and men wear their blue fardas. There are also whit̶ farda outfits that are worn during festival times, during the highly demanding "dance works," those grueling, yet often in the end deeply satisfying, all-night marathons of dancing and singing hymns that I was exposed to a bit later.

You don't have to enter into this complicated and fascinating religious world with anywhere near the level of ignorance that I did. Therefore, without any further fanfare, I point you (yet again) to "Santo Daime 101" (www. liquidlightbook.com/santodaime), where I offer an extremely compressed and terse overview of the history, beliefs, practices, and institutional structure of the Santo Daime.

2

Philosophical Reflections

FIRST-PERSON WRITING AND THE NATURE OF CONSCIOUSNESS

I'd like to pause a moment here to say a bit about why I've chosen to write in the first person. An experientially grounded perspective is, in my opinion, absolutely critical for any nuanced understanding of ayahuasca spirituality in general and of the Santo Daime tradition specifically.

You can read all about the chemical constituents of ayahuasca; you can read scientific studies replete with colorful pictures of brain scans of other people who are taking psychedelics; you can read impeccable academic papers analyzing, with reams of statistical data, the social behavior and psychological fitness of those who have taken entheogens. All of this literature serves an important function in this world of ours in which it seems that nothing is taken seriously unless it comes blessed with the mantle of scientific respectability and rigor (and there are, increasingly, highly skilled people who feel the call to do this sort of work). But if all that you ever did was to read "objective" analyses of psychedelics, I think that it's safe to say that you wouldn't have a clue as to the depth and quality of the shifts in consciousness that can and often do take place when you drink Daime, or take any other classical psychedelic substance—ideally with an uplifting set of attitudes (such as hope, desire for self-knowledge, trust in the process) and within a supportive setting (that is, in surroundings that are safe, peaceful, and beautiful and with experienced and caring guides)—all the while also paying close attention to the amount of Daime that is ingested.

My intention, therefore, is to switch the angle from which we often approach these experiences—to let go, at least for the moment, at looking at psychedelics from the outside-in (that is, looking at them from a third-person perspective) and to embrace instead what taking psychedelics (in this case, ayahuasca) feels like from the inside-out (that is, from a "first-person" point of view). And yes, it is true: you are reading about what happened to someone else, and in that way, these descriptions of my inner life are still no substitute for the vivid, incandescent immediacy and convincing force of personal experience. I openly acknowledge that it is extremely difficult, if not impossible, to convey in words the energetic reality and textures of this quality of experience. (As the philosopher William James was famous for pointing out, one of the classic marks of a mystical experience is its "ineffability."[1]) Therefore, I explicitly want to honor what my descriptions have missed; what my words have left out; what simply, inherently, couldn't be communicated. And yet, I also have faith that even imperfectly crafted words can serve a valuable function. In this case, at minimum, they can point in a certain direction and say: Here's what I discovered. If you feel inspired, go there and see what you find.

I would suggest that this sort of first-person exploration is crucial to any adequate knowledge of what psychedelics have to offer. And in fact, first-person exploration (ideally, an exploration that is rooted in a subtle and profound philosophical foundation and also as phenomenologically nuanced as possible—investigating with as much precision as possible the intricacies of what appears to our consciousness) is crucial to any adequate exploration of consciousness in itself. Because it has to be said: examining consciousness is not like examining objects in the external world. Human beings, throughout our time on this planet and in all cultures, have primarily and, it appears, increasingly had to focus our attention almost exclusively on what was going on in the external world simply to survive. So, evolutionarily, biologically, it makes sense that we are, as it were, "hardwired" to look outside ourselves and that we believe that this realm of experience is what truly counts, what truly matters. (Notice the high value that is given, even linguistically, to what is quantifiable and physical.) Human beings, biologically, and certainly culturally, are primed to figure out, and therefore utilize, material objects—objects that are assumed, at least tacitly, to possess clear-cut boundaries and to have specific locations in space; objects that can, therefore, be weighed, measured, and quantified; objects that are assumed, at least by most intellectuals of the modern era, to be constituted, underneath it all, by mathematically calculable, mechanical interactions of infinitesimally small particles and patterns of energy—and these particles and energy patterns are, in turn, assumed to be completely insentient. That is, really smart people take for granted that these particles and streamings of energy lack even the slightest degree of consciousness. The physical sciences are based on very sophisticated strategies for how to best gain reliable knowledge about this sort of "stuff" (for example, methodologies that revolve around quantifiable data attained during replicable experiments in controlled laboratory settings). And our increasingly sophisticated technology emerges out of this external focus and in turn appears to validate it, as if to say, "Look how much this emphasis on mastering the external world has given us!"

However, the hard problem remains, as all philosophers of mind are aware: how does consciousness emerge, as the vast majority of academics assume, from the brain, given that the brain is also, like all physical objects, assumed to consist, underneath it all, of nothing but highly complex patterns and interactions of completely insentient particles and energy?[2] That is, how is our undeniable, first-person, direct awareness of the fact that we're aware, right here, right now, even possible if it comes from matter and energy that is, again, assumed to be completely insentient or devoid of consciousness? (Amazingly, there are several highly respected philosophers of mind, adherents of a perspective termed "eliminative materialism," who even go so far as to deny that we actually *are* conscious; they are so committed to the idea that the entire universe is, at its foundations, insentient—to them, therefore, consciousness itself can be, and is, nothing but an illusion.[3])

However, this sort of philosophical blindness is immediately refuted by the moment-to-moment conscious experience of each one of us. Of course we are conscious! Nothing else is so immediately self-evident and undeniable. In-and-through all of Western culture's emphasis on externality, consciousness remains—unseen, but seeing. Unheard, but hearing. Untouched, but touching. Unknown, but knowing. There is something utterly mysterious about consciousness, something that makes it (and it is not an "it"—which is why it is so difficult to examine) so easy to miss, so easy to devalue. Consciousness is not an object to be studied. Rather, consciousness is what allows us to study anything at all. So when "we" (whatever that is!) attempt to explore consciousness, we are exploring that which is the precondition for any exploration at all—even of the external world. When we try to look deeper into consciousness, that looking itself is consciousness exploring itself (and again, it is not an "it").

It's impossible to grasp consciousness, because consciousness is not a physical object. It doesn't have a discrete location. It doesn't have boundaries. Exploring consciousness is entering into an *Alice in Wonderland/Through the Looking Glass* exercise in reversals, paradox, displacement, and reflexivity. Exploring consciousness is exploring the depths, the foundations of ourselves. If we are exploring consciousness, we are looking at the process of looking; seeing the seer in the process of seeing itself; examining what makes examination itself possible.

Consciousness itself is also, inherently, first person, immediate, and direct. And only consciousness has this quality. While we can acquire an enormous amount of secondhand, third-person, knowledge about the externals of, let's say, another person (her height, weight, ethnicity, life story, etc.), only that person knows, from within, what her conscious experience feels like.

And notice (and here things get even more complicated), even all of that third-person data that we can acquire about someone or something else is only possible because we are *conscious*; it is only possible because we are consciously experiencing the sights, the sounds, the smells that come together within our consciousness to create our *experience* of the external world. The flux of our first-person conscious experience is the basis, really, for *all* forms of knowledge— *both* our knowledge of what is going on within us (our feelings, our thoughts, our memories) *and* our knowledge of the external world (which is always a complex fusion of our sensory experiences woven together with a tacit background of memories, thoughts, and beliefs that help us to interpret and make sense of these sensory experiences).

So, it has to be said: any examination of consciousness without first-person exploration, followed by nuanced, subtle descriptions of what was found in that exploratory process, as well as thoughtful, ideally heartfelt, ruminations on those vividly felt experiences, misses the boat entirely.

And again, it has to be said: psychedelics are amazing gifts to those of us who feel called to enter into that process of inner exploration. Stanislav Grof, a crucially significant psychedelic elder, rightfully pointed out: "Psychedelics, used responsibly and with proper caution, would be for psychiatry what the microscope is for biology or medicine or the telescope is for astronomy. These tools make it possible to study important processes that under normal circumstances are not available for direct observation."[4] (I must note, however, that microscopes and telescopes reveal a world that anyone/everyone can see, whereas psychedelics reveal worlds that are only directly visible to each individual psychonaut.) And make no mistake: there's a *lot* to explore within the depths of our consciousness— much that, ironically, we are not conscious of. (It is one of the great puzzles of consciousness: How is it that so much of consciousness is either preconscious or subconscious? How is it that so much of consciousness, which is inherently self-revealing, is hidden, as it were, from "itself"?) There are layers upon layers upon layers of consciousness within—literally worlds upon worlds, countless dimensions of consciousness, that can be accessed via psychedelics—if we are willing to approach them with care and respect.

However, before deciding to work with psychedelics, it is crucial to educate ourselves about these mind-manifesting substances. Many people carry a multitude of unseen prejudices against psychedelics that have been inherited from our cultural milieu. Almost all of them, like most prejudices, are based on either misinformation or all too often propaganda and even flat-out lies, spread in a wide-ranging, systematic, self-serving attempt, starting, for the most part, in the mid-1960s, to discredit psychedelics and to harshly penalize those who sought to use them.

I'd once again like to focus your attention on "Psychedelics 101" (www .liquidlightbook.com/psychedelics), my attempt to counteract some of this misinformation and propaganda—a short, focused discussion of what anyone should know before choosing to work with these powerful, mind-opening, "mind-manifesting" (the literal translation of "psychedelic") substances.

THE RELATIONSHIP BETWEEN THE BRAIN AND CONSCIOUSNESS: WILLIAM JAMES

A key philosophical issue needs to be addressed when discussing psychedelics: the relationship between the brain and consciousness.[5]

Many, if not most, people in our culture tend to think that when someone takes psychedelics, they experience hallucinations; that is, many people believe that psychedelic substances alter the neurochemical processes of the brain in a pathological way, resulting in delusory experiences that do not correspond with reality. However, for people within cultures that value these sacred substances (and for countless people in our culture who have taken them with respect and care), psychedelics are *not* hallucinatory. Rather, they are understood to bring about visions of sacred beings; or to initiate profound insights into the hidden dimensions of reality; or to catalyze transformative experiences of communion, or even union, with the divine Source of it all—that is, psychedelics are thought to generate experiences that are inherently valuable, true, and spiritually transformative.

I would argue that the assumption that psychedelics produce hallucinations is closely connected to a deeper assumption: that the neurochemical activity in the brain is what produces consciousness. At first glance it would seem that what I just said is a truism: "Well yes, of course the brain produces consciousness!" Nonetheless, this assumption becomes much less obvious if we examine it carefully through the lens of two profound thinkers: the American philosopher and psychologist William James (1842–1910) and the French philosopher Henri Bergson (1859–1941). These thinkers offer us another, equally persuasive way to understand the relationship between the brain and consciousness.

James, for example, in his early essay "Human Immortality: Two Supposed Objections to the Doctrine," notes that there is, of course, a relationship between the brain and consciousness.[6] As he points out, different types of drugs have the power to alter our state of awareness and the stimulation of various parts of the brain will often provoke changes in our consciousness. However, James goes on to emphasize that the exact nature of the *relationship* between the brain and consciousness is not readily apparent.

What James suggests is that this relationship can be understood in two rather basic ways. The first is what he terms the "productive" theory. This theory, which the vast majority of scientists and intellectuals today typically take for granted, postulates that consciousness is "produced" by the various complex neurochemical interactions that take place inside the brain.

James notes, however, that there is a second, equally respectable alternative: it is also possible that consciousness preexists the brain, and that the role of the brain is to mold that preexistent consciousness into various forms. James refers to this relationship between the brain and a preexisting consciousness (often understood as universal in scope) as the "transmissive" theory. From this perspective, the brain's task is to receive and transmit limited forms of this consciousness in much the same way as, to use an anachronistic example, a radio receives portions of preexisting radio waves and then transmits them, suitably modified, through the air as sound waves. (James's own example is of a prism or lens that receives the energy of light and then limits and modifies it.[7])

James insists, I think correctly, that it is just as logical and scientific to postulate that the brain receives, limits, directs, and shapes preexistent states of awareness as it is to postulate that the brain produces different states of consciousness. *Both* theories (and this is crucial) account for the complex neurochemical activity of the brain. They only differ in their understanding of what that activity is accomplishing. The productive theory insists that brain activity is what generates consciousness. The transmissive theory says that brain activity is indicative of the complex processes at work that limit, shape, and direct some sort of preexisting, larger consciousness. (James does not explicitly mention this, but it seems clear that both theories would also be able to acknowledge that the brain performs numerous other functions as well.)

According to James, although it might not be immediately apparent, "The theory of production is . . . not a jot more simple or credible in itself than any other conceivable theory. It is only a little more popular."[8] Indeed, James claims that in some ways the transmissive theory has certain theoretical advantages over its more popular competitor. For instance, if the transmissive theory of consciousness is accepted, then consciousness "does not have to be generated *de novo* in a vast number of places. It exists already, behind the scenes," intimately connected with this world.[9] In this way, the transmissive theory, especially when aligned with philosophical systems such as transcendentalism or idealism (as well as the panpsychism that James adopted toward the end of his life), can be philosophically quite fruitful, in that it does not need to overcome the gulf between mind and matter that is assumed by a Cartesian dualism, nor does it have to explain how the activity of the material brain—understood by most advocates of the production theory as inherently insentient and nonconscious—somehow magically transforms into our conscious experience. (While there are differences between transcendentalism, idealism, and panpsychism, each of these philosophical perspectives emphasizes the key role of consciousness, often seen as some sort of cosmic Mind, for any adequate understanding of reality.)

James points out several more apparent advantages of the transmissive theory of consciousness over the productive theory. For example, if the transmissive theory is correct, and consciousness is not utterly dependent upon brain activity, then it follows that consciousness could exist in some form after the death of the physical body. Individuals who assume the productive theory, however, have to insist that postmortem survival of consciousness is impossible, given that their theory insists that consciousness is solely the product of brain activity.

In addition, the transmissive theory is able to account coherently for a wide variety of phenomena that the productive theory has difficulty explaining, such as "religious conversions, providential leadings in answer to prayer, instantaneous healings, premonitions, apparitions at time of death, clairvoyant visions or impressions, and the whole range of mediumistic capacities."[10] (As the president of the American branch of the Society for Psychical Research, James studied all of these phenomena, and more, with great care.) But if the transmissive theory is accepted, these sorts of phenomena are at least somewhat more comprehensible, in that consciousness is understood to be inherently free of spatial limitations.

Over time, these sorts of reflections prompted James to articulate his own nuanced and sophisticated philosophical vision of the world—a world consisting of a complex, multilayered, plurality of existents that, at bottom, were interconnected with a deeper, unseen world (a vision of the world that is, to my mind, completely congruent with psychedelic experiences). In the conclusion of another important essay, "Confidences of a 'Psychical Researcher,'" James speaks of this vision:

> Out of my experience, such as it is (and it is limited enough) one fixed conclusion dogmatically emerges, and that is this, that we with our lives are like islands in the sea, or like trees in the forest. The maple and the pine may whisper to each other with their leaves, and Conanicut and Newport hear each other's foghorns. But the trees also commingle their roots in the darkness underground, and the islands also hang together through the ocean's bottom. Just so there is a continuum of cosmic consciousness, against which our individuality builds but accidental fences, and into which our several minds plunge as into a mother-sea or reservoir. Our "normal" consciousness is circumscribed for adaptation to our external earthly environment, but the fence is weak in spots, and fitful influences from beyond leak in, showing the otherwise unverifiable common connexion [sic].[11]

James recognizes that this type of panpsychic belief is only the bare bones of a theoretical structure that needs fleshing out and that many questions remain:

> What is the structure of this common reservoir of consciousness . . . it's inner topography? . . . What are the conditions of individuation or insulation in this mother-sea? . . . Are individual "spirits" constituted there? How numerous, and of how many hierarchic orders may these then be? How permanent? How transient? and how confluent with one another may they become?[12]

THE RELATIONSHIP BETWEEN THE BRAIN
AND CONSCIOUSNESS: HENRI BERGSON

We will be exploring many of these questions raised by James in much more detail and depth later on in this text, but for the moment, it seems important to note that James's "transmissive" theory of the relationship between the brain and consciousness is echoed in the work of Henri Bergson as well. Like James's work, Bergson's metaphysics not only dramatically challenges the philosophical materialism that is for the most part tacitly assumed by most academics in Western culture, but it also opens the door to a re-visioning of the origins of a wide range of nonordinary experiences, including psychedelic experiences.

However, before plunging into an examination of Bergson's understanding of the genesis of *nonordinary* phenomena, it is important to become acquainted with the basics of his theory of *ordinary* perception, as the former emerges, quite organically, from the latter.[13]

Our commonsense understanding of how we come to know the objective world around us is that physical stimuli from the external world impact our sense organs, and these organs then send signals to our brains via the nervous system. Our brains, receiving these signals, promptly translate them into our conscious perceptions. The problem with this commonsense understanding, however, is that our consciousness appears to be qualitatively different from the physical matter that constitutes the brain, as well as the senses and nervous system. Consciousness, on the face of it, is inherently nonspatial, inner, subjective, and private, whereas the material world and the brain are inherently spatial, outer, objective, and publicly accessible. We are therefore presented with an urgent philosophical question: How are these two very different "stuffs" related? How is it possible that the neurochemical activity of the brain somehow manages, almost magically, to change into our conscious perceptual experience? (As we saw earlier, these questions are differing attempts to articulate the hard problem in the philosophy of mind.)

Bergson offers an ingenious, albeit difficult to grasp solution to this philosophical dilemma in his second book, *Matter and Memory*. He begins by positing a universe that is, below the level of appearances, a pulsating, interconnected field of images. (The term "images" can be misleading, in that it does not refer simply to visual perceptions, but rather to any/all perceptions.) These images possess qualities that are similar to how both matter and consciousness are often understood. Like matter, at least as matter is articulated in quantum mechanics, images are dynamic patterns of energy, vortices of vibrations that radiate outward, contacting and affecting other complexly patterned vortices. Understood in this way, the physical world is an interconnected, dynamic continuum of becoming, in which "numberless vibrations, all linked together in uninterrupted continuity" travel "in every direction like shivers through an immense body."[14]

Bergson postulates that this transmission of energy-information is, moment to moment, passed on to other images, automatically, fully, without hesitation. It is this measurable, predictable, lawful interaction of images that, according to Bergson, is the basis for the stable, objective world of matter, a world rooted in the dependable, repeatable patterns of cause and effect studied by the natural sciences.

However, unlike how matter is typically understood, according to Bergson, the overlapping fields of vibration that make up the universe are neither inert nor non-aware, but instead are a type of "virtual" or "latent" consciousness. As he puts it, "The material universe itself, defined as the totality of images, is a kind of consciousness," and therefore, consciousness, in a latent form, is already present in this universe of images.[15] It is this assertion that forcibly calls into question one of the Western world's most central (and typically unexamined) metaphysical assumptions about matter, that is, that matter is insentient, non-aware.

In Bergson's vision of the universe, consciousness is not a mystery to be solved. Instead, consciousness is always present in the very heart of matter itself. Consciousness is not somehow inexplicably and almost magically produced by the interactions of insentient matter. Consciousness is not secretly added into the mix at just the right moment. Instead, it is already there under the surface as a latent aspect of the very tangible and material "stuff" of the universe—Bergson's images.

The benefit of Bergson's model of perception is that the genesis of our conscious perceptions does not have to be explained, since everything in the material world, as the totality of images, is at all times *already* a type of latent or virtual consciousness. According to this model, the brain does not *produce* consciousness; instead, it receives and responds to those preexisting fields of consciousness in ways that serve its own practical needs.

From this perspective, one of the primary jobs of the sense organs, nervous system, and the brain (which, it is important to remember, are also all images) is to receive the pulses of virtually conscious vibrations from the other images of the universe and then, from this infinitely complex, interpenetrating field of latent consciousness, to select out and actualize only those vibrations that serve the needs of our particular organism, letting the rest of the information from the universe pass through unimpeded. In *Matter and Memory*, Bergson postulates that our personal, subjective set of images occurs when we select out and actualize only a tiny percentage of the infinitely complex, interpenetrating, multilayered, vibratory field of virtual consciousness that surrounds us. Our personal perceptions are therefore the result of a radical truncation, a culling process by which we ignore most of what we might potentially know. As a result, we perceive only the "external crust" or the "superficial skin" of what actually surrounds us.[16]

According to Bergson, it is important to remember that the creation of our perceptions is intimately linked to the physical activities taking place within our bodies (especially within our brains and nervous systems). He argues, however, that the relationship between the activity of the brain/nervous system and perception is not the simple, one-way, causal relationship that is often assumed by most philosophers, psychologists, and scientists. These theorists often act as if it is self-evident that the neurochemical activity of the brain/nervous system *causes* our perceptions of the world around us; however, as Bergson notes, strictly speaking, "all that observation, experience, and consequently science, allows us to affirm is the existence of a certain *relation* between brain and mind."[17]

As George Wald, a Nobel Prize–winning physiologist from Harvard pointed out in 1987:

> There is no way of knowing whether the brain contains consciousness in the sense that it is producing it or whether it is simply a reception and transmission mechanism which, as Bergson has argued, has the function of selection and realization of conscious images and not the production of such images. As a neuroscientist, one can only intervene in the brain and record whether the intervention in particular parts of the brain results in the evocation or abolishment of conscious experience.[18]

Wald, rather insightfully, compares the brain to a television set. It is clear that there is an intimate relationship between the electrical and mechanical activity of the television set and the programs that are appearing on the screen. But no one ever claims that the program that is appearing on the screen has been *produced* by the television. Instead, a television set receives, limits, directs, and shapes pre-existing electromagnetic signals of various frequencies into the programs that we watch on the screen. Similarly, as Wald notes, if we "pull a transistor out of [our] T.V. set and it no longer works," we would not (or at least should not) "conclude that the transistor is the source of the program" (nor, one might add, is the television set as a whole), any more than we are forced to conclude that the brain is what produces consciousness simply because of the fact that when a person's brain has been damaged by a severe organic illness or trauma, that person's cognitive abilities are often severely impaired.[19]

Nonetheless, from a Bergsonian perspective, the brain still possesses a crucial role, in that it continually acts to filter out the vast majority of the streaming universal flux of images in which we are immersed. If we were to perceive and attempt to act upon the physical world as it exists at its most fundamental vibratory level, we would become incapacitated. If, for example, we no longer saw an oak table as a solid structure of wood, but instead consciously perceived and responded to the flux of almost infinite energetic patterns that underlie the table, we would become lost in the "moving immensity" of what previously had been a motionless, rectangular solid object.[20] We are therefore continually, on subconscious levels, carving out manageable islands of stability in the onrush of universal becoming by choosing to focus only on that level of experience that best serves our needs.

The creation, therefore, of our moment-to-moment experience of the world is fundamentally pragmatic: we perceive and interpret only a select subset of the universal flux that surrounds and interpenetrates us, that is, only those aspects of the universe that are necessary in order to act in any given situation. But if this is the case, if our predominant mode of attunement with the world and each other is pragmatic, then it becomes possible that numerous other worlds of experience might also exist. Bergson addresses this possibility in the following memorable passage:

> Nothing would prevent other worlds corresponding to another choice, from existing with it in the same place and the same time: in this way twenty different broadcasting stations throw out simultaneously twenty different concerts which coexist without any one of them mingling its sounds with the music of another, each one being heard, complete and alone, in the apparatus which has chosen for its reception the wave-length of that particular station.[21]

In these remarkable lines, we have what I call Bergson's "Radio Reception Theory of Consciousness." From this perspective, our mundane level of consciousness is simply one channel out of theoretically unlimited alternate possibilities, a channel of consciousness whose function is simply to play the music that is appropriate to our day-to-day practical functioning in the physical world.

It is crucial, however, to recognize that according to Bergson, these channels of consciousness are not made of some sort of Cartesian mental substance that is ontologically distinct from matter. While *Matter and Memory* emphasizes the functional and practical differences between mind and matter, in the final analysis, Bergson asks us to conceive that both mind and matter are simply differing manifestations of a unified (albeit continually changing and intrinsically pluralistic) reality: the universal dynamic flow of consciousness writ large, consciousness understood as the underlying substance of reality itself.

However, similar to Bergson's radio analogy, this dynamic stuff of becoming is not monolithic; reality does not take place on a single plane. According to Bergson, there are multiple dimensions of experience, multiple levels of reality (quantum, molecular, mineral, vegetal, animal, human, and perhaps higher), each possessing a unique, albeit ever-changing, temporal rhythm; there are countless levels of experience other than our own; there are countless "planes" or, if you will, "channels" of this Cosmic Mind. Tuning in to these other channels we are able to experience *extra-ordinary* phenomena—phenomena that ordinarily pass above or below our pragmatic experience but are neither unreal nor, with the right tuning, inaccessible to our conscious experience.

Bergson theorizes that the task of the brain is not just to filter out the flood of images that pour in and through us from the physical world. In addition, the brain also attempts to screen out a concurrent, perhaps even more extensive, torrent of coexisting, interpenetrating memories, thoughts, and feelings. To a certain extent these subconscious memories, thoughts, and feelings correlate with our personal biographies. However, Bergson emphasizes that our minds, in a way that is far more pronounced than matter, overlap and interpenetrate each other—and in fact transcend spatial boundaries altogether.

Bergson argues that "consciousness is not a function of the brain"; therefore, it can and does transcend physical boundaries.[22] This freedom from spatial limitations means that it is quite possible that our minds are continually blending and overlapping with other minds in a reciprocal flow of mental information just below the surface of our awareness. However, if this mental "intercommunication" is indeed continually taking place under the surface of our everyday awareness, then he suggests that it is quite possible, even likely, that certain images might occasionally slip past the "filtering" mechanism of the brain, leading to moments of telepathic and clairvoyant knowledge.

As a scholar of religious studies, I am struck by how Bergson's philosophical perspective offers a nuanced and sophisticated account of the genesis of the numerous nonordinary experiences that fill the pages of religious texts and ethnographies (not only telepathy and clairvoyance, but also mediumship, visionary encounters, and, importantly, psychedelic/entheogenic experiences). Seen from a Bergsonian point of view, these types of powerful and often transformative spiritual experiences no longer have to be understood as the meaningless result of the mechanical neurological activity within the brain, nor do they have to be seen as nothing more than the sum total of the psychological, economic, and cultural factors at work within an individual.

Rather, what this Bergsonian point of view allows us to do is to note that, while we need to give careful attention to physiological, psychological, economic, and cultural factors in understanding the genesis of these types of experiences, we can *also* posit that there could be transpersonal, transcultural, transhistorical factors at work as well. From a Bergsonian perspective, we can suggest that these nonordinary types of experiences are moments when, for a variety of reasons, individuals "change channels" and tune in to dimensions of reality with which they are already connected subconsciously. We can argue that our own subconscious may well overlap with countless higher and more inclusive "superconscious strata" of awareness and volition; strata of consciousness that we typically filter out of our daily conscious awareness but that nonetheless might well occasionally manifest themselves powerfully within the minds of mystics, shamans, visionaries, and mediums; levels of consciousness that, while interpenetrating our own, might well also possess their own ontological distinctiveness and agency.

Ever since the rise of the philosophical Enlightenment with its stress on the primacy of reason and sense experience, paranormal and religious phenomena have been frequently ignored; or have been dismissed as superstitious relics of backward, irrational cultures; or have been reduced to nothing more than a conflux of various psychological, sociological, cultural, economic, or physiological forces. Given the fact that many, if not most, of the Enlightenment and post-Enlightenment theorists of religion internalized a highly positivistic and materialistic set of presuppositions, these reductive explanations of paranormal and religious phenomena make quite a bit of sense. However, given a different set of foundational assumptions about the nature of external reality and the nature of the mind, we can easily begin to understand these types of "a-typical" phenomena in much more nonreductive, albeit equally complex and sophisticated ways.

Seen from a Bergsonian perspective, we are (subconsciously) connected with the entire universe, and the apparent clear-cut separation between objects is not ontologically real but instead is created by the filtering mechanisms of the brain as well as by unconscious, deeply engrained patterns of memory and belief. Given this alternate set of metaphysical assumptions, it makes sense to posit that different spiritual disciplines (chanting, fasting, meditation, dancing, ritualized ingestion of sacred plants, and so on) can serve to open up the inner floodgates in a ritually controlled and culturally sanctioned fashion, allowing practitioners to more easily and effectively absorb and integrate the powerful flux of information that is pouring into them from different currents of the ocean of the ever-changing images that make up the universe as we know it. From a Bergsonian perspective, therefore, it can be argued that many visionary/mystical experiences and, importantly, psychedelic experiences are indications that it is possible to see and to know *more*, and this suggests that we can see and know *better* than is typically possible from within the context of our everyday levels of consciousness. This Bergsonian understanding of nonordinary experiences allows us to claim that it is quite likely that many, if not most, nonordinary phenomena are not delusions or superstitious nonsense; in fact, we can argue that they might well be manifestations of a *more* profound, *more* inclusive quality of perception, or at the very least a level of perception that is an equally valid and valuable alternative to our more prosaic modes of experience.

It is also important to emphasize that it is not only the more "spectacular" forms of paranormal and/or religious experiences that can be reevaluated from a neo-Bergsonian metaphysical framework. If we can begin to let go of the idea that we are bounded, atomistic, billiard balls of dead matter that bump against each other in mechanistically predictable ways, if we can begin, instead, to view ourselves as something closer to a relatively stable whirlpool in a surging sea of consciousness, then it also becomes increasingly possible to make sense of a wide range of more prosaic levels of intuitive awareness as well, modes of experience that frequently occur within many of us but that we often choose to ignore or to deny.

For example, this Bergsonian point of view allows us to argue that our intuitive insights, while not inevitably accurate, are also not simply psychological in nature, but rather have a deeper ontological dimension as well. Coming from this perspective, we can legitimately claim that our sense that someone is sexually attracted to us (or conversely, the sense of danger or wrongness that we pick up from someone) is not irrational, nor is it simply based on subtle bodily cues, but instead may well be rooted in an accurate perception of what is actually occurring under the surface of our normal sensory perceptions.

This Bergsonian perspective also gives us a framework from which to suggest that something more than psychological quirks underlie those trance-like moments when we are composing a song or painting a picture or playing the piano or writing a story and it seems as if something or someone else is working in-and-through us: perhaps we are in truth inspired by some deeper strata of the universe and/or deeper levels of our selfhood. Similarly, we can posit that our empathetic feelings about our pets or even wild animals are not subjective anthropomorphic projections unto other species but actually reflect a genuine, albeit muted, awareness of a deeper underlying ontological connection with these beings. We can argue, in a rational, sophisticated fashion, that it is quite possible that all of these phenomena, in actuality, are simply varieties of ways in which we are tuning into and acknowledging the flow of subliminal information that we constantly receive from the mysterious universe that surrounds and interpenetrates us, but which we, for a variety of evolutionary, cultural, and psychological reasons, typically ignore or choose not to see.

Importantly, as mentioned before, this theory can help us to make sense of what is happening within us when we take psychedelics. Aldous Huxley in his well-known work, *The Doors of Perception*, explicitly draws upon Bergson to help make sense of the experiences he had while taking mescaline for the first time.[23] He suggests, like Bergson, that the main function of the brain is *not* to create our conscious awareness. Instead, the primary function of the brain is actually to protect us from being overwhelmed and confused by the torrent of information that ceaselessly pours into us from the cosmos, a cosmos that Huxley saw not as a soulless machine but as something closer to an all-pervasive Mind. Understood in this way, each of us is, under the surface of conscious awareness, linked to this (to use Huxley's phrasing) "Mind at Large," but in order to make biological survival possible, that Mind-at-Large, for the most part, needs to be funneled through the reducing valve of the brain.

That valve can, however, be opened by psychedelic compounds or by the various spiritual exercises advocated by different visionary/mystical traditions. Seen in this way, the changes in the neurochemical activity in the brain that are catalyzed by the ingestion of various psychedelic substances do not produce aberrant hallucinations. Instead, they "disclose dimensions or levels of existence that are otherwise screened by the rational ego";[24] they serve to open up an individual's awareness to dimensions of reality that already existed but were previously screened or filtered from our ordinary level of awareness, bringing about, at least potentially, visions of extraordinary beauty or a glimpse into the infinite meaningfulness and glory of Reality.

Seen from this perspective, we can theorize that entheogens such as the Daime are simply a way to change the channel of the television of the brain so that it can receive information from other, and in this case "spiritual," dimensions of reality. If we are willing to accept Huxley's filter theory of the relationship between the activity of the brain and changes in our states of consciousness (a theory that he shared with Henri Bergson, Fredric Myers, William James, C. D. Broad, and many others), then the visionary/mystical experiences that take place after ingesting various entheogens can be understood as potentially valid and valuable, and not, as many in our culture would want us to believe, delusive psychopathological hallucinations.

A JAMESIAN THEORY OF VISIONARY/MYSTICAL EXPERIENCES

James's philosophical perspective can also help us to better understand the typically unseen and/or misunderstood dynamics of how mirações and psychedelic/visionary/mystical experiences more generally are generated within us. (Bergson's philosophy is also quite helpful, but for the moment I'm just going to focus on James's work.) However, before we plunge into the genesis of mirações, we first need to get a grasp on how our everyday conscious experience takes place. If James's theories can help us to better understand some of the previously unseen dynamics that are at play in-and-as our own immediately felt day-to-day ordinary levels of experience, then perhaps those same theories might then be usefully extended to nonordinary experiences such as mirações as well.[25]

James emphasizes that our "normal" conscious experience is actually an intricate interweaving of two qualitatively different strata of knowledge: "knowledge-by-acquaintance" and "knowledge-about." Knowledge-by-acquaintance is immediate and direct knowledge, knowledge that feels indubitable. Knowledge-by-acquaintance occurs when our knowledge of an object is primarily based on our sense experiences (what we directly see/hear/taste/smell/touch) or in the case of visionary/mystical varieties of this type of knowledge, when we experience or feel something with an immediacy and vividness that is analogous to, or perhaps even ontologically prior to, sensory experiences. Knowledge-by-acquaintance is a preverbal, directly evident, unmediated knowledge of the simple "thatness" of something. When we know the color blue or when we taste an apple, we are experiencing knowledge-by-acquaintance.

Knowledge-about, on the other hand, is conceptual knowledge and is linked to the "whatness" of something. Knowledge-about is either explicitly or implicitly structured around language and is operative when we give the blue that we are seeing or the apple that we are eating a name (let us say "navy" or "Granny Smith") and bring to these sensory experiences (our knowledge-by-acquaintance) the wealth of cultural information that we possess about, for instance, colors or fruits. Knowledge-about analyzes, compares, contrasts, explains, and describes the qualities of an object.

Implicit in James's work is the acknowledgment that there are actually two levels of knowledge-about: the level that we can become consciously aware of within us and the level that is continually operating *beneath* the level of our conscious awareness. The preconscious level of knowledge-about gives the "brute facts" of sense experience a condensed, multilayered, typically taken for granted penumbra of meaning; it fills in the "scaffolding" of sense experience with the multifaceted richness of understanding that we have internalized from our culture (especially via the process of learning a shared language) and through the never to be repeated specificity of our life experiences (for example, growing up as a short, skinny Italian girl in the Bronx in the 1960s, with an alcoholic father and a clinging, ineffectual mother, gives a unique knowledge-about "lens" through which to view life.)

James illustrates the distinction between knowledge-by-acquaintance and knowledge-about when he notes that "a blind man may know all about the sky's blueness, and I may know all about your toothache, conceptually; . . . But so long as he has not felt the blueness, nor I the toothache, our knowledge, wide as it is, of these realities, will be hollow and inadequate."[26] According to James, knowledge-by-acquaintance cannot be described and it cannot be imparted to anyone who has not experienced it already. As he points out, we cannot tell a blind man what blue is like or give an accurate account of the taste of a pear. According to James, knowledge-by-acquaintance gives us information that is qualitatively different from the information we receive via knowledge-about, even though every moment of experience is always, to different degrees, a fusion of *both* forms of knowledge.

To illustrate this complex perceptual process, it might be useful to analyze what happens when we, for example, pick up a smartphone. Many people would assume that when we do this nothing more is occurring than a complex mechanical procedure in which our senses relay information to our brain, in effect communicating data that the phone is such and such a height, weight, color, texture, and so on. A careful examination of that process of perception, however, reveals that much more is occurring below the surface than we might assume. When we look at the phone, on some preconscious level we know what the phone's function is; we associate the phone with past experiences of reading text messages or seeing amusing videos. When we look at the messages appearing on the phone, we don't see shapes of electromagnetic energy; we see letters, words, and sentences that are meaningful. When we pick up the phone, we are subtly aware, on some level, of our role as readers, speakers, and listeners. None of these conceptual associations occur in isolation. Instead, they are fused with the information that comes through our senses in such a way that is impossible, except perhaps retrospectively, to determine which part of the final perceptual package comes from the senses, and which part comes from our tacit conceptual background. In this way, as James repeatedly stresses, we do not passively receive information through the senses. Rather, at least on a preconscious level, we are in a very real sense cocreators of the world that we experience.

From a Jamesian perspective, therefore, while we all inhabit the same physical universe, it is safe to say that each of us *experiences* a very different universe—a universe that is, to a degree that is difficult to ascertain, partially (yet powerfully) shaped by the unique and constantly changing lens of how we *interpret* our world.

However, even if all concrete moments of experience are always complex fusions of knowledge-by-acquaintance and knowledge-about, it is analytically useful to maintain the distinction between these two types of knowing. Knowledge-by-acquaintance provides information that knowledge-about simply cannot replicate; tasting a pear is fundamentally different than knowing about pears, even if these two processes are interwoven during each bite.

This analytical distinction can also help us to gain a more subtle understanding of the genesis of mirações, and psychedelic/visionary/mystical experiences more generally. Let's imagine, for example, a daimista during a powerful mediumistic work. Her eyes are rolling back in their sockets as she feels herself pulled upward, only to find herself seated in the center of a subtle yet not subtle at all world—an extremely tangible world; a world with vectors of directionality (there are angles everywhere); a world filled with aliveness; a world impregnated with a sense of portentous meaningfulness and significance. Then, slivering into this space from the left comes a rippling, sensuous, green dragon-like being: massive, with a bright gold heart of glowing light—a heart like a furnace—and a dragon-like face. It has a clear form, even if that form is extremely dynamic and flowing with no clear-cut edges.

Using our Jamesian categories, we could say that the knowledge-by-acquaintance aspect of that miração manifested as the in-your-face thatness of that dragon-being; as the daimista's strongly felt sense that this being was coming to her of its own accord, possessing its own inherent, preexisting autonomy; as the exquisite, detailed, constantly shifting beauty of its golden-green scales—all of this and more—gave that daimista a categorically unique type of information, information that she could never have gained from years of reading books (such as this one!) on the doctrines and practices of the Santo Daime.

Nonetheless, this daimista was not a blank slate: when she saw that dragon-like being (that is, when she experienced its knowledge-by-acquaintance thatness), she was also preconsciously, without any effort, overlaying onto that powerfully felt, spontaneously emerging, detailed "otherness" a preconscious extract of any/all of her memories that (somehow!) helped to make sense of that thatness. She was, without any conscious intent on her part, seamlessly interweaving a highly condensed, multilayered, linguistically structured network of meaning onto all of that detailed sensory-like information—that is, her knowledge-about. This knowledge-about, for example, might emerge from years of reading fantasy novels, seeing dragons in movies and on television, and playing video games with heroines flying on the backs of similarly shaped beings; whatever the case, this knowledge-about helped her to turn that shifting flux of images into an experience that had context and significance, an experience that was taking place in "another world," with a dragon-like being. All of those conceptual understandings, to one degree or another, were inextricably intertwined with and helped to shape the particular form of the miração itself.

As usual, however, although our categories appear to be clear-cut and straightforward, experience itself isn't that neat and tidy. Looking at the dragon being, for example, how much of the "angularity" of that subtle world was inherent in the knowledge-by-acquaintance aspect of the experience— was that world inherently "angular" and angular in just that way? Or was that angularity itself a metaphorical depiction of a quality of experience that simply couldn't be grasped by our young daimista's mind? I'm not sure how we could ever know. Similarly, it seems to me quite likely that the golden heart of the dragon being perhaps acted as a metaphor for that being's innate nobility, goodness, and radiance, but who really knows? Maybe it just literally had a glowing golden heart. And even though meaning and significance is the hallmark of knowledge-about, I bet our daimista would say that the portentous meaningfulness and significance that she felt in that world was actually a clear example of knowledge-by-acquaintance, in that it was immediately and powerfully felt.

Therefore, proceeding carefully, with a keen awareness of the inherent limitations (and potential power!) of our theoretical structures, I'd like to suggest that a miração is formed in roughly the following way: First, "something" appears within the consciousness of a daimista—something that possesses a certain degree of objectivity, a clear sense of "otherness." This something feels very much as if it exists independently of the daimista: it is something that the daimista finds or that finds her. (Admittedly, however, as we will see later on, the question of where the sense of self begins and where it ends isn't always so clear in mirações.) This "more-ness" that comes to daimistas during mirações, as well as to visionaries/mystics of all traditions, seems to appear of its own volition. And that more-ness is directly felt, without any need for words; it shines with what James calls, at least in my "buffed-up" version of James' Victorian prose, "immediate luminosity." And that more-ness, when it comes streaming into the daimista's consciousness, often comes just like the onrush of our ongoing and overlapping sense experiences; it can and often does manifest itself in highly specific and intricately detailed ways.

Nonetheless, all this powerful influx of more-ness always comes into consciousness intimately fused with the daimista's knowledge-about and is therefore structured by the daimista's cultural and psychological categories of understanding. Below/above the daimista's conscious awareness, her cultural and psychological assumptions are almost magically filtering and shaping that more-ness into forms that she would expect to perceive or forms that would make the most sense to her, given her unique set of life experiences. Again, it's always both/and. This young woman might never have expected to have a dragon being appear to her in this specific, highly detailed, knowledge-by-acquaintance way; nonetheless, her knowledge-about still helped her, as in ordinary sense experiences, to make sense of what she was experiencing, and perhaps to a certain extent, underneath her conscious awareness, helped to shape that experience itself.

To give another example, let us "envision," a young female daimista who is ecstatically immersed in a miração. In that participatory, joyous, expanded state of consciousness, a radiant form of the Virgin Mary suddenly appears within the consciousness of the young woman, radiating grace, blessings, and forgiveness. From a Jamesian point of view, we could say that the entire time that this daimista was joyfully beholding the grace-bestowing form of the Virgin Mother, she had an experience that was a fusion of knowledge-by-acquaintance and knowledge-about. The knowledge-by-acquaintance components of the experience entered her awareness with a high degree of objectivity; they came without her conscious instigation; they felt "factual" rather than made up—undeniable, really there.

Yet this miração also possessed important elements of knowledge-about. For instance, knowledge-about was present in the set of powerfully persuasive cultural assumptions and personal memories that were operating beneath the surface of the conscious awareness of this young woman, perhaps taking the form of her rarely examined and deeply buried sense of shame and unworthiness; her internalized expectations of what it would feel like to interact with the Virgin Mary (she will be merciful, forgiving, etc.); her preconscious understanding of why she was drinking Daime; what she hoped would happen within her, and so on—this entire complex web of linguistically coded memories that effortlessly, almost miraculously, helped to cocreate (or draw to her?) a visionary form of the Virgin Mary instead of, for example, the serpents or jaguars that might more likely have been seen by an indigenous shaman, even if our young daimista and the shaman were drinking the exact same amount of similarly constituted ayahuasca.

Nonetheless, I simply have to say it again: these categories can only take us so far. For example, when our young daimista felt the Virgin Mary "bestowing grace" during her miração, did that knowledge-by-acquaintance feeling itself carry with it the inherent, nonverbal knowledge that grace was being transmitted, or was that label "grace-bestowing" the result of her prior knowledge-about—all of her previous understandings of what grace "means"? Or—here's a thought—perhaps both were happening simultaneously. Perhaps the knowledge-about conceptual overlay that helped to create the experience of grace-bestowing within our daimista somehow fit the inherent, mystically apprehended, immediately felt quality of the nonverbal) grace/mercy/love that our daimista felt flowing from the Virgin Mother. In this case, we could say that the word "grace," as it were, "clicked into" its ontological source/substratum. (What can I say: drinking Daime tends to make Neoplatonists out of many of us. As with Neoplatonism, experiences of this world can increasingly begin to feel as if they are emanations of and/or emerging from something Higher, something Deeper.)

And don't get me started on the epistemological status of the Virgin Mary in that scenario. Was she experienced in a knowledge-by-acquaintance sort of way, as inherently divine? That is, did that experience bring with it the immediate, nonverbal gnostic "Knowing" that this female figure was intrinsically and always a She? (My money is on yes.) And what was all of this about virginity? Here I tend to think that our daimista leaned rather heavily on her knowledge-about—there's certainly a lot of deeply human, and hence often distorted, theological baggage that comes with the term "virgin." (Nonetheless, even here I might be convinced that, in-and-through all of the sexual distortions and misogyny that often comes with that term, it might well also symbolize/express something deeper: innate Purity.) And finally, did our daimista experience that female figure as inherently, ontologically, linked to the historical mother of Jesus of Nazareth or is it possible that underneath that knowledge-about overlay She was also (or She was actually) the Divine Mother—the Source of all Divine Mother figures who have appeared in different cultures throughout history? (Maybe both? Neither? Beyond any and all of it?) One way or the other, it seems clear to me that in almost all mirações, real Light is shining through a psychologically and culturally constructed stained glass window.

This Jamesian understanding of the genesis of mirações offers us a way to affirm the cultural and psychological uniqueness of each visionary/mystical experience without denying the possibility that perhaps underneath all of that particularity, something "more" exists as well (to use James's own delightfully ambiguous term), something "more" that underlies and empowers all of that difference and specificity. Even though this undefinable, but directly felt, higher power will always be perceived in a multitude of ways (as various entities, gods/goddesses, higher levels of selfhood), the energy of that more-ness directly or indirectly is what catalyzes and undergirds every visionary/mystical experience. Drawing upon James, we could also hypothesize that this felt sense of more-ness itself has a very deep, very real, ontological source—or better, a plurality of such sources, or even better, a plurality of sources that are all rooted, in different ways, in one Source—and all of this ontological fecundity can be found in the depths of our own consciousness, in what James calls the "mother sea" of consciousness, a Consciousness that connects us all, under the surface of our conscious awareness.

From a Jamesian point of view, it is difficult to say precisely to what extent we make our experience and to what extent experience makes us. However, even this recognition of the difficulties that are inherent in any philosophical investigation of visionary/mystical experiences, especially their entheogenic varieties, can move us toward a more subtle and more nuanced understanding of the interactive nature of these types of experiences.[27] They can let us speak, hopefully with humility, about the genesis of visionary/mystical experiences, while at the same time providing visionary/mystical experiences with the opportunity to speak back to us in their own, often surprising ways.

As soon as we begin to acknowledge the ways in which our experience is shaped, below the surface of our conscious awareness, by numerous social, cultural, and psychological forces, we are able to take the first steps toward genuine empowerment in which we can gradually begin to make lasting, beneficial, and transformative changes in our lives. Instead of letting ourselves be shaped by these forces, we can, instead, choose to creatively and consciously reconfigure those previously unconscious "scripts" that have created so much unnecessary suffering, both for ourselves and for others. By consciously rewriting our understanding of what is real, what is valuable, and who we could and should become, our life experiences can become more profound and beautiful than we had previously imagined was possible. Increasingly, with hard work and grace, we can actually begin to create and inhabit a magical and sacred world, a literal Heaven on Earth; we can consciously invoke a heavenly quality of experience that can illumine/transform all of the challenges that life can bring. This book is a conscious attempt to share the "Good News" of our capacity to claim authorship of our experiences.

THE MORE-NESS OF VISIONARY/MYSTICAL EXPERIENCES

There is strong evidence suggesting visionary/mystical experiences are more than a simple product of the cultural and psychological assumptions of the visionary/mystic. To begin with, visionaries and mystics have repeatedly challenged some of the most central, taken for granted, and powerfully held cultural assumptions of the times and places in which they lived—often offering, instead, compellingly new and creative visions of what could and/or should be. What flowed into the consciousness of those religious founders and cultural innovators (James's "religious geniuses") wasn't simply a rearrangement of the old; their visions were not simply reiterations of preexisting social values and beliefs. Instead, many of these charismatic figures challenged some of the most fundamental values of the societies in which they lived, inspired to do so by the immediacy and the indubitable Power and Light of what they were experiencing. As James emphasizes, it is clear that at times the more-ness that manifests within the consciousnesses of visionaries/mystics can override their psychological and cultural expectations and can create unanticipated and powerfully persuasive experiences that, in turn—as history has shown us time and time again—have the potential to alter the cultural and psychological landscape that the visionary/mystic inhabits.[28]

It will be fascinating to see how this creative impetus will unfold within the parameters of the Santo Daime itself—how much of the older ritual structures and conceptual assumptions will be maintained, and how much "newness," often inspired either directly or indirectly by the Daime, will ultimately be incorporated within that religious tradition. (Later in the book I will discuss in more detail the crucially important tension within the Santo Daime between the stability of tradition and the—inevitable?—changes brought about through the revelations/inspirations that are catalyzed by the Daime.)

In addition, the most striking evidence, to myself at least, that visionary/mystical experiences are not simply rearrangements of the visionary/mystic's cultural and psychological background is the fact that there are numerous accounts of visionary/mystical experiences, entheogenic or not, that have given a visionary/mystic detailed information about other cultures and/or times, or even startlingly correct information about the biological functioning of exotic forms of life—information that the visionary/mystic did not know before and often *could* not have known without years of disciplined study in arcane fields of knowledge.[29] I am keenly aware that many readers might well have difficulty accepting the validity of these claims. All I can say is that having carefully examined the evidence (and there is a lot of it, often quite rigorous and persuasive), I have moved firmly from the camp of "agnostic skepticism" to "reality seems to be much stranger and more mysterious than I once thought."

3

Next Steps on the Path

After the Self-Transformation retreat, interested in pursuing the Santo Daime tradition a bit more, I called the phone number of a Santo Daime elder (the revered Ms. Liz) that a retreat participant had given me. Ms. Liz, in her typical gracious yet no-nonsense way, helped me to arrange a time, about a month later, to make my way to a Santo Daime church in order to drink Daime again. After a few more requisite phone calls, and the mandatory orientation/screening process, and the required filling out of official forms, I found myself taking part in another Santo Daime work, not realizing at the time that this work, as well, was rather nontraditional, in that it was a completely outdoor, hardcore mediumistic work—a "St. Michael" work that was done in three separate outdoor, beautiful, and secluded sacred spaces (*terreiros*) with only a very rustic, minimalistic altar, all while drinking a *lot* of *very strong* Daime.[1] Not surprisingly, less than an hour into the work, all sorts of rather wild mediumship phenomena quickly began to manifest, with many participants starting to whoop and holler and spin, gesticulating forcefully and jerkily moving their bodies, with all of this atypical bodily movement spontaneously emerging and subsiding in wave after wave as we sang hymn after hymn after hymn.

At a certain point, deep into the work, when I was hunched over in my seat with my hands twisted and my face contorted into an ugly grimace, and when I was feeling as if I could barely endure the Force that was pouring through me, Trevor, the leader of the work, came up to me and started softly whispering in my ear, "Welcome friend. Welcome. You are very welcome here." He then, much to my dismay, proceeded to offer me a small amount of Daime, which I (exceedingly reluctantly) drank.

It wasn't until after the work was finished, when I was informally debriefing with Trevor, that I learned, despite my issues with mediumship, that he had seen that I was, without consciously realizing it, manifesting a "suffering spirit" and had offered that small drink of Daime to that spirit to help it to leave my body/mind and move on to a higher dimension. I for one didn't have a clue that any of this was happening. All that I had felt was that I could barely tolerate sitting there in those woods, writhing away, clenched and grimacing on my plastic chair, each hymn sonically assaulting me, with wave after wave of too-muchness pouring through me, again and again and again.

It was truly puzzling to me, therefore, when Trevor began to whisper those words of welcome into my ear. (I remember asking myself: "Who is he talking to?") However, from my current vantage point, I'd have to say that Trevor got it absolutely right, even if at that particular point in time I didn't have the cognitive capacity or spiritual discernment to tell that what I was feeling was the energetic overlay of a suffering spirit, rather than any upwelling of feelings emerging from my own normal conscious personality.

A month or so later I returned to the church that Trevor led for my first "real deal" Santo Daime church work—a "Concentration" work in which everyone sat in chairs, men on one side of the room and women on the other, where it was clear that you'd be rather firmly chastised if you crossed the invisible but strongly felt "line" that separated the two domains; a work in which almost all of the participants wore uniforms; a work in which everyone was encouraged to sing the hymns rather than do what I kept wanting to do, which was to lie down for hours.

Up until this point, I thought that *all* Santo Daime works were designed to provide ample time and space for mirações. And it certainly would appear that Concentration works such as this one would fit the bill, in that, unlike dance works, they are rituals in which people are able to spend a prolonged period of time seated in a chair (usually highly spartan folding or stackable chairs, carefully arranged in clearly defined rows). In addition, the central intention of a Concentration work is to turn one's attention within, for at least two rather prolonged periods of meditation, even if these inwardly directed contemplative time periods are inevitably sandwiched in between *lots* of hymn singing. However, as I was soon to discover, the real focus of a Concentration work is less about providing prolonged time in which to become immersed in inner experiences and more about structuring a time and place in which you can gradually learn how to become increasingly present, grounded, and firmly centered within yourself *as* you meditate. (And, of course, as you sing. There's always a lot of singing in Santo Daime works. That's a given.)

This work took place in a small, nondescript, two-bedroom house in a suburban neighborhood. Soon after I arrived, still a bit bleary and weary from my grueling trip, members of the church, mostly white countercultural types in their late twenties and early thirties, were already busily carrying out the furniture from the living room and setting up the salão (the central ritual area). In the very center of the salão was a large rectangular table covered with a white tablecloth—the *mesa* (literally, "table," but more accurately "altar"). The altar/mesa is the axis of the salão, and the "spokes" of energetic influence that radiate out from that axis fill the entire room and beyond. And at the very center of the mesa (the axis of the axis, as it were) was an impressively large, probably two-and-a-half-feet-tall, double-barred cross: the cruzeiro. The cruzeiro was in turn surrounded by four large taper candles, pictures of various Santo Daime elders, and a vase of flowers. There was also a handful of chairs around the mesa itself where the various male and female "important personages" sat once the work began, while the rest of us lower-ranking participants sat in our assigned places in one of the rows of folding chairs that were carefully set up on the male and the female sides of the salão.

In most Santo Daime works, there is also some sort of dedicated space (the "healing room"—one for men and one for women), where you can lie down if you simply can't remain seated because the Force is too strong. And it didn't take me long, probably about a half hour into the initial round of a cappella hymns (that were at times grindingly off-key), before I felt compelled to exit the salão, unsteadily hoisting myself up from my chair, trying my best to navigate the rather cramped space on the men's side without bumping into anyone, and intently focused on making my way toward the tiny back room in the house that served as the men's healing room. Before I got there, however, a young fardado stopped me and in a low, somewhat intense tone, informed me that the room was already occupied. That stopped me in my tracks: "So what do I do now?" I asked. Heaving a sigh, he told me to stay where I was, and after quickly unrolling a yoga mat onto the wooden floor of the narrow hallway that was directly in front of the healing room, he grabbed my upper right arm and not exactly gently helped me down to the mat, where I finally managed, to my extreme relief, to lie down on my back.

Most guardians that I've known in Santo Daime churches are very energetically attuned and skilled in working with new people. This young man, however, was not yet in those ranks. A guardian during a Santo Daime work has several important jobs: filling the glasses of water on the central altar; keeping the candles lit; and crucially, accompanying those who are struggling with the Force, helping them in whatever ways are needed. For example, if someone needs to throw up/"get well," the guardian will be there with a well-placed and well-timed bucket, and afterward will typically offer a much-appreciated tissue. But sometimes, especially if guardians are relatively new, they can get a little, shall we say, overzealous. And in this particular case, not long after I had, oh so gratefully laid down on the mat and was just beginning to be carried deep within, the guardian knelt down beside me, touched me on the shoulder, giving me quite a start, and said, in a way that was overtly quiet but that energetically carried a massive charge of irritation, "If you can do it, it would be good if you could get up and come back to the salão." Well, at this point I didn't even know what a salão was. However, being the good boy scout that I was (yes, sir!), I somehow managed to find the inner resolve to slowly and oh so carefully, rouse myself and to totter back to my seat, and hours later I finished the work.

A month or so later I attended my first "Dance work" at this same church. Once again, I accomplished the rather daunting, hours-long journey to the church, only to discover that this time the work was taking place in a rented dance studio. This time, having been reassured that it actually was OK to go to the healing room when needed, as soon I felt the Force kicking in I quickly headed for a mat in the "off to the side" section of the dance floor that served as the rather rudimentary men's healing area. I gratefully collapsed on it, eager to dive into the rapidly unfolding astral worlds that I was feeling powerfully drawn into. However, after a precious bit of well-appreciated time engaging with the visionary experiences that were rapidly and forcefully opening up within me, this same eager beaver guardian, yet again rather firmly encouraged me to get up off my mat and to come back to my place in line.

I later learned that the "subtle" encouragement I received from this guardian was perhaps, at least in part, fueled by the commonly held daimista assumption that if you're absent from the salão for too long, you are, as it were, "creating a hole" in the flow of the Current that circles around the room, and therefore, you are reducing the energetic intensity, both quantitatively and qualitatively, of everyone else's experience in the room. Or seen another way, the assumption is that your absence makes the work more difficult for others, since they are, as it were, "taking on more"—your unwillingness to remain in the salão means that others are having to work harder to keep the energy smoothly and powerfully flowing in the room.

It is clearly easier to keep dancing and singing if your brothers and sisters are singing and dancing together with love, joy, and vigor. Nonetheless, I also have to say that it is simply not my experience that I am "out of the Current" if I'm not dancing or sitting in my chair singing the hymns, even if I also have to say that I very much prefer to stay in the salão, especially during dance works. (I typically only leave to take a serving of Daime or during an "interval"—the long break that occurs in the middle of dance works.) Yes, there *is* something powerful and special that circulates in the salão during a work, but at the same time, I often feel completely bathed in the Divine Presence when I'm lying down in the healing room or taking a break to walk outside for a bit. I honestly don't think that we can "box" the Force of the Daime into the spatial parameters of a room.

At this point in my Santo Daime journey, more than fifteen years after my first Dance work, when I sense the Force strongly and I feel the desire to lie down, I try to tune in and see what's called for in the moment, and then I act according to my deepest guidance. While I take the input of others I respect quite seriously, at the same time, I think that it is also crucially important for me to make my own spiritual choices, moment to moment, from my inner depths. That is, while I realize that I need to remain open to the possibility that I may not be seeing things correctly, nonetheless, I choose to live my spiritual life by aligning myself to that Source as best I know how, trusting that if I make a mistake, the Daime will take that opportunity to teach me a valuable lesson.

After receiving this "encouragement" to come back to the salão, I once again managed to heave myself up and make my way back to my highly circumscribed and assigned place in my row on the men's side so that I could join everyone else and try to sing the hymns and try to dance. (Even the extremely basic back-and-forth steps didn't come easily to me in my "barely on this planet" state of consciousness). And I truly tried. But I was still reeling in the Force, and so, to me, it was almost laughably difficult to figure out the exceedingly basic dance steps (the main one: stepping left one, two, three, then pivoting right on four, and then repeating the same pattern going the other way—basically a march step; or less often: swaying back and forth to a one, two, three waltz beat; and even less often: standing facing left for a couple of beats and then pivoting to the right and standing for another couple of beats—the mazurka). It wasn't easy to keep dancing back and forth in my spot, in my row, for hours, while holding a hinário (hymnal) in one hand.

I was also strongly encouraged by the guardians to sing along with the Portuguese hymns as they barreled forward, one after the other after the other for hours and hours, in a rush of (at that time, for me) difficult to pronounce Portuguese words, and since it was all a cappella, it was often torturously off-key. The Portuguese alone was daunting. Still, I wanted to understand what

I was (oh so valiantly!) trying to sing, so in the interludes before and after the hymn when we'd keep dancing but stop singing, with only the sharply rhythmic shaking of the maracás (ceremonial rattles) providing the background cadence, I would hastily attempt to glance at the English translation on the other side of the page from the Portuguese lyrics. But given that I was so strongly in the Force, the words on the page had a laughably annoying tendency to transform into outposts of fifth- and sixth-dimensional streamings of meaning that were shimmering over the pages of the hymnbook.

SENSING AND RIDING THE WAVES OF THE FORCE

I'd like to say a bit more about the issue of how long to stay in the healing room, at least from the vantage point that I have now, after playing all sorts of roles in the official and unofficial hierarchies of this tradition.

To begin with, I think that it's crucial, in the right moment, with a lot of sensitivity and heart, to know how to encourage someone who has been in the healing room for a long time to discern, within themselves, whether it is perhaps time to go back to the salão. I know that, for myself, as the years passed during my time in the Santo Daime, I increasingly began to welcome the gentle and loving nudges that I would receive from well-trained guardians. And one of the main reasons that I began to value those periodic taps on the shoulder is that they prompted me to ask myself: OK—am I done? Or perhaps better phrased: Is the Daime done with me?

To explain what I mean by "done," I first have to note that over the years I have increasingly been able to perceive that the energetic pulsation of the Daime frequently has a temporal rhythm, a sort of energetic cohesion, a beginning, middle, and end associated with it. Here's how it often goes: the Force will suddenly surge up within, really powerfully, which at least for me is often a signal that it is time to make my way to the healing room. Then, usually fairly quickly after I lie down, a series of powerful mirações will open up within like the slow-motion unfurling of a cotton pod. It's possible, especially if you're somewhat new to working with the Daime, to stay "horizontal" in this intermediate phase of the energetic "wave" of the Daime for quite a while. The Daime doesn't seem to mind manifesting one astral splendor after the other. However, at some point in my time in the Santo Daime, it also became clear to me that the wave of the Daime has its own organic reabsorption time period, a sort of energetic ebbing back—and when I am really attuned within myself, I can feel that soft-edged closure manifesting within myself as the subtle but unmistakable sense of: OK, it's done. It's time to get up and rejoin the others in the salão.

In a way that's very similar to riding a physical wave in the ocean, working with the Daime is all about timing. It's actually crucially important to learn how to *not* give into each and every desire to go lie down. There's a type of "inner muscle" that you need to develop as a daimista, the ability to somehow find reserves of strength that you didn't know you possessed—the strength to keep going, even if it seems impossible. But it is also crucial to learn when it *is* time to stop resisting the powerful waves of the Force that are clearly and strongly pulling you inward. Dancing and singing the hymns is, in and of itself, wonderful, but sometimes you just need to lie down. Why? So that you can have a powerful series of encounters with a wide panoply of spiritual beings; so that you can receive, with awe and gratitude, illuminative metaphysical insights that feel sacred and true, insights that seem to come from the "place" where Sacredness and Truth live; so that you can receive energetic openings and "rewirings" of your subtle body—for all of these reasons and more.

In other words, you don't always have to say *no* to that urgent inner tug, even if some daimistas (many of them very high up in the institutional structure) think that you should. But it can be difficult at times to discern how much of that "saying no" is actually valuable and noble, and how much of it is nothing more than a manifestation of psychological and sociological rigidity.

I also have to point out that in my years in the Santo Daime I have begun to recognize that the rising and falling of the waves of Force tended to become more compressed as my firmness (*firmeza*) began to develop.

As one of the most important developmental trajectories within the Santo Daime, firmness is the ability to remain centered, grounded, and in your heart, even as you are also powerfully feeling the Force. Firmness can also be understood as maintaining an ongoing connection to the will of the divine/higher self, and not being swayed by the whims of the ego, with its desire for comfort and/or its unwillingness to endure discomfort.

Over the years, I slowly began to realize that, going from work to work, I'd often see the same cycle repeating itself: *a powerful Force arises; I go to the healing room and have many mirações; I eventually rally myself and guide myself back into the salão.* However, as my firmness gradually began to deepen, this cycle has shortened to something close to the time it takes for two or three hymns to be sung. This more trimmed-down process is still extremely powerful: as soon as I lie down, or sometimes just sit down if it's a dance work, and close my eyes, I will typically find myself plunging into a torrent of mirações—mirações that, as it were, had been knocking on the door during the work for quite some time, since

I try to wait for what feels like "just the right moment" to go lie down. During this time in the healing room, lying down with my eyes closed, these visionary encounters can (at last!) come pouring through and be gratefully received. And when the cycle completes itself, these visionary manifestations can then be equally gratefully released.

To complicate matters somewhat, riding that wave is less about visionary experiences and more about welcoming and receiving, with love, the "entrance" of some being who wants to manifest itself within my *aparelho* (the Portuguese term means something like "tool" or "instrument," but in mediumistic circles it refers to the total gestalt of our body-mind and subtle body). At times it's almost as if this being (and I will be writing *much* more about who/what I think these beings are later on) arrives with bugles blowing and flags flying within, as it comes into my aparelho with a sudden, surging, upwelling of Force, often accompanied by swirling geometrically intricate patterns of color and an almost shrill "note" of insistence ("Look at me! Notice me!"). It can often feel as if the being *really* wants to encourage me to give it some time and space to "stretch out" a bit, to strut its stuff, to do whatever mysterious, sometimes viscerally felt, task it has to do within me or within my conscious field of awareness, or simply within/as my bodily movements themselves. This is where the realm of mirações meets the phenomenon of mediumship—with both of their complexities and wonders.

FIRMNESS

I also have to say that my ability to sense the rising and receding of the Force of the Daime within me began to deepen as I started to work in earnest to remain in the salão (and it was sometimes *really hard* work) rather than leave it to go lie down. I think, especially during my first few years as a daimista, that I perhaps often erred too much on the side of just gritting my teeth and willing myself not to give in to the desire to go lie down—a way of working with the Force that is often advocated in the Santo Daime, a mindset that goes something like this: *These moments are tests, so you need to get tough—don't give in, don't abandon your brothers and sisters in the current, keep participating, "man-up," stay firm.* And I have to say that even though at this point I'm not a big fan of pushing yourself forward with sheer will, the fact that I worked really hard over many years of works to not give in too soon to the urge to go to the healing room allowed me, with the grace of countless Beings, to be able to build a type of inner muscle, a the slowly growing capacity to just be present in a way that was more and more centered, calm, grounded, and in my heart with whatever was arising as the Force came pouring in-and-through me, in wave after wave of sheer Power.

I was developing my firmness.

Firmness is, as I mentioned, one of the most important developmental goals of a daimista. And to me, the slow, almost cell by cell growth of that inner muscle of firmness is an utterly fascinating combination of self-effort and grace. On the one hand, deepening in firmness does take work—prolonged steady effort over time. And it takes the willingness to keep coming to the works, again and again. It takes the genuine desire to give yourself fully to each experience— even (especially!) the really challenging ones—and to be increasingly, fully, here, now, with whatever. And if it's at the end of a *long* work, when you're really, really tired, firmness means you remain standing, even if you'd just *love* to sit down. You gather yourself; you stand up straight; you find your inner connection to the Divine; you ground yourself in the earth; you rest back into your heart; you take a breath; and you keep going, you keep singing, even if it seems almost impossible.

And developing this capacity to reorient ourselves to the guidance of the *Eu Superior* (literally, "the Superior I," the higher, completely divine Self, or the I Am that shines within everyone) is crucial. It not only gives us strength when we didn't think it was possible to keep going, but it also prompts us, as a Daime brother said so well in a letter to me: "To the activity that would be most beneficial in the present moment: concentrating, receiving, singing, channeling, assisting, taking out the compost toilets, filling water glasses, dimming lights, speaking to a new person, quieting thoughts, releasing emotion, praying with attention, etc."

All of this is true. Nonetheless, there's also an *equally* important quality of the process of developing firmness that comes from learning how to open; to not resist; to float on the inner tides with more and more trust; to stay softly observant; to energetically relish each passing moment in the Force. Developing firmness from this angle means that we learn how to say *yes* from within, over and over again, communing with each moment of experience as it flowers within us. Here the lessons are about timing, grace, and alignment with the subtle pulsations and bubbling inspirations of the Force as It (He? She? They?) flows in-and-through us. Here we learn the art of diving into the liquid, often semi-inchoate flux of what is rising and descending of its own accord within us. Here we learn how to let go, how to surrender more and more fully, with trust and gratitude, to that enormous Presence and Power that wants to work in-and-through each one of us, at each moment. Here we learn how to embrace, without holding back, that Grace, that Mercy, that Love that is seeking with such tenderness and compassion to heal and transform each of us.

From this perspective, firmness isn't about "toughing it out," or gritting your teeth, or sheer (manly!) endurance. It's something that is much more subtle, but also much more powerful and spiritually efficacious than simply pushing forward with an effort of will, which is what many, many well-meaning daimistas think firmness is all about.

Developing firmness is also, importantly, about learning (again, with a fusion of grace and self-effort) how to firm ourselves in different "strata" of spiritual Beings or divine qualities. Many hymns in the Santo Daime speak about firming ourselves, for instance, in the sun, the moon, the stars, the earth, the wind, and the sea. They talk about firming ourselves in Christ, in Mary, in Mestre Irineu. And to me, this very refined and exalted level of discovering what firmness means has been quite a journey. It has been so beautiful, for example, to discover, within myself, what it feels like when I firm myself in the sun; that is, when I energetically link up with the Sun (the Source of Sun-ness Itself); when I experience within myself what it is like to feel, directly, forcefully, the specific conjunction of qualities that stream from the divine Being of the Sun, that Being who Shines, who is Radiant and Glorious and Noble.

And it has also been beautiful to learn just how different it is when I firm myself in the Moon—when I link up with the divine Being that is the underlying Source of Moon-ness Itself—to feel within myself the unique energetic quality of that Being who shines so softly, so beautifully, so tenderly, with such exquisite Power and Presence.

Each different divine Being or Energy that we can connect with during the process of developing firmness is qualitatively unique. As we link up with each of these specific Beings or divine qualities, we are given the gift of communing with, and feeling ourselves enlivened by their irreplaceable and incomparable energetic qualities and we discover that each of these Cosmic, Archetypal, manifestations of the Sacred comes to us in the Force, as a quality *of* that Force.[2] Each of these icons of divinity radiates out its own inimitable vibratory signature of divine Energy.

This capacity to firm ourselves in different qualities or energies of divinity is, in certain respects, an expression of the intrinsic link between the Santo Daime tradition and the powerful Presence of Nature from which it emerged and within which it remains embedded. For daimistas, God can be experienced in every aspect of the natural world. Most daimistas, therefore, have a profound reverence for Nature, a reverence that is expressed again and again during works in the form of *vivas* (loud and collective "hails") that are offered fervently to the Sun, the Moon, the Stars, the Earth, the Wind, and the Sea. Daimistas also seek to experientially link up with the Beings that undergird and empower these various aspects of the natural world when, at certain times during specific Santo Daime works, the *Orixás* are sonically invoked in-and-through the hymns—the divine Powers, often understood as various Gods and Goddesses (that historically emerged from within the West African Yoruba tradition and that are also worshipped within Santería and Candomblé in the Americas). The Orixás are expressions of the innate divinity of, for example, a flowing waterfall, or a roaring flash of lightning, or a gentle breeze rustling the leaves of a tree.[3] For daimistas, at least implicitly (since many/most daimistas do not give a lot of conscious attention to theology), the Santo Daime tradition is rooted in a type of panentheism—the understanding that God pervades and transcends the cosmos; the belief that the universe is God's body, and that while there is always a "more-ness" and a "beyond-ness" to divinity, at the same time, and crucially, God is fully present in every natural object.[4] In this way, a small green bird chirping on the limb of a tree can be seen simultaneously as a biological being as well as a hierophany—a shining manifestation of the sacred.[5] For daimistas, that delicate, utterly precious being sings its song *in* the sacred, *as* the sacred, and *for* the sacred—the sacred that also shines fully within each and every one of us, simply by virtue of being human.

Firming ourselves in each of these differing divine qualities or energies brings with it an energetic "rewiring"—a capacity that is ideally ever increasing to tolerate higher frequencies (larger amounts?) of Force. Our firmness deepens, organically, when we consciously and intentionally align ourselves with various strata of divinity. (And sometimes, it has to be said: it isn't always that simple and straightforward. It's quite possible to be *flattened* by the Force even if you've developed a *lot* of firmness. The Daime seems to like to give periodic reminders about who's really in charge.)

What I've also discovered is that my firmness, at least at this point, receives its deepest infusions *not* when I'm forcing myself to do anything, but rather when I "lean back" into the deepest/highest level of divinity that I know. And for me, as a daimista, that level of divinity is the Christ Consciousness: the supremely steady, unwavering, yet simultaneously ultra-dynamic and transformative force of Divinity Itself that descends into this level of reality to transform and redeem each one of us; that One who comes to take on extremely dense and dark energies in order to free them; that Being who is here, now, within each and every person, shining the Light of unconditional Love on the immensity of the world's suffering. To me, that is what I want to be aligned with, in-and-through grace, as much as possible. And what I've discovered is that the more that I keep invoking that Christ Consciousness, and then resting back into that enormity, the more I'm able to remain present, with my heart open and my hand steady at the helm in the rushing river of the Force. To me, that's firmness.

Although I tend to say, "the Christ Consciousness," I'm equally at ease with saying "my Buddha nature," or "my divine Self," or "the Divine Mother," and so on. I'm not saying that I don't, as a religious studies scholar, know that historically and culturally, these phrases have been used in very different ways. I am very aware that the assumptive worlds that they emerged from vary tremendously. I'm not a straightforward perennialist. While I am willing to affirm that the mystical depths of each tradition emerge from a single Source (or perhaps interconnected Sources?), I am also keenly aware that "influxes" from that Source (those Sources?) always come to mystics in-and-through the psychological and cultural lens that they have internalized.

The academic literature on perennialism is vast. See Aldous Huxley, *The Perennial Philosophy* (New York: Harper Perennial, 1990); Martin Lings and Clinton Minnaar, *The Underlying Religion: An Introduction to the Perennial Philosophy* (Bloomington, IN: World Wisdom, 2007); and a recent insightful contribution: Jeffrey Kripal, "The Future of the Human(ities): Mystical Literature, Paranormal Phenomena, and the Contemporary Politics of Knowledge," in *Consciousness Unbound: Liberating Mind from the Tyranny of Materialism*, ed. Edward F. Kelly and Paul Marshall (New York: Rowman and Littlefield, 2021), 359–405.

Therefore, I recognize and affirm that *any and all* words that are used when attempting to describe as accurately as possible these subtle and rarified levels of Reality/Attainment simply aren't going to adequately represent that level of Being. In this way, I have a very strong apophatic perspective on divinity. I believe that there is always *so much more, infinitely more* to what That Is (or should I say who They Are?) than any words, no matter how exalted, can ever express. And since I'm using words to claim that the divine is beyond words, this paradoxical affirmation of the inherent, unimaginably transcendent dimension of divinity (its apophatic dimension) gives me the freedom to be somewhat casual with what word I choose to use whenever I talk, for example, about the Christ, or the Atman, or the Tao, or the Buddha Nature.

JURAMIDAM

Most (all?) daimistas believe that the Christ Consciousness has incarnated within the physical liquid of the Daime itself.[6] Understood in this way, the Daime is a true sacrament.[7] When daimistas drink the Daime, it is an opportunity to feel, viscerally, a deeply intimate communion with the Christ Consciousness. Daimistas even have a name for that liberative, transformative, redemptively divine Christic Power: *Juramidam*.

There's a whole set of typically implicit, overlapping theological assumptions that are associated with Juramidam, but for now, let's just say that Juramidam is not only the Christic Presence and Power that is manifested in the Daime, but it is also understood by most daimistas to be Mestre Irineu's "name in the astral," which means that for most daimistas, Mestre Irineu (the founder of the Santo Daime) is seen as the continuation of the full incarnation of the spirit of the Christ that first took place in-and-as the person of Jesus of Nazareth. In this way, Mestre Irineu is often understood as the replanting, the reflowering of that Christ Consciousness, this time shining forth in the middle of the Amazon rain forest, in the person of an almost seven-foot-tall, illiterate son of former slaves.

Now I have to confess that when I first heard this belief expressed to me by a fellow daimista I was a bit taken aback. At this point, however, I have to say that I'm completely at ease with this theological perspective, as long as Mestre Irineu is not understood to be the *only* manifestation of that Christ Consciousness. I mention this because, at least to my way of thinking, all of us have that I Am Christic Presence within us, as the Eu Superior, as our Higher Self—it's just that some human beings, like Mestre Irineu, are arguably much more "awake" to this inner reality; some human beings, like Mestre Irineu, have established a living, ongoing connection to that "I Am" within.[8] And at this point, I am completely comfortable with this faith stance. I have Mestre Irineu's picture on my altar, and there have been countless works in which I have been able to link up with divinity, powerfully, quickly, simply by connecting energetically with Mestre Irineu while looking at his face glowing from a picture in the salão.

Nonetheless, I have to confess that early on in my participation in the Santo Daime, I was, shall we say, rather skeptical about the divinization of Mestre Irineu that I saw within the Santo Daime tradition (and as I point out in my website discussion of Mestre Irineu's life, found at www.liquidlightbook.com/mestre, many of his closest followers who knew him best also resisted this tendency). However, I also rather quickly learned that the Santo Daime tradition isn't at all about indoctrinating others. Daimistas typically don't attempt to convince others of the superiority of Santo Daime beliefs. There is no catechism in the Daime; there are no popes ruling on correct doctrine; there is no standardized set of rigid dogmas that everyone is subtly or not so subtly pressured to accept.

Instead of a clearly articulated, unanimously affirmed, set of beliefs, what daimistas *really* care about are profound, deeply personal, highly transformative, spiritual *experiences*—experiences that are firsthand and glowing with Light; visionary interactions with an enormous range of nonphysical beings; moments of mystical union (and/or identity with) Divinity Itself; revelatory insights and gnostic teachings that pour into our consciousness, right from the Source (albeit always expressed in-and-through the complex set of filters, assumptions, values, and tacit beliefs that each one of us have internalized.)

Daimistas *also* deeply and passionately care about ritual protocol—how to act within the different ritual spaces in a way that is disciplined, thoughtful, and ideally as impeccable as possible: knowing the hymns well; singing them correctly; embodying within your behavior and comportment all of the nuances of how a daimista should act, on every level, in every situation, within a Santo Daime ritual.

Nonetheless, the Santo Daime wouldn't be a religion (and it most certainly is one) if it didn't have a certain cluster of more or less accepted beliefs that most practicing daimistas basically take for granted. And one of the central Santo Daime beliefs, one that most daimistas would probably have some loose sense of, is that Juramidam is the spirit of the Christ that is sacramentally present within the Daime and that Juramidam and Mestre Irineu are closely, mystically, intertwined.

Furthermore, those in the lineage of Padrinho Sebastião might have also heard that Juramidam is a combination of two sets of understandings: "jura" and "midam," with "jura" representing God the Father (or, more broadly, the transcendent aspect of God) and "midam" representing all of us (or, as I would phrase it, the immanent aspect of God).[9] In this understanding, *all* of us, especially those who drink Daime, are, as a collective whole, a crucially important manifestation of Juramidam. I would say that the Christ Consciousness/Juramidam is always there, albeit, in a hidden way, within everyone (and really everything), but as a daimista, I would *also* say that Juramidam is mysteriously *especially* present (or *especially* evident/manifest) in those who drink the Daime, in that, as we drink this sacrament, we consciously and intentionally enter into an extremely intimate communion with God and are therefore prompted, from within, from our own depths, to work—slowly, patiently, and over time—to incarnate within ourselves, more and more fully, with fewer and fewer impediments, that Christ Consciousness, so that, according to the Santo Daime tradition, we can grow into our rightful stature as mature Daughters and Sons of God.

We're talking divinization here folks. Just like the early Church Fathers taught (and probably Mothers as well, but that's a bit more difficult to discover), way back when, in the first few centuries of the Christian era. Back then, and now, at least for some, divinization was *the* goal of the Christian life, since, in the words of Athanasius of Alexandria, slightly updated for our modern gender sensibility, "God became a human being, so that human beings could become God."[10] That's *really* what daimistas are aiming for, consciously or not: how to realize, in our day-to-day lives, what it means to be a full-fledged Daughter or Son of God. How to more and more fully ground that Light, that Love, on this earth, at this time.

THE SANTO DAIME AS A RELIGION

It is important to remember that the spiritual transformations catalyzed by the Daime do not come automatically or easily.[11] Instead, they emerge gradually from within the context of Santo Daime works. These works often take place quite frequently—in the Santo Daime liturgical calendar, Concentration works, for example, take place twice a month (at least ideally), and during certain festival periods, works are often held several times a week. And these works last anywhere from a minimum of two hours (for *Missas*, or "Masses") to the all-night dance works that can take up to twelve hours or more to complete. In this way, committed daimistas do not just drink Daime every now and then; they don't drink Daime if and when they choose; and they don't drink Daime by themselves. Instead, by taking part in the communal rituals that are an integral part of the Santo Daime tradition, daimistas are given the opportunity to immerse themselves, with discipline and commitment, in a regular way, within the intense, highly rarified, vibratory space of Santo Daime works. And in this way, they offer themselves the chance to commune with the Daime in an extremely powerful, uplifting, and cocreated group context.

Daimistas are given the gift of not having to re-invent the wheel, since they have inherited the polished, intricate jewel of the tradition itself—the cumulative distillation of the divine guidance received by Mestre Irineu, and then Padrinho Sebastião; guidance that both leaders drew upon during the decades during which the Santo Daime tradition emerged and developed, culminating in the ceremonial structures of the Santo Daime tradition itself—rituals that are followed by thousands of daimistas around the globe; rituals that can and do act as strong and beautiful alchemical cauldrons for the often turbulent and highly dynamic energies and states of consciousness that daimistas willingly plunge into, again and again and again.

And Santo Daime works are not called "works" for nothing. They are not for the faint of heart, nor are they for those attempting to run away from their problems or from the world. Santo Daime works are not about partying or getting high. Instead, in the context of these works, a group of people gathers together, with great respect, to take a sacrament. Then, over time, with tremendous self-effort and discipline, little by little, daimistas learn how to become increasingly translucent conduits of Divine Power, Light, and Love, and they do this not just for their own healing and self-transformation, but also to serve others and the world.

And, on a slightly more prosaic level, it takes a lot of work simply to learn the intricate subtleties of Santo Daime ritual protocol. Daimistas are not given a handbook that clearly states how they should behave within the salão. Instead, they learn the nuances of these behavioral norms by cultivating a particular set of virtues, especially the value of paying attention and the need for humility. By putting their egos to one side, and by paying close attention to what is going on around them, daimistas gradually figure out, for example, what gestures to make during communal prayers and when; they learn when and how to step forward in the serving line for the Daime; they learn where to face when drinking the Daime; they learn how to enter and leave a row during a dance work; they learn when it is important to remain in their places and when it is important to leave the salão, as well as how to dress, how to play the maracá, how to dance, and all of the other components of attending Santo Daime works.

In addition, most full-time daimistas will eventually learn hundreds, if not thousands, of hymns. Dedicated Daimistas will often spend an extensive amount of time studying these beautiful and inspiring transmissions that are understood to come from the Astral realm, practicing these hymns with focused effort and devotion so that they can be sung with precision and heart during the works. For most committed daimistas that I know, there is nothing more important in the Santo Daime tradition, with the exception of drinking the Daime itself, than the ability to sing the hymns, with clarity and love, in tune, on the beat, unifying your voice with all of the other voices in the salão, allowing yourself to be carried forward by the beautiful melodies of the musicians, and letting yourself be uplifted and transfigured within that surging, rapturous chorus of devotion and love.

And importantly, being a daimista also means being part of a fellowship, part of a community. The rituals of the Santo Daime are intended to cultivate a deep and abiding communion not only with the divine Beings and with Nature itself, but also, and crucially, with other daimistas as well. The Daime therefore is always taken in a ritual context, in the company of others. This communal context means that Daimistas are given numerous opportunities to learn how to love and respect their brothers and sisters, even if some of those brothers and sisters can at times be somewhat idiosyncratic and/or difficult to deal with. In fact, in-and-through the hymns, daimistas are repeatedly taught the importance of not speaking ill of someone behind his or her back; how to forgive others for being less than perfect; how to forgive themselves for their own limitations; and how to have patience with the countless subtle and not so subtle expectations and demands of others. Daimistas quickly learn that it is crucial to see beyond the off-putting or irritating aspects of their Santo Daime brothers and sisters in order to appreciate the deeper perfection that shines in-and-through all of that messy humanness.

In all of these ways and more, the Santo Daime is a real-deal religion—a religion with well-established institutional structures, a multilayered set of historical and mythological narratives, and a complex web of normative beliefs and ritual practices. It's not an "I get everything exactly as I want it" form of spirituality.

I remember, all too well, that when I was first exposed to the Santo Daime tradition I almost ran screaming from the room when my daimista friends would talk about their "religion." The last thing I wanted at that point was to be part of another religious tradition. But besides the fact that the U.S. Constitution protects the freedom of religion and not the freedom of spirituality (and the Santo Daime probably needs all the legal protection that it can get in the all-too-often close-minded and fearful world that we currently live in), it is also true that there are real benefits that come from taking a psychedelic substance in an explicitly religious context.

Admittedly, the explicitly religious aspects of the Santo Daime can often rub people the wrong way. Nonetheless, having to deal with the at times jarringly abrasive, ritual-based, communal, and institutional aspects of the Santo Daime offers daimistas ample opportunities to allow their egos to be challenged, especially their insistent need to feel completely in control. When you are a committed member of a religion, you don't get to decide how to run rituals. You don't get to decide who is in charge and who isn't. You don't get to decide what to do or what to sing. When you are a committed member of a religion, you simply have to find a way to deal, with as much integrity as possible, with aspects of ritual structures and belief systems that you don't feel totally comfortable with and that don't "fit" your sense of how you would do things and how you see the world.

I was often, from the get-go, rather uncomfortable with some of the top-down patriarchal organizational structures of the Santo Daime and with the, to my mind at least, overly militaristic emphasis on ritual rules. But the primary focus for my impotent wrath, at least during my first few years in the Santo Daime, was how long and arduous the dance works were. During dance works I would often find myself stewing about how completely ridiculous and over the top it was to have to sing *all* of the hymns of an elder. But I soon figured out that this obsessive mental agitation was nothing more than wasted energy. It was like complaining in a baseball game that I should get five strikes instead of three. It just doesn't work like that. Therefore, I chose, instead, to change what I actually could change: my attitudes toward the rituals themselves. I chose, instead, to give myself fully to each hymn, focusing on the hymn we were singing in the moment, and singing it with a focused mind and an open heart, rather than anxiously wondering how many more hymns were left and squirming around for hours in the toxic sludge of self-created resentment and bitterness.

Especially in my early years, I also tried my best to ignore the hymns that emphasized divine punishment, original sin, and depictions of God as some sort of wrathful and condemning judge. At this point, however, I am not overly bothered by these less than-easy to deal with hymns, and at times, I can actually appreciate them. This shift in my attitude arose not only because I (slowly, reluctantly) began to realize the value of these hymn-based "wake-up calls" and reminders of our perhaps hard to admit human failings, but also because I figured out over time that I needed to focus my attention less on the overt subject matter of these hymns and more on the energy that they carried within them. With this change in attitude, everything shifted, and I often began to revel in the powerful, shake you to your core energy that these hymns could/would generate within the Current that circulated throughout the salão as they were being sung.

Santo Daime rituals have been, at least in part, established to create a space and time that is set apart from ordinary life in order to create higher-order positive change within. Therefore, if we either implicitly or explicitly say *yes* to these ritual structures; if we can simply relax into the ritual process with an attitude of openness and acceptance, it can become much easier to plug into the Force that is generated by that ritual and begin to genuinely reap the benefits of this ritual process. On the other hand, Santo Daime rituals, even if approached with an exemplary attitude, are often extremely challenging, both mentally and physically. I don't particularly enjoy having to wear a tie that squeezes my neck, or sitting in hard chairs, or being too hot, or being too cold, or throwing up, or having to deal with the "loud" energetic configurations of the people around me, or singing so many hymns. Even given all of that, what I've learned is that when all of us together have agreed that it's worth it to be uncomfortable in these specific ways—when we can, more or less, open into what is, with faith and trust—then we can create something magical, or at the very least, we can create a context in which something magical *could well* appear. This is, after all, a tradition in which grace is centrally important.[12]

Ironically, it is exactly the hard-edged, spiky, and difficult to deal with aspects of the Santo Daime that, at least potentially, offer us gifts that a completely self-governed spirituality simply cannot. Consciously having to deal with all of that uncomfortable otherness can, if approached thoughtfully, become a real opportunity for us to grow and to become more internally spacious and accepting. It isn't a simple task to find our places, with integrity, in a religion that isn't always accommodating, that makes real demands of us.

Being part of religion also comes with a whole set of potential pitfalls. For example, I can certainly recognize within myself how tempting it can be at times to simply ignore my doubts and reservations about certain aspects of the tradition and instead simply do what I've been told to do. It's much easier to simply mirror what others are saying and doing rather than to raise uncomfortable questions. However, if I'm going to err, I'd prefer to err on the side of remaining faithful to what Mestre Irineu and Padrinho Sebastião taught (although even here, things are not so simple, in that Padrinho's way of working with the Daime—for example, including mediumship and working with cannabis—was often quite different from Mestre's original teachings). To me, aligning myself, with trust and faith, with the traditional ritual forms that have been passed down through the generations has its own inherent value, purity, and power.

But faithful and openhearted trust in Mestre Irineu and Padrinho Sebastião is quite different from unquestioning adherence to the dictates of an external authority, which at times can come hand in glove with a subtle or not so subtle form of dogmatism and/or ritual rigidity. At times daimistas can unknowingly develop an us-vs-them mentality in which "we" are the good guys who are fighting on the side of Light against evil, and all too often, "evil" becomes "those who disagree with us" or "those who do things differently than us." In these cases, it can become all too easy for us to believe that the anger we feel rising within us when others are doing things differently is righteous and justified, since it seems so painfully obvious to us that these "others" are threatening "our" religion. It can be all too easy, in the name of protecting the religion that daimistas love, to proclaim, with utter certainty, "So and so is no longer in the Doctrine." (The Doctrine is the energic matrix from which the Santo Daime emerges and is sustained.)

There are some daimistas in the Alto Santo line (those people, led by Mestre's widow Dona Perigrina, who attend works in the church that Mestre built, in the Alto Santo neighborhood of Rio Branco) who have at times disparaged the followers of Padrinho Sebastião, saying, at least implicitly: *Padrinho Sebastião did things differently than Mestre Irineu did. He gave Daime to people in Rio, and to people from Europe and the United States: Mestre Irineu never did that. He introduced mediumistic rituals into the Santo Daime: Mestre Irineu never did that. He was open to investigating other sacred plants (especially cannabis): Mestre Irineu never did that.*

There are indeed differences between the Santo Daime of Mestre Irineu and of Padrinho Sebastião. However, the issue of Mestre Irineu's link to mediumship is complex. While it is true that Mestre Irineu did not support the practice of mediumship in the Santo Daime, there is compelling evidence that in the early days, before the first works of the Santo Daime, that Mestre Irineu engaged in a form of ayahuasca-based mediumship with a group called the CRF: the *Círculo de Regeneração e Fé*—the Circle of Regeneration and Faith.

For certain daimistas in the Alto Santo line, any changes that took place in the Santo Daime tradition after the death of Mestre Irineu are by definition wrong, and daimistas who follow Padrinho Sebastião's line (the ICEFLU line of the Santo Daime—the current iteration of what was once called CEFLURIS, the lineage begun by Padrinho Sebastião) are seen as "expansionists" or "innovators," and these terms are almost always cast as negatives.

However, all religions, everywhere, throughout time, have always changed, so why should the Santo Daime be any different? (Admittedly, the changes that took place in different religions rarely came about easily, and not all changes were for the best.) It seems quite likely that the Santo Daime will also change as well, especially as it expands into cultural and social worlds that are far different from the Amazonian rain forest world of northwestern Brazil in the mid- to late twentieth century. And perhaps even more importantly, it seems futile to want to stop these changes: do we truly want to cap the fountainhead of boiling ecstatic inspiration that is the Daime? If someone like Padrinho Sebastião, who is deeply established in the Santo Daime; who is spiritually mature and sincerely wishes to follow the inner guidance that she/he has received from the Daime—if someone like that wants to introduce a new ritual form into the ongoing flux of the Santo Daime tradition—it should be encouraged, as long as others are benefiting from that innovation and as long as there can be spirited yet respectful conversation about the pros and cons of this change, rather than resorting to hurling antagonistic verbal "bombs" at one another.

For daimistas, the Daime is deeply aligned with (is identical to?) the Source of genuine revelatory insights, so it seems deeply problematic to ignore and/or to disparage Daime-inspired insights when they're received, in good faith, with discernment, by those who are energetically aligned with that Source. May many more such spiritually mature innovators emerge in the years to come—those who, with minimal ego, are confidently yet selflessly willing to create new ritual forms and/or to offer new theological/metaphysical understandings that speak to the needs of the current cultural/historical configuration.

On May 13, 2018 (Mother's Day), I received my twenty-seventh hymn: "Oh Mother God." I had been having an extremely vivid and powerful dream in which I was seated with a large group of friends in front of a huge brass cauldron—perhaps fifteen feet across—that was sunk into the earth. The cauldron was filled with serpents that extended up from the cauldron like five- or six-foot-tall slithery pillars—dancing, intertwining, very alive, very potent. But then someone had the not so great idea to put a brass lid on the cauldron, and things then immediately went badly— a stream of poisonous ooze began to seep out from under the lid of the cauldron and began to flow out toward all of us. Immediately, however, those of us who were gathered around the cauldron began to sing the words "Oh Mother God" to calm and heal the situation. When I awoke, those three words flowered into the rest of the lyrics of the hymn that I was receiving. To me, the teaching of this dream was all too apparent: putting a lid on our own Life Energy—or the Life Energy of the Daime— isn't exactly a great idea.

Nonetheless, having a strong and well-earthed alchemical cauldron in which those energies can dance and move also makes a *lot* of sense. Clearly there is a profound value to linking up with and faithfully following the ritual forms and protocols of a religious tradition, especially a tradition such as the Santo Daime, that is, it could easily be argued, plugged into an ongoing, genuine Source of divine revelation. And the time, energy, and genuine effort that it takes to maintain that ritual continuity carries with it real rewards: few things can unite a community as much as regular, heartfelt participation in a highly charged and energetically alive ritual process.

Therefore, I don't think that any changes made to Santo Daime rituals should ever happen without careful discernment and plenty of divine guidance. It can be extremely difficult to say which changes are valuable and which are not. It is not always an easy task to tell the difference between the conceivably expendable outer cultural trappings of the Santo Daime and its inner, pulsing, sacred heart. This discernment is made especially challenging because not all cultural/historical specificity is inherently problematic. In fact, I think it would be a real loss if all of the Santo Daime's cultural otherness was smoothed over; if it was adapted to "fit" who we are in our culture to such an extent that it lost something that was genuinely precious. To me there is something that is irreplaceable, and wonderful, about the specific cultural heritage of the Santo Daime. I can't imagine a Santo Daime that was purged completely of the lilting words of Portuguese; or a work in which I could not smell the scent of sage burning in the salão; or a work where I did not see the women in their white fardas with their streams of rainbow-colored ribbons and the pipe-cleaner crowns precariously perched on top of their heads.

For myself, the major problem isn't the outer, culturally specific institutional forms per se. Rather, it's *attachment* to those forms; it's mistaking and/or substituting the outer forms for the inner heart; it's the anxious desire to cling to the past at all costs rather than having faith in the wisdom that seeks to express itself in-and-as the free-flowing, uncontained divine energy that is the Daime.

And yet, being a both/and person, I have to ask myself: Is everything really open to change? And if so, at what point do we say that the Santo Daime has changed so much that it is no longer the same religion? Personally, I'm willing to live in the fruitful tension of balancing sameness/tradition and newness /inspiration. I want to participate in traditional forms with all of their cultural exoticism (although I'm still a bit wary of mistaking that exoticism for what really matters in the Santo Daime) *and* I want to take part in powerful works that are relatively *new* creations of trustworthy elders in the tradition—elders who appear to be responding to genuine inner guidance and who are willing, with heartfelt courage, to offer these new works to their respective communities. (Although I will admit that I sometimes shake my head in wonder when some of these same elders critique the ritual innovations of *other* elders—all in the name of protecting the sanctity and stability of the tradition.)

I am clearly in favor of a thoughtful, careful, and ongoing examination of what aspects of the Santo Daime tradition are cultural and contingent, and what aspects of the tradition are essential and irreplaceable. But let's recognize that different well-intentioned and well-informed people can come to different conclusions and that we're better served by engaging in this difficult and demanding process with an underlying attitude of mutual respect and a willingness to genuinely listen to and be changed by those who have different perspectives from our own, rather than attempting to subtly or not so subtly pressure others into agreeing with us.

If space allowed, I would share more about my experiences in Brazil with daimistas who were (and are) creating new ritual forms in which drinking Daime is centrally important. (If you make your own Daime, or if you have unimpeded access to the sacrament, then even if other daimistas—perhaps understandably—say that what you're doing is "wrong" or "not in the Doctrine," then what do those opinions really matter?) Given more space/time, I would write more fully about a Daime–bioenergetics retreat that I attended in the mountains outside of Rio de Janeiro, cosponsored by Baixinha and a very close disciple of hers who is a bioenergetics therapist—a retreat with no prayers, no hymns—in which the participants (mostly patients of this therapist) drank Daime and meditated while listening to beautiful music or while communing with the natural beauty that surrounded the retreat site. (I have to say that I really missed the prayers and the hymns.) Or I would write about the Spiritist center in the middle of an impoverished *favela* (Brazilian urban ghetto) that would open up its doors every Wednesday afternoon for several hours, welcoming in people from off the streets (often prostitutes and drug addicts), offering them, completely free of charge, opportunities to work through their suffering, anguish, and despair via heartfelt mediumistic encounters with the beings/energies that were afflicting these individuals. During each of these weekly therapeutic encounters, the mediums would all be dressed in white; after drinking Daime and giving each other energetic "passes" to clear off any negative energy, they would arrange themselves, seated in chairs, around a long table, with hymnals in front of them, ready to sing hymns and/or to incorporate spiritual beings if directed to do so by the primary facilitator, a deeply skilled and loving therapist. Or I would describe how a Santo Daime eco-village in Florianópolis (one of the largest residential Santo Daime communities in Brazil outside of Céu do Mapiá), in addition to doing the full liturgical calendar of Santo Daime works, also sponsored and participated in deeply traditional Lakota sweat lodges, vision quests, and Sun dances. This community also periodically took part in all-night *Fogo Sagrado* (Sacred Fire) ceremonies in which participants would begin by smoking hand-rolled, prayerfully made, cigarettes made of native tobacco. They would then later eat small palmfuls of carefully prepared dried peyote, washed down by a drink of San Pedro brew, which would be followed in turn, hours later, by drinking Daime. This is all done in the church itself, with the central altar put off to one side and a huge bonfire built right on the ground (the concrete floor under the altar having been jackhammered off to expose the earth below). The coals were arranged throughout the night into fantastical shapes (dragons, phoenixes, butterflies, and so on) by the fire-tender—all this within a ceremony that was periodically punctuated by participants, having received the ceremonial "talking stick," offering up a hymn, or saying a prayer from their hearts into the circle. All of these deeply moving and transformative ritual forms were consecrated by the Daime, and yet none of them were orthodox Santo Daime ceremonies. But then neither was my first Santo Daime work with Jonathan Goldman, or the *Caminhado* ("Walkabout") work that I took part in during my time in Céu do Mapiá, or the *Umbandaime* work (a fusion of Umbanda and Santo Daime works) that I did there as well. (For a description of the Caminhado work, see "Jardim da Natureza Work" in the "Supplemental Materials" section of the website; www.liquidlightbook.com/jardim.)

CONCENTRATION WORKS

On May 26, 1930, the first official Santo Daime work took place in Rio Branco.[13] This small gathering—only Mestre Irineu and two of his friends, and perhaps his wife of the time, Dona Francisca—took the form of a ritual that later became known as a Concentration work. And even though the external form of this work has undergone numerous modifications since that time, what has been there from the start remains: an emphasis on meditative stillness (*concentração* in Portuguese is perhaps best translated as "meditation"). Concentration works are the ritual hub of the Santo Daime liturgical calendar, in that they typically take place, at least in more established Santo Daime churches, on the fifteenth and thirtieth of each month. And although Concentration works, like all other Santo Daime works, have plenty of prayers and hymns, the primary focus of this particular work is meditation.

Concentration works are opportunities for daimistas to turn within, to immerse themselves as a community in prolonged periods of often an hour or more of silent meditation—meditation sessions that are saturated with the energy of stillness and sacred Presence. Concentration works do not typically contain many explicit teachings on meditative techniques (in the Santo Daime, teachings are transmitted through the hymns, and even more fundamentally, come from the Daime itself, which is seen as the Teacher of Teachers). Nonetheless, a set of teachings associated with several meditative traditions is at least implicitly present in the Santo Daime, given the fact that in 1961 Mestre Irineu decided that his community should become affiliated with the Esoteric Circle of the Communion of Thought, a spiritual organization founded in São Paulo in 1909 that disseminated a variety of teachings drawn from yoga, Theosophy, and Spiritism.[14]

The Santo Daime, especially in the CEFLURIS lineage, has explicitly identified itself as an "eclectic" religion that is open to the teachings of a wide variety of different religious traditions, and the CEFLURIS (now ICEFLU) lineage has for decades nurtured an affiliation with what is known as the "Oriental line" of yogic teachings. (Currently Padrinho Alex Polari is, arguably, the elder in the tradition who has most overtly cultivated a connection to this line.[15])

From my early days with the Santo Daime, I recognized that there was an intimate "fit" between the Santo Daime and these yogic/tantric meditative traditions—traditions that had been the basis of my own spiritual practice for decades before I became a daimista. And I acknowledged that fit by keeping two altars in my home office. One altar affirms my spiritual roots in the yogic/tantric tradition with a multitude of small statues of Hindu deities (Ganesha, Lakshmi, Saraswati, and Hanuman), as well as a picture of my former guru (Swami Muktananda) and a small statue of his guru (Swami Nityananda). The second altar, dedicated to the Santo Daime, contains statues of Jesus and the Virgin Mary, pictures of various Brazilian elders of the Santo Daime religious tradition, a glass candleholder, a small cruxeiro, along with various crystals and small sections of dried curling "jagube" vines from the Amazon. And I have never had any problems with having altars that are dedicated to both of these two strikingly different spiritual paths. For myself at least, both traditions are completely congruent.

Over the years I have noticed that many daimistas often have a wide assortment of religious icons in their homes—usually some combination of Christian figures, Native American symbols, esoteric imagery, and yogic artwork. Some scholars might dismiss this iconic interplay as an indication of a "cafeteria-style" of spirituality, while others might even accuse daimistas of cultural appropriation (although this accusation is made less plausible by the fact that the Santo Daime was founded by a black son of former slaves who himself engaged in the quintessentially Brazilian task of synthesizing diverse religious elements into a cohesive, and one might even say inspired, whole.) Personally, I see such artistic exuberance as a visual representation of the "eclectic" nature of the Santo Daime path itself (at least within the ICEFLU line). And I would suggest that this eclecticism is completely congruent with a mode of reasoning that emerges from the powerful experiences that the Daime itself engenders. For once we have known, powerfully, directly, a state of consciousness that takes us—at least to a certain degree—beyond the limitations of culture, and even beyond time and space as we know them; once we have been shown that no social/historical form of religiosity can fully and accurately represent what has been experienced so forcefully within; then it seems completely legitimate to (ideally respectfully) combine these various limited and local religious beliefs and practices into a hopefully uplifting and coherent thematic whole.

As the years have gone by, I have increasingly appreciated how Concentration works are ritual manifestations of this hybridic interplay. For myself, Concentration works have repeatedly provided a context, in a regular, disciplined way, in which to open up my consciousness to levels of visionary/mystical awareness that I had occasionally experienced during my time within the yogic/tantric traditions, but not with the frequency and ritual continuity that immersion in the Santo Daime ritual calendar provided. And in certain respects, this opportunity to be carried deep within by the Daime in order to experience these wondrous mirações is one of the most important purposes of Concentration works.

And yet, as I've increasingly grown to realize, there is another perhaps more subtle but equally profound purpose of Concentration works—a purpose that is also completely aligned with the yogic/tantric traditions—in that these works offer daimistas a context in which to practice being present in a heartfelt way with *whatever* arises within their consciousness.

Personally, I consider the Daime to be a spiritual Force of almost unimaginable intensity that, with masterful intelligence, often works to bring layers of old, often quite painful, buried psychic material to the surface of consciousness. And for myself at least, when the Daime manifests in this way during Concentration works, it can be quite helpful to have a philosophical outlook that can offer some much-needed perspective on how to work most effectively with the turbulent and often wrenchingly difficult emotional "stuff" that can grip my body/mind during these prolonged periods of meditation. I've been thankful to have internalized a set of teachings from the yogic/tantric traditions that, as it were, elevate these experiences of suffering, so that even though my body/mind might be hunkering down under the onslaught of wave after wave of raw and painful "gunk," on a deeper/higher level, I can recognize that the Daime is bringing up these *samskāras* (to use the yogic term) from my subconscious so that these dense and contracted thoughts and feelings can be acknowledged, accepted, and transformed. In this way, even in the middle of all of this suffering, I can usually, on some level of my being, realize that what is arising within me is in fact a gift brought to me by the Daime; I can, at least most of the time and to a certain extent, maintain the meta-awareness that whatever I am feeling, no matter how difficult it is to bear, is in fact there to be compassionately welcomed and ultimately transformed.

I don't think that anyone will deny that meditating with the Daime definitely adds something to the mix. Especially early on as a daimista, I found that there were times when it could be quite a challenge to keep my mind still and focused during Concentration works, in that I was often swept away by the Force that I could so powerfully feel surging in-and-through me. Nonetheless, as I continued to participate in Concentration works, I increasingly gave thanks for the opportunity to deepen my meditative capacity as I slowly, step by step, learned how to "navigate" in the rushing current of the Force during those hours of meditative stillness.

During Concentration works I was given a context in which to return, again and again, to the rhythm of the breath, as well as a chance to repeatedly sink back into the vastness that I was often able to discover within as I focused on the pauses between each breath. Concentration works also provided me with an opportunity to repeatedly renew my focus on the experiential specificities of each passing moment—grounding myself, centering myself, coming back to my heart, letting go of my mind's tendency to obsess over the past and fret about the future. Instead, I could plunge over and over again into the felt concreteness of the present moment—a present that was saturated by the uplifting energy of the Force of the Daime that I could feel streaming in-and-through my body/mind. As the years have passed, Concentration works have offered me the opportunity to learn how to rest naturally and at ease in the Self-luminous Presence that, with the grace of the Daime, I was increasingly able to discover shining within the depths of my own consciousness.

For years before becoming a daimista, linking myself to this Presence was my central spiritual practice. This form of meditation had been the foundation of my spiritual life and continued to be so even after becoming part of the Santo Daime tradition. Nonetheless, becoming a daimista clearly added something special to my meditative practice—not just the purifying and spiritually potent gift of the Daime itself, but also, crucially, the communal nature of Concentration works. During these works, as daimistas, we are given the chance to link our minds and hearts together, energetically settling into that One Source and letting *That* shine in-and-through each one of us. Each work, in its own unique way, provides the opportunity for all of us, together, to go as deep as we know how. It offers the opportunity to open ourselves up to the Force within a space and time that has been explicitly created for the purpose of giving birth to the highest possible levels of spiritual transformation.

More and more, Concentration works are opportunities for me, with my Santo Daime sisters and brothers, to hold the highest intentions that I know (for healing, spiritual transformation, and awakening), not only for myself, but for everyone. During each of these works, I attempt, with the grace of the divine Beings and hand in hand with my daimista sisters and brothers, to help to cocreate a ritual setting and spiritual intentionality that provides optimal conditions for a powerful awakening of our divine nature, that enables us to practice being, as the Santo Daime tradition expresses it, Daughters and Sons of God and the Divine Mother.

Concentration works, indeed, any Santo Daime work, also offer each one of us a ritual context in which we can, together, with the grace of the Daime, at times almost literally open up an interdimensional portal through which we can begin to explore other worlds and interact with other beings. They provide times during which we can firm ourselves in higher "octaves" of our being as well as opportunities to offer our bodies/minds as portals in-and-through which those divine Presences can infuse their energies into our world. Concentration works give each of us the chance, in a disciplined, active, conscious, and communal way, to participate in the process of the sanctification of the Cosmos. They offer us the opportunity, together, to break open the husk of illusion and let the divine Light that was previously hidden within shine forth with increasing clarity and freedom.

Concentration works offer me, in the company of my daimista sisters and brothers, the space and time to simply be at ease, resting in my body, and savoring each moment with these beloved people. These works offer me the chance to remain in the center of the enormously complex, dynamically interweaving "strands" of spiritual energies that are operative in the salão. They give me the opportunity, as much as possible, to remain aligned with the Source; to stay centered, calm, and in my heart; to go for the highest and deepest level of experience that is possible in each and every moment—and with time, doing so with less and less effort. These works give me the opportunity to learn how to relax deeply into that ongoing divine Presence, that spacious Stillness that surrounds each thought and feeling; to learn how to increasingly rest back into my divine nature during the dynamic unfolding of the work itself.

And from that place of stillness and heart, it is easy for me to feel genuine appreciation and love for different people in the salão and to offer these church members (literally the "members," the "limbs" of the church) my very real, sincere, and deep respect. I will often feel in these works as if, in-and-through my body/mind, the healing Love of God and the Divine Mother is effortlessly flowing forth from my heart, allowing me to simply cherish them, as they are, with all of their idiosyncratic quirks; to love them fully, as someone in process, as someone who is less than perfect, as someone who is oh so beautifully human. And these works also give me the chance to extend that permission to be less than perfect to myself as well, while also recognizing that, as a daimista, it is my job, it is my privilege to seek to evoke the highest and deepest level of heart and consciousness within myself; to hold the highest possible intention *for* each moment, *in* each moment, and *as* each moment.

During Concentration works I have also frequently experienced how the combined spiritual intentions of all of us in the salão can at times come together to create a type of shining energetic "temple" that to my Daime-infused spiritual "eyes" manifests as a crystalline sphere of Light, something that looks like a shimmering, iridescent buckyball that surrounds and irradiates the salão. I vividly remember one Concentration work in which the salão became transfigured in this way. All of us had just emerged from a prolonged and radiantly still period of meditation. We then began to sing this beautiful hymn, straight from our hearts, all of us linking into the streaming beauty of the vibratory Current that flowed through those words, letting it carry us where it wanted to go—all of us singing those words with our hearts wide open—words that, somehow, almost magically, invoked the Presence of Beings of Light, inviting them into the salão. And each of these Beings shone forth as overlapping parts of a prismatic, ever-shifting, temporally formed spectrum of energetic "tones" that rang out within the salão, uplifting and transforming us all. And sitting there, I could clearly see the flows of energy that were emerging from and entering into everyone in the salão, forming that radiant, living crystalline sphere. I felt so present, so interconnected with everyone, as I effortlessly reached out and touched them with my heart *and* received back the gift of the utterly unique patterning of energies that flowed forth from their precious individuality. It was such a giving and receiving of Love, of Light—all of us interpenetrated by these Beings of Light; all of us creating together, effortlessly, within the Force of the Daime, this radiant, ever-shifting, crystalline matrix.

I wasn't clear, even afterward, if all of this had happened when my eyes were open or shut; the experience was just so clear and real that it was like sense experience squared. That shining crystalline sphere of energies was just such a seamless interpenetration of visionary experience and sense experience that I couldn't tell whether I had been uplifted into an archetypal/higher dimensional world or whether in that moment that "other" dimension had "descended" into the physical reality of the salão, enabling me to see more clearly the intermingling of that dimension, as it and countless others were overlaid upon and infused the physical space and time of the salão.

Nonetheless, although such powerful mirações (visionary/mystical experiences) can at times emerge this effortlessly and naturally, at this point, Concentration works, for me, are primarily about remaining firm, alert, and poised in my center, in my heart. My main practice and my main experience during these works, as well as during my "normal" life, are to simply rest in my Sonship, with ease, grace, and humility; all I am asked to do is to flow with and celebrate the never to be repeated textures of each ongoing moment. That's my job. That's my joy. To just stay in my heart, and to stay in *the* Heart. Just breathing in Love and breathing out Love; breathing in God and breathing out God; being God, breathing God. That's more than enough. That's the real work; that's the real delight. To practice, consciously, with others, what it's like to be a Son (or Daughter) of God and the Divine Mother; to simply rest, fully, within mySelf, as myself—at ease, delighting in every moment, extending my heart out to embrace everyone, all while being established in a deeply felt, very tangible, internal relationship to God within.

During one of those exalted but utterly ordinary moments while I was practicing being a Son of God during a Concentration work, I had a powerful insight that to be the Christ fully (which we're all called to be, according to the Santo Daime tradition, as part of the Second Coming of the Christ Consciousness in the world) does not mean some sort of generic Sameness or Oneness. Instead, it means being fully yourself, utterly individualized and unique, while at the same time being completely connected to and expressing the Divine in each moment. I could "see" how each one of us is fully the Center of the Universe, fully Divine; yet each one of us is also manifesting that divinity in our own irreplaceable, ever-changing way. [For numerous depictions of similar experiences by other daimistas, see *Christ Returns from the Jungle*.] Years later, looking back at this experience, I find myself wondering: what would I call it? It wasn't a miração, at least not in the way daimistas normally think of these types of spiritual experiences. That is, it wasn't a vision of some distinct otherness, which for me might manifest as colorful and intricate geometric designs unfurling within; or the surreal architecture of some celestial city; or a Green Lady embracing me with pure love. There was really nothing visionary about opening into the experience of being a Son of God, in that my perception of the external world was not altered in any significant way. Nonetheless, I *was* having numerous in-sights (the ongoing fusion of humanness and divinity within us; the inherent value of remembering and linking up with our higher Self/the Christ within, etc.). And, as with mirações, at least as they are more typically understood by most daimistas, resting in my Sonship was clearly catalyzed by the grace of the Daime, in that it came unexpectedly and felt like a gift. In addition, it was a striking alteration in my consciousness (if anything, it felt higher, more significant, more valuable, than many visionary mirações I have had). So I have to wonder: was resting in my Sonship a type of miração, or does that quality of experience actually belong in a different category? (I'll talk a lot more later in the book about the issue of ranking various types of spiritual experiences.)

Despite all of the expansive inner experiences, sometimes it is also *tremendously* challenging to take part in a Concentration work (or any Santo Daime work!). At times, I'll find myself reeling in the turbulent, densely textured, interweavings of pain, fear, anger, and unsatisfied cravings that will, all of the sudden, be coursing through the salão—and I'll feel as if I'm saturated by all

that suffering, as if I'm marinating in it, to the point that it can be really difficult to rise above those moments of raw, seemingly unending suffering and find
my bearings.

What I'll somehow manage to do, in-and-through all of that energetic (and at
times external) tumult, is sink into my feet; I'll reestablish my "vertical connection" to the divine Source, the I Am. I'll find my heart, my center, and by doing
this I'll ground that Light. Then, without any force or pressure, I will simply sing
out the note of my being (complexly interwoven with and co-emerging from
the energetic notes of everyone in the work); I will simply be present with these
rhythmic pulsations of energies, letting the stillness that I feel within calm what
was charged; untangle what was knotted. And in this way, with the grace of the
divine Beings, I become a steady, inaudible, yet ongoing bass note that carries
with it the unspoken message that right here, right now, we are all loved and
cherished, just as we are. This is a time and place where we can flourish; this is a
time and place where we can begin to learn, within our own experience, what it
means to be a true Daughter or Son of God.

RECEIVING MY STAR

It was the end of September 2009. I had about four and one-half years of Santo
Daime works under my belt. And after studying Portuguese with my tutor
Cristina for a year or so, with a year of prior language study on my own, I was
beginning to think that, at least linguistically, I was ready for my first big fieldwork experience in Brazil, scheduled for the summer of 2010—my two-and-
a-half-month stay in Céu do Mapiá—the village in the middle of the Amazon
rain forest that was/is the international headquarters, the mecca (if you will)
of the CEFLURIS lineage of the Santo Daime, the lineage that was established
by Padrinho Sebastião after the death of Mestre Irineu. (Again, this line is now
officially known as ICEFLU, but for many years it was known as CEFLURIS, so
I will often use the latter term.)

But before I headed off to Céu do Mapiá I needed to receive my star. I needed
to become a fardado. That was crystal clear to me.

For a detailed discussion of the history and symbolism of the six-pointed Star
of David (adorned in the middle with an eagle taking flight from a crescent
moon) that is the "badge" of a fardado, see www.liquidlightbook.com/mestre.

For my first four years in the Santo Daime, I had been quite content to come to works wearing my visitor whites. I really wasn't sure that I wanted to join another religious movement. I had already done that, with enormous fervor, during my more than seven years living in various Siddha Yoga ashrams or meditation centers. I sort of liked hovering at the edges of everything related to the Santo Daime. And besides, I figured that if I was supposed to wear a farda (a uniform), that is, if I was supposed to become a fardado, an initiate of this religion, if I was supposed to receive my star, well then, I was fairly sure that I'd receive some pretty clear-cut inner guidance to do so. And I wasn't wrong.

I vividly remember that evening. All of the sudden, I just knew: you need to receive your star. That level of clarity didn't come simply because I was planning to go to Brazil and I knew that doors would open for me as a fardado that wouldn't if I remained in my whites. And that level of certainty didn't arise as a simple one-to-one response to my bone-deep uneasiness with certain life choices that I had been making at the time, although that spiritual malaise clearly factored into that inner recognition on some tangential level. No, this knowledge ("you need to receive your star") came flooding into my consciousness from some extremely deep, transpersonal level within and arrived with a Force that left no room for questioning or doubts. It felt as if a benevolent, but highly insistent astral bulldog had grabbed me by the scruff of my neck and was shaking me, making sure that I got the message.

And when my inner guidance is that clear, I almost always say *yes*. So, that very evening I called up Jonathan Goldman. I spoke to him about receiving my star and I found out when the next work was in which I could become a fardado. I then ordered my white suit (an essential part of the "white farda"/uniform used for the more formal "Dance works") online, and I bought my plane ticket to Oregon. A couple of weeks later, on October 9, 2009, in Jonathan's church, I officially become a fardado. My *fardamento* took place during a dance work graced with the presence of two elders from Brazil: Padrinho Alex Polari and Madrinha Sonia. Nonetheless, it was Jonathan who actually pinned the six-pointed brass star on the right lapel of my white suit.

The first half of that work was extremely tough. There were several times in which I felt like I simply could not continue dancing, but I basically willed myself to keep going. Finally, after four hours of going back and forth, trying my best to sing hymn after hymn of Mestre Irineu's hinário, the *intervalo*, or break, arrived, and I headed straight to the men's healing room. And for the next hour and a half, I lay there on a thin mat, lined up side by side with several other men. I was almost writhing with self-loathing, doubt, and fear. It felt as if I was thrashing around in a cesspool that was filled with layer upon layer of energetic black goo that kept oozing up and out from within my cells. Over and over again I prayed to Christ, asking for help. It just didn't seem possible to me that I would ever be able to stand up there, in front of everyone, with joy in my heart, and receive my star.

But then ten minutes before the actual star ceremony began, something miraculously shifted; the black tar of negativity began to drain away; and when I finally did stand there, and everyone was singing a hymn to celebrate the moment, and Jonathan was pinning my star on me—I was genuinely happy, filled to the brim with a sense of rightness and goodness and inner solidity.

And that sense of rightness extended even to the little things: such as how good it felt to wear that farda; how good it felt to dance in my row with my other Santo Daime brothers; how good it felt to have said *yes*: this is my Path.

Several months later, when I was in Céu do Mapiá, after my first dance work, I had a miração during which a Star Being manifested within my inner sight, a Star Being who I somehow sensed was the Consciousness of an actual physical star. He consisted of scintillating, crystalline Light; he was shimmering, shifting, utterly beautiful; and he radiated out countless, ever-changing crystalline "points" of Light: they emerged and shone forth from his center, from his heart, in all directions. These rays of Light were his way to bless me, to connect with me, and they filled me with purely pleasurable waves of golden Light, beams of Light that were not like physical light, in that they were somehow organic, alive. These beams were inherently geometric: they had edges and points; they had planes and angles, even if none of this angularity was rigid or hard. This was a Crystal Star Being. Moreover, and I felt this strongly, this was My Star—this was the Being who had united with me during my Star ceremony when I became a fardado; the Being who, on some really deep level, *was* Me. The arrival of this Crystal Star Being was, I just Knew, the culmination of the process of receiving my star (the process that I began during the work in which I became a fardado). Now I had received it directly, and fully, from the Astral.

4

Mapiá—Beginnings

HEADING TO THE HEART OF THE AMAZON RAINFOREST

In the middle of June 2010, I finally made it to Brazil. Cristina claimed that I was fluent in Portuguese; however, as I quickly learned, it's one thing to have a slow back-and-forth conversation with an educated Brazilian and quite another to have to make sense of the gushing, slang-filled, strongly accented Portuguese of, let's say, a taxi driver. Nonetheless, I was as ready as I could be. I had all my shots. And I was lugging three huge suitcases, one of which was filled to the brim with gifts (clothing, medicine, etc.) for the people in Céu do Mapiá.

Céu do Mapiá was hacked out of the jungle—literally, with machetes—in the beginning of the 1980s with the blood and sweat of a highly dedicated group of daimistas who, with tremendous faith and courage, had followed Padrinho Sebastião into the rain forest. A few years earlier, after selling most of the property they owned in Colônia Cinco Mil (the 5000 Colony), an agricultural settlement on the outskirts of Rio Branco, a large group of his followers had followed him into *another* section of the Amazon rain forest that they called Rio do Ouro—the River of Gold. There they managed, with enormous effort, to create a Santo Daime community. They put up houses, erected a church, planted crops, and established rubber-tapping trails; doing all of this while at times not having enough to eat and at one point enduring an extremely debilitating and dangerous onslaught of malaria (only 40 of the

260 inhabitants did not catch the disease, and 3 ended up dying). Unfortunately, due to the ambiguities and ineptitude of Brazilian bureaucracy, two years after taking possession of this swath of virgin rainforest, they were informed that the land they had been officially told was theirs and that they had worked so hard to cultivate and make their own was actually the property of a wealthy rancher from southern Brazil. When Padrinho Sebastião heard this news, he didn't hesitate. It was clear to him that they needed to find a new location. And therefore, several months later, with the approval of and assistance from the Brazilian authorities, they finally "landed" on the banks of the Igarapé Mapiá, a small stream that emptied out into the River Purus, which is itself a branch of the Amazon River. In this new location, this small but highly committed group of daimistas, once again, with enormous faith, courage, and hard work, started the process of creating a community in the middle of the Amazon rainforest. And once again, it wasn't easy. (One elder told me that most of the early settlers at Céu do Mapiá basically lived for months on crackers, since there wasn't a lot of wildlife, and it took a while before any crops were ready to be harvested.) But three decades later, when I managed to make it to Céu do Mapiá, what I found was a more or less self-sufficient, spiritually oriented, eco-village with about six hundred inhabitants; a cluster of small shops; a modern school; and an internet café. (I tell the story of the creation of Céu do Mapiá in much greater detail in "The Historical Development of the Santo Daime: Section Two—The Life and Work of Padrinho Sebastião," www.liquidlightbook.com/padrinho.)

I had flown from Dallas to Rio de Janeiro and then on to Brasília, the capital of Brazil. Then, after an overnight stay, I had taken a much smaller plane to Rio Branco, the capital of Acre, a state on the westernmost frontier of Brazil. Everything had been planned out carefully: I was going to be met at the airport by a man that a knowledgeable American daimista had recommended. This man was supposed to take me to a nearby hotel where I'd stay for a few days, getting to know this small city where the Santo Daime had emerged in the early 1930s.

But when I arrived at the airport in Rio Branco, all of those carefully made plans disintegrated, in that I was actually met by this man's brother, and it soon became clear that he had driven all the way from Boca do Acre to pick me up. (Boca do Acre is a small frontier town several hours away from Rio Branco—it's where I had planned to hire a boat to take me to Céu do Mapiá). It took me a while to finally "get" that, in his mind, he was there to take me all the way to Boca do Acre, which meant that I either had to tell him that this wasn't the plan" and then ask him to drive all the way back (which also meant I'd have to just wing it in terms of getting myself there), or I'd have to shift *my* plans. I ended up shifting, and after haggling a bit about prices, I ended up loading all of my luggage into his "taxi" (an old, extremely dusty, mud-caked Volkswagen sedan), and we headed off to Boca do Acre.

At my request, we first stopped at Alto Santo, located on the outskirts of Rio Branco. This is where the tomb of Mestre Irineu is located, as well as his original church. I quickly discovered, to my dismay, that Mestre Irineu's tomb was closed for construction. (The old tomb, I found out later, needed to be expanded so that it could handle more people at festival times). Nonetheless, a few hundred feet across the street from the construction site I spotted a building that certainly looked like a Santo Daime church, and after walking up to the gate and (bold as brass) peering into the open-air structure for a bit, I was finally noticed by an extremely kind and welcoming man from the church. We talked for a while, and he eventually opened the gate and showed me around the church. (In this case, doors literally opened for me due to my prior contacts: almost immediately after he discovered that I knew the work of Matthew Myer, an American scholar of the Santo Daime who had lived with their community for an extended period of time, he said, "Any friend of Matthew's is a friend of mine!" and let me into the church grounds.)[1]

I was a bit awestruck: this was *the* church, Mestre Irineu's church. I didn't really have the time to do much more than gaze in wonder at the simple, but beautiful architecture and to walk around the grounds, grinning from ear to ear, thinking to myself, for example: *I bet those are the orange trees Mestre Irineu refers to in his hymn!*[2] My guide even attempted to introduce me to Mestre Irineu's widow, Madrinha Peregrina, but it ended up that she was asleep, so he encouraged me to drop by later on my way back from Céu do Mapiá. (This guide's welcoming invitation was itself, I knew, a bit unusual, since the Alto Santo "line" is rather different than the CEFLURIS "line" of the Santo Daime, and apparently it was all too common for members of the Alto Santo line to be somewhat less than welcoming to daimistas who were heading to and from Céu do Mapiá.)

After less than an hour in Alto Santo, I reluctantly said goodbye (I could tell that my taxi driver was beginning to get a bit antsy), and we drove off, heading to Boca do Acre. The first hour or so of the drive was in the state of Acre, where the roads were paved, and the landscape was surprisingly open, the original rain forest having been cut down decades ago to make room for extensive, gently rolling fields for cattle, punctuated here and there by a few really beautiful, tall trees. However, immediately after we entered the state of Amazônia, the previously paved road shifted, rather abruptly, into a rutted clay "road" that the taxi bumped and bounced along for the next four hours, frequently swerving around or splashing through pond-sized puddles. Apparently, according to my driver, a bulldozer and other assorted road equipment had gone through the countryside a few years earlier and did the initial work that was needed to create a paved, two-lane road. However, construction simply stopped. (My driver claimed that there had been funding to complete the road for years, but that all of that money had gone into the pockets of crooked politicians.) The bottom line was that there was only a very narrow section of the clay road that was sufficiently packed down to be drivable. This was where the rather numerous trucks and cars went, jockeying for space, bouncing through bone-shaking potholes, honking exuberantly, weaving back and forth from one side of the fairly wide swath of cleared clay earth to the other, accelerating through some "puddles," while going very, very slowly through others, and avoiding yet others altogether—with me utterly bewildered as to how they knew which was which.

We didn't get to Boca do Acre until after dark. I'll admit that town was rather intimidating. I felt like I had suddenly been transported into the Wild West of Brazil, filled with seemingly sullen, slouching lowlifes, and here I was, this exhausted and frazzled, well past middle age North American who was praying silently to himself, asking for both internal calm and external protection.

The driver stopped at a "restaurant" (more like a dingy bar with a few scattered tables and a blaring television) where, about an hour later, after barely being able to choke down the stringy meat and tasteless vegetables that I was finally served, we made our way through the mostly unlit town until we finally arrived at the Hotel da Floresta—a hotel run by daimistas that my American daimista contact had recommended. Unfortunately, the hotel itself ended up being pretty grim—peeling paint; young toughs hanging around outside the front door and in the lobby; no hot water in the shower—not even a towel until I explicitly, and rather testily, asked for one. Nonetheless, it had one supremely redeeming feature: to my surprise and delight, Rick and Ron were there waiting for me.

Rick and Ron were two easygoing young men in their thirties who I knew pretty well from our times together during my previous Santo Daime works in the United States and genuinely liked. I had known that they were coming to Brazil around the same time I was, but I had assumed that I would meet up with them in Céu do Mapiá. But as often happens in these sorts of journeys, they had been forced to stay in Boca do Acre longer than they had expected, because Rick had had difficulty using his Mastercard to get money. And as fate would have it, during that time they had run into two other Brazilians who were also planning to go to Céu do Mapiá: Jorge and Soraya.

Jorge was a tall, baby-faced man in his thirties, while Soraya was a tiny, wiry, petite, tough-as-nails woman in her mid-thirties who rapidly took us under her wing. (She had been to Céu do Mapiá several times and "knew the scene" there.) Early that evening we all huddled together in Rick and Ron's bedroom upstairs to talk logistics. That was when we heard from Soraya that the house that the three of us had planned to stay in had been broken into; it didn't have electricity; and it really wasn't very secure. (We had arranged to stay in the house more than a month earlier, based on my American daimista friend's recommendation, as well as after a labyrinthian back and forth with various intermediaries.) Welcome to the rain forest!

That distressing news was followed, the next morning, by an extremely difficult interaction with a young man (Eduardo) that the owner of the house had sent to Boca do Acre to act as her representative. He had, unfortunately for us, spent the night before getting drunk, and had shown up at Rick and Ron's room unannounced and had begun shouting at them in extremely rapid, and somewhat slurred, Portuguese. Because Ron didn't know any Portuguese and Rick only understood a bit, they tracked me down, and I did my best to make sense of the difficult to understand prices that Eduardo was trying to shove down our throats. ("You owe me this amount for this; and this amount for that . . .") As I was listening to this rather hostile young man, red flags began flapping like crazy within me, so I quietly exited the room and finally managed to find Soraya, not an easy task at the best of times. Thank goodness for her tenacious, streetwise self, in that she helped us to finally make sense of Eduardo's monetary demands, and then went on to help us to negotiate a face-saving alternative. We had by that time decided there was no way in hell we were staying in that house. We ended up paying him not the 1000 reais he had demanded (about $500 at the time), but instead, a token amount of money for the time that he had spent coming to Boca do Acre.

During my first days in Brazil I was a bit discouraged with my Portuguese skills: it was just so clear to me how much I didn't understand and how difficult it was to communicate easily with others. (Nonetheless, my Portuguese *was* good enough to hear the cab driver who drove me from Rio Branco to Boca do Acre tell the hotel clerk that I didn't really understand much Portuguese.) At one point I told Soraya that with my "working knowledge" of Portuguese, in charged conversations like the one with Eduardo, it was like I had my hands held in front of my face. My fingers were overlapping, so that I could see something through the gaps, but a lot of my vision was blocked. Still, my confidence rose a few weeks later, after I had finally arrived in Céu do Mapiá. Many people, very politely I'm sure, kept complimenting me on my Portuguese. One man even said that I already spoke better Portuguese than many of the people in Mapiá. (I wasn't sure if this was a compliment to me, or an insult to them!)

That morning in the hotel, I began to feel rather shell-shocked, not just from the trip and the energetically heavy and charged interactions with Eduardo, but also because I had finally figured out that, before getting on the boat, we needed to buy enough food for us to live on during our time in Mapiá—without really knowing what sorts of food we should even purchase. (We ended up getting rice, beans, spaghetti, carrots, onions and other staples, along with an all-important hammock for each of us.) We also didn't have a clue whether the amount of food we bought would even last. (I was going to stay for two and a half months, whereas Ron and Rick were planning to stay for six weeks.) And before we could do any of that, Rick had to figure out how to get money with a Mastercard that no ATM in Boca do Acre would accept. (He was finally able to locate a supermarket manager who was willing to accept his Mastercard in exchange for food.) It was, to put it mildly, a rather stressful morning.

While all of this was taking place, Soraya negotiated with the boat drivers and the porters. We ended up each paying about 150 reais so that the five of us and a few small bags could go in one canoe, while the excess luggage and the food supplies we had bought would all be transported in a second, slower canoe. (That canoe didn't arrive at Mapiá until early evening of the next day—a delay that, by itself, created some rather thrilling zings of anxiety within me.)

Nonetheless, by eleven o'clock that morning, our band of five intrepid travelers descended the rickety wooden stairs down to the dock and after the inevitable waiting around and not knowing what was happening, we finally officially set off down the River Purus in, to my mind at least, a rather less than ample metal canoe/boat that was maybe fifteen feet long, with a driver named Júlio who had lived in Mapiá since he was two (at that point he was thirty-two). Júlio stood at

FIGURE 4.1   Boat to Mapiá

the back of the canoe steering and deftly maneuvering the small, but extremely loud motor—a motor that was rigged with a long handle so that it could be quickly and easily lifted from the water if, as was often the case, we had to navigate around hidden logs or other obstacles. Soraya sat in the front seat, Jorge and I sat in the middle, and Rick and Ron sat behind us.

TAKING THE BOAT TO CÉU DO MAPIÁ

The first part of the canoe ride, in which we made our way down the River Purus, was actually relatively relaxing. The river was extremely wide (I'm guessing around two hundred feet across); the greenish-brown water was so still that it was almost glassy (it was even hard to tell which way the current was flowing, although I later found out that we were going downstream); and the riverbanks on each side rose, steeply vertical, at least thirty feet above the river. The small boat rode very low in the water (I could easily dip my hand in) and we were

completely exposed to the elements. (Throughout the journey I would periodically send up a quick prayer of thanks that it wasn't raining.) Fairly soon into
our journey I began to feel the sun's radiation pressing strongly on my exposed
skin, so I quickly lathered myself with sunscreen and then passed it on to the
others. Nonetheless, to my surprise, it was actually rather cool as we made our
way down the river, since the movement of the boat itself helped to generate a
soft and deeply appreciated breeze.

I also hadn't even thought about food. I had just assumed we'd stop somewhere. But luckily Soraya had brought some bananas and oranges, along with
some stale bread and oily cheese, as well as a few cheap chocolate bars, and she
was happy to share with us, which was fortunate, because that was all the food
that we had.

I should emphasize that we were basically in the middle of the rainforest as
soon as we started down the River Purus. After the initial remnants of the outskirts of Boca do Acre disappeared, we quickly began to see numerous dugout
canoes drawn up onto the narrow yellow-sand beaches on the right side of the
river, along with occasional very primitive huts on stilts that, every now and then,
would appear on the high bluffs. But mostly it was just us, the river, and the
forest.

And for hours I breathed in that sense of immensity as we kept, quite loudly,
moving down the river. And kept going, and going, until finally it dawned on
me that there wouldn't be any official rest stops. (I'm actually somewhat embar-
rassed to admit just how ignorant I was about even the basics of this journey.)
So, whenever the driver stopped the motor to refuel, we'd hop out on a sand-
bar and quickly pee. (At one point, Ron's bladder was so insistent that—as we
hooted and teased him mercilessly—he accomplished the rather tricky task of
peeing off the side of the moving canoe.)

About four hours into our trip, we finally, with little fanfare, turned up a tiny
tributary (the Igarapé Mapiá). At that point, everything changed. All of the sudden the river was dramatically narrower (maybe thirty feet across) and shallower
(I could frequently see the sandy bottom), and the trees were much, much closer
to the river, often overhanging it, as if we had entered a shimmering green tunnel.
The sound of the motor also became much more intense as it echoed off the trees,
creating these eerie, almost alien overtones that were extremely insistent and at
times oddly compelling. (Nonetheless, I quickly handed out all the earplugs that
I had brought with me—and being the boy scout that I am, I had several—which
the others gratefully received.)

We had also entered into a world in which the tributary twisted and curved,
over and over, in a seemingly infinite variation of sameness, while Júlio deftly

navigated the canoe diagonally from point to point (perhaps to avoid the stronger current in the middle?). I was quickly struck by how steering a canoe is quite a bit different than driving a car: there are no brakes, and the "road" isn't solid, so there has to be an exceedingly subtle and highly attuned relationship between the driver, the boat, and the river. All of this weaving back and forth meant that we often had to duck our heads down to avoid being hit in the face by the branch of an overhanging tree. At one point we even rammed an enormous log in the river and got stuck for a while, but in the end, Júlio, after some choice curse words muttered under his breath, jumped out of the canoe, and stood, not quite up to his waist, in the reddish-brown water, thrusting his weight against the side of the canoe and tugging backward until he finally managed to extricate us.

Júlio was, to be frank, a rather intense, tightly coiled, piece of work. At another point, farther up the tributary—we were going upstream—another canoe filled to the brim with a family was coming downstream (our first time seeing other people!), and he basically played "chicken" with them, or at least it seemed like he did, in that he didn't slow down a bit, and barely moved over to the left at all, which meant that as they roared past us on the right, water swept into our canoe and we were flung around in their wake, while the family in the other canoe suffered through the exact same indignities. Neither boat driver seemed to bat an eye at any of this.

It was really hard for me to "read" Júlio. Was he playing with us? Was he trying to freak out his North American passengers? Was this the normal speed that he would go in the boat, or was he upset that we were late and was therefore pushing things? It sure seemed to me that he was going as fast as possible, but I was acutely aware of how little I actually knew about his opinion of us. I'll be the first to admit, however, that all of that high-speed dodging, weaving, and ducking at the last minute *was* thrilling—and it definitely meant that we all had to be extremely alert and fully present, if for no other reason than to prevent any unnecessary injuries.

During our time on the igarapé I was also surprised not to see much wildlife— just a few kingfisher-type birds, some cranes, and a few tiny caimans. Nonetheless, the presence of the forest, especially the lush plant life, was extremely strong and beautiful. Over and over again throughout the journey, I reminded myself: just breathe it all in. On the whole, the journey itself was a very powerful and spiritual process for me—an opportunity to stay present; to harmonize with the energy of the other people; and to open myself again and again to the immense Force that I could feel pressing upon me from the rainforest that surrounded us on all sides.

CÉU DO MAPIÁ: FIRST IMPRESSIONS

Finally, just before it became pitch dark, (around 6:45 p.m.), we arrived at Céu do Mapiá. I could immediately tell that we were there. The green enclosing canopy above and around us opened up; the sound of the motor quieted; and we glided under this seemingly professionally built, extremely sturdy (and long!) wooden bridge that crossed the igarapé until Júlio beached the canoe on the narrow sandy beach immediately to the side of the bridge.

My heart leapt: we've arrived! Nonetheless, it was dark, and I for one didn't have a clue as to what to do next. And yet again, Soraya came to the rescue. Almost immediately after we were pulled up onto the riverbank by a group of young men who appeared to be waiting there for us, she quickly hopped out and after about half an hour, she returned, saying that she had managed to find a place for us to stay—an "inn" (the Pousada 2000) run by Padrinho Alfredo's

FIGURE 4.2 Padrinho Alfredo.

Courtesy of the Goldman collection.

extended family (his own house was just across the dirt road). (Padrinho Alfredo, one of Padrinho Sebastião's sons, is the current head of the ICEFLU lineage of the Santo Daime.) Thankfully, it was slightly cheaper than the original place we had planned to stay, and much more secure, in that there were always people there, and each room could be locked.

After hiking up a rather steep dirt road that led from the bridge to the inn, we had an impromptu dinner. It tasted *wonderful* after the boat food. And the people at the inn were extremely friendly and welcoming—which was fortunate, because it quickly became clear that in many ways we were actually staying at their home, since we simply joined them at their dining room table and ate the same food they did, which they had cooked in the rather spacious and surprisingly well-equipped kitchen just off the dining room area (although I later found out that they didn't have a refrigerator: no electricity!).

The inn was two stories tall and probably had about twenty bedrooms, although a couple of the rooms were where the people who helped out around the inn stayed. I was given an upstairs room, which I later learned was a boon,

FIGURE 4.3 Inn in Mapiá

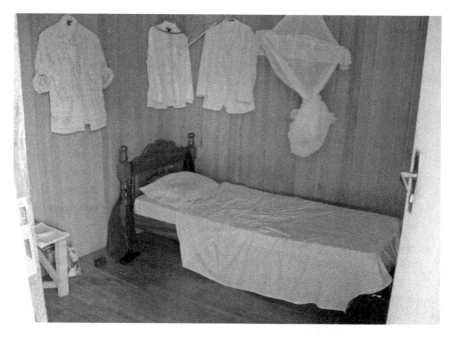

FIGURE 4.4 Bedroom in Inn

since the creepy-crawly things (and there were a lot of them!) usually tended to congregate in the lower rooms (less distance to crawl). My room, like Rick and Ron's, reminded me of something out of an army barracks—it was small, and very simple. It was furnished with nothing more than a stark wooden bed frame and a thin mattress, which I later covered with the mosquito net that I had purchased in Boca do Acre. The walls of the room were made of dark hardwood planks that were painted yellow, and it had "windows" that were actually square or rectangular holes cut into the walls, equipped with sturdy wooden coverings, painted blue, that you could slide open, via grooves in the wood, when you wanted light and air, and that you could slide shut when you wanted protection from the elements—and from potential thieves. Everything was solid, and yet open. The walls didn't go all the way up to the ceiling—which was actually the underside of the corrugated tin roof—which left a couple of feet for air to circulate—and plenty of room for lots of bats to fly around. (I confess that I really liked those manic, yet graceful, and highly efficient insect catchers.)

The human–insect interactions in Céu do Mapiá were often quite dramatic. One night, Ron, Rick, and I were sitting around a small fire in the front yard of the inn. Ron at some point left to go to bed, but a minute or so later, we all jumped up from our log seats, having heard a really loud, high-pitched scream coming from the darkness. We soon found out that the scream came from Ron: a *huge* spider, at least as big as his hand, was splayed out on his door. Unfortunately, Ron had discovered his close proximity to his arachnid neighbor without a flashlight: he had basically been eyeball-to-eyeball with the massive hairy thing. (I'll admit that I took a brief moment of satisfaction, hearing him "scream like a girl"—given that this was exactly how he described how I had sounded when I had almost stepped on an equally huge spider on the path in the dark as we were coming back from an earlier visit to one of the elders.) Anyhow, Rick was laughing at Ron's hysterics. Ron's voice was really high, and he was going on and on about how the spider was going to jump on him and eat his face if he came near. He was trying to rally his courage: he had gotten a flyswatter from upstairs and had put a blanket down under the door of his room so that if/when the spider got knocked down, it wouldn't scuttle under the door and get into his room. If the spider did that, Ron swore that he'd never sleep in the room again. Ron finally summoned his courage and did indeed swat the spider down and apparently it, in Rick's words, began to "gallop" away down the concrete hallway in front of the rooms after apparently attacking the flyswatter. Rick then chased after the spider with his camera to get some photos, and the spider finally had enough and turned around and reared up like a bucking bronco, moving his two front legs defiantly, seemingly daring Rick to come any closer. And as if that wasn't enough, Ron had been dealing, almost every night, with a bat defecating on his bed. I teased him over breakfast the next morning, saying that he must have felt like he was under attack from the forces of evil.

After dinner, I decided that I'd sleep better if I had a shower before bed. Tereza, the manager of the inn, showed me where the two bathrooms were located: they were both on the first floor, around the corner from the kitchen, on the back side of the inn. Braving the bathroom that night was quite an adventure. When I slowly opened the creaky wooden door, carefully balancing all of my toiletries and my flashlight, a small green frog that was perched on the wall to my left leaped through the air, seemingly aiming right at my face. (It's hard to tell who was more startled, me or the frog.)

The shower of the men's bathroom was actually nothing more than a faucet jutting from the faded, slightly peeling, mustard-yellow plaster wall, along with a showerhead that was positioned slightly higher up the wall. The toilet was only a couple of feet away, cheek-by-jowl with the shower.

The only light in the bathroom that night came from the flashlight that I had (wisely!) brought with me and from the soft glow coming from a small white taper candle that Tereza had set on an empty tin can that was placed on the top of the wall that separated the men's side of the bathroom from the women's side. As in the rest of the inn, the walls didn't go all the way up, so as I discovered to my dismay the next day, any and all "bathroom sounds" were all too vividly shared if both bathrooms happened to be occupied at the same time.

I also quickly discovered, not surprisingly, that there wasn't any hot water for showers, even if the water was actually not quite as ice cold as I had feared.

After finally braving the cold water of my shower (accompanied by plenty of yips and yells) and now feeling invigorated and alive, I ascended the stairs back to my bedroom. Despite the mugginess of the night, I actually slept well, at least after I navigated the somewhat delicate process of climbing into the mosquito net using my flashlight to guide me. (The mosquitoes typically only buzzed outside the netting for a short period of time, right after sunset—otherwise, they were not in evidence.) After about an hour, it actually got rather cool, a pattern that repeated itself most nights.

I was awakened the next morning, and basically every morning afterward, by the sound of roosters crowing. I quickly discovered that life at the inn was typically filled with activity and noise: chickens almost continually clucking around in the sandy yard; young kids running around outside in their underwear shouting and playing; harried yet indulgent mothers yelling at the kids; Tereza and other women (friends? neighbors? both?) chatting downstairs in the kitchen; everyone laughing and joking around the dining table. It was quite a communal experience at the inn: shared bathrooms, shared meals, people that didn't live there stopping by to bring Tereza some food, or to take some greens from the greenhouse out back, or to deliver news. And sometimes people came by simply to help out. On our first full day at the inn, for instance, Dona Raimunda from down the hill cooked the lunch, just because she knew that Tereza was feeling a bit overwhelmed.

Not surprisingly, at times that sense of communality also morphed into something a bit less idyllic, such as when Damião, a young man who hung around the inn, and who every now and then, seemingly only when he felt like it, helped his young wife Solange to sweep the floors and do other odds and ends, kept "borrowing" the flip-flops that I used to walk around the inn, especially to the showers, doing so without bothering to ask me, and only sheepishly shrugging when Tereza later lovingly confronted him about it. Or when Raimundo, another young man who also hung around the inn (he was much more rough-edged, compact, and intense than Damião), would occasionally hop on the placid horse that was tied up out back and gallop off with a lot of panache, whipping the flanks of the horse with a rope—no saddle, just a blanket and a crude bridle—doing all of this, I discovered later, with a horse that wasn't his. He was just "borrowing" it from the people who lived next door.

Céu do Mapiá, I soon discovered, was a place that was continually overturning my typically ill-founded expectations. For example, as I mentioned, there were few if any mosquitoes during the day. And even the heat, which really began to build by 10:00 a.m., wasn't *quite* as oppressive as I had anticipated, especially under the shade of the trees. (Even though by the middle of the afternoon I'd be drenched in sweat and for a few hours each day I typically only wanted to either laze around in a hammock or cool off in the igarapé).

Céu do Mapiá was also much more open, expansive, and beautiful than I had imagined it would be. It was filled with interweaving paths, dappled sunshine, and hills with exquisite views. In my thoroughly uninformed mind I had thought that Mapiá would be this collection of ramshackle huts on stilts under a thick canopy of trees, but what I quickly discovered was that it was actually closer to India or Hawaii, at least how I imagine how Hawaii must have been before the dawn of tourism. There was lots of lush vegetation, and the village as a whole was very domesticated and comfortable. There were even quite a few nice, real-deal homes scattered throughout the village—inevitably made with the ubiquitous hardwood planks for walls, along with modern tile floors, and as I discovered after I had been invited into several, often filled with well-made furniture and attractive artwork.

But not all of Céu do Mapiá was beautiful. In fact, on my first full day there I was astonished to discover that there was litter everywhere. The beaten-down, barely even brown grass of the central town square was covered with a thin but extensive layer of small pieces of trash: bubblegum wrappers, cellophane covers, and ice cream labels, punctuated by larger offenders such as potato chip bags and empty liter-sized Coke bottles. I later learned that an enterprising and idealistic young woman in the community had organized a group of people who set up trash cans throughout the community, and they had placed these trash cans everywhere, accompanied by signs filled with inspirational exhortations about the importance of cleanliness. And this same group of people even had an site just off

FIGURE 4.5   Home in Mapiá

the plaza where community members could exchange plastic trash for powdered milk for their children, and this mound of plastics was then ingeniously used to fashion items benches and other items that the community could use. Nonetheless, throughout the community, and extending far into the forest, it was clear that for many people in Mapiá, the ground itself, and the igarapé, was one big trash can—one that they used openly and unapologetically. Therefore, somewhat upset by this situation, Ron, Rick, and I got into a habit of picking up trash as we walked around. Several daimista "old-timers" noticed and informed us that there was a type of "war" going on in Mapiá around the topic of trash. On one side were the more educated, economically well-off daimistas who had moved to Mapiá from the south (e.g., from Rio de Janeiro and São Paulo), while on the other side were the *caboclos*—the less-educated and less economically privileged, typically mixed-raced people who were beginning to relocate to Mapiá.[3] (Why *wouldn't* you want to live in a place that—unlike anywhere else for hundreds of miles—has an extensive, strikingly modern, and up-to-date school for the children?)

Céu do Mapiá reminded me a lot of what it was like when I spent two years— from 1976 to 1978—in Swami Muktananda's ashram (residential meditation center) in rural India, outside Mumbai. But Mapiá was like an ashram without any walls to separate it from the more secular surrounding village. Céu do Mapiá consists of an inner core of intensely spiritual, highly idealistic, extremely disciplined people who are willing to dedicate their entire lives, without holding back, to a lifelong, full-time journey to realize and embody the Light, Power, and Love of God. And this core of deeply committed fardados, many of them long-time followers of Padrinho Sebastião, are interspersed with people who really aren't all that interested in anything spiritual; who'd rather hang around all day and chat, or watch TV, or scoot around the village on motorcycles, or drop litter anywhere they please. Because, in truth, who could/should stop them? No one officially owns the land in Céu do Mapiá, so anyone can come and build a house, and raise some chickens, and/or start a little store. When Céu do Mapiá was, again, quite literally, hacked out of the forest with machetes and axes in the early 1980s, everyone who lived there was willing to risk everything to follow Padrinho Sebastião into the depths of the Amazon rainforest. They wanted to inaugurate this deeply communal, almost literally communistic, share and share alike, quasi-utopian, divinely inspired, village. By 2010, however, life had become much more complicated and messier. Céu do Mapiá was, by that time, nowhere near as cohesive and harmonious and idealistic as it had been even a decade or two before.

YOUNG PEOPLE IN CÉU DO MAPIÁ

One of the most pressing problems that old-timers in Céu do Mapiá had to deal with was how to integrate the young people of the village into its religious life. The vast majority of these young people had not, of course, come to Mapiá voluntarily—instead, they had been born into daimista families who were idealistic enough to want to live full-time in the Amazon rainforest. And, unlike their deeply committed daimista parents, many of the young people weren't exactly thrilled at the idea of living in an isolated village in the middle of the rainforest. In addition, they were also not exactly keen on drinking Daime. To many of them, the Daime was, quite literally, a bitter medicine that their relatives kept urging them to swallow. Not surprisingly, therefore, I saw a fair amount of typical teenage behavior rearing its head during my time in Céu do Mapiá: sullenness, resistance, resentment, foot dragging, passive-aggressive behavior, coming late, and doing the bare minimum.

There were many astonishingly committed and deeply spiritual young people in the community as well. And I have to say that even the young people who were, at best, ambivalent about the Daime, quite often did come to works, and almost all of them could sing each of the hymns from memory.

In general, the presence of the young people in Mapiá was very "in your face": they loved to congregate in little packs, laughing among each other. I'd see them lounging around; or walking around playing video games on their handheld units; or zipping around the village on their motorbikes. Nonetheless, I would often see these same typically dressed teenagers come into the church for works all decked out in their fardas. They might come in late, and they might come in with an attitude, but they showed up.

The older generations of the community in Mapiá were crystal clear that if the village was going to remain focused on the Santo Daime path, then the young people needed to continue to drink Daime, and they needed to drink it because they wanted to and not because they were forced to do so. Therefore (and I was genuinely impressed by this), the older people went out of their way to respect their teenagers' need for autonomy and even tolerated quite a bit of open rebellion. Their children were given enormous space, even while the elders, in a subtle, yet ongoing way, also encouraged the young people to go to church, at least occasionally.

From what I've been told, difficulties with the young people in Céu do Mapiá continued in the years after I left. Attempting to deal with these problems, the community initiated several innovative and worthwhile programs: apprenticeships for artisanal craft-making; internships in the Center for Forest Medicine in Céu do Mapiá; and the Lua Branca (White Moon) Center for Culture, Sports and Recreation, which offers teens the possibility to become credentialed instructors in the capoeira school located in the village: the Golden Vine Capoeira Academy. And apparently even more initiatives are planned.

MORE IMPRESSIONS OF CÉU DO MAPIÁ

The multilevel complexity of the lived reality of Céu do Mapiá was embodied and expressed by the noise levels of the village. For example, the generators that kept the electricity going in the small town square were almost always running and made a huge racket. But these generators allowed the shopkeepers in the cluster of small stores that were located around the edges of the square to sell the at times almost life-saving refrigerated items such as *sorveche* (Brazilian ice cream), Coke, and (my favorite) the quintessential Brazilian soda Guaraná. The electricity that was generated also enabled the shopkeepers, for much of the day, to sit around with a small cluster of other men watching TV—particularly tele-novelas and soccer.

And the generators were nothing more than a gentle background burble com-pared to the noise that would periodically erupt over at Padrinho Alfredo's house when they cut the grass of their quite extensive, albeit somewhat scruffy, lawn with a gas-powered weed whacker—a sonic torment that would at times go on for hours, only to be repeated the next week. Mapiá was a place that liked loud noises: not only generators and weed whackers, but also loudspeakers broadcast-ing tinny instrumental music that sounded like it was piped in from a carnival hurdy-gurdy; the large brass bell of the church that was enthusiastically clanged; and the smoky din of exploding firecrackers and fireworks that were frequently set off for almost any excuse.

Nonetheless, at other times, Mapiá was deeply quiet and serene, with the cool breezes of the morning and the evening rustling the leaves of the huge shady trees; the underlying whirr and hum of distant unseen insects; and (especially at night) the haunting, poignant cries of some unknown creature (a bird? a frog?) echoing from the thick and enveloping darkness of the nearby forest. (I still vividly remember walking back to the church from the inn one night after an intervalo—the long break that took place in the middle of an all-night dance work—in which I simply had to stop, for several minutes, lost in the beauty of these limpid tones coming from an unseen creature—haunting and otherworldly notes that felt like drops of sonic pleasure.)

The nights in Mapiá were quite simply magical—as well as quite cool (a major blessing after the humidity and heat of the day). The stars were *so* bright there. I had never before seen a night sky that vivid, that lit up. And it was a joy to join Ron and Rick sitting around the small campfire that we'd make almost every night in front of the inn when there wasn't a Santo Daime work, where we would sing hymns (the inn's staff would often join in), and clap along to the strumming of Ron's guitar and Rick's ukulele.

And the young children were often a delight. Early on during my stay, just before going to bed, I was lying in a hammock upstairs, relaxing, when Raquel, a young (probably around four years old) daughter of Padrinho Alfredo came dashing into the room and basically shooed Jorge out of his hammock, which was hung next to mine. She then proceeded to get me play with her for about twenty minutes. I would reach out with my leg from my hammock and try to get her, either with my "toes of death" or nudge her with my foot under her hammock, as she screamed and laughed and tried to avoid me. Then she had me swing her, via a rather complicated process involving ropes and a certain timing of when to pull and when not to, that enabled her hammock to just soar, as she lay on her belly perpendicular to her hammock, her arms outstretched as if she was flying, yelling in delight, urging me to send her higher and higher, until I became a little concerned that she was coming perilously close to the stair banister. I finally had to call it quits, mainly because others were going to bed and we were being rather rowdy.

TEMPORAL DISCURSION

During my entire stay in Céu do Mapiá, I was never really sure what time it was. During those two and a half months, I repeatedly had to confront, within myself, how unsettling it was to not be able to pin down the time. Every clock that I looked at, every watch that I consulted, gave me a slightly or sometimes dramatically different version of the time. And no one in Mapiá seemed to be all that bothered by this inexactitude. The people there tended, on the whole, to be rather relaxed about when something should begin. It didn't matter if it was a party or a Santo Daime work. People would just sort of drift in, and when a critical mass of important people had finally arrived, things would get going. And if the actual beginning time, at least as represented on my watch, was an hour or more later than the beginning time that had been formally announced, well—"No problem." *Tranquilo...*

As someone who is saturated in the thought of Henri Bergson (and arguably no one has a more insightful understanding of the nature of time than Bergson), I was struck by how just living in Mapiá underscored within me, so powerfully, the artificial, man-made notion of mathematical "clock time." No one in Mapiá, of course, had smartphones. It wasn't like living in the United States, where all of our iPhones are interconnected and chronologically synchronized. It became a little easier, therefore, for me to spot within myself, as I was dealing with all of this temporal ambiguity, my tacit, ethnocentric assumptions about time— my unquestioned sense that time itself is inherently split up into utterly regular, mathematically precise, continuously repeatable temporal units (seconds, minutes, hours), temporal units that are the same for anyone, in any place (a second is the same in New York as it is in Cairo—an assumption that allows our global economy to function). But that seductive yet laughably two-dimensional sense of time had little to do with the immediacy of my *experience* of time in Mapiá. And during the experiential flux of my time in Mapiá, time moved forward with a type of rhythmic pulsation to it—each moment inherently different than the next, yet no moment separate from the other—seamlessly connected and continuous with the next as time flowed, moment to moment, from the past (living in the present as memory) into the open-ended and ceaselessly new future—a future that only emerged in-and-as the present, in-and-as the Now, at each instant.

My experience of time in Céu do Mapiá was all this, *and* it was intricately intertwined with, and punctuated by, the strikingly powerful and dramatic experiential shifts catalyzed by the Daime itself, as well as by the experiential shifts catalyzed by my subconscious yet ongoing interaction with the multitude of beings/energies/consciousnesses that filled the rainforest. In that cascading experiential flux, temporal moments would ripple forth, wave after wave of potent difference, and my experience of time, uplifted by the Daime, by the Force of Nature, would often become transfigured, infused with a sacred quality of divine Energy and Presence—time in this way becoming exalted; becoming, as it were, Time Itself: sheer Becoming unfurling its unpredictable newness at each moment.

Yet I also experienced time in Mapiá in a way that was predictable, steady, and dependable: the almost unrelenting sameness of when the sun rose and when it set (on the equator, the length of each day is always the same; days don't get longer and shorter during different seasons of the year). Time experienced in this way—"astronomical time," as it were—offered an unvaried linchpin for the rhythm of my life in the village to unwind. And it took me a while, but after several weeks, I could notice within myself a nagging sense of unease rooted in my awareness that the days weren't getting any shorter or longer. And the longer that I stayed in Mapiá, the more I could spot my increasing distaste for this almost inexorable grinding temporal sameness. You could depend upon the fact that when the sun was shining at a particular angle in the sky, the temperature would always be the same, day after day after day. When I finally returned to the United States, where the length of a day would gradually shift, I could almost feel my cells sighing with relief.

MY FIRST FULL DAY IN CÉU DO MAPIÁ

Right after breakfast on our first full day in Céu do Mapiá (breakfast was typically a thermos of weak coffee, a pitcher of hot milk, a basket of individual loaves of white bread, some margarine, a basket of oranges, apples, and bananas, and if we were really lucky, a few fresh eggs), Soraya, Jorge, Ron, Rick, and I did what was customary for people newly arrived in the village: we went over to Madrinha Rita's house to pay our respects. (Madrinha Rita is Padrinho

Sebastiao's widow, and the matriarch of the ICEFLU line of the Santo Daime.) As we made our way up the long tile walkway to her house, we were greeted by a lovely older man who was, and there's simply no other way to say it, filled with Light. He was sweeping the walkway so joyfully, his face completely lit up, and when he saw us, he welcomed us with *so* much love. Madrinha Rita's house, as well as many others, was surrounded by a large, open veranda—everything about it was simple and aesthetically pleasing. She was sitting on one side of the veranda, this almost ninety-year-old woman fussing with an old Singer sewing machine that Jorge helped her to fix. It was so heartwarming to be welcomed by her so sweetly as we all went up and introduced ourselves, and to receive her blessing the traditional way: by kissing her hand. Everything about that encounter was very relaxed, very mellow.

No one rushed us off the veranda. Nonetheless, probably due to our American "let's get things done" mentality, after hanging out for a while on Madrinha Rita's veranda chatting with the people (mostly women), we said goodbye and headed off to the feitio house—the location where the Daime was made during certain specific times of the year. We were welcomed there by the *feitor* (literally, the "overseer,") the person who was in charge of the *feitio*, the entire, extremely

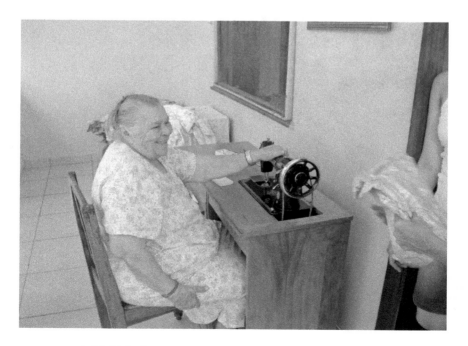

FIGURE 4.6   Madrinha Rita

FIGURE 4.7 Feitio sign

FIGURE 4.8 Jagube vines

FIGURE 4.9 Chacruna bush

arduous process of making the Daime. He was very warm and informative and spent well over an hour with us, taking us through the process of making the Daime step by step. He also invited us to feel free to help out, since the feitio itself was just beginning. The three of us decided to join in, which in this case meant helping the handful of men who were sitting there on stumps in the open-aired,

corrugated tin roof–covered area. Our job was to pick up one of the approximately one-foot-long sections of the *jagube* vine (*Banisteriopsis caapi*, one of the
central ingredients of the Daime, together with the leaves of the *chacruna* bush,
Psychotria viridis—also called *Rainha* or "Queen") that were piled in a heap on
the floor, and then to scrape off lichen, moss, spider webs, or rotten parts of the
vine. I sat there for about an hour on a special stool they had made that had
this extra extension of wood that jutted out between my legs, where I could rest
one end of the vine while I scraped off the gunk with my knife. (I had actually
remembered to bring my Swiss Army knife, which worked perfectly.) The three
of us made quite a little pile.

PADRINHO ALFREDO'S VERANDA

A few weeks later, the three of us, accompanied by Soraya, had a chance to hang
out on Padrinho Alfredo's veranda soon after sunset. We joined a bunch of men
who were already there, talking quietly among themselves. The night rather
quickly began to get darker and darker, although that darkness was soon illuminated by an exquisitely beautiful full moon. It was therefore rather difficult
to distinguish one face from another (and besides, there were, as usual, so many
friends and family members that kept coming and going in that huge rambling
house that it was, at the best of times, hard to keep track of who was who). But at
some point, Soraya figured out that one of the shadowy faces on the veranda was
Padrinho Alfredo himself. So, in her inimitable way, she pushed me forward, and
I introduced myself to him. He was extremely kind and soft-spoken. He asked
me where I was from and how long I had been drinking Daime. I answered his
questions and then told him that I was a professor of comparative religion and
that I was planning to write a book on the Santo Daime. (When he heard this he
smiled and gave me a big thumbs-up.) I even made a joke with him that (amazingly!) everyone laughed at. (In one of Mestre Irineu's hymns, he advises his disciples to listen much, and talk little, and so I said that I like to listen a lot and write
a lot as well.) I apologized for my still at times rather rough Portuguese, but he
laughingly said: "Don't worry at all—you're doing just fine." The whole conversation probably lasted no more than a few minutes, but it was a lovely, very relaxed
way to begin to establish a connection with him.

Many weeks later, I received an invitation to join Padrinho Alfredo and his
family at his house. I was, not surprisingly, simultaneously touched and thrilled.
When I arrived that evening, around 7:00 p.m., Tereza directed me to the side

porch, the same porch where I had first been introduced to Padrinho. Once again it was dark, and it took me a moment to realize that Padrinho Alfredo was sitting there, casually chatting with a group of people that I didn't know. I pulled up a chair and sat somewhat close to him, but it was not the easiest task to hang out there for the next half hour. I had to work hard with myself, trying to figure out how to be comfortable in my own skin. They were just bantering among themselves, so the Portuguese was filled with slang, half-formed sentences, and jokes, and it was just barreling forward a mile a minute. I could barely manage to follow what was being said, even as I was, simultaneously, sensing all of these energetic undercurrents. I kept getting "whiffs" of the complexities of the charged familial interactions that they'd had with each other over the years—their layered, intricate history with one another, the vast majority of which I will never, and need never, know. Nonetheless, during that whole time, almost out the corner of my eye, it seemed as though I was catching glimpses of energetic eddies that were washing around the people on that porch. I was subliminally sensing the highly compressed, tacit messages that were being transmitted by tone of voice, bodily posture, and that much more difficult to communicate "feel" of the complex, ever-shifting configurations of energy that were increasingly ebbing and flowing around me on the porch.

All of this subtle sensing was rather awkwardly intermingling with how genuinely ill at ease I was feeling. I just didn't quite know the "rules" of the social interaction there. I was also hyperaware of how this visceral discomfort was a mirror of times in my past when I'd find myself in situations where everyone but me knew what the game was and had played it multiple times; situations where people were just gabbing to each other in a purely social way, and I'd just want to wriggle out of my skin. So I sat there, painfully aware of how I didn't really fit in, knowing all too well that it simply wasn't going to be possible to have an intimate, heartfelt conversation with anyone. Not surprisingly, I once again ended up staying very quiet—trying to be attentive; trying to consciously breathe in and out; trying to relax into the moment as much as possible; trying to let go of any worries about what others might be thinking about this stranger who had been inserted into their world.

5
Feitio—The Ritual of Making the Daime

Oddly, Rick, Ron, and I never returned to the Feitio House during our stay in Céu do Mapiá. I'm not actually quite sure why. I think we were so swept up in the day-to-day intensity of our experience in Mapiá that we "conveniently" blanked out that the feitio was happening. However, at this point in time, more than ten years later, I've had the privilege of participating in three feitios—my first during my six-week stay at Céu do Patriarca in Florianópolis, Brazil; my second during my monthlong stay at Céu do Mar, in Rio de Janeiro, Brazil; my third during the almost three-week-long Daime Dharma retreat with Padrinho Alex Polari de Alverga and his wife, Madrinha Sonia Palhares de Alverga—two shining Santo Daime elders—that took place at Céu da Montanha in Visconde de Mauá in the summer of 2015. I'm focusing on this last feitio not because it was any better or worse than the other two, but simply because it was during this time that I felt like I finally received a new level of understanding of at least some of the depth and complexity of this alchemical, deeply sacred process.

In Mauá, the feitio "officially" began on the afternoon of July 15. It had already begun informally, yet crucially, much earlier than this, when a dedicated and skilled crew of men went into the rain forest and began to harvest the jagube vines. I wasn't part of that expedition during any of my three feitios—my best guess is that the last thing they wanted or needed was some less than young, utterly inexperienced North American. It took the bone-deep knowledge and commitment for these (mostly young) men to be able to find the jagube and distinguish it from the countless other vines that fill the rain forest. It took those who were willing and able to clamber up enormous trees, likely filled with insects, using their machetes to cut/pull down the vines (selected for their age and size) with the vigorous help of another group of men on the ground who would then chop the vines into manageable sections of about four feet in length and stuff them into large fiberglass bags. These heavy, bulky bags would then be hauled for long distances back to the feitio house. The harvesters always left plenty of younger vines to gather later and/or "sprigged" the ground with small sections of vine that would years later be ready for another feitio.

The feitio house itself, like all of the other feitio houses that I have seen, was a rather large, no-nonsense, utilitarian, open-air, simply built structure with a white tile floor that could be easily cleaned. In Mauá, the feitio house was constructed with vertical metal poles—poles that held up a corrugated tin roof adorned with dangling fluorescent light bulbs. And again, like all the feitio houses that I've seen, this one was divided into several distinct sections. The *bateção* area (where the vines are "beaten") was a rather circumscribed rectangular space with low white half-walls, around four feet high, in which twelve sections of thick, shiny, dark-brown tree trunks (approximately three feet high and a foot thick) were arranged in two rows of six each in front of rough wooden benches. The *raspação* ("scraping") area, where the vines were cleaned, was next to the bateção space, and was basically an open area with some benches and chairs and a blue tarp on the floor. Next to this was the central area of the feitio house, a slightly raised, spacious area in which the Daime was cooked—an area dominated by the long rectangular row of six huge (hundred gallon?) aluminum pots, placed one after the other in circular openings over the *fornalha* (the wood-burning "furnace") that for hours would be roaring underneath. The rest of that open "cooking" area was used for several other crucial tasks—pouring/straining the Daime into large plastic jugs; storing large jugs of various concentrations of *cozimento* (literally, "cooking"; the liquid base that is used in lieu of water to cook Daime); and another tiled area off to the side held the big plastic tubs that were used to wash the chacruna/Rainha leaves, a utility sink, and so on.

The feitio house, situated at the end of the road, was surrounded by the Atlantic rain forest of that region and was raised up about fifteen feet from the road. The fornalha was situated on the ground level of the feitio house, with the "mouth" of the furnace opening out about waist high so that the firekeeper could easily insert the logs that he would select from an unruly pile on the ground beside him, carefully and efficiently inserting them into the fornalha itself (which extended underneath where the pots were placed in the cooking area in the level above), skillfully, almost artfully, arranging the logs with an approximately twenty-foot-long iron rod so that the fire would be at exactly the right level of heat for each of the (up to) six cooking pots. This ground level of

FIGURE 5.1 Bateção area

the feitio house was almost constantly filled with young men hacking away at logs with axes, sharpening axes, or splitting the logs with wedges. And the pile of wood they were working on would constantly need replenishing.

While all of this male-dominated activity was taking place, the women were busily picking the Rainha leaves from a small grove of the bushes located behind the kitchen/dining room area and then sorting and cleaning them in the church. I only spent a small period of time in Mauá helping to pick leaves, but in Florianópolis, this (typically women's work) was actually my first assignment. (I had actually been shocked to have been invited to pick leaves with the women in Florianópolis, having understood that the various tasks in the feitio were strictly gender segregated, a segregation that was/is based on the notion that the leaves are linked with female divine energy and the vine with male divine energy— but apparently in this case, and in Mauá, practical necessity trumped theoretical "purity.") After having been served Daime in the back of the church, I was given a small cloth bag and followed the six or seven women in that morning's leaf-picking group to the small "plantation" of these kissing cousins of the coffee bush that was located just down the road. I was given a crash course on how to properly pick the Rainha leaves: with reverence and respect; primarily staying quiet (unless there was a practical question that needed to be addressed); making sure to not pluck the final three leaves at the growing tip of each branch (in Mauá we were told to leave four: the two at the end to keep the branch growing, and the two before that as their "protectors"), and if you happened to accidentally break off that tip, then you needed to be sure to place it on the ground at the foot of the bush so that it could replant itself. We worked for hours in silence, with some of the women periodically singing hymns. Then, as our small bags became filled, each of us would transfer the leaves within the bags into a much larger fiberglass bag that, on that day at least, I hauled on my back like a beardless Santa to the office where the leaves were weighed and properly recorded. I never participated in the subsequent ritual of sorting and cleaning the leaves in the church, but on several occasions I saw small groups of women seated cross-legged on the floor of the church, gathered around a blue tarp with a mound of leaves on top of it, quietly at work cleaning spider webs off the leaves or throwing away any leaves that were browning, all while periodically singing hymns together.

RASPAÇÃO: MAUÁ

My primary task in the feitio in Mauá (and also in Florianópolis and Rio de Janeiro) was the raspação—the scraping/cleaning of the vines. This was a men-only process. When I arrived at the feitio house in the early afternoon of the first day of the feitio, I was served a reasonable-sized amount of reasonably strong Daime by one of the men in charge of the feitio. (Each time someone new arrived to the feitio house, they would be served Daime—so the feitio participants were basically constantly in the Force throughout the more than weeklong feitio.) I was then motioned toward a bench in the raspação area, where I joined the few other men who had arrived before me and were already hard at work. We all sat there, in silence, with our feet tucked under the blue plastic tarp that covered the floor. We each had our respective small piles of jagube vine sections to be scraped. I was glad that I had brought my Swiss Army knife so that I didn't have to use one of the small pieces of bamboo cut in a V at one end that were available.

I actually loved the raspação process, especially, when I began to feel the Force of the Daime within me and I'd take in some deep breaths of appreciation for the natural beauty that surrounded us. In the Force, I even appreciated, albeit with a rueful smile to myself, the less than idyllic sounds that came my way: the ongoing, forceful shoosh of a power-washer (with its low-pitched gasoline-powered chugs) that was used to wash off a large tangled pile of thin (less than finger width) jagube vines that were then chopped into three-foot sections by a man sitting on a stump whacking away with his machete, which were then given to a man wearing goggles who fed the long, thin pieces of jagube into a small gasoline-powered wood chipper that emitted an earsplitting grinding roar, all while another man gathered the finely chopped pieces of the vines spat out by that eager-beaver little machine into a large, tough, white fiberglass bag. These pieces were then put into porous and seemingly equally tough sacks and were boiled for hours in water, along with some Rainha leaves, in the large aluminum pots that were positioned in their respective circular openings over the (unseen) fire of the fornalha—a process that eventually produced the liquid base (the cozimento) that was poured over alternating layers of cleaned and washed leaves, as well as cleaned and scraped and beaten vines. Then all of that simmered for hours in order to make the Daime.

There are various types of cozimento. Cozimento is *also* created from the initial boiling (with water) of the layering of beaten jagube vines and Rainha leaves in the large pots. That first cooking is not Daime, but is actually cozimento, the "daime-esque" liquid that is the fluid base for a *second* cooking (with fresh layers of vine and leaf), a cooking that does eventually result in Daime. But cozimento is also created from amply used piles of vine and leaf (in the CEFLURIS line, the vine/leaf is cooked and recooked numerous times with varying levels of concentrations). That is, cozimento also comes from vines/leaves that the feitor (the head of the feitio process and chief chef of the Daime) has determined can no longer produce Daime but can still be used to produce the liquid substratum that is added to other layers of vine/leaves. All of this cooking, and recooking, with leaves and vines of varying degrees of "previous cookedness," combined with cozimentos of various degrees of intensity and varying origins (with each pot then cooked down to differing levels of concentrations, ranging from a translucent golden amber–reddish brown Daime to an almost muddy brown density of a thickly concentrated Daime) leads to a mind-blowingly complex collection of "recipes" for the Daime. This requires that the feitor possess a level of culinary knowledge and sophistication that I can only compare to a chef in a four-star restaurant (a good feitor should also possess, at least ideally, a corresponding level of spiritual depth and heart).

Meanwhile, back to the raspação: all of that noise, testosterone, smoke, chopping, grinding, and grunting went on for hours, all while we were in the Force, working away, together, surrounded by the trees of the spellbindingly beautiful forest whose leaves, in quieter moments, I could hear rustling in the soft breeze. And I was just breathing it all in. And feeling deeply contented.

I truly loved the raspação. It was (is!) a deeply meditative and peaceful process in which a no-nonsense group of men could gather together, for hours, while hymns were playing on a small boom box, steadily working away, communing with the vine, each one of us sitting quietly, using both our knives or bamboo stalks and small plastic brushes to remove the dirt/lichen/mold/moss/rot off the vines, focusing especially on the grooves and crevices of the vine.

To complicate matters a bit, as I first discovered in Florianópolis, raspação can at times be a rather delicate balancing act. The trick is to find that sweet spot where you've cleaned off all the gunk, but you haven't taken off too much of the outer layer of the bark, where most of the spiritually charged "good stuff" in the vine is located. And there are at times differing, and perhaps even frayed and fraught, opinions as to which (i.e., getting rid of gunk or saving precious bark) has priority. There were also differing, often strongly held beliefs as to how much scraping is not enough or way too much. And all of this discerning was all too often communicated in a type of grunting, speaking the bare minimum in strained whispers manner. At times, this all would take place with a simmering, intertwining, subtly shifting, undertone of hostility, frustration, puzzlement, and misunderstanding communicated via looks and gestures and only partially understood words. It was sometimes challenging to respond with clarity and an open heart and to stand my ground when needed. It was not easy to let go of my sense of rightness and to not get unnecessarily hooked into someone else's drama. I had to work to let everything just roll off my back and return to the present. And throughout it all, I realized that it was important to do this inner work, and I think I was not alone in thinking this, because I wanted to make sure that the highest, most refined energy possible was flowing from me into the Daime. I think it's fair to say that all of us knew that our attitudes/feelings were infused into the Daime itself, and this background awareness of our responsibility for our inner state meant that even in the most challenging moments, everyone attempted to shift these difficult interactions toward a place of harmony and acceptance and openheartedness. (And I need to emphasize that these more challenging moments were actually extremely rare.)

At one point during the weeklong process, I also participated in washing the Rainha leaves. A large sack of leaves that had already been cleaned and picked through by the women in the church was dumped into a big blue plastic tub (it looked almost like a kid's outdoor swimming pool—the same sort of tub that was at times used to store the cozimento—about three feet tall and maybe seven feet in diameter). The tub was then filled with water using a hose attached to the large work sink in the feitio area. Then, working with one of the young men, I'd dip my arms into the cold water and "agitate" the leaves, almost like a relaxed, rhythmically oscillating washing machine, so that the dirt on the leaves would be rinsed off and settle to the bottom of the tub. After doing this for perhaps ten minutes, we'd then use a similar motion of our arms to scoop the leaves out of the water, shaking the large handful that we'd gather above the tub to get most of the water out, and then putting the leaves back into the tough plastic woven bag that they had arrived in.

BATEÇÃO: MAUÁ

The bateção isn't for the faint of heart.

The bateção in Mauá typically happened in shifts that lasted two to four hours, depending upon how many vines needed to be beaten to fill the pots. During one early bateção shift, twelve guys (most of them young and fit—with a smattering of older folks like myself) were selected in a jostling, causal, joking sort of way—and this time, I was chosen to be part of the crew. The twelve of us then stood around the entrance to the bateção area, taking off our shoes. We all then quietly entered that rather narrow rectangular space and picked a wooden mallet that seemed right for our own individual physique from the assortment of different sizes that lined the top of the walls. We sat down on rough stools in front of one of twelve large (probably three feet high and one foot in diameter) shiny dark-brown tree trunk sections that acted, in essence, like massive, extremely sturdy, pounding blocks for the vines. As I mentioned earlier, the tree trunk sections and the rough stools were set up in two rows, six tree trunk sections in each row (each of us therefore would beat the vines facing another man). These tree trunk sections had been used a *lot* before, so they were extremely smooth, and the almost polished top of each tree trunk was more or less horizontal.

One of the young men then passed out twelve shot glasses and one of the head feitio guys walked around with a glass pitcher filled with dark brown Daime, stopping in front of each of us, pouring the Daime. Each man drank his serving in a way that was strikingly similar—simultaneously reverent and casual.

There was a long rectangular pile of already scraped, brushed, and cleaned jagube vine sections (about one foot long) on the ground in front of the two rows of tree trunk sections. I leaned forward to gather a small handful of the vines, which I then arranged carefully on the far-left side of my trunk/tabletop. Then, still fumbling around a bit, I selected a piece of the vine from that small pile; I positioned it in the middle of the stump—bisecting the stump horizontally; I held it steady with my left hand and while glancing around me to make sure that I was doing all of this in harmony with the other men, I raised my mallet high with my right hand. Then, as one of the head feitio guys began to sing one of Mestre Irineu's hymns, all of us dropped our mallets down on the vines—simultaneously—our twelve voices joining together to sing that hymn, as twelve heavy wooden mallets were simultaneously held up high by everyone, our right arms straight and aloft, and then forcefully and rapidly allowed to descend—the same sequence happening over and over and over again.

And everyone worked really hard to remain in sync with everyone else. But that unity didn't always come easily. For example, if (as occasionally happened) someone was singing or pounding a bit off-rhythm, or if someone started singing a hymn and it wasn't aligned with the beat of the young men who set the pace of the bateção, someone in charge would shout out something to help correct the rhythmic imbalance. But usually, even in those more challenging moments, the overt drama was minimal—if something was slightly off, then most of us simply stopped for bit until everything got worked out.

We all basically worked hard to honor the strong intention that undergirds the bateção: that everyone should hit the jagube together, in rhythm, on the beat. And there were times when everyone was in sync; when our voices were linked up with the rhythm of the beating of the jagube; and then it was magical and powerful. The bateção, at its best, was men working hard together in the Force; aligned with each other; laboring as an organic whole with shared intentions for a truly noble cause; singing strongly and with sincere hearts; our mallets rising and lowering as one with a satisfying thud, over and over again. At those moments the bateção was suffused with quintessential male energy, energy that shone forth in its archetypal goodness and power. In a world that is filled with highly distorted manifestations of maleness, it was refreshing and hope-giving to have an opportunity to participate in a spiritually potent ritual that celebrated, and encouraged, positive experiences of male community.

I wasn't surprised to hear from one of the elders in Céu do Mapiá that Padrinho Sebastião received most of the hymns of *O Justiceiro* (his first hinário) when he was taking part in the bateção. Here's how I envision him: deeply in the Force; doing that sacrificial labor; offering himself up to God; asking that the hard crust of his sense of separation from God be beaten down by the repetitive, continual pounding; giving himself fully to the heavy thuds of the Force descending from above. I see him: his heart unfurling in Love and Ecstasy as he shares in this Sacred Work with his friends and disciples, uniting (in song, in rhythm, in forceful intention) with those who have given themselves—body, mind, and soul—to him, their Padrinho.

And there are also times when the bateção is just an enormous chore. It's really strenuous and demanding. And it just goes on and on and on and on, and if you've got a sixty-year-old body, and have had lung surgery in the past, and have had numerous pneumonias, some fairly recently (as I have), then you probably shouldn't be shocked to discover just how little stamina and breathing capacity you have compared with some of the others.

I could only hit the vine about three or four times before I'd have to take a break. And it seemed perfectly fine to periodically do so. Rearranging my little tabletop pile of vines was my favorite way to still be doing something rather than lifting that mallet, a mallet that seemed to possess the mysterious ability to grow increasingly heavy. During these "breaks," I'd take in a couple of deep and conscious breaths, pausing for a bit to gather myself before beginning again. Then I'd sit up straight, breathe some more (deeply, consciously), and start to sing the hymn, joining my voice with the others, once again raising my mallet high and letting it descend, aligning myself once more with that repetitive collective thud.

And, at least for me, there was a rather steep learning curve that came with participating in the bateção. With help from the seatmate on my right, I finally figured out that I didn't need to forcefully slam my mallet downward using my muscular strength. Instead, after raising the mallet high, I just let gravity do the work. But sometimes my mallet would land ineffectually, almost bouncing off the vine. And sometimes the vine was thin and the wooden mallet would come crashing onto the rock-hard polished wooden surface of the tree trunk, and that ringing impact would send shocking, deeply unpleasant, vibrations ringing up my arm. And sometimes I'd find myself tightening up, forcing too much. So, I'd attempt to switch, to sink into the present, and gradually, breathing deeply, I'd begin to access the weighty, deeply earthed sensations of my physicality; I'd recenter myself; I'd realign; I'd take yet another deep conscious breath; I'd gather new resolve; and I'd continue.

And then I'd be served more Daime.

And sometimes the Force was almost overwhelming, and I'd feel myself becoming more and more fatigued, and my right arm would be getting really tired, and I began to seriously wonder if I would be able to continue, but then something would shift, and I'd find myself riding on the wave of the Force instead of being hammered by it, and I'd continue, uplifted and strong, for another couple of hours. (During the retreat in Mauá, Padrinho Alex described during a sharing session how Padrinho Sebastião told someone who was really struggling with exhaustion, doubt, and fear during the bateção: "Don't worry my son, you won't fall through the floor.")

In the bateção, we worked hard, we worked to overcome our limitations, each of us unified—vibrationally, intentionally, with all the other men, until little by little, the knotted twisted cords that made up the vine unraveled, and the previously tough and knotted vine became a bundle of almost straight fibers, almost like thin straws that I could hold together in the encircling palm of my left hand.

I'd then put that bundle of fibrous stalks on the floor to my left, letting that pile gradually build as, hour after hour, I beat vine after vine. And when I was finally done, when I had beaten my allotted pile of jagube vines, I ended up with two new piles on the floor—one pile of light brown, tough, fibrous stalks and another pile composed of the "dust" (the pó), the potent reddish-brown threads of the outer bark and the softer material of the vine that had been separated from the fibrous stalks through the pounding of the mallet; dust that slowly began to build up on the floor around my pounding block and was, in the end, gathered up and swept up into a pile.

After that bateção, for the next couple of hours, I could barely open the fingers of my right hand. I was grateful that I at least had brought a pair of cotton gloves, unlike some of the other men. Even so, my fingers were still extremely stiff and sore the next day. The bateção was, in certain respects, an ordeal. I was just exhausted. I could barely manage to take my shower after I returned to my dorm. All I wanted to do was to lie down on my bed and not move for hours.

I therefore had, and have, enormous respect for those men who, with dedication and devotion, somehow managed, unlike me, to do the bateção, day after day, for hours each day. They were doing all of this while, along with the rest of us, also taking part in full-bore, pedal to the metal Santo Daime works that often followed the hours of strenuous work at the feitio. (We did some sort of Santo Daime work almost every other night during the feitio portion of the retreat in Mauá and had works even more frequently after the feitio concluded.)

COOKING THE DAIME: MAUÁ

As I mentioned earlier, it was during my time in Mauá, while participating in my third feitio, that I finally turned a corner in my understanding of the depth and sophistication of the process of cooking the Daime. Something really snapped into place within me during the night when, having finally prepared enough vines and leaves, the feitio crew began the cooking process.

Earlier that day I had watched from my perch in the raspação area while Padrinho Alex layered one of the enormous aluminum pots with the vines and leaves that we had previously prepared. He started with three to four inches of the fibers in the bottom of the pot. He then added a similar thickness of leaves, then a layer of the *pó* (dust), then more leaves, then more fibers or pó, and so on, all the way up to the top, often stopping to push it all down with his hands so that the entire mixture was really compressed. After this was done, he ended the layering process with a "dome" of fibers. In essence, the bottom layer of fibers kept the other ingredient layers from burning, while the top layer of fibers kept the liquid from bubbling out and boiling over.

That night, the layering process having been repeated with several other pots—then and only then was the cooking of the Daime ready to begin. To be precise, what actually was begun was the first cooking of the leaves, vines, and water that together created the cozimento, which was then poured into the pots for the first cooking of the Daime itself. And that alchemical moment would only happen much later that night. All of the retreat participants were invited to watch this first cooking of the vines and leaves. Some of the young men had carried quite a few white plastic chairs from the church to the feitio house to set up two seating areas: one for the women on one side of the raspação area, and one for the men on the other, with the overflow for both men and women in the batação area.

That night we sang the *Oração*—a selection of Padrinho Sebastião's hymns— in the feitio house. And we all watched as Padrinho Alex and Lonnie, the leader of the church in the United States that had sponsored the retreat, stood by the pots, steam rising and curling around them, each holding a long, thick, two-pronged

FIGURE 5.2   Brewing Daime

wooden staff used to periodically poke, stir, and inspect the pots of pre-Daime/ cozimento that were simmering away. The scene felt so ancient, so primordial, with those two men wreathed in daime-scented steam, so at ease, so settled into the moment. And I don't know about anyone else, but I was feeling the Force strongly. The night sky was brilliant with stars, the forest was rustling in the cool breezes, and I was feeling deep reverence and awe.

FIGURE 5.3 Padrinho Alex Polari

And then, after the Oração was over, having decided that I'd like to hang out for a bit, I watched as a line of people walked along the winding clay road back toward the center of the retreat site. I watched as they chattered casually to each other, most of them carrying a few white plastic chairs (some of the younger guys carrying tall stacks of them balanced on top of their heads). Eventually, there was no one left except for Lonnie, Padrinho Alex, and some of the key feitio guys.

Padrinho was seated on the rumpled, cloth-covered padded chair that they'd set up for him near the small altar where the Daime was served, right at the entrance of the slightly raised cooking area where the pots were bubbling away, and I asked him if it was okay for me to enter. He smiled at me, clear-eyed and kind, and gestured for me to come in.

Lonnie was standing over one of the pots, talking quietly to Marcos, the head feitor. Then, in his quiet, calm way, Lonnie came over and asked me if I wanted to hang out with them for a while. And so, after being served some Daime, for the next couple of hours I just stood around, watching this amazing dance of synchronized male competence.

Because it quickly became clear to me that the feitio house was an extremely pure expression of male energy. Everything was no muss, no fuss. It was all straightforward, to the point. There was hardly any talking. It was just men working hard, with discipline; men working with metal; men working with fire; men working with things that were heavy—things that needed to be manhandled, hoisted, adjusted with wrenches, and wrangled into place. And they were doing all of this with deep care and reverence.

That night I spent several hours shadowing Lonnie. Most of the time I'd simply stand there, still, attentive, trying to be present and attuned, working hard to not get in anyone's way, while also (ironically) working hard to rest easy in my body, reminding myself that I'd been invited in, that I belonged. And Lonnie, in his tall, lanky, low-key way was just so relaxed about everything that it was easy for me to remember to take some breaths and to center myself in the flow of the moment, all the while paying close attention to what everyone else was doing. The whole time I tried to tune into when to speak and when to remain quiet, which meant that every now and then I'd ask Lonnie a question, which he would invariably answer in his quiet, succinct way. Lonnie would also at times show me something or give me some choice tidbit about the subtleties of making the Daime, always reminding me with his "at-easeness," and by the fact that he refrained from unnecessary talk, to calm my energy down; to consciously breathe in the steam that was rising from the pots; and to settle into the moment as the reddish liquid bubbled up through the compact layer of the jagube fibers.

I spent hours watching Lonnie and Marcos poking the fibers or thrusting their long two-pronged staffs down the side of a pot they were examining, lifting the fibers up (while another guy would shine a flashlight into the pot) to see the level of the liquid, or bending over the pot, wafting the vapors toward their faces while inhaling deeply. (Is it ready? By this time of the night they were no longer cooking cozimento, but rather, the very first pots of Daime.)

Finally, when it was time (and apparently there is no formula to know when the Daime is ready—just a sensing/knowing that combines a good dose of intuitive insight and divine guidance with practical experience as to how the liquid should look and smell), Marcos hit the side of the pot three quick solid times with his staff. (Lonnie afterward told me that the three strikes symbolized "Sun, Moon, Stars"—one expression of the Santo Daime version of the Holy Trinity). That was the signal that told the nearby group of men to wheel over a tall, forest-green, fabricated metal frame, which looked something like a thick swing-set on wheels. An electric winch was permanently attached to the top bar of the frame. The frame itself was then slowly, carefully, positioned over one of the large aluminum pots. The thick steel wire that was rolled inside the winch was unwound and then attached to the metal handle that arched over the pot. The pot, with all of its precious cargo, was then hoisted up, the winch making a loud, grating metallic protest about the weight it had to tackle. Then, while Marcos stabilized the pot, two other guys rolled the winch-frame, a bit awkwardly but carefully, away from the rectangular fornalha area, the frame squeaking and creaking and groaning.

The pot finally arrived at the other side of the cooking area, where it was positioned in front of another fabricated metal creation: a shining metal "sluice" (like a wide slide). After a thin, but strong green metal band was positioned around the sides of the pot, like a sturdy metal belt in two parts that cinched together, and after an (again metal) filter was attached to the top of the pot, the pot was turned over. The metal filter kept the fibers and leaves in the pot but permitted the reddish liquid to flow out in a thin but steady stream, down the polished metal runway of the sluice into a smaller aluminum pot that was waiting on the tile floor, the top of which was covered with a thin cheesecloth, held in place by Marcos, that kept out any stray fibers or pieces of Rainha leaves.

Since the pot that had been emptied out onto the sluice had officially been determined to contain Daime, everyone in the feitio house, except for the man appointed to keep the fornalha fire going at just the right temperature, gathered on both sides of the sluice and sang a hymn to the Daime as the sacramental liquid flowed into the smaller pot on the floor. We all sang "The Daime Is the Daime," one of Padrinho Alfredo's hymns in his first hinário, with such deep reverence (everyone's hat was taken off).[1] All of our voices blended together, as we sang the hymn slower than normal, in a way that was so heartfelt. All of us were witnessing and affirming the mystery and power of this magical sacrament as it was concretely manifesting in the world in this liquid form. (A few years earlier, when taking part in the feitio in Céu do Mar, I had been given some of that "first degree" Daime to drink—it's quite an experience to drink hot Daime straight from the pot.)

Afterward, I was asked to help transfer the hot Daime from the smaller pot on the floor into a translucent, thick blue plastic, three-gallon jug. Before setting the empty jug on the ground and placing a large red plastic funnel into it, Marcos poured about three inches of cozimento from another large plastic container into the jug; he covered the open top of the jug with his hand; and then he swirled the cozimento round and round, symbolically coating the entire inside of the jug, before emptying the cozimento back into its prior container. I then held the jug and the funnel steady on the ground as Lonnie ladled a large aluminum dipper into the Daime, and carefully, consciously, transferred it from the pot into the jug.

After the first batch of Daime was cooked (all Daime that is cooked with fresh leaves and vines is known as "first-degree" Daime) and was then poured off and stored, the raw material in the pot was then used to make more Daime, with cozimento poured into that, and cooked until, once again, the liquid in the pot was ascertained to have become Daime. But this time, it was "second-degree" Daime. (I'm not sure how many "degrees" of Daime there are: one participant said that they make nine degrees of Daime, another said twelve.) And each of those varying concoctions was carefully noted, and each of the large immaculate plastic bottles that stored the Daime was clearly marked with the description of the type of Daime it was, the date it was made, and so on and so on. Everything was done, as throughout the feitio, with clarity, focus, and attention.

And when it was determined that the vines and leaves could not produce any more Daime, that mass of vegetation was still cooked and poured out, over and over again, to make more cozimento, which was itself poured into different degrees of Daime. (The second- and third-degree Daime was often reduced down, so that it was more concentrated, thereby making it, at times, perhaps even stronger than first-degree Daime. And those various degrees of Daime were themselves at times concentrated down to various specified levels: for example, "two to one" Daime (in which, let's say, one hundred liters of the original liquid was boiled down to fifty liters) or "three to one" Daime (in which, one hundred liters would be reduced down to thirty-three liters)—each more potent and sweet than the last, until you finally reached *mel*, Portuguese for "honey," a thick, syrupy, highly concentrated form of Daime.

And all of that Daime, created with so much love and enormous hard work, would then be reverently imbibed in later Santo Daime works in the church; or it would be distributed, with each drop accounted for, and with no one making any profit, to other churches that were in need of the sacrament.

Knowing all of this, when we finally finished our tasks late that night/early in the morning, I felt such a sense of satisfaction and accomplishment. The feitio guys slowly ambled off; and the very last thing that Marcos did as he closed down shop was to blow out the candle on the altar. And then the two of us had a wonderful walk and talk under the brilliant stars, heading back to the dorm.

6

Early Works in Céu do Mapiá

Back in Céu do Mapiá: Later during our first full day in Céu do Mapiá, after participating in our little "mini-feitio," we three Americans had a hearty lunch. Lunch is the major meal of the day—usually the ever-present rice and black beans and some spaghetti, along with some sort of meat—most daimistas, at least in Brazil, are not vegetarians—as well as some fresh greens from the garden they cultivated behind the inn. Afterward, we napped for a few hours in the upstairs common area where we hung our hammocks.

Resting in the hammocks was *such* a luxury. It felt *so* good to not have anything that I had to do, no deadlines to meet. I immediately thought to myself: hammocks are truly gifts from God—just slowly rocking back and forth, feeling like I was cradled in a cloth womb, with the fabric of the hammock softly molded to my back, as if my back and the hammock were made for each other (by the way: you actually lie down diagonally in the hammock). I rested so deeply, my arm draped to one side, my legs completely relaxed, usually one extended out, and one curled under, periodically pulling on a rope that Rick and I had tied to the window to keep the rocking motion going, thereby creating at least the semblance of a breeze to soften the impact of the sweltering heat.

After our nap, Rick and I made our way through Padrinho Alfredo's yard down to a branch of the igarapé and cooled off in the shallow Daime-colored (yes!) water, splashing around with a small group of kids, most of them around five to seven years old, who were there with their mothers, Rick and I pretending to be *jacarés*—that is, caimans—who wanted to eat them, the kids screeching and running away in mock terror while the mothers were hard at work washing clothes in the stream.

Then, after going back to our rooms and changing into our blue fardas, Rick, Ron, Jorge, and I went down the hill, crossed the bridge, and made our way to the church. It was our first visit, and we arrived there around six o'clock in order to sing the Oração, the hymns that are sung every day in Mapiá by a small group of people in the church.

The church was, not surprisingly, the most important physical structure in Céu do Mapiá. It was located a short walk from the center of the village (the collection of small shops and an administrative building that were clustered around an open grassy plaza close to the igarapé). After walking past a small pond (an aborted attempt, I discovered later, to raise fish) and making our way up a small hill, we saw to our right a large (probably eight- to ten-feet-tall), solid concrete, white cross with two cross beams (the cruzeiro), that was set on top of an eight to ten feet in diameter, blue, six-pointed star-shaped concrete base, with a little niche in the front that sheltered a tall white lit candle. We stopped there for a moment, to be silent, and to make a quiet prayer.

FIGURE 6.1 Cruzeiro in Mapiá

FIGURE 6.2 Tomb of Padrinho Sebastião

Just to the left of the cruzeiro was a small white-walled building: the tomb of Padrinho Sebastião, the founder of this community and its patron saint. The door to the tomb faced the entrance of the church. As soon as I stepped inside the tomb I could feel the power of Padrinho's presence. It wasn't subtle. My eyes were immediately drawn, not surprisingly, by the imposingly large, rectangular, tile-covered, white raised structure where Padrinho was buried. A framed picture of Padrinho was hung over this tiled burial place, and its slightly sloping top was adorned with a small statue of him, some flowers in a vase, a small wooden cruzeiro, and some lit candles.

Directly in front of the Padrinho's rectangular burial structure, on a small table covered with a white cloth, was a life-sized statue of a lamb, perhaps symbolizing Padrinho's link with St. John the Baptist, who is often pictured as a boy carrying a lamb. In front of the statue, there was a lacquered, twisted, approximately three-feet-high piece of jagube. (Another, much larger, and un-lacquered piece of jagube was underneath a life-size picture of Mestre Irineu that hung on the wall to the right of Padrinho's burial enclosure.) Further to the right, in a connected, somewhat smaller, anteroom, another important figure in the Santo Daime was buried: Padrinho Corrente. His room was a slightly smaller version of Padrinho's tomb.

When we finally left Padrinho's tomb, to the right, and just behind the cruzeiro, was a small greenhouse-like structure surrounded by an abundance of flowering plants, where Madrinha Cristina, another important Santo Daime elder, was buried.

The wooden steps that led up to the church entrance were part of a covered but open-air deck/hallway that formed one "point" of the church. The church itself was built in the shape of an enormous six-pointed Star of David. (I had previously seen a photo of the church taken from high above: it looked then, and felt at that point, very much like a glowing star-shaped spaceship ready to take off from the small hill where it sat.) The deck/hallway was made of the same weathered gray hardwood planks that formed the walls of the church. Hanging over the entrance to the steps up to the hallway was a large, tarnished brass bell that I later discovered was frequently rung before ritual works as a way to summon the community. (Fun fact for daimistas: according to Vô Nel, a respected elder in Mapiá, Padrinho Sebastião's hymn "Dem Dum" refers to the ringing of the church bell—and thus, symbolically, refers to the inner call that rings out within each of us, drawing everyone back to the divine Presence.[1]) On both sides of the steps leading into the church were low walls with decorative carvings of stars, crescent moons, and suns, three key symbols within the Santo Daime, cut out of the wooden planks of each wall.

When I peered through the main entrance of the church, with its intricately carved doors—huge, solid, probably two inches thick, made of dark brown/almost black wood, that opened up to either side—I immediately saw a large, probably twelve-foot-high and six-foot-wide, green rectangular image of Padrinho Sebastião's face, hanging like a curtain, filling the doorway, but back a few feet. The image, which had been transferred from a photograph, was on a type of translucent canvas, so the light shone through it, which meant that his face hung there, glowing, looking both outside the church and into it, almost as if he was taking care of both what was going on in the day-to-day existence of the community and the innermost spiritual life of his people. This massive image—his sternly commanding face topped with a large hat and his impressively long white beard cascading down his torso—was created with thousands of green dots: it was like a digitalized Impressionist presence, shining forth from the white canvas, and it was flanked on both sides of the doors by two flags: the flag of Brazil and the flag of the Santo Daime.

When I first entered the church, I was genuinely stunned. It was so vast and open—the central room where the singing and dancing and praying took place (the salão) was, like the church itself, six-sided, and probably almost one hundred feet across and about forty feet high in its centermost peak. There were wooden benches scattered here and there along the walls, as well as along the sides of various other wings/star points of the church. When the three of us went into the church, however, arriving a few minutes before the time of the Oração, which took place every day just after 6:00 p.m., there were just a few white plastic chairs stacked against the walls. I later saw that during the larger seated works these stackable white plastic chairs would be neatly set up in rows in each of the six pie-shaped sections of the church that radiated out from the central altar/table/mesa. But on this day, we all just went and got our own chairs from the few that were stacked against the walls and lined them up in a row, quite close to the central altar, since only about ten to twelve people would typically come for the daily Oração.

The floor of the church was concrete. Years ago, the floor had been painted green, but since that time there had been so many all-night dance works that much of the paint had disappeared under the persistent pressure of shoes shuffling back and forth during the dances. The floor also had a grid of white painted lines that helped to define the six major sections of the church—three of the sections were for the women, and three of them were for the men—that radiated out from the center in roughly pie shapes, with a whole other set of more or less horizontal lines that bisected each of the pie-shaped sections, thereby creating clearly defined rows—rows that indicated either where the plastic chairs were placed during the seated works or where people danced during the dance works.

The walls of the church were made of the ubiquitous hardwood planks—but seen from the inside, the boards were a rich honey brown instead of the bleached-out gray of the planks seen from the outside. (The walls were only one board thick, since the same boards served as both inside and outside walls—there was no need for insulation). Here and there on the walls were large pictures of important spiritual figures in the Santo Daime.

The altar table, located right in the middle of the church, was about ten feet across. Like the church itself, the altar was in the shape of a six-pointed star and rested on a six-sided platform that was about three feet high. The altar top, incredibly, appeared to have been cut from a single slab of wood—a weighty reminder of the tree trunk from which it came. It was at least four inches thick, and its deeply dark, smooth, dense, polished wood was strikingly similar to the wood of the massive front doors of the church. This solid hardwood altar top was also,

FIGURE 6.3 Church in Mapiá

FIGURE 6.4 Altar in Mapiá

FIGURE 6.5 Church in Rio de Janeiro

again like the doors, intricately carved: row upon row of raised lines in the wood (perhaps representing lines of Divine force?) streaming from and interconnecting the elaborate carvings of a crescent moon, a five-pointed star, and a sun, and all of these carvings were, in turn, interwoven with depictions of jagube vines.

The altar itself was surrounded by twelve sturdy wooden chairs that during the festival dancing works were covered with a thin, bright green cloth. These were the chairs that, during the more important works, were reserved for the elders of the tradition, as well as for the group of young men who played guitars (both electric and acoustic and an electric bass) during the works and, at least occasionally, an older man who played the accordion.

There was not a lot on the altar top during the time of the Oração on that day, except for a small, simply made, dark wooden cruzeiro that faced the main entrance of the church (it was replaced during the major works with a much larger cruzeiro). The altar top was much more elaborately festooned during the larger works—filled with tall white taper candles, vases of flowers, framed pictures of key Santo Daime figures. During the Oração, the altar top also had a reused plastic gallon milk jug equipped with a little spigot that was filled with Daime. At the beginning of the Oração, we were each served a tiny, ceremonial thimbleful of this Daime by Sergio, an elderly, dark-skinned, glowingly happy guitarist who led the Oração.

Emerging straight out of the center of the altar and thrusting upward to the ceiling was an impressive faux jagube vine looking a lot like a curling two feet in diameter grayish-green tree trunk. This was clearly the symbolic, and perhaps actual, central pillar of the church. And acting as a symbolic tree canopy above the vine/trunk, forming a type of huge, glass, six-sided, colored bowl, were a series of six, lit from within, identical, quite large, equilateral triangular pictures of Madrinha Rita, that faced out toward each of the six sections of the church. (The tree trunk and the glass "bowl," seen together, also appeared to form a type of huge maraca/ceremonial rattle in the center of the church.) In each photo, Madrinha Rita was depicted as a smiling, relaxed, benevolent presence floating above us all, adorned in her full white farda, gazing lovingly down upon us, with the full moon behind her head serving as both as a type of celestial halo as well as a symbolic reminder of her connection with the Divine Mother.

Extending out from each of these pictures of Madrinha Rita, draped from the ceiling in relaxed U-shapes, were row upon row of blue and white paper streamers. This mass of blue and white drooped away from the center of the church ceiling toward the walls, which in turn led to a similar explosion of row upon row of tightly packed paper in all of the colors of the rainbow. The entire mass of draping colored paper shapes formed a type of alternate, cloud-like, floating, dimly lit, ethereal world above. All of these paper streamers (as well as cloth buntings placed on the top of the walls, surrounding the entire church) appeared to have been put up quite a while ago and were a bit faded, well worn, and slightly disheveled. Nonetheless, they appeared to represent a heartfelt attempt to fill the echoing vastness of the church with what seemed, at least to me, to be a symbolic evocation of the Astral world.

The church itself was often rather dimly lit, at least during the time of the Oração. It wasn't until it got completely dark outside that, seemingly reluctantly, someone turned on the six rather old fluorescent lights that hung from the ceiling, as well as the lights behind Madrinha Rita's pictures. Then, at some point much later, someone finally got around to turning on the newer, much brighter, compact fluorescent bulbs, as well as the incandescent bulbs that illuminated the pictures on the wall.

The echoing vastness of the church was filled, not long after we finished singing the Oração, with a whole troop of young girls who had been herded in at the very end of the Oração by a couple of elderly women. They were, with much giggling and squeals of protest, lined up in their "young female" section and soon started to sing various hymns—a sort of ragtag Santo Daime choir. I was immediately struck by the unique way that they sang: the sound of their voices was sharp-edged, nasal, and piercing. It was actually quite powerful and even in certain ways beautiful, but it was also intense. I thought to myself: I'll bet these are *puxadoras* in training (puxadoras are the women who lead the singing of the hymns during works; it's really crucial that everyone can hear their voices, so soft and gentle sounds are not all that useful). Comically, sometimes the girls didn't get a certain musical phrase right, and they'd suddenly stop and burst out laughing. They were like a gaggle of little goslings, all clucking and chirping together. And then, when these young girls finished singing, boom, they all got up at the same time, very quickly putting away their chairs and exiting the church en masse. No lingering for them!

AN OVERABUNDANCE OF MATERIAL

Before I launch into my description of some of the Santo Daime works that I attended during my time in Céu do Mapiá, I would like to reemphasize that I stayed there for slightly more than two and a half months.

And every day of my time in Céu do Mapiá was extremely rich—it was a *lot* to digest. So, attempting to do justice to that rushing river of time could easily devour this whole book. (I'm envisioning that huge plant in *Little Shop of Horrors* saying: "Feed me!") Therefore, I've had to make some extremely hard choices—what do I leave out, and what is absolutely essential for me to describe?

Struggling as a writer with an overabundance of material to work with is similar to a related difficulty: how to adequately communicate the ongoing, longitudinal, moving slowly through time nature of taking part in the Santo Daime religious tradition. Being a daimista is not like going to a two-week ayahuasca tourist retreat in Peru (however genuinely amazing and transformative that might be!). Participating in the Santo Daime is not a one-shot event. In the Santo Daime, the works just keep coming; each one huge, each one downloading massive amounts of learning into your cells—information that you need time to integrate, even if at times that integration process simply has to be postponed because another work is getting ready to happen. And another one. And then another one.

And each work is highly structured and repetitive. You soon figure out, for example: "here's what happens on the Night of St. John." As a daimista, you become conversant in what to expect with different specific works ("Oh, we always ring the bell when we sing that hymn"), since the major rituals follow a clear liturgical calendar and take place more or less in the same way, at the same time of the year, every year. As a daimista you also frequently shake your head in amazement at how each of these supposedly the same works is actually, on the level of personal experience, strikingly new and unanticipated.

However, as a writer making hard choices, I've had to more or less ignore this never-ending sameness within difference, as well as the implacable "ongoingness" of the Santo Daime, except by occasionally, such as right here and now, alluding to this inescapable, utterly central, decidedly temporal, over and over and over again dimension of the Santo Daime.

So, I just want it to be explicitly said: in my descriptions of my time in Céu do Mapiá, I have consciously, intentionally, chosen to leave out relatively massive chunks of material to focus on some of the events, both internal and external, that I finally decided were the most powerful, transformative, and at times, flat-out dramatic. A *lot* took place during my time in the boiling cauldron of spiritual Force that is Céu do Mapiá. But I'm only going to present a highly selective but illustrative and accurate spoonful of that potent brew. (I have included a few sections that I ended up cutting from this text—for example, "The June Festivities," a description of the celebration of the June Festival in Mapiá—in the "Supplemental Materials" section of www.liquidlightbook.com.)

THE NIGHT OF ST. JOHN

It was the night of St. John—the most important day of the year for the Santo Daime church (although I've also heard that said about the Day of Kings, in January). The night of St. John—the time of transformation, when the energy gets really intense and during which we sing and dance Mestre's beautiful hinário, all night. (If you want to read an account of the festivities leading up to this important celebration go to www.liquidlightbook.com/junefestival.)

The energy of that transformative spiritual fire of St. John was incarnated and expressed, quite powerfully, with the heat and visceral impact of physical fire itself: a *huge* bonfire was burning right in front of the church.

The day before the festival, during the *mutirão* (the weekly communal work session that usually happened on Monday mornings), a group of young men had unloaded a truckload of logs, typically around ten feet long and between six and eight inches in diameter, throwing them down in a loose pile, the logs ringing like wooden bells as they hit one another. These logs were then stacked up horizontally, very tightly, one on top of the other between four upright logs (about fifteen feet tall) that were stuck into the ground, and this whole edifice was held together loosely at the top by a strand of barbed wire. This compressed stack of logs was then lit, just before the Dance work began, with a "small" (about four foot high) bonfire in front of it, which meant that the fire itself started from the ground, in the middle of the stack, and worked its way up, creating a type of fire-womb, or a cave of fire, as the inner/lower logs began to turn bright orange, their material solidity transforming into the blazing heat and light of the fire of transformation.

The four log pillars didn't burn much, which was amazing, given the heat that radiated from that fire. They must have been freshly cut trees, filled with sap. And that fire burned, full bore, all night long, lingering on all the next day and night, and even some of the following day as well.

The church was crowded with when the work began. Unlike many of the other works, which would often begin with only a few dozen stalwart daimistas in attendance (typically elderly women), with many of the elders and their families, especially the young men ready to rock with their electric guitars, only arriving after the two hour or more interval in the middle of the dance work, for the night of St. John the church was packed with fardados and fardadas, right

FIGURE 6.6 Madrinha Julia

from the start. And all the elders were there—Padrinho Alfredo, Madrinha Nonata (Padrinho Paulo Roberto's wife, and the youngest daughter of Padrinho Sebastião), Madrinha Julia, and others.

Madrinha Julia is an elderly matriarch of the church who is one of Madrinha Rita's sisters. I was told that she had just arrived back in Mapiá the day before—apparently she had been ill and had needed time away to recuperate. I liked her right away: when she came into the church, she just strode down the aisle to the altar/table and sat down on one of the central green-cloth-covered chairs, and it was immediately clear that she was in charge. She looked a lot like my grandmother on my father's side: small, thin, bent over, lots of wrinkles, mostly white hair, wizened, tough. There was something hawklike, demanding, and ferocious about her; she didn't tolerate much nonsense. She was famous (infamous?) for her tough discipline within the church works.

For this Dance work, I was put in the section of the church that was reserved for other men who were, like us, visitors to Céu do Mapiá. Each of the church's hexagonal pie-wedge sections that radiated out from the central six-pointed-star central altar/table was designated in this way for a different group of people. To my right was the section for the men who lived in Mapiá, and to my left was the section for the young men/boys. On the women's side, there were the same three sections, with corresponding distinctions (so the men in our section faced the women who had arrived from outside Mapiá, and so on).

Both Rick and I were really struck by how different the Santo Daime works were in Céu do Mapiá, as compared with works in the United States. In the United States, if you want to drink Daime, you typically have to drive, sometimes for hours, to attend a work, so when you're there, you're there to do the work and nothing else. But Céu do Mapiá is a community where people live and work. So, in Céu do Mapiá, if people were coming and going during the works: no problem. If kids were running around outside, yelling and laughing during the works: no problem. If teenage boys were lounging around in the wings of the church, tinkering away on the guitar during the works: no problem. In Céu do Mapiá, if you needed to sit out long sections of the dancing because you were exhausted: no problem. It was as if they were saying: we've got a large enough cohort of people here who are really dedicated, really committed, who will sing their hearts out, who have memorized and internalized these hymns and are completely aligned with their energy: this is all that's needed.

I was guided by one of the guardians to stand in the second row back in my section, right by the aisle. The men and women in each row were arranged by height, with the tallest to the right. In my case, I was the tallest man in my row (there were only four or five of us).

For this Dance work, we drank Daime right after the opening prayers (an Our Father and Hail Mary—in Portuguese of course—along with some other longer prayers asking for God's blessings). The men and women were served in their own respective wings of the church. The men's serving area for the Daime was to the right of the salão itself, whereas the women's serving area was to the left.

If you wanted to be served Daime, and unlike most Santo Daime churches in the United States, there were no clear-cut serving times for Daime during the major works in Céu do Mapiá, you would go up to the large open "window," basically just a large rectangular open area cut into the wooden wall, and someone would serve you the Daime. He would press the nozzle of a dispenser, and the Daime would flow out into a large clear shot glass (a typical serving might be about an inch high.) The Daime in Mapiá looked and tasted slightly different than in the United States—lighter colored, less syrupy, and more tangy/vinegary (probably due to Céu do Mapiá's lack of refrigeration). But one thing was the same: it was still difficult to drink. I tried to drink it as quickly as possible, but not so fast that I might throw it up.

At the far end of the men's Daime-serving wing of the church, there was a large earthen-colored container that was filled with drinking water, as well as a few metal cups that were communally shared. Beyond that were the bathrooms. These were crude but clean, two or three open stalls with squatting places, and one stall at the end with a Western toilet (with no seat). On one wall of the bathroom were two long group urinals. The only water to wash your hands afterward was right outside the door—an iron faucet that was set into the wall about two feet up from the floor, with the water emptying into a rough bricked-in basin in the ground.

In the wing of the church where the healing room was located, at the very end of the hallway, there was a huge gong (the end of the hallway, like all of the other of the wings, was open-air: this was a church that let air and energy pass in and out—no sealed-up spaces). Suspended from the ceiling, and extending from the gong, as if aiming toward the main body of the church, there was a large, several feet in diameter, twisted tree trunk that looked very much like a jagube vine, (even though it wasn't). Looking at it with my religious studies' eyes, it felt very much like the symbolic representation of a huge, smooth-skinned anaconda—perhaps a preconscious nod to the "rainbow serpent" of the earlier *ayahuasquero* traditions.[2]

Right from the beginning of the work, I knew I was in for a powerful night. (That intuitive clarity might have been at least partially due to the fact that I was given a full shot glass of rather dark-brown Daime.)

At first, all was going well. Like all the other men, I was wearing a white, lightweight suit and a navy-blue tie, clutching a spiral-bound hymnbook in my left hand and trying my best to keep the beat with the maracá in my right hand. I felt comfortable easing into the rhythmic back and forth of the dance steps, little by little letting go of my underlying, low-grade anxiety that I wasn't playing my maracá correctly, and just letting myself sing, from my heart, the lyrics of those hymns that were already becoming familiar to me. We danced together in the church in expanding concentric circles that radiated out from the center altar/table, forming rotating rings that circled in unison, back and forth, around the central altar/table (and the pillar/trunk that extended up into the ceiling).

More and more I began to sync with the rhythmic beats of the maracá and softened into the oscillating repetition of the dance steps. And the more that I danced and sang, the more that I could slowly feel my personal energetic boundaries softening, and I was increasingly able, with periodic stops and starts, to sink into something bigger, until—for several distinct instances, lasting a few minutes each time—my consciousness encompassed and then merged with the whole room as the hundreds of men and women in their white farda finery swirled around with choreographed precision, my consciousness expanding to wrap within itself the voices of hundreds of fardados, singing from their hearts those uplifting musical messages from Mestre Irineu, singing and dancing in the Force. Over and over again I felt myself almost bodily uplifted by the sounds of the hymns (their words, their melodies, their rhythms) as they were sung with such clarity and heart, as hundreds of us were swept up in the surge of the Current as it circulated round and round and round the salão, dancing back and forth around the central pillar, moving as if we were unified parts of one organic bodily whole, as if we were within the oscillating movement of a magical mystical Santo Daime washing machine, all of us being churned back and forth, receiving our cleansing.

When you're in the Force, singing hymns that are powerful and uplifting; when everyone joins in (many of the people in Céu do Mapiá know hundreds, if not thousands, of hymns by heart), and everyone is moving together, often with a lot of vigor and emphasis, the voices merging and fusing into one multi-faceted, full-throated, heartfelt communal voice that is both everywhere and nowhere in particular; when you're sinking into the weighty, visceral, and repetitive, back and forth of the crisply executed dance steps, the beat punctuated by the insistent rasp and whir of the maracas; when all of this is taking place and you've drunk a lot of Daime, it is very common to begin to sense a powerful force/current circulating back and forth in-and-through everyone, often flowing, very specifically, counterclockwise around the circle of people, entering from the left and flowing to the right. And it's not unusual to begin to feel interlaced with everyone, your boundaries dissolving, melting and merging into the larger, pulsating, sonic whole as you are lifted above your normal physical limitations in a powerful state of ecstasy that is often accompanied by a sense of deep inner stillness, a feeling of being centered and present, grounded and rooted in the earth as your legs and feet hit the concrete in the repetitive, hypnotic dance steps.

However, at times Dance works can be rather rough. For example, singing the Confession (Hymn 17 of Mestre Irineu's hinário, "My Divine Father of Heaven") was not exactly a walk in the park. This hymn was sung three times, each time followed by three Our Fathers and Hail Marys. Everyone was standing there, all in their places in line (this hymn isn't danced) in their fardas. It was really hot and humid, the church was packed, and all were holding lit tapers in their right hands, pouring out their hearts, offering up their wrongdoings to God, asking for forgiveness, singing the Confession a cappella, slowly, ponderously. It just went on and on and on. Increasingly, it became difficult for me to remain standing. The energy in the room felt dense and difficult to deal with. It was like I was viscerally taking on the enormous weight of massive amounts of toxic energy pouring in-and-through me, all of it having been released into the Light that filled the salão, all of it offered up for transformation. In this way, the Confession was serving as a focal point for the hard-core spiritual energy cleansing that daimistas take on, especially on the night of St. John.

Then, after that hymn, there was more singing, more dancing, with me at one point feeling, in my bones, that the exertion itself was an essential aspect of the experience, that it was an opportunity, step by step, to move the energy of the hymns and the teachings that they were transmitting, in-and-through my body. It seemed that dancing and singing each hymn was a chance for me to embody, note by note, the vibratory lessons that they were expressing. And so many of the hymns were *so* beautiful and powerful, *so* uplifting. I frequently felt genuinely ecstatic, my heart pouring out my love for God, my eyes beginning to roll back into my skull as I'd feel myself, rapturous, energetically swept up into a swirling mass of blue and white and gold sparkles of inner Light, with such joy, with such a sense of innate fulfillment.

At times during the singing and dancing, my voice would, of its own accord, descend deep into my chest and lower in tone, and I would begin to feel the words that I was singing start to reverberate from the center of my body. As the hymns were intoned from my heart, my body began to resonate, like a tuning fork, with the echoing vibratory overtone of everyone singing and dancing in the church, as I increasingly began to attune myself to the dynamic interwoven wholeness of the church as we all sang as one. During those moments, it felt like I was singing from some very deep, centered space around the middle of my chest; and yet, simultaneously, it was as if I had expanded outside of my personal boundaries, connecting to everyone as we all were swept up in the Current, carried forward on shimmering waves of hauntingly beautiful and deeply heartfelt music.

This process of letting go into the greater Whole, of aligning with God's presence and with your inner depths, is by no means always easy, especially if you've drunk a lot of Daime. At times it felt like I was having to grow new Daime "muscles," bit by bit. I was learning how to stay present and grounded, while simultaneously opening up and softening into this insistent, surging, circulating Force. And during dance works in Mapiá, especially when the Force was strong, it was at times difficult to navigate all of those surges of energy, especially when I'd feel buffeted here and there, like I was being swept away and at risk of losing myself.

During this night in particular, over and over again, I'd find myself viscerally resisting what, on another level, I knew I needed to do: to surrender, to relax into the currents of the Force that were moving in-and-through me, often very insistently. Time and time again, I'd feel myself hunkering down, trying subconsciously to put on the brakes by inwardly inner clenching and bracing. And I'd notice myself tensing up and would again and again somehow, remind myself to trust, to relax, to breathe deeply and fully, to open up to the Force and welcome it, with every breath. But then another huge wave of Force would come rolling through, and I'd quickly find myself battening down the hatches yet again.

During this work, while dancing, I would also often find myself needing to consciously, slowly take really deep breaths. I would expand my lungs forcefully with air, right up to the very tops of my lungs, and then hold my breath there for a few moments, strongly yet effortlessly, as I felt the life force carried by that breath insistently pressing even farther upward and outward from the center of my chest.

And I kept wondering why in the world they were not turning on the overhead fans—these large, old-fashioned, rotating fans that were mounted just outside Madrinha Rita's "tree canopy" that looked down on us? Because even though many of the women were fanning away with their hand fans, and some of us men were opening our jackets and using the "wings" of the jacket to fan ourselves, the overhead fans were never turned on.

I worked really hard during the first few hours of the Dance work to not focus on how many hours were left and how many hymns remained to be sung. Instead, I would try to make each hymn an opportunity to call myself back to the present, to Presence, to remember God, to remind myself that it was a chance to sink into my heart, to open into my Center. I actually welcomed this opportunity to stay deeply quiet inside while simultaneously opening up to the increasingly Forceful energy that was surging in-and-through me.

And that sort of inner orientation mostly worked. I would concentrate on the words of the hymns, not only trying to get the Portuguese pronunciation correct, which can be quite a task in and of itself, since the words often come very fast, but also using the meanings of the words themselves to orient in the various "directions" that they were indicating: the need to trust God and to have faith; the beauty of asking for forgiveness; the value of living life fully and with joy; the gifts that come from discipline and from paying attention to the guidance of the Divine Mother; the blessings that pour into us when we thank all the Divine Beings, when we praise the beauty of the Sun, the Moon, the Stars, the Wind, and the Sea—on and on, an ever-renewed torrent of spiritual teachings and reminders.

SANTO DAIME "THEOLOGY"

During my time in Céu do Mapiá, it became clear to me that many, if not most of the daimistas who lived there were not all that focused on the *meanings* of the hymns. Instead, their focus was on ritual excellence: singing (and dancing) the hymns well; memorizing and internalizing and singing (accurately and with gusto) literally hundreds, if not thousands, of hymns. This theological "casualness" hit home to me one night after singing the Oração on the veranda of the house of an important person in the historical unfolding of our lineage: Vô Nel. (After the first few weeks of going to the Oração at the church, Rick and I were invited to sing the Oração at Vô Nel's house along with other members of his family and a few close friends, a practice that we continued almost every evening—it was quite an honor.) I mentioned to Vô Nel that there were a few phrases in some of the hymns in the Oração that were a bit unclear to me. (By the way: being the humble man that he was, Vô Nel preferred for us to not call him "Padrinho" Nel. Instead, he asked us to refer to him as "Vô Nel" or "Grandad Nel.")

FIGURE 6.7 Vô Nel

I then asked if he would mind helping me to understand some of these verses better. He seemed open, and so (with several family members standing nearby) I asked him about a verse that stood out to me, a verse in "Eu Vou Rezar"/"I'm Going to Pray," (no. 7 in the *Oração*) that says: "My Master, He does not hide; / I'm always attentive; / with the most holy sacrament." I immediately noticed that everyone there seemed a bit startled when I asked him, "What does this verse mean to you?" It was clearly either a question that they would never have asked or had never thought about. Vô Nel himself seemed a bit stumped as to what to say, but two of his adult children, each of them central figures in the Céu do Mapiá religious hierarchy, quickly jumped in—talking about how that verse of the hymn speaks about how Mestre's presence is always there, especially within the Daime.

I went on to say that the hymns often seem to have different levels of meaning—some more obvious, others more subtle—and that I wanted to be as clear as I could about those more subtle levels of meaning. That observation seemed to open the conversation up a bit more, in that we quickly got into a discussion about exactly who the Mestre is that is referred to in this hymn. At first one of Vô Nel's "children" said: "It's the Daime." But then a bit later, he added, "Well, it can also refer to Mestre Irineu, or Juramidam." And another one of Vô Nel's "children" then piped up and said, "Or Jesus Christ."

I also asked about a passage in another hymn ("Peço Que Vós Me Ouça"/ "I Ask That You Hear Me," no. 10 in the *Oração*) that goes: "The boat which sails in the sea; / Sails within my heart." Again, at first they smiled and/or laughed at my question, but then one of Vô Nel's adult children went on to say, very confidently, that the verse refers to the time of Jesus, and to the boats on the sea of Galilee. (Padrinho Alfredo, during a visit to a U.S. church that I frequently attended, had a similar understanding, underscoring that the boat is actually in the astral, but—multiple layers of meaning!—that it also referred to the boat of the brothers who were instructed by Jesus as to where they should throw their nets.) But then Vô Nel said that he heard Padrinho Sebastião speak about a boat that is there in the astral realms, a boat that manifested in this world as Noah's ark—and when he said this, everyone lit up. I then said that I thought that perhaps the verse was also referring to all of us who are part of this fellowship, gathered together, riding over the ocean of illusion—and they seemed to like that interpretation as well.

Walking back to the inn, I spoke about this conversation with Rick, and we both agreed that it seemed as if many of the people in Mapiá were not especially concerned about the different possible meanings of the hymns. Instead, there appeared to be a type of tacit, collective set of assumptions about what the hymns meant, assumptions that were rarely, if ever, explicitly discussed. So at first, my asking those types of questions had seemed a bit odd to them. However, it soon became clear that individual daimistas had divergent interpretations of the hymns and that, if prompted, they actually seemed to enjoy discussing these more overtly "theological" topics. Seen from my current vantage point, I also think that it's safe to say that many of the elders within the tradition *are* keenly interested in the meanings of the hymns and are happy to share these insights with those who ask.

REFLECTIONS ON HYMNS

The centrality of the hymns in the Santo Daime simply cannot be overstated.[3]

During the ritual of the Night of St. John, I was struck by how there is, quite clearly, a highly specific "Daime-feel" to each of the hymns—this unique vibratory "signature" that is communicated in-and-through the rhythm and melody of the hymns. So even though each hymn is very distinct, they all began to seem as if they were just different musical phrases in one long, unified (even while extremely diverse and ever-changing) hymn.

Nonetheless, thinking about hymns from my current vantage point, it also seems that there is a quite distinct "flavor" to each hinário. For example, I think that Padrinho Alfredo's hinários are direct, ongoing, transmissions from the highest level of the Astral worlds, transmitting the Christ Consciousness into this world in a sonic, rhythmic form—each hymn so unique, and yet each one bringing with it a very elevated, high vibratory frequency; each hymn in its own way seeking to connect each of us with that Light; each hymn so clear, poetic, beautiful, lyrical (often invoking the flowers, the Moon, the Stars, and especially the Sun). In his hymns, it seems that the inner Sun and the outer Sun merge, the light that illuminates our world fusing with the luminous Source of spiritual illumination.

Padrinho Sebastiao's hinário *O Justiceiro*, however, is often much more challenging for me. It's as if the hinário, as a whole, twists in upon itself like a jagube vine. And quite often, the words of his hymns can seem opaque to me—they rebuff any easy understanding, in that it is often not clear who is speaking to whom or about what. And for me, the words themselves, even when they are clear, are at times hard to accept: they often speak, forcefully, about punishing liars, bringing the whip, and other ideas that can be difficult for me to accept. Therefore, his hymns, again, albeit only at times, can be hard to swallow, like the Daime itself. But like the Daime, even when my body clenches and rebels against those hymns, I can recognize and respect their underlying energy, the demanding, intense Power as it works within me, insistently, forcefully—often catalyzing mediumistic energy. Over the years, therefore, I have learned how to look beyond, or underneath, the overt meanings of some of Padrinho Sebastião's hymns, focusing instead on how to let myself be swept up in the turbulent currents of the liberative Force that his hymns bring.[4] And fascinatingly, at least to me, his later hinário, *Nova Jerusalem*, has a very different energetic quality to it—it is very joyous, free, clear, and uplifting, and yet equally potent.

Mestre Irineu's hinário *O Cruzeiro* also carries its own energetic "note." For me, his hymns are like standing underneath a crystal-clear waterfall; they are a pure, powerful, descent of grace, direct from the highest levels of the Astral. His hymns are songs of praise, of joy, of reveling in life, of seeing the Divine in all things. They are multifaceted, typically up-tempo, limpid praise poems, glorying in the beauty and fecundity of the Divine Nature, often hymns of thankfulness to the Divine Mother, each hymn cascading and crashing upon the next, carrying wave after wave of blessings and benedictions.

And so, within each hinário, each and every hymn is in its own way a precious gem: a highly compressed and polished node in an interconnected net of other gems, similar to the diamonds that make up Indra's Net.[5] Each of these sonic pulsations of Beauty and Power emits the Light of the Source that they are plugged into, that they are expressing and transmitting. Each hymn is a highly individualized conduit of the Doctrine: the energetic Matrix of the illuminative teachings of the Santo Daime.

BACK TO THE NIGHT OF ST. JOHN

During the Night of St. John work, around hymn 50 in Mestre Irineu's hinário, I exited my line in the proper way, that is, after the hymn was finished and before the next one began, making my way down the line, mumbling my pardons to the people I squeezed past, until I got to the aisle. I then received another serving of Daime. Like the first one, this was also almost a full cup, and it was again dark brown. Not surprisingly, almost immediately after drinking the Daime, I could barely bear it: every cell in my body wanted to reject it. I had to lean against the half-wall of the serving wing, my face scrunching up, grimacing, like it was twisting away, trying to escape from the taste.

Not long afterward, I was not able to dance anymore. I was simply feeling the Force too strongly. So I once again stepped out of my line and made my way to the edge of the salão, where I sat down on one of the benches, feeling almost like a boxer going back to his corner in the ring, preparing for the next round of punches. Determined to stick it out, I didn't stay on the bench for long—just

Fireworks and firecrackers were a striking feature of life in Mapiá (as well as throughout Brazil). They'd often explode during certain key hymns. Although the locals were well aware of exactly when the flurry of these explosions would take place, as a relative newbie, I would frequently find myself jolted back to earth just as I was floating off into the Astral.

a couple of hymns. When, to my relief, hymn 66 arrived—this is a hymn to St. John, sung three times—lots of fireworks were set off by the boys waiting outside; the church bell was rung again and again; and then (at last!) there was a break, the intervalo.

By the time of the interval, I had been dancing with everyone for over four hours straight, with hardly a break, going back and forth in my designated spot, in my designated row, in my designated section, in the dense, humid heat, and I was totally wrung out. Instead of trudging for twenty or thirty minutes across the town square of the village and up the rather steep hill to my little room in the inn, I staggered off to the small storage area in one of the side wings of the church, which doubled as an informal healing room for the men. Jair, an elderly and beaming guardian, managed to locate a thin foam mattress that was tucked away on a shelf in the back of the room, unfolded it on the bare concrete floor, and very sweetly helped me to lie down. He even helped me take off my shoes so that I'd be more comfortable. When I stripped off my jacket to lie down, it was drenched in sweat and reeked with this odd sort of bodily odor. (I'd never smelled anything like it before, sort of like straw, but also acidic and vinegary.) And that pungent, sharp smell intermingled with the lingering bleach smell of my white farda.

After I crumpled down on the mattress with an enormous sigh of relief and a quick muttered prayer of thanks, I found myself stretched out, unmoving, flat on my back with my eyes closed, feeling completely gripped by the Force as vision after vision unfurled within my inner sight, as if they had been eagerly waiting for the opportunity to emerge. These mirações were extremely powerful and profound, but throughout it all, I felt awful: extremely hot, flushed, uncomfortable, and even mildly itchy. My stomach/intestines were protesting, and I was feeling the gnaw of hunger. But the exhaustion kept me from getting up to get something to eat.

As time passed and I didn't begin to feel any better, I started to worry that I might be dehydrated. So, with an enormous effort of will, I managed to force myself to get up and gulp down several glasses of water, which unfortunately didn't seem to help much. Almost immediately afterward I collapsed back onto the foam mat and lay there, praying from the depths of my heart for help from God and the divine beings; asking for energy; asking to be recharged. I was beginning to think that I would never be able to get up. A couple of times I did manage to at least get up on my knees so that I could bend down and pray, but then after a few minutes, I would sink back down again to the mat.

Then, over half an hour later, lying there wrapped in pungent-smelling clothes, swept away in a torrent of visions, I finally began to notice that my bladder was beginning to urgently insist that I get up. However, given my level of exhaustion, I also wasn't completely surprised to discover that my body simply would not/ could not move. It was as if the inner electrical circuits connecting my will to my muscles had been short-circuited.

At first I was not overly perturbed by this semi-paralysis. I had, after all, finally managed to wiggle my fingers—a fairly major accomplishment given the current state of affairs. I also knew that dramatic physical phenomena were not unheard of among those who drank Daime. I was used to just riding out whatever the Daime brought to me, having faith that everything would eventually work out as it should. But increasingly, I began to wonder, in an oddly detached way, if perhaps this situation was a bit more serious than I had imagined. Perhaps I had simply not drunk enough water during the past few hours. (Looking back, I would say that assessment was probably right.) I began to think that perhaps this quasi-paralysis was not just a manifestation of the Daime at work within me but was also (instead?) a physiological symptom of a fairly major case of dehydration. I feared that I might not be able to replenish my electrolytes and that I would spiral down and there would be no way for me to get any intravenous liquid.

It began to sink in that I was in the middle of the rain forest, with not a doctor or hospital to be found for miles and miles. I then realized that even if I eventually was able to drink some more water, I wasn't really sure that it would make a significant difference. Bit by bit, I began to accept that it was quite possible that I might actually die that night, that I might become one of those morbidly interesting stories that you'd read about on the internet. (I could see the title of the story in my mind's eye: "American Religious Studies Professor Dies in the Amazon Rain Forest While Taking Part in a Hallucinogenic Religious Ritual.")

Looking back, I'm actually amazed that I didn't panic at the possibility of my perceived impending death. But incredibly, I was quite calm. I was completely clear that I didn't want to die, that I wasn't ready to make the transition into whatever it was that awaited me after death. But I also figured that if I did everything in my power to make sure that I continued living on this earth (including eventually managing to get up and drink some more water) that the rest of it was all in God's hands. And so, as I lay there, unmoving, strangely peaceful, I began to ask myself: "If I really do die tonight, what would I regret not having done with my life?" And one of the answers that arose, very strongly, very clearly, was that I would regret not having written the book that you are reading now.

I finally managed, after several abortive attempts, to haul my severely weakened body up to a sitting position. Leaning on one arm, I reached out and grabbed the liter-size Coke bottle filled with lukewarm water that I had brought with me into the storage room and, slowly this time, drank it down. After that, walking extremely carefully, still reeling in the Force, I made it to the bathroom, where I stood for a moment, leaning against the wall, seeing one of the few external visual effects that I've ever had with the Daime: a series of intense, darting, thin lines of light that come with the underlying sense that they're an indication of the fault lines in the fabric of the universe; indications of a world that is, as it were, splitting apart at the seams; indications that I was about to finally see the Light that is behind/underneath the world that we normally live in, seeping through the cracks.

When I finally made it over to the urinal to pee, Rick suddenly appeared beside me. I looked over at him (I'm sure I was quite a sight), and said, "Hey man, I don't want to alarm you, and I might be mistaken, but I think that I might be really dehydrated, and maybe even suffering from heat exhaustion. This could get really bad. I could actually die here, tonight." Rick stood there, in his completely chill Rick way, and said, very calmly, "But you won't." I worked to let that sink in, and then I told him, "I'm really clear that I don't want to die. I've got a lot of work still to do here in this world. I'm definitely letting God and all the divine Beings know that I want to stay here in my body."

Then, after making my way back to the healing/storage room and somehow (slowly, so slowly) managing to put back on my tie and jacket and plopping myself down on one of the plastic chairs that were scattered along the sides of the walls of the church, I sat there, stunned, gripped by the Force, and utterly exhausted. I then saw Antonieta (a revered elder in the community) and Rick talking together in the church, and I tottered over toward them to let them know that I was really struggling. (By this time, it was probably about 2:30 a.m., and the intervalo had been going on for well over two hours.)

Antonieta immediately pulled over a plastic chair for me, indicating that I should sit down. She then drew another chair toward her and sat down across from me. She was clearly a bit concerned about what I was going through, and at some point she got up, heading off to get someone else who she thought could help me. About five minutes later (as Rick hovered nearby), she returned, bringing with her this tiny "force of nature" woman—Olivia. Olivia promptly sat down in the chair facing me and began to work with me energetically. She held her right hand out, with her palm facing me, and I could tell that she was sending me this lovely energy of peace, of calm. She then told me, in her musical, raspy, low-voiced Portuguese: "You need to shut the doors to your aparelho (the mind/body/spirit of a medium) and open up to your higher Self. Be calm, remember that the Daime is Beauty." (This was a good reminder—at that point the Daime was feeling pretty funky within me.) She then almost cooed to me, saying: "It's good to sing in the festival, the Queen of the Forest likes it; it's a joy to align with Mestre Irineu through his hymns." She then said, "*Com licença*" (she was asking for permission to come closer), and when I told her, "*Claro*" ("For sure!"), she stood next to me and began to work a bit more overtly with my energy field, making rapid hand "passes" over my body, with occasional mediumistic flourishes—the clicking, the finger-snapping, the whistling, as well as occasional sudden, yet modulated, semi-seizures that rippled through her. And I was responding in kind—at first my body jerked and shook while I was seated there in my chair. I then began to brush myself down, rapidly, breathing heavily.

But gradually, I began to become calm, quiet, centered. And then, feeling a sense of closure within me, I thanked her, and I said that I'd try to follow her advice (to find my Center, to align myself with Mestre Irineu, with God) but that it was sometimes not easy to do this when the Force is so strong. She held my hands, looked me in the eye, and said: "If you want it, you can do it. Have courage. You are a man. You are a Son of God. Be strong. Trust." As she was walking away, I asked her if I should drink any more Daime. She looked at me, paused, and then said: "Don't rush. Go very slowly. You need to recharge your aparelho. Maybe later in the work." (I took her advice: no more Daime for me for the rest of the work, and none was needed: the Force stayed with me for hours afterward.)

Both Antonieta and Olivia then, almost simultaneously and with great vigor, sent me off to the fire. Antonieta told me: "This fire is very magical; it contains within it the power of transformation." And when I got there, the fire *was* utterly amazing: by that time of night it was almost all glowing orange coal, but coals that formed a sort of fire-filled structure, about ten feet tall and several feet thick. The logs were like the shining leg bones of a giant lodged within a glowing, orange-ribbed womb. And the fire was topped with blue flames, each of them several feet high, that occasionally turned green or even purple as some of the people gathered around it threw some powdery substance into it. (I never found out what that was.)

I sat down on a plastic chair, about twenty feet from the fire. There was a small group of other daimistas sitting together at ease, talking and laughing, playing around with drums, absorbed in the beauty of the fire. I didn't join them; I just sat quietly in my chair for about thirty minutes, sinking into myself. I was still pretty tired, and part of me was amazed at the energy level of the people who were sitting nearby. (Ron at some point came up and joined me, sitting quietly beside me.)

The work finally started up again, signaled with three loud, long clangings of the bell, each one spaced about fifteen minutes apart. This was done because people had gone back to their homes to rest or shower, and they needed to know that the work was about to begin, so they could have time get their fardas on and walk back. The interval, from beginning to end, was probably three hours long. Taking a few deep breaths, I went back to my place in line and stayed there for about ten hymns, really linking up with the power and beauty of the hymns, playing my maracá. But eventually, I had to leave the line to sit down on one of the plastic chairs. Sitting there, I began to grimace as I moved my shoulders up and down and rotated them backward and forward, trying to free up an insistent, highly localized pain that was gripping the upper right side of my back, just under my shoulder blade, like some sort of energetic angry crab. I was so tired that I couldn't even sing. I settled for just sitting there mouthing the words (often I couldn't even manage that simple task). I was aware that the guardians were checking me out, sometimes subtly, other times less so: at times standing nearby, at times asking me how I was doing. But they didn't insist that I dance (which I couldn't/wouldn't have done even if they had insisted).

While sitting there on my plastic chair, all sorts of doubts and waves of intense negativity arose within me. I thought to myself, *What the hell am I doing here? I just want out. I hate this. Do I really want to do this? I just don't seem to have the capacity. Why am I here? This level of work is insane. This is just brutal. It's too much. Is this really what God wants me to do? Is this really worth it? There is no way in hell that I'm ever coming back to Mapiá, forget about staying here for six months.* And on it went. It felt as though my physical and energetic body was flushing an enormous amount of black, gooey, toxic gunk. The waistband of my pants was really tight with my gas-bloated Daime belly, and I just wanted to tear off my necktie—the collar felt so constricting. It was like a pair of hands were squeezing and shutting down my breathing.

Nonetheless, at the same time, in-and-through the exhaustion, the doubts, and the torrent of negativity, I would also find myself, almost begrudgingly, savoring the majestic, awe-inspiring power of the hymns. I'd sit there stunned by the surging vortex of the dancing, filled with gratitude for the skill of the musicians. (They had appeared after the intervalo. The first part was a cappella.)

I somehow managed to stand during the closing hymns of the work, which (to my rather jaded perception) just went on and on and on, and I didn't even recognize about three-quarters of them. Then around 6:00 a.m., after the close of the work, I trudged home (after greeting Padrinho Alfredo, who was really glowing, in the salão); I stripped off my stinking farda; I opened the shutters that covered the windows in my room; and I collapsed on the bed.

THE FIRE BURNS HOT IN MAPIÁ

My first couple of weeks in Céu do Mapiá were rather disorienting. It took that long for me to even begin to put together, bit by bit, some sort of rough and ready internalized map of the place. There was something so elusive, shifting, and hard to grasp about the village. For the first week or so, I'd be walking around with Rick and Ron, and afterward I wouldn't have a clue about how to get back to where we had just been. There was just so much to take in, so much that I had to do in order to function in that world that was so foreign to me, that it seemed that there was simply not enough "mental room" to put all of those experiences away into some tidy cubbyhole.

And adding to that mental overload was the fact that there was just something about the layout of Mapiá that made the topography of the place difficult to grasp. The trails and pathways went up and down and round and round. They curved, twisted, and veered sideways and opened up suddenly to expansive vistas. The sun was also beating down on you with this insistent force, and the heat would infiltrate my bones and lay on top of me like a heavy wool blanket. Sweat would be pouring down my back, and the insects would be singing in the lush and florid and shiny-leaved vegetation. And generators would be roaring and motorcycles would be chugging past and clusters of children would walk by chattering away in a language that I could only sporadically understand. The flies would be buzzing around my face like crazed kamikaze pilots, while the gnats would be nipping at my ankles. And my mouth would get dry, and a vaguely familiar taped hymn of young women singing in loud, nasal tones would be blaring out of the house that I just walked past. Nothing in Mapiá was tidy; nothing was precisely delineated. Barbed-wire fences were just temporary markers—polite requests addressed to the anarchic fecundity of life in this village.

And I was, even then, hyper-aware of how this experience overload that I was going through was intimately overlaid with and infused by my own inner state: how my confusion, delight, depression, wonder, and anxiety were all in the mix, seeping into each moment—and all of that "much at onceness" was boiling away in the middle of the pressure-cooker energy of Mapiá—that uncomfortable, never-ending, encircling, almost literal pressure; that jaw-tightening intensity that got under your skin. It never stopped cooking me, as I was being pushed and pulled here and there by these powerful unseen forces, and I was bouncing off all the other chickpeas in the pot, and it was hot as hell, both physically and spiritually.

I'll just say it: the spiritual "fire" was really hot in Mapiá. I'd feel such a strong desire to get the hell out of there (Right now! While I still can!). I'd watch those thoughts arise, so strong, so insistent. And I'd think to myself, *This path is not for me, what was I thinking, I can't bear it a moment more.* And yet, I'd also know that those thoughts and feelings would, probably very soon, shift into something radically different, where I would find myself marveling at the beauty of a sunset from a hill high above the village; feeling myself filled with gratitude at the shimmering Divine Presence in the waxy leaves shuddering in a cool breeze; rocking and swaying with love and gratitude while singing those urgently ardent hymns in praise to God, right there in the temple in the very heart of the Santo Daime, singing out from my depths those inspired, often hauntingly beautiful words that touched me so deeply, that uplifted me, that helped me to soar into communion with the Flowing Divine Light that filled me and poured through me.

I must admit that in no other spiritual path have I had to struggle with so much inner resistance. When I was participating in both of my prior spiritual paths (Siddha Yoga and in the IM School of Healing Arts), I always felt a simple and easy *yes* resounding in my heart. That *yes* would basically always be there, suffusing everything, shining underneath it all, even during moments of difficulty and suffering. But with the Santo Daime, especially in the beginning, it was different. For years, my relationship to the Santo Daime as a path was very similar to the way I'd typically feel when I drank the Daime itself: an entrenched, nonrational part of me was almost viscerally repulsed by certain aspects of the Santo Daime, similar to how my body would at times become nauseated when I drank the Daime itself. Yet simultaneously, also like my experience of drinking the Daime, there'd also be this miraculous golden-petaled flowering of awe and wonder within me, along with deep gratitude at the Beauty, Divine Presence, and Power that was being revealed and bequeathed to me. From the very beginning, hand in hand with the knee-jerk resistance, there was also this deep inner tug to be part of the Santo Daime path. There was this bone-deep Knowing that this path was truly good, that it was Right for me, that it was in fact a path like no other—incomparable, stellar, miraculous. And during my time in Mapiá, those two extremely powerful yet opposing feelings toward the Santo Daime itself were frequently jostling together within my psyche.

I swear that I wasn't suffering from some sort of spiritually ennobled bipolar disorder. Rather, everything just seemed magnified there, and I needed so much patience; so much willingness to just tough it out through the rough spots; so much trust that even when I *really* did not want to be there, when I was filled with doubts and negativity and second-guessing, just around the corner there'd be a gift, a reminder of why I'd come to Céu do Mapiá in the first place.

SANTA MISSA IN CÉU DO MAPIÁ

On Monday, July 4, I took part in my first Santa Missa, my first Holy Mass. It took place at four in the afternoon, in a relatively small, perhaps fifteen foot by twenty foot crudely framed, rectangular, open-air, corrugated roofed structure in the middle of the Céu do Mapiá cemetery. In the middle of the structure they had set up a small table, and a group of (primarily) older women was gathered around it. Rick, Ron, and I arrived, decked out in our blue fardas, just slightly after the Missa had begun (it began, as always, with a *terço*: a repetition, while standing, of Our Fathers and Hail Marys in a certain order, guided by the rosary). We were served just a tiny amount of Daime in an equally tiny plastic cup as the rosary continued. Everyone else who arrived (and many more came after us) was also given a small serving of Daime.

After the rosary finished, everyone sat down. We sat on the men's side on a rough, somewhat uncomfortable, wooden bench, while others sat on the ubiquitous white plastic chairs. Several more of these chairs were brought in as more and more people kept arriving. The configuration of where people were seated, and on what, continued to shift for about the first forty-five minutes, until finally everyone who was going to come had arrived.

The cemetery itself was fairly small. It was the opposite of American cemeteries with their manicured lawns, imposing tombstones, and wide-open spaces. In Mapiá, the graves seemed crammed together; some graves were marked with just a simple wooden cross adorned with a hand-lettered name; and throughout much of the cemetery there was a profusion of small plants scattered around or hanging over the graves. Everything was a little bit wild and unkempt. Nonetheless, there was still a strong sense of reverence and remembrance during the Missa. I was especially struck by how often, when people arrived, they would stop at a grave site; they'd put candles and/or flowers on the grave; and then they would stand there for a while, praying quietly to themselves.

The mass is celebrated in the Santo Daime, at least in Mapiá, on the first Monday of every month. It is a work of charity, offered to the souls of the dead, an offering of prayers to help them in their afterlife journey. This Missa lasted two hours. After reciting the rosary, we sang ten hymns (mostly of Mestre Irineu), each one followed by three Our Fathers and three Hail Marys (as well as a few other less well known prayers). These hymns were all sung a cappella. They were all extremely slow and sober and "heavy." As we sang, time itself seemed to slow down, to get really thick, like some sort of temporal molasses.

The "heaviness" of the mass was amplified by the fact that, again, a lot of the ideas expressed in the hymns were difficult for me to accept or relate to—a repeated emphasis on having "offended" God, asking forgiveness for our sins, and so on. Not being raised a Catholic, I was pretty certain that God is never offended by anything that I have done. I was also not a big fan of the (repeated!) emphasis on repenting for one's sins. I thought then and continue to think now: we do need to recognize mistakes, sure. We do need to become aware of the need to change our way of life, absolutely. But flogging oneself with guilt: not so much. And yet, there I was, singing those hymns and trying to be as heartfelt and sincere as possible. To cope with this incongruity, I kept telling myself, *Clearly these hymns emphasize notions of sin and offending God that I have problems with, and yet I can't change any of that. What I can change, however, is how I respond to them.* In an ideal world, I perhaps could have recognized that, at their best, these hymns are about humility; that they help us to remember that each one of us is imperfect and that we need to open ourselves to divine correction. However, at that point in time, about the best that I could muster was to stay in my heart, to stay connected to the Divine, and to send my best wishes to all beings, in material form or not, all the while telling myself, *I'm fine to sing these hymns, if for no other reason than because singing them is what is expected—that's the ritual protocol.* Such ritual adaptability made a lot more sense to me than refusing to sing hymns that I had theological trouble with (and at that point I needed all the hymn singing that I could get!)

7

Mirações—Visionary/Mystical Experiences in the Santo Daime

A POWERFUL SERIES OF MIRAÇÕES

Earlier in this text I offered a neo-Jamesian outlook on the genesis of mirações. Nonetheless, there is a *lot* more that needs to be said about these subtle and deeply fascinating phenomena. However, before diving into the philosophical implications of mirações, I would like to offer an account of one extremely lengthy and powerful series of mirações that I had (or that had me!) a few years before I went to Céu do Mapiá.

I am not offering this account to imply that this type of experience is typical or common among daimistas. It's not. It's not even typical or common for me. I'm also not making any normative claims about how "high" or "low" these mirações were—the question of how to rank experiences, and by what criteria, and whether the very notion of ranking itself is helpful, will simply have to wait until later. But I want to offer a detailed description of one extremely memorable interconnected series of mirações to provide a robust, multifaceted, conglomeration of visionary/mystical material—as a neo-Jamesian, I think it's always a good idea to ground any/all theorizing in data that is as explicitly empirical as possible, with the provision, again following James, that our empiricism is open to visionary/mystical experiences as well as sense experiences and hence is a "radical" version of empiricism. The image I have is of a strong and broad tree trunk, made up of vivid, compelling depictions of visionary/mystical data that are enveloped by the lush, overlapping vine-like tendrils of ideas, questions, proposals, theories, and insights.

I should emphasize, however, that most daimistas tend to be rather reticent about sharing their mirações, and understandably: it probably *is* a good spiritual practice to treasure the sanctity and profundity of our spiritual experiences; to not casually throw them around; to not cheapen them by speaking of them carelessly or flippantly, especially if we are, knowingly or unknowingly, using our descriptions of these wondrous inner gifts as a way to subtly or not so subtly puff up our ego. But it has seemed clear to me from early on that a crucial aspect of what I am called to do when writing this book *is* to share some of these experiences with others and give these experiences a polished, crystalline "body" of words so that others can at least get a glimpse of what can, at least at times, take place within the consciousness of a daimista (or at least the consciousness of this one rather idiosyncratic daimista).

BEGINNING THE PROCESS OF TAKEOFF

Plunging right in, here's my only slightly edited account of these mirações (drawn from my "Daime Diary")—mirações that took place, interestingly, *after* the work was complete. In other words, they occurred when I was alone in the house of my hosts, dressed in my sweats instead of my farda, for the most part lying down curled up with one of my hosts' cats (Honey) snuggling up in the crook behind my knees, leaning softly into me.

Honey stayed there, for quite a long time, even as I was tensing up, bracing against the Force of the Daime that was still surging within me. I was shivering from my core. It was as if I was freezing cold, when in reality the room was, at most, only somewhat cool. Occasionally guttural groans and moans would emerge—involuntarily, almost spasmodically—from my chest, alternating with deep shuddering breaths.

Then, after a certain point, something shifted, and instead of bracing, I was suddenly able to relax—deeply, fully. It was almost as if I became physically paralyzed, but without any need or desire to move. And almost exactly at this point, right when I was somehow able to soften inside, and truly open myself to the Force, the Daime, with its impeccable timing, upped everything, dramatically, and the Force began to swell (and swell and swell) within me. I somehow knew that the Daime was beginning the initial process of "takeoff" and that the underlying and ever-building pressure of divine Light and Power that was cresting within me was simply the preparation for something Huge.

RELAXING INTO THE DAIME

I'm again struck by how often relaxation is the key to opening the door to receiving mirações.[1] In this case, it was almost as if my ability to let go of my previous knee-jerk hunkering down against the onslaught of the Force somehow gave permission to the Beings who were working in-and-with the Daime to powerfully up the wattage level of the experience, while simultaneously shifting the feeling-tone of that experience from "overwhelming too much-ness" to "radiantly accessible." I'm also fascinated by the interaction, in this case, between grace and self-effort: did my conscious intention to relax "open the valve" within me, letting grace pour in, or did grace itself, operating above/below the threshold of my conscious awareness, prompt/empower that (now suddenly possible) ability to relax? One way or the other, it is often the case that if and/or when I am able to relax/open/say *yes* within myself, the hell realm of nonspecific suffering that I had previously been experiencing will disappear and the same Force that I had previously attempted to repel will, all of a sudden, be welcomed by every cell of my body. It is as if my previous clamping down itself had been a type of visceral saying *no* to the Force that not only kept it from fully unfolding its Splendor but also, ironically, led to the very suffering that I had preconsciously been seeking to avoid via that tightening itself.

Sometimes, therefore, it does indeed seem that we can "stop" the Daime from unfurling within us by bracing against it—or conversely, with a shift of attitude, we can open the doors to what certainly can feel like higher/deeper levels of experience. It often does seem, therefore, that the Daime, at least at times, listens and responds to what we are asking for. Nonetheless, as any daimista knows, there are also times when our overt desires seem to have nothing to do with what is happening within us; times when the Daime is going to give us what it has to give us. There are moments when it's going to take us where it wants to take us— perhaps even opening the Gates of Heaven within. Nonetheless, I'd like to think that when we are given these wondrous unfoldings within us, it happens only after a *yes* on the highest levels of our being. I'd like to think that the Daime in this way respects, and in fact helps to manifest, our spiritual sovereignty. During those exalted moments, the deepest strata of our being—our "I Am Presence"— merges with the Daime itself. It is from this place of spiritual unity that Mestre Irienu said "The Daime is me, and I am the Daime";[2] it is in this place where our will, and the Will of God are one. In this place there is only the Christ Consciousness: radiant and resplendent.

ROCKETING INTO THE ASTRAL

Continuing on from my Daime Diary: *As the Daime opened—powerfully— within me, I just took off, soaring into the Astral.* [By the way, the term "the Astral" is simply the Santo Daime way to refer to a vast, multidimensional "realm" of nonphysical reality. I'm *not* using it in the way that theorists like Ken Wilber do to refer to only one, rather low-level, "layer" of that multifaceted spiritual "world."][3] *And merciful God, it was like: "Here we go!" I felt plugged in, just wired to the max, swept away in this rushing current of Light and Power. And I just dived into it, holding nothing back. It was just up, up, and away, and I was plunging into the cosmos; I was surging up and out into the infinite; I was inwardly cheering, jubilantly alive. I was a daimista space surfer, riding the undulating waves of the universe, given full permission to navigate those realms, to explore, to play.*

I was almost literally rocketing into the Astral. It felt like I was in some hyper-real science fiction movie. I was enclosed in something like a capsule, or some sort of high-tech subtle world space probe. It was like 2001: A Space Odyssey seen on acid, but this time I was not watching images on a screen. Instead, all of these surreal experiences were actually happening to me—they felt utterly real. And I somehow "real-ized" this fact with every fiber of my being.[4]

At one point I even remember laughing to myself, thinking "The Daime is just showing off!" There was just such an onrush of creative exuberance. It was like a peacock spreading its plumage for the sheer joy of doing so. Everything was high velocity and I was heading up, up, and away, entering into world after inner world. Nonetheless, I also increasingly became aware that I was not making this journey alone. Instead, I recognized, thankfully and joyously, that I was accompanied by several powerful and innately benevolent presences, Beings of Light who, in a way that transcended words, were willing and able to teach me how to consciously navigate the multiple worlds of the Astral, Beings who helped me to familiarize myself with the qualitatively unique textures of these different Astral worlds, and who, wordlessly but directly, facilitated and were present during the numerous interactions that I began to have with a whole slew of deeply fascinating beings who lived in these alternate dimensions of reality.

For example, at some point in my inner journeying, I became aware of this "demigod" (at least that's the title that I'm going to use). This being (let's call him Loki, the Nordic god of anarchical chaos, since he was clearly some sort of amped-up trickster god) was just so cocky, so full of pride. He possessed raw unfettered confidence; he crackled with Power and Light; and he was plunging gleefully through the cosmos, unimpeded, free, and alive. I was shown by my "guides" that this being was somewhat similar to what the Neoplatonists described as the "Powers and Principalities" in that it had a specific assigned task, and it was actually doing that crucially important work just by being itself. I was shown how even if, as often happens, Loki causes tremendous pain and hurt to erupt in our world with all of his careening through the cosmos like a manically gleeful pinball wizard, nonetheless, the Beings of Light gave Loki the freedom to create chaos, to stir things up. I was shown, to my amazement, how all of the suffering that we're experiencing at this time on Earth is actually arising in order to be seen, to be acknowledged, and to be forgiven and redeemed. I somehow Knew that, seen from the vantage point of a higher/deeper level of reality, what Loki was doing was completely perfect; it was all an expression of God's freedom and creativity; and even his cocky turbulence was part of the divine redemptive and transformative work.

I'm reminded here of another miração I had a year or so earlier than this series of mirações, in which I saw/felt Earth irradiated with Light. The impact of that intensity of Light and Presence was actually prompting foul black ooze to rise to the surface throughout the world, bubbling up subconscious layers of hate, fear, and ignorance that caused unimaginable suffering to all of us on Earth (manifesting as environmental degradation, political upheavals, and so on.) The Good News is that I was also shown that all of this darkness was arising in order to be transformed, to be turned into Light by the Light.

During all of this "Loki download," I wasn't watching everything take place from a far-removed distance. Instead, the boundaries between myself and this being kept blending and separating, and my consciousness, as well as, more subtly, my sense of identity itself, kept morphing, kept shifting its boundaries. I watched, from some deeper place within me, fascinated, as I was, as it were, hitching a ride with Loki, the "two-as-one'" of us taking the form of this rough, wild, and free "biker of the astral"; the "two-as-one" of us surging utterly uninhibited through huge black storm clouds, as well as through vast stretches of space dotted with shining stars.

At other times the two of us semi-separated and I was something closer to Loki's "biker-chick" (but without any of the gender-reversals that this title might imply)— my arms wrapped around his waist (subtle beings can have waists!) as I rode behind him, feeling the rush of speeding forward in delight as the two of us soared and roared through the cosmos, brilliant crystalline colors streaming off on both sides and behind us like a comet's tail, both of us laughing with fierce abandon at the pleasure that was surging up within—the pleasure of possessing raw, untamed, and unleashed Power.

Amazingly, at least to me, throughout the whole time that I was, "superimposed" upon Loki, another dimension of my consciousness was simultaneously present, in which I was resting, without thought, in a very open, spacious state of being, filled with deep peace, calm, clarity, and compassion. And from that "place" of seemingly boundless compassion, stirred by the immense suffering I was feeling from the earth, I "spoke" to Loki, "telling" him: "Let's just take some breaths, OK? Calma. Calma. Let's just calm everything down a little." Even as I was giving Loki the space and freedom to be who he was, at the same time I was radiating out a soothing, gentle, tempering, maternal energy (at this point "I" was strongly identified with/supported by/infused with the Divine Mother, or some divine female Being), and I somehow just knew, on some nonverbal level, that this energy of Peace that "I" was transmitting to Loki would, in important ways, ripple out and down, and have a beneficial effect on the sufferings of our world.

I had an "echo" of that encounter a few years later during an informal healing work in Padrinho Alfredo's home toward the end of my stay in Céu do Mapiá. His family had been going through some painful struggles, and I felt honored to be invited to participate in this extremely intimate *Cura*, or healing work, with his family. At one point during the work I had a vivid miração of a being that felt something like a lower octave of Loki's trickster energy— the leering, long, gaunt, maniacal face of this being reminded me quite a bit of the Green Goblin from the Spiderman movies: cackling with glee; charged with energy; entranced with and exulting in his own power; flying through the inner "skies" with an almost (perhaps literally) fiendish delight. That Green Goblin being kept "banging into" the Sphere of Light I was resting in, almost as if he was trying to frighten me, in order to create a fissure in that Sphere so that he could "get at" me. But I simply kept calm and centered and in my heart and radiated the energy of blessing (and even at times, the energy of amused appreciation) to that being. Neither the Green Goblin nor Loki seemed evil to me. Rather, they felt utterly amoral, even if, underneath it all, they were also part of a deeper underlying Perfection.

At some point during my interactions with Loki, I began to laugh, because I was rapidly becoming convinced that these miraçoes were giving me a whirlwind turn of a level of archetypal reality that I was convinced was the ontological source for many (most?) comic book characters and superheroes—the "realm" that various writers for

Marvel comics often psychedelically, tapped into when they were creating.[5] (At one point during this part of my journeying I even reached out energetically to my friend Jeff Kripal, sending him my appreciation and gratitude for all of the insights that his work on the psychedelic and paranormal origins of comic books had given me.) Skyrocketing through those realms felt like I was inhabiting a comic book that had come to life; or as if, as I mentioned earlier, I had been inserted into the middle of a science fiction or fantasy movie. Everything was filled with drama, intensity, color, verve, and a whole cast of vivid and eye-catching characters.

At some point, having left "Loki" far behind, I began to enter into new "dimensions" of this flux of pulsating beauty and ever-new sensations (at one point I remember touching, with great reverence, the throbbing, living walls of the Divine Womb of creation itself). On some faraway level of my being, as all of those Astral fireworks were taking place, I was also vaguely aware that I was physically lying there on the bed, feeling flattened by the Force. And every now and then I'd mumble out loud: "I say yes" (while simultaneously "shouting" it out within), and that reaffirmation of my ongoing intention to give myself as fully as possible to the Force helped to anchor me.

Buoyed up and propelled by that rather relentless torrent of ongoing mirações, I nonetheless felt extremely present. I was not swept away, but rather, I felt focused and deeply centered—maintaining (easily, naturally) an ongoing awareness of what was occurring, moment by moment, even as the mirações kept unfurling within me. Again and again, I found myself keenly aware of the interactive nature of what I was experiencing, knowing that these mirações were manifesting, in my consciousness, in a way that drew upon my own cultural background, my philosophical education, my spiritual training. (In a sort of meta-moment, I realized that even this realization itself would most likely only happen within someone with my level of academic preparation.) I was conscious of how I was helping to shape the experiences, and/or how I called them to me, and/or how those experiences emerged as various levels of astral reality were attuning themselves with the utterly unique energetic configuration of who I was at that moment. Throughout it all, I was very clear that I was not just passively receiving something outside myself, something ready-made and stable that was simply sitting there waiting for me to discover it. And yet, it was also clear to me that those levels of experience really did exist, outside my typical conscious awareness—that they were not in any way my own arbitrary subjective creation. Instead, I was crystal clear, right in the middle of these mirações themselves, that I was taking part in a highly interactive, deeply participatory, process, a process in which the inside and outside merged and separated; a process through which previously unimaginable levels of experience and insight (and wonder and delight!) were ceaselessly and freely being created.

In addition, as all of this was happening, I was consciously, intentionally, attempting to engrave everything that I was experiencing into my memory, because from multiple past experiences with the Daime, I knew that it was highly likely that I would, at best, be able to retain only a fragment of what was unfolding within me. And so, in order to have the best possible chance to remember as much as I could within all of this high-intensity "all-at-once-ness," I (at least implicitly, albeit rather forcefully) told myself: "Notice how real (hyperreal!), how vivid (hyper-vivid!) this moment is. Notice how pristine and radiant your consciousness is right now. Pay attention to the minute specificities of what is happening, right here, right now, in this level of reality." I was giving myself this inner pep talk because I knew, from multiple past experiences with the Daime, that later, after emerging from these mirações, most of what I had experienced so vividly would appear almost unreal; it would feel vague and dream-like and distant, an insubstantial wisp of memory that would all too quickly fade in comparison to the solid facticity of my everyday waking life. I also knew that my current level of neurochemical (and energetic) "wiring" simply wouldn't be able to retain those memories, since the startlingly new events that were unfurling within my consciousness simply had no one-to-one correspondence with any nameable event that I had previously experienced in my ordinary existence. Nonetheless, I also knew that my efforts to keep myself poised, alert, and attentive were not in any way wasted; I somehow knew that my ongoing intentional attempts to remember what was taking place were themselves an integral, indeed crucial, phase of my inner training.

At this point I would say that training myself to remember extremely rarified levels of mirações was, itself, part of a wider and deeper transfiguration: the subconscious/trans-conscious creation of a higher-level subtle body. In order for "me" to enter and explore, with full awareness, some of these preexisting, high-frequency archetypal realms of being, my vibratory matrix first had to be readjusted.[6] This was a quite complex and lengthy process, one that was assisted by my subtle-world guides, in which I repeatedly and joyously said *yes* to and consciously synced with subtle energetic levels of my selfhood that were apparently "waiting in the wings" in those higher dimensions for me to reclaim them. Once I accomplished this task, I was no longer "Bill Barnard" as I entered into those often overtly heavenly realms. Instead, I was a "higher octave" of myself, a centered matrix of consciousness that "fit" the energetic parameters of the world that I was entering into and engaging with. I was also shown that this reconfiguration and upgrade of my energetic matrix would allow me not only to journey in those realms, but also to create and sustain a trans-dimensional doorway that increasingly would permit ongoing cross-communication between those high-level, hyperreal dimensions or levels of consciousness that were always active above my normal awareness and the steady, dependable, quotidian events that were taking place in my ordinary world.[7]

There were several distinct time periods within this onrush of miraçōes in which I would take a breath; I would recenter and reorient within myself, making sure that I was consciously going for the deepest and the highest dimensions that were possible. I'd return, again and again, to my heart; I'd link up with God, with my own divine nature; I would set my intention: "I want God; I want enlightenment; I want awakening—not only for myself, but for all sentient beings." (Hurrah for the bodhisattva vow!) And again and again, the clarity and force of that intention helped to ground me in the moment; it helped to orient me in the swirling "much-ness" of the torrential river of miraçōes that I was navigating.

And the Daime responded to that high-level intention, joyfully carrying me deeper, farther, opening up numerous portals into different Astral, and at times heavenly, worlds. One of the most memorable "shifts in scene" in that archetypal reality was when, like the crippled doctor who, at least in the mythological world-view of Marvel comics, hits his cane and is magically transformed into the Norse god Thor, I also underwent a sudden and dramatic transformation, in which, simi-larly, I was suddenly able (at last!) to remember my divine origins.[8] I was (finally!) able to return home; I was, with the grace of the divine Beings, permitted to journey higher, entering into overtly godlike dimensions of reality. And I was able to revel in what I was beginning to discover.

At one point, I entered into one these realms and discovered, to my joy and amazement, that I was a prodigal Son returning back to his rightful kingdom, liter-ally stepping through a golden gate made of the Light of Sacrality itself. And when I entered within, I was greeted with a massive and joyous roar of celebration by the Beings who belonged there, as I was bathed in and was uplifted by the waves of Love that flowed from them to me, and from me to them. And then a surge of celestial jubilation erupted as I—with joy and utterly at ease—stepped fully and willingly into my Sonship and claimed my divine heritage.

(As Mestre Irineu's hymn 113, "I Follow in This Truth," says, probably echo-ing and transmitting a similar experience, "When I arrived in this house, they gave me a roar of applause. / My leader received me, the owner of the whole empire.")

I know that I have only retained in my conscious memory the barest outlines of what actually occurred during this close-to-final sequence of inner events that took place during this torrent of miraçōes. But I have deep faith that on another level of my being, those higher dimensions are always available to me, that in fact, I am *always* there. As are we all. The ongoing sense I have received from drinking Daime is that we're all divine beings who have forgotten our true heritage as Daughters and Sons of God and the Divine Mother, and we are all also, miraculously, simultaneously, already being welcomed Home. (As Mestre Irineu's hymn 119, "Trust" says: "This is the golden salão of our True Father. / All of us are sons and daughters and all of us are heirs.") And so, each of us in a unique way and with unique timing, is increasingly able to remember more of his or her True Nature. Certainly for daimistas, little by little, at least in part through the influx of Light that can and does arrive, in just the right time, in just the right way, through powerful miraçães, the Daime as the Master Musician plays differing permutations of the melodic phrases of "Awakening" and "Divinization" over and over again within us. And over time, we are increasingly able to open up to our Christic nature; over time, we are able to begin learning our own unique ways to "just say *yes*" to what it means to be a true human being, to be a full-grown Daughter or Son of God; over time, we are increasingly able to let the Power, Truth, and Holiness of the higher dimensions pour through us, with increasingly fewer obstructions and distortions—dimensions that are illuminating our everyday existence here in this world.

At some point around 9:00 p.m. (the work had ended around 5:00 p.m., so I had been "traveling" for almost four hours), I managed to actually surface, rising up from under the covers on the bed. And then, still reeling in the Force, I carefully made my way into the living room. As I slowly moved forward, step by tentative step, I kept seeing a multitude of afterimages of my hand/arm as it moved through space, almost as if I was seeing the movie reel of perception itself shuddering. Thin and intense "lines" or "cracks" kept appearing and disappearing in my visual field, as if the world of my perception was about to break open under the intensity of the Force. It felt as if my whole external world was shimmering and subtly shaking, and this energetic throbbing was accompanied by a very high-pitched vibratory thrum, a thrum that I could hear not with my ears, but rather heard from inside—a type of sonic reverb, a high-frequency overtone entering in from the margins of perception and then surging back, as if it were a vibratory waveform of sound before sound itself.

I somehow managed to make my way into the kitchen, and washed a handful of cherries, and sat upright in the couch, abstractedly eating them one by one. The cherries tasted almost unreal, waxy, as if I was eating them from a distance. I then

FIGURE 7.1 Sandra's mandala

tried my best to sit up, get a bit more grounded before I talked on the phone with my wife.

(Several hours earlier, in the middle of that torrential onslaught of miraçōes, I had "reached out" from within to my wife Sandra, and almost immediately, this extremely beautiful, pulsing, organically cohesive, mandala-like form of swirling vibrant colors appeared, blessing me with its Presence, and I somehow knew that I was being given the gift of seeing the radiance of her spiritual/Astral body. Years later I had a skilled artist paint a mandala for her that at least approximated the energy/beauty of that encounter. It now hangs in her office.)

The next morning, after I woke up, I was still feeling quite tired, as if on some level I was quivering from the aftershock of the spiritual tsunami I had undergone the day before. Nonetheless, I also felt cleansed and flushed out, as if some sort of cosmic Roto-Rooter had washed out all of the psychic debris from the inside of my energetic channels. I also discovered that I had lost two pounds.

THEORETICAL REFLECTIONS ON MIRAÇÕES

Again, I have described these mirações, because, like James, I believe that a careful examination of magnified and heightened levels of experience can be helpful in my attempts to relay an accurate and inclusive sense of the depth and range of visionary/mystical experiences—that is, to begin to make sense of realms of experience that are found far beyond the limits of our typical, rather truncated and pedestrian, conscious experience.[9]

Nonetheless, I want to emphasize that most people (again, myself included) don't typically tend to have such prolonged or numerous mirações during Santo Daime works. If mirações do occur, they usually tend to last for only relatively brief periods of time. (I would guess most of my mirações typically last, at most, for only a couple of minutes.) And again, mirações can also often feel rather evanescent—more like fleeting glimpses (as if "seen through a glass darkly") of Something More rather than a full-fledged immersion into higher levels of consciousness. It is often as if we are only catching the faintest glimmers from the corner of our inner eyes of levels of reality that remain tantalizingly hidden from our sight.[10] I even know several long-term daimistas who have *never* had any mirações, as well as other daimistas whose mirações have been extremely sporadic and were not really all that crucial to their spiritual lives. (I know for myself that there have been many works in which, after the work was over, I was glowing with gratitude at the transformative power and beauty of what I went through in the salão—all without having experienced a single miração.)

But I can almost guarantee you that *all* daimistas will have felt the Force—often, and powerfully. They will have experienced that feeling of being plugged into Something More, that tangibly felt awareness of a Power that surges through the physical body that is almost always there during a work. Nonetheless, even here, there are exceptions. There are some works in which the Force can feel rather mild, even if you drink a *lot* of Daime, and conversely, there are some works in which just a sip can send you flying. Drinking the Daime is not like taking, let's say, insulin. There simply is not a one-to-one, predictable, causal relationship between dosage and level of experience. Although dosage (and set and setting) are clearly factors that influence the depth and quality of a daimista's experience, clearly Something Else is also at work: the Daime Itself, understood in this case as a divine Power of infinite Intelligence that has its own clear sense of what is needed within each person who drinks it.

Furthermore, during most works, most daimistas, especially those who have been around for a while, are able to function quite efficiently; most daimistas, even if they are feeling the Force quite strongly, will typically perceive more or less the same world that someone who has not drunk Daime sees—there are rarely dramatic external shifts in the way in which daimistas before, during, and after a work perceive the world around them. In other words, I don't know too many daimistas who have seen purple elephants dancing in the corner or any of the other frightening or silly images used to portray psychedelic perceptions of the external world. The primary difference when someone has drunk Daime is that her or his perceptions are usually overlaid with the visceral feeling of the Force.

Admittedly, there are also, at least occasionally, moments in which daimistas will perceive alterations in the external world (such as during the miração that I just described, where I saw afterimages of my hand/arm when I finally got up from the bed). Another "open-eyed" miração that I have experienced somewhat often is the transfiguration of the world around me, when everything feels saturated with Significance, Sacredness, and Presence. I vividly remember during one work in Mapiá, I was looking out over the waist-high wall of the men's Daime serving wing during the interval. Then, almost as if a veil had been lifted, I suddenly felt as if I could finally see everything as it truly was: charged with sacred Significance, transfigured, overtly holy, radiant, and calmly resplendent. In the distance, women in their fardas were walking up the wide white-tiled walkway that led to Madrinha Rita's house, and as they passed through the open wooden gates, it was as if I was perceiving a terrestrial echo of the gates of heaven. There was an air of hushed reverence to the scene, and yet everyone was also utterly at ease. I had this achingly powerful sense of nostalgia; the almost-grasped, yet fleeting memory of entering into Paradise—a world where we all belong, completely; a world of beauty and peace that is our true and natural home, now and always.

And so, daimistas rarely (if ever?) have hallucinations. That is, their perceptions do not become pathologically distorted, rendering them incapable of distinguishing what is illusory from what is real—a reality that most people tacitly assume to be a stable, objective, external world made of insentient particles/energy that obeys the rules of Newtonian physics; a world that can, at least for the most part, be publicly verified via the perceptions of one's waking consciousness. Instead, daimistas, at least at times, can and do experience and feel profoundly blessed and transformed by miraçōes: again, a range of often spectacularly vivid, powerfully convincing, innately true feeling, visionary (and/or auditory, gustatory, olfactory, etc.) experiences; encounters with levels of reality (often filled with nonphysical beings) that often feel, if anything, *more* real than our ordinary experiences of the physical world. And, by the way, most of these mirações happen with closed eyes. They are primarily experiences that arise deep within the inner recesses of a daimista's consciousness and emerge in a way that does not—at least in any obvious way—depend upon the activity of the sense organs.

MIRAÇÕES AS POTENTIALLY VALUABLE SPIRITUAL GIFTS

I think that it is quite likely that many, if not most people, drink Daime, at least initially, to have mirações. The possibility of having powerful visionary/mystical experiences almost on demand can be, to put it mildly, quite tantalizing. I would be the first to say that a daimista needs to be careful to not become attached to having mirações. (Later on I'll say more about the dangers of "spiritual materialism.") Nonetheless, I also do not think that mirações should be considered unimportant or utterly irrelevant to our spiritual lives. (I think, for example, that some Zen Buddhists make this mistake with their frequent dismissal of visionary experiences as illusory and/or distracting *makyo*.[11]) Paying attention to mirações, if done skillfully, can actually be a wonderful way to immerse ourselves in the richness of the ongoing and flowing present moment (when else could mirações possibly arise?). In fact, mirações do not necessarily take us away from reality, as much as they enrich and deepen our experience of what reality actually is, under the surface. Valuing mirações does not necessarily mean that we're attempting to run away from the difficulties of life (although there's nothing wrong with an occasional vacation) or that we're necessarily becoming entranced by what we are often told is the ultimately superfluous and gaudy flash and glitter of low-level visionary experiences (for some spiritual thinkers, it is almost as if anything less than completely merging with the Absolute is hardly worth bothering with).

Instead, I think that mirações are perhaps best understood as gifts—and why in the world would we be so rude as to ignore a gift so lovingly given? Or they can be thought of as blessings raining down upon us from some hidden Source or as episodic infusions of grace. Mirações, understood in this way, are vivid, energizing, and meaningful glimpses of levels of reality that are in striking contrast to the prosaic, often gray and lifeless perceptual world in which many (most?) people live. Mirações can give us hope; they can enliven our spiritual practice and kindle our longing for communion/union with the divine; they can show us—directly, immediately, forcefully—just how multidimensional the universe actually is; they can offer us convincing and intriguing encounters with numerous spectacularly wild, weird, and wonderful beings; they can energize and reconfigure our subtle bodies so that we can, over time, become increasingly transparent channels of Love and Light (and a host of other divine qualities); and at their best, miraçôes can open us up, repeatedly, in numerous different ways, to powerful, awe-inspiring, and even life-altering experiences of our Oneness with, and even identity with, divinity.

I would suggest that, as daimistas, there are many times in which it can be difficult to say whether what we just experienced was a "miração" or whether we had a mediumistic experience. Typically, miraçôes are thought of as moments in which we "go up" and, like shamans, travel in various Astral dimensions, whereas mediumship is typically thought of as the descent of nonphysical beings into the body/mind (aparelho) of the medium. But it seems clear to me that this up/down way of thinking is much too simplistic. I would propose, instead, that we think of spiritual experiences with the Daime as an interactive flux of spiritual bidirectionality. To give just one example: Let's "envision" a shining, iridescent green lady as she "descends" into your field of consciousness, filling your body and mind with Her Presence. In this quasi-mediumistic phase of the experience, you feel yourself infused with divinity, filled with joy and awe as She bestows Her grace upon you. Then, however, through the blessings of that grace itself, you feel yourself almost literally lifted up, expanding beyond any prior sense of confinement within your physical form. In this miração-esque phase of the experience, you find yourself soaring in the Astral, washed by wave after wave of golden Light and bathing in Her Love. And so, how can we best categorize the totality that experience when examined as a whole? Was it mediumship or was it a miração? Or was it both? And if so, did this bothness happen sequentially or simultaneously? Or was that experience beyond either category?

Therefore, I think that our understanding of who we are and what reality actually is can deepen enormously if we take the time to examine miraçôes carefully. But I also think that it is crucial to recognize the inability of our words and theories to reflect fully and accurately what miraçôes can reveal.

There have been times during some powerful miraçōes when I've felt like a goldfish that has been scooped out of the comforting confines of my prior goldfish-bowl world. There I'll be, flopping and wiggling in response to all of that overwhelming too-much-ness, just shaken to my core by the ontological immensity, wonder, and strangeness that I'm so forcefully encountering. And when I'm finally put back into my so well-known and comforting goldfish bowl, with its plastic sand floor, plastic castle, and plastic palm tree, the contrast between those two qualities of experience can be quite dramatic and at times somewhat disorienting. I might try to knit my world back together again with the help of words or labels, but time and time again I have been struck by the impossibility of saying anything, no matter how elegant or well-crafted the language, that even comes close to fully and accurately representing the rich complexity, beauty, and sacredness of what these miraçōes can reveal with such convincing force and immediacy.

> James is famous for listing "ineffability" (along with "noetic quality," "transiency," and "passivity") as one of the major qualities of a mystical experience. And in this way, I'm clearly a Jamesian—or at the very least, a neo-Jamesian.

Nonetheless, the relationship between spiritual experiences and our ideas about spiritual experiences is enormously complex, and I think that we are well served by looking closely at this intricate interweaving of "raw" experience and our ideas about our experience (we're back, yet again, to the Jamesian relationship between knowledge-by-acquaintance and knowledge-about.)

To begin with, I think that it actually *is* wonderful, in the right context, with the right attitude, to attempt to communicate to others as clearly, accurately, and sincerely as possible what we have experienced; to share, from our hearts, the intricacies, the complexities, the sheer beauty of these visionary/mystical experiences. Talking or writing about our miraçōes can be a rich and rewarding way to share our gratitude, to reveal our bewilderment, to express our wonder, to help us overcome our doubts and confusion. This type of communication can also nurture a profoundly intimate connection to others, one that is based on shared values and uplifting ways of understanding who we are and why we are here. And this includes talking about our miraçōes and the questions they raise for us in ways that are thoughtful, inquisitive, humble, and vulnerable. For much too long our culture has muzzled us, it has convinced us that if we talk freely and openly with others about profound and deeply intimate experiences that we'll either be ignored or mocked. And so, let's have the courage to break free from the shackles of our culturally engrained fear of speaking, ideally with subtlety and insight, about the depths and nuances of our nonordinary states of consciousness. Let's come out of the closet as real-deal visionaries and mystics.

Thoughtful and heartfelt words about our spiritual experiences can, at their best, be powerful gifts to ourselves and to others. They can act as linguistic life-lines to Something More; they can help us to reconnect energetically with the Source of our visionary/mystical experience; they can become channels through which the transformative Power and Beauty that we have experienced in, for example, our miraçōes, can once again flow. Our thoughtful and heartfelt words/ideas in this way can not only, at least to a certain extent, accurately reflect the contours of even subtle states of consciousness, but they can also—magically—help to cocreate, to generate, and to shape levels of consciousness that were previously inaccessible to us. Communicating in a clear, open, and connected way can itself become a magic carpet that we and others can ride back to those deeper and higher dimensions of reality and selfhood that were once, and still are, our spiritual home. Inspired and inspiring ruminations about our miraçōes (as well as visionary/mystical experiences more generally) can help us to link up with that vibratory Influx that the miraçōes (and other spiritual experiences) themselves originally emerged from and that they carried with them. In this way, thoughtful, heartfelt, and inspired words can, as it were, transcend themselves and become translucent windows through which Something Real can shine.

At the same time, it is also true that even if we are speaking and/or writing with as much clarity of mind as possible, even if we are as spiritually tuned in as possible—even with all of that—ineffability remains, at least for me. There simply is a radical divide between the quality and depth of what I experience in powerful miraçōes and the ability of *any* words to communicate accurately and fully the profundity of that quality of experience. And I think that this "inevitability of ineffability" is itself rooted in something deeper, something ontological, in that (and I'm consciously aware of the paradox of talking about ineffability) there's always something More to what is Ultimately Real. There is an inherently transcendent "beyondness" to the divine nature, something that cannot be captured by any words, any images, any ideas, no matter how beautiful, persuasive, or complex. In this way, it is good to remain keenly aware of the limitations of words, as well as their potential magical power to shape and cocreate countless worlds of experience.

MAPS OF SPIRITUAL PROGRESS

In my own attempts to use words in a way that is illuminative and fruitful, I would like to begin with a nod of appreciation to theorists such as Ken Wilber, Stanislav Grof, and others, who have created carefully reasoned and clearly articulated "maps" of various "levels" of nonordinary states of consciousness.[12] We find in their work precise descriptions of discrete stages of the spiritual journey inward (for example, the movement from "psychic" levels to "subtle" levels, to "causal" levels). We find clearly delineated steps on the "ladder" of spiritual experiences, each one higher than the next, each stage thoughtfully constructed from a comparative analysis of visionary/mystical states drawn from numerous mystical traditions. These various maps offer us useful analytical markers by which we can better understand what it means to progress spiritually toward increasingly subtle and more profound states and stages of spiritual experience.

Wilber's and Grof's work (albeit differing on various details) offers a helpful starting point for those of us who think that there might well be meaningful underlying patterns to be discovered in the rich profusion of visionary/mystical experiences that have occurred across history, in various cultural settings, and (in the case of Grof's work especially) that have been accessed with the assistance of entheogens. Nonetheless, I also have to say that I'm rather wary of any overly tidy analytical categorization and ranking of visionary/mystical experiences. (In this way I'm like James again. At one point he wrote that when he read the highly rational, architectonically precise theoretical systems of some of his philosophical colleagues, he felt like his collar was tightening around his neck.)

I have to admit: my experience of the Daime doesn't seem to fit all that well within the theoretical confines of any of these explanatory systems. The Daime, perhaps in part because it emerges from the florid hyper-abundance of the rain forest, is much "wilder," much less predictable than what we would expect from these theories. There is a sort of rough around the edges, quasi-anarchic quality to the Daime wherein almost anything (or nothing) can happen during a work. There are so many sudden switches and reversals to the way mirações emerge and unfold from work to work, if they even arise at all, to say nothing of the frequently rather dramatic movements to and from different levels of experience/reality within each work itself—and the ways in which mirações can blend together differing "levels" of experience into one complex whole—that it can at times be hard to see how useful these much more static and carefully delineated maps of inner experience actually are.

For example, during a Santo Daime work, I might be writhing in intense suffering—albeit a suffering that is undergirded by a vast Presence of kindness and compassion—and then boom! Suddenly my eyes are rolling back at the joy I'm feeling as I'm singing a new hymn and I'm feeling almost literally uplifted as the Force surges powerfully within me as I stand upright, my arms raised upward in praise and gratitude as golden Light pours in-and-through me and then— boom! We begin to sing a new hymn, and I'll make my way back to my seat, and my mind is profoundly quiet, while the golden Light continues to suffuse my inner sight and I'm leaning back within myself into a vast spacious Openness and Love.

It is difficult to say how these various states of consciousness, differing as they do from one another and emerging and then shifting rather rapidly within the temporal flux of a work and often arising with various categorical levels superim- posed upon one another (e.g. the subtle golden Light blending seamlessly with the causal Openness and Love), can be meaningfully said to be higher or lower than what had come before. In fact, I'm not convinced that making that assess- ment really matters, at least in the short term.

Nonetheless, I very much believe that spiritual growth is possible (as long as we recognize that assessing that growth is a complicated issue, since as James would say, these assessments are always made "on the whole" and over the long run).[13] I also believe that we can and should think clearly about what some of the indicators of that growth actually are. And to me, one of the key signs of spiritual progress is the ability to give ourselves fully to what is emerging, sponta- neously, from the divine Center. It is the ever-deepening ability to celebrate *each* quality of spiritual experience as qualitatively unique, unrepeatable, and simply what is—each moment of experience a perfect manifestation of the Buddha nature, the ongoing flow of Suchness, the birthing forth of the Mother. Unlike the implicit (or explicit!) understanding that time spent in the causal level of reality/experience (for example, resting in a formless state of Knowing divinity by being divinity) is somehow innately and always superior to time spent in the psychic level of reality (for example, interacting in mediumistic ways with suffer- ing spirits), from the perspective that I'm endorsing here—let's call it "equality consciousness"—there is no "better" or "worse" state of experience; nothing is inherently higher or lower. More and more it seems to me that whatever quality of experience that emerges naturally within the Force is perfect, just as it is; it is exactly what should be happening in that moment. (Actually, more inclusively, whatever quality of experience that emerges, period, Force or no Force, is exactly as it should be.)

And to possess the deep faith that whatever the Daime is bringing to us, and to everyone in the salão, is exactly what is needed in that moment, can trans- form everything. Then, if we find ourselves immersed in interpenetrating fields of dense, gnarly, and contracted energy, instead of wishing we were somewhere else (or someone else), instead of longing for some prior state of Light-Filled Causal Emptiness, we can give ourselves fully to what actually *has* been given to us. We can see that experience of suffering as an opportunity to open our hearts, to offer compassion. We can recognize those periods of suffering as a chance to assist in the Christic work of transmuting dense dark energies into Light, instead of wishing that we could fly away into the subtle heavenly realms in an attempt, usually hidden even from ourselves, to escape from the suffering that we were feeling so strongly.

However, if the Daime *does* end up carrying us to those heavenly realms, then hallelujah. I have to admit that if I'm in a state of union with God/the Goddess; if I am glorying in my divine creative capacity to effortlessly and joyfully body-forth my own being in-and-as extremely rarified and utterly Beautiful Cosmic patterns of Light, Love, and divine Presence—well, that quality of experience does indeed seem to be innately higher or deeper than the quality of experience that takes the form of, for example, aching and moaning in response to an ongoing influx of diffuse, dark, and dense contracted energies of sheer, unremitting suffering.

Let's just say that I'm a "both/and" sort of person. From one point of view, there is no higher/lower, and everything is the absolutely perfect expression of the divine, everything is simply the unfurling of another beautiful petal of the lotus of the spiritual life. On the other hand, I think that it is important to affirm that we actually can and do develop spiritually; that our hard work really matters; that there actually are states of consciousness (corresponding to ontological realms of being) that are higher or better than our ordinary levels of awareness in this realm of illusion, separation, and suffering. Therefore, personally, I prefer my metaphysics, as James would put it, a little "loose-limbed." I'm fine with a little ontological/cosmological messiness in my theoretical constructs. Life almost always, it seems to me, breaks the bounds of any overly tidy philosophical systems. Our lived experience rarely fits "just so" within the confines of our self-created linguistic/cognitive/theoretical boxes.

"DIABOLICAL MYSTICISM"

Given all of these caveats, I am willing (again, in a loose-limbed sort of way) to create some "good-enough" analytical categories of various types of miraçōes—to articulate a categorization that is not simply a phenomenology of visionary/

mystical experiences (that is, an analysis that is not just a neutral listing of different patterns of experience), but which also, at least implicitly, offers a "soft-edged" normative assessment of their positions on a hierarchical ladder of visionary/mystical experiences. (James had his ladder of mystical experiences, I have mine.[14])

But before I move onto this ladder, I want to say something about the apparent similarities between the visions of someone who is severely mentally ill—visions that in certain respects resemble, in a fractured funhouse-mirror sort of way, the visionary/mystical experiences that appear higher on the ladder. (James evocatively referred to the visionary experiences of the mentally-ill as "diabolical mysticism."[15]) A schizophrenic, for example, might see visions, or hear voices, or feel energy moving within. However, these often quite powerful and convincing inner visionary (or tactile, auditory, and so on) experiences typically come interwoven with complicated and knotted strands of that person's unresolved fear, anger, or grandiosity. And so, while these experiences might *seem* similar to "authentic" visionary/mystical experiences, they are actually quite different.

However, I would suggest that it is also quite possible that some, if not all, of the visionary experiences of those suffering from severe mental illness, as distorted and pain-filled as these experiences often are, might well contain elements of something "more." That is, I think that someone who is suffering from a severe mental illness might well, in reality, be extremely sensitive and open to psychic or subtle or causal levels of consciousness/reality. However, I would further suggest that the powerful energies and insights that can stream into the consciousness of individuals who are suffering from psychosis can, at least typically, only arise into awareness after going through the heartbreakingly difficult to cope with distortions of that individual's psyche, resulting, for example, in leering diabolical faces where there might once have been visions of benevolent and beautiful deities and persecutory and demeaning voices where there once might have been words of comfort and love.

My wife and I witnessed the complicated overlap between schizophrenic delusions and visionary/mystical experiences many years ago in a woman who was a regular member of our meditation community. This experienced and openhearted meditator would often, like many of us in that community, feel a powerful energy moving through her; or she would feel trustworthy guidance arising from some ineffable Source; or she would sense the presence of numerous nonphysical beings radiating blessings in the meditation hall. However, within a highly compressed phase of time, this woman went through a period of enormous stress when, among other things, she lost a stable and well-paying job that she enjoyed and she broke up with her long-time lover. Pushed over the edge by these and other traumatic events, her "visionary" life changed.

Now instead of hearing the soothing and loving voice of the Divine Mother, she began to hear persecutory voices telling her how worthless she was and how little other people were to be trusted. Now, instead of feeling a gentle nudge from within to call up a friend to enquire how they were doing, she felt compelled by the hateful voices she was hearing to make dramatic public declarations of her "profound" insights. Now she felt impelled to perform actions that debased herself, in order to clearly show everyone just how worthless (and yet simultaneously Chosen) she truly was. (For example, one day she showed up unexpectedly at the door of the carriage house where my wife and I lived, completely disheveled and distraught, wearing only one shoe, and pushing a grocery cart filled with trash. We later discovered that the walls of her apartment were smeared with her own excrement.)

The intersection between the visionary/mystical experiences of daimistas (and, more generally, those who take entheogens regularly) and the highly charged nonphysical perceptions of individuals who are suffering from severe mental illness is extremely multilayered and nuanced, and I am unable to adequately deal with this complex and delicate topic here. However, at the very least, I think that it is crucial that we do not attempt to understand miraçōes through the lens of pathology. There is a qualitative difference between the internal projections of unresolved/raw psychic material that people suffering from severe mental illness have to deal with and the profound visionary/mystical experiences that can arise within daimistas. Just because people who take psychedelic substances can often and powerfully see visions, or hear voices, or feel attuned to inner guidance, and/or sense pulsations of energy coursing in-and-through their bodies, these nonphysical experiences are *not* (at least necessarily) indications of mental illness, especially if these individuals, as is usually the case, are otherwise high-functioning people. (In fact, I would say, speaking personally, that most of the daimistas that I know are *more* high functioning—clearer, more hard-working, more loving—than the majority of mainstream Americans.)

Nonetheless, as a way to show just how complicated this issue can be, it is not uncommon for daimistas (and others who use entheogens regularly) to spend many, many works actively attempting to consciously address and to transmute an enormous amount of extremely challenging and difficult to bear intrapsychic material that they can find arising within their psyches. Daimistas will often work with this dense and contracted subconscious material with the faith that all of this inner "gunk" is emerging within them in order to be transformed, and that inner attitude makes all the difference. It can at times be exceedingly difficult for those who are suffering from severe mental illness to extricate themselves from

insidious "loops" of highly negative thinking, even as they will often, simultaneously, deny that they are in need of any psychological healing; whereas daimistas
who are taking on the crucially important, yet extremely taxing work of healing
themselves on all levels, for the most part are actively and consciously working
to address these issues within themselves, *and* they are, at least typically, rooted
in the awareness that this transformative process itself is catalyzed and skillfully
guided by the divine Light and Love that is embodied within the Daime itself.
And how we choose to interpret and deal with the subconscious psychic material
brought up/amplified by the Daime makes all the difference to our mental/emo-
tional health, both within works and in our daily lives.

During the orientations that are given to people who are interested in participating in a work with one of the North American churches of the Santo
Daime, potential participants are asked if they have struggled with severe
mental illness in the past. If they say *yes*, then they are informed (hopefully as
gently as possible) that the Daime is not appropriate for them. (For more on
these orientations, see "Santo Daime Churches in North America" at www
.liquidlightbook.com/northamerica.) I have to say that I agree with this pru-
dent restriction on who can and should participate in Santo Daime works.
While the Daime, at least anecdotally, appears to be tremendously helpful
for individuals suffering from various addictions, depression, anxiety, and
PTSD, in my opinion it is simply not the best option for individuals whose
personal sense of selfhood is fragile or unbalanced.

VARIOUS LEVELS OF MIRAÇÕES

One of the lower rungs of the ladder of mirações is the realm of inner light shows.
These types of mirações, while perhaps filled with flash, verve, and color, as well
as a type of startling, in-your-face specificity, at times can also feel somewhat flat
and empty. This is the realm of a whole host of rather bizarre cardboard-cutout
characters that, at least at times, can possess an almost carnival-like quality. Or
here, we can see rather stilted dreamlike scenes arising within. Or here, we can
become fascinated with the seemingly endless unfolding of countless geometric/
organic matrices that appear before us. (The possibilities appear to be endless.)
However, these inner images do seem to have a certain type of "objectivity" to

them, in that they arise within the inner "screen" of our consciousness without any overt intention on our part. Nonetheless, there doesn't seem to be a lot of substance to these images—they are all flash. These types of experiences, somewhat similar to idle daydreams or moments of fantasy, appear to be little more than the flotsam and jetsam of the subconscious emerging into consciousness, and to this extent, they are, if anything, actually rather "subjective," in the sense that they seem to primarily emerge from the depths of the psyche and appear to have little inherent "ontological selfhood" to them.

When these types of fleeting images emerge within me during a work, I try not to give them a lot of attention. It rarely, if ever, feels spiritually valuable to let my mind get carried away by this level and quality of images (at most, at times I'll smile at them rather ruefully, almost like an indulgent parent tolerating the antics of a misbehaving child). And if they persist, I'll often consciously work within myself to reorient; to sink deeper into my heart; to ground myself; to find my center. Or I will consciously and intentionally ask the Daime to please take me deeper. This is the level of mirações in which the Zen critique of visionary phenomena as illusory and distracting makyo makes a lot of sense (whereas I do *not* think that those critiques apply, at least in the same way, to the higher levels of mirações).

I will admit that although I have profound faith in the cosmic intelligence of the Daime, I still have to ask: what function, if any, does this inner parade of seemingly meaningless images serve? Honestly, it is not immediately apparent to me what value they possess, if any. Is the Daime perhaps clearing out psychic debris? Or is the Daime giving me the opportunity to learn how to train my mind so that I can discern between worthwhile mirações and those that are simply distractions? It's really not clear to me.

At a higher level of mirações, we find a whole range of radiantly beautiful, intensely compelling, visionary unfoldings. Here it can almost seem as though the Daime is reveling in its creative potency—almost as if it were joyously displaying its astonishing ability to unfurl, effortlessly, scene after scene of stunning beauty, each arising in a way that is unanticipated and utterly unique. For me, these mirações are often like watching an extremely vivid, fascinating, and emotionally charged movie playing out on the inner screen of my consciousness. But in this case, unlike the lower-level light show mirações, the more vivid mirações often feel quite substantive and inherently valuable. With this level of mirações, I am aware that what I'm seeing (and at times, to different degrees, hearing, feeling, and so on), is taking place "over there," just like in ordinary experience. There is a quality of inner distance between me the beholder and the vision that I am beholding. Just like in ordinary experience, I'm perceiving an otherness that has spontaneously and forcefully arisen (and continues to arise) independent of my conscious intentions. And that otherness has come to me (or I have arrived where it is), and now we two, the knower and the known, the subject and the object, are interacting with each other in a way that clearly isn't a figment of my imagination, a daydream, or a fantasy. There's a sense of objectivity about what I'm seeing, even if that objectivity, just like in every moment of ordinary existence, always takes place within my own consciousness.

The "objective" computer that I'm typing on right now, for example, if examined carefully, is also an experience that takes place within my own consciousness (or, said in another way, that manifests *as* a form of my consciousness). I didn't make up the computer; it's clearly a "not-me," but nonetheless, I only know that computer in-and-as my experience of a computer. All I really know is the synthesis of my sense experiences of the computer (that is, knowledge-by-acquaintance) overlaid and interwoven with my highly particular, yet deeply informed by culture, preconscious, primarily linguistic, webs of interwoven assumptions, beliefs, and expectations about computers (and myself, and what it means to be a human being). I assume the computer is made of solid matter; I act with it as if it is made of solid matter, but if examined closely, drawing upon the assistance of decades of philosophical study and inquiry, I can ascertain that the computer that I know is not actually an utterly other, third-person object that is something completely external to me, but rather, the computer that I experience is always, inescapably, a form of my own consciousness; it is always, inescapably, "something that is known by me." When it comes to experience, notions of "inside" or "outside" don't really work all that well. For example, is my experience of this moment happening within this room, or does this room exist within my experience of this moment? I tend to lean, rather strongly, toward the second option. If life, in its totality, is made up of anything, I would say that it is made of experiences

It is clear that even miraçōes on this level (and perhaps all levels to an extent?) are deeply intertwined with my own typically preconscious and perhaps even subconscious attitudes, assumptions, prejudices, and so on (again, just like in daily life.) As I will underscore later in my discussion of mediumship, at times it can be hard to assess the actual ontological status of various visionary encounters. Let's say, for example, that a thrillingly exotic, shimmering green lizard being, adorned with magnificent swoops of gold and red around her/his eyebrows, has suddenly appeared within my inner world. What is that being actually? Is it a quite unimaginable conflux of energies and vibrations emerging from another dimensional level of being—a conflux of energies that is molding and adapting itself to my own assumptive knowledge-about inner meaning-making world, an assumptive world that contains, among countless other layers of information, the shape of lizards, the size of scales, what red looks like, and so on? Or is that "pre-encounter" lizard being already, well, sort of "lizard-y" in its own environment? (My best guess is that it is some magically mysterious combination of both of these factors, as well as a whole lot else that is quite literally unimaginable.)

The power and the vivid immediacy of the types of experiences that are possible at this level of miraçōes means that it is important for us to keep our wits about us, both when we're having these experiences and after the fact. Everything depends upon the meanings we overlay on these starkly compelling experiences. The exact same inner forms that are emerging and changing moment to moment on our inner visionary screen can easily be interpreted to mean radically different things. For example, let's say that a woman who is relatively new to the Santo Daime is having a miração in which she sees the "Green Goblin" figure I described earlier, flying around her, cackling and leering and laughing. Let's imagine that she is bringing to that experience multiple layers of preconscious assumptions from her earlier fundamentalist Christian upbringing about devils and demons. In such a scenario, it would be all too easy for her to imagine that she is being attacked by sinister forces of darkness and, consequently, for her to react with a type of knee-jerk jolt of fear instead of, as would ideally be the case, remaining calm and secure, knowing that she is completely protected by the Daime and the Beings of Light who are with her at every moment during the work. And then afterward, it would (again) be completely understandable if she might feel a lot of anxiety, combined with a visceral reluctance to take part in other Santo Daime sessions.

Decades ago, psychedelic therapists learned the crucial importance of "coaching" people, before a session, as well as in the immediacy of the visionary encounter itself, on what attitudes to bring to such powerful and challenging inner interactions.[16] It soon became clear to these psychedelic therapists that it was crucial to encourage people to breathe deeply; to remember that they are completely safe and protected; to turn and face what is frightening them, perhaps asking that monstrous figure what it wants, what it is trying to show them. And this sort of inner attitudinal preparation (as well as on the ground interpretive and emotional support) was often critically important in the immediacy of such moments (as well as after the fact), in that those calm, reassuring words often made all the difference between someone spiraling out of control into a full-blown anxiety attack and someone who ended the session feeling uplifted and transformed, having been empowered to face his or her fears and overcome them.

In much the same way, within a Santo Daime work, helping people in the immediacy of the moment as well as afterward to challenge and/or reexamine some of their perhaps less than helpful interpretations of what they are going through (and/or went through) during a work is a crucially important task of a skilled guardian or church leader. Reminding participants that they are completely safe; telling them that everything that arises within them during a work does so only with the permission of the Daime and the Beings of Light; and encouraging them to ground themselves, to find their hearts, to breathe. Words of calm reassurance (especially if they emerge from someone who is herself/himself radiating an energetic field of clarity, faith, and love) can make all the difference for someone who is struggling during a work (*and* can help to contribute to the cohesiveness and clarity of the overall energetic "tone" of the salão itself). Our beliefs matter; helping someone to choose which knowledge-about interpretive cluster of ideas to overlay on their mirações can make all the difference between a "hellish" experience and one that, although perhaps difficult and challenging, will ultimately be seen as deeply rewarding.

In much the same way, even powerful mirações that are much more overtly benevolent can, at least at times, bring their own set of challenges. Again, let's envision a young daimista who, perhaps unknown even to himself, tends to see the world through the lens of a type of emotional neediness; someone who has a craving for self-validation; someone who possesses a seemingly endless need to (somehow!) fill the inner emptiness that torments him under the radar screen of his conscious awareness. In this case, if the glowing form of a godlike being, shining with love and radiating approval, should appear to this young man during a work, he might naturally interpret this vision to mean that he, as an egoic self, is somehow spiritually special, that he has been chosen by God for a special mission. And so the interpretive lens that he superimposed onto that overtly benevolent experience might well create a (typically preconscious) tendency toward grandiosity; it might well cultivate a sense that he is somehow superior to others, somehow better than everyone else.

This tendency of powerful and often genuinely benevolent mirações to kindle, at least at times, an undercurrent of grandiosity within daimistas is an all too frequent occurrence within the Santo Daime tradition. And I'm not even talking here about the full-blown messiah complexes that sadly can at times develop (these are difficult enough for any spiritual community to deal with). Instead, what I'm referring to is something that is more subtle, something that even well-meaning and spiritually developed daimistas might have to struggle with periodically during their spiritual unfolding—that is, the tendency for a person who has had a powerfully convincing and luminously benevolent miração to somehow manage, typically beneath the surface of conscious awareness, to co-opt these experiences as a way to shore up an innately fragile egoic sense of superiority.

It doesn't have to go this way. There are times when powerful mirações can transmit the deeply true and profoundly transformative recognition that we are, indeed, completely divine, just as we are, warts and all, but instead of using that insight to shore up a fragile ego structure, we can instead draw upon those mirações to deepen our conviction that *all* beings are utterly precious Daughters and Sons of God—enabling those mirações, in this way, to deepen our sense of solidarity with everyone and everything rather than to inflate our precarious sense of egoic entitlement.

Let's face it: there's a huge difference between the not exactly ideal belief that you, in-and-as your egoic self, are the chosen by God savior of all and the inherently positive act of waking up, again and again, to the awareness of your innate divinity. Sadly, however, at times these two radically distinct outlooks can become confused. In the aftermath of a full-bore miração, it's not always easy to catch our ego's tendency to grasp onto that universally applicable Knowledge of our divinity in order to prop itself up ("Look how special I am!"). The miração comes, bringing the liberative force of awakening, but our ego is only too happy to shrink and distort that transformative insight.

To give another (unhappily rather frequent) example: how do daimistas learn how to discern the difference between crystal-clear messages from their inner Guidance and what is actually (or at least primarily) their own confusions and distortions masquerading in the guise of their "Guides"? I vividly remember Padrinho Alex Polari addressing this exact issue in a question-and-answer session that took place during the almost three-week Daime-Dharma retreat that he led with his wife Madrinha Sonia Palhares de Alverga in the community of Mauá in the mountains outside Rio. During that session, Padrinho Alex strongly cautioned people to not make impulsive decisions based on the guidance that they received during Santo Daime works, saying that while we can in certain instances receive trustworthy guidance from Beings of Light—especially during particularly powerful and luminous mirações—we need to carefully examine how much of the guidance coming from these visionary encounters is actually coming from a divine Source, and how much of it is coming from our own unacknowledged and often distorted psychological baggage.[17]

And yet, to be fair, I also have to say that I have seen many daimistas who have made amazingly liberative and deeply healing life choices (for example, leaving dysfunctional jobs and relationships) by following their inner guidance with courage and faith. In fact, I think that one of the most profound gifts of the Daime is the gradual cultivation of an increasingly refined capacity to tune into and trust our intuition. It's just that developing the ability to discern the difference between genuine intuitive Knowing and our own egoic desires doesn't come automatically or easily, and it's important that we keep our wits about us and remain humble. (One of my favorite mantras, shamelessly stolen from Roshi Bernie Glassman: "I could be wrong.")

We all need assistance in developing this sort of inner discernment. It can at times be difficult to navigate the frequently turbulent waters of mirações—knowing how to avoid the whirlpools of pride, anxiety, self-doubt, projection, or transference that can arise with and even help to shape the mirações themselves. It's important therefore that those of us who are learning how to captain our inner vessels have the opportunity to share our concerns with others; to speak from our hearts about what we've experienced and how we understand these experiences; to ask questions and then listen, hopefully with as much humility as possible, to words of wise counsel; to know how to trust our intuition, even when it goes against the advice of others *and* how to remain ever-vigilant to the very real possibility that our intuition itself might not be infallible. There are simply countless ways in which, daimistas (or as anyone else who is deeply immersed in a powerfully illuminative spiritual path) have the opportunity to develop spiritual discernment. But that development doesn't necessarily come without concerted, sustained over time effort, effort that is itself rooted in the sincere desire to purify our hearts and minds so that Light and Love can flow through us with fewer and fewer distortions.

And it is exceedingly difficult to hone this capacity alone. The process of clarifying our discernment is, at least ideally, nurtured in a grounded, mature community of deeply committed spiritual seekers (and finders) who can act as spiritual mirrors to one another, lovingly teaching one another, and learning from one another; people who care enough about themselves and their spiritual brothers and sisters to speak up in community meetings and sharing sessions; sisters and brothers who are willing to ask questions, listen to answers, and offer their own heartfelt insights. Although the tendency to overshare and/or share as a way to inflate our own sense of importance is, of course, something to be watchful of, both within ourselves and within others, I for one am deeply grateful for the opportunities we are given, as daimistas, to be part of a larger community in which we can share our experiences, either as a group, whether small or large, formal or informal, or in intimate one-on-one conversations about some of the best ways to walk the spiritual path with as few impediments as possible.

Again, I keep coming back to the sharing sessions that took place in Mauá with Padrinho Alex, remembering so vividly the way in which he would kindly and thoughtfully answer our questions and skillfully address our concerns. Over the years I've learned so much from such sharing sessions—sessions that were, for the most part, orchestrated by skilled and loving elders who not only had the capacity to offer helpful and subtle insights, but who did so as we were all sitting together in the "afterglow" of a powerful Santo Daime work, and who spoke to all of us while remaining rooted in the calm, radiant, open Presence and utter naturalness that they had developed through long years of intensely disciplined spiritual practice in the Santo Daime. (There have been times when certain elders have—sadly—acted in less-than-ideal ways, but even that sort of relatively rare behavior can, if approached with transparency and courage, become rich fodder for further spiritual discernment and open dialogue within various Santo Daime communities—even if that process itself might well be extremely challenging.)

The need for discernment doesn't disappear even in some of the higher levels of miraçōes. In fact, the need for discernment may grow more acute due to the increased Power and deepening sense of innate Truth that miraçōes possess at these higher levels. Here it can become even more critical to learn how to disentangle any lingering egoic distortions or/and latent cultural prejudices from the Power-full Knowings that we can receive in-and-through these often genuinely revelatory and often life-changing miraçōes.

During these higher-level miraçōes, we can merge with Beings of Light and be granted a glimpse of the purity and profundity of their diamond-like, love-suffused vision of the cosmos. In this way, our vibratory rate can be radically upgraded via a streaming of divinity manifesting as rays of radiance itself. Or our physical/emotional ailments can be healed via the shimmering and yet exceedingly potent crystalline presence of compassionate spiritual "doctors." Or, as I mentioned earlier, in these innately higher/purer realms, you can have the direct realization that you are no longer "you"; at these levels, you are not simply watching an intricately patterned unfolding of visionary colors unfurl (although this, in itself, can be wondrous, beautiful, and innately rewarding). Instead, you discover your Self in the very center of that unfolding; you Know that "you," in the higher "octave" of your being, are the Source of all of that visionary beauty— beauty that radiates from you and then pours back into you; beauty that comes imbued with intrinsic feelings of joy, wonder, and delight, as well as downloads of mystical insight that feel inherently True. Here you are (ecstatically) taken into some preexisting, extremely high, vibratory level of reality—a level in which "you" have already, and always, been living. Here the previous identification with the smaller "ego-self," or even the self-contained, energetically bounded soul-self, falls away, and you know yourself to be a vast divine Being (if not Being Itself), effortlessly creating and sustaining a heavenly world—a world of sublime beauty that is itself a radiant manifestation of your own divine nature. Here there's no egoic knower and no separate object that is known. Here Knowledge itself is an expression of divine creative Potency.

At this level of miraçoes, we are often no longer simply seeing an inner scene. Rather, each of our spiritual senses (our inner ability—without physi- cal sense organs—to see, hear, taste, touch, and smell) is operative. And these elevated senses are seamlessly unified within our spiritual experience, and all of them are present—just more self-luminous, more refined, clearer than our everyday sense experiences. And all of this uplifted quality of experience itself unfolds within the embracing, enveloping matrix of a preexistent, fully formed archetypal world, a world that is itself an upgraded outpouring of our own consciousness.

And this innately higher world is not cut off from our daily lives. Rather, it is profoundly and intimately linked with our ordinary world—it is, in fact (we can discover), one of the countless creative matrices of this world: our love, our joy, our health, our life, and our wisdom are, as it were, choral reverbs from the Songs that stream forth from those worlds. In fact, our daily life, below/ above the level of our conscious awareness, is ceaselessly aligned with these higher realms of Being that interpenetrate and overlay this world, and these "imaginal" worlds (and "imaginal" selves and "imaginal" others) ceaselessly and joyously infuse our world with the juicy Goodness of Life—especially if we consciously work to open ourselves up to these levels.[18] (Which, by the way, is *exactly* what is taking place in a Santo Daime work as we attempt to align ourselves with the Astral.)

In these archetypal worlds, we have bodies of Light, and we live in a world of Light. Here we are "raised" into a higher, innately sacred, realm of experience that is not foreign to us. Here we just Know: this is my place; I belong here. In these worlds we are fully divine beings, with corresponding visionary bodies, engaging in adventures that make, for example, the Marvel superhero movies seem rather tame and pedestrian. In these worlds, we find that, in-and-as higher "overtones" of our being, we are, right here, right now, ardent students in an ancient school of magic that makes Hogwarts seem boring and humdrum. In these worlds, right here, right now, in-and-as higher "overtones" of our being, we are luminous bodhisattvas gathering together in a Pure Land of our own Creation, listening joyfully to the chimes of Enlightenment that ring out—each of us mutually kindling each other, each of us awakening each other. In these worlds, right here, right now, "above our heads," we are hierophantic initiates, receiving our Crown, taking into our hands, as our rightful possession, the scepter of Light or the sword of Fire. In these worlds, right here, right now, we are unexpectedly, suddenly, "Waking Up" within God's house, and seeing God Himself/Herself— recognizing, to our delight, that we also are fully divine.

As a way to offer an example of a miração that exemplifies this level of visionary/mystical experience, I would like to return, to my experience in Céu do Mapiá. Right after the St. Peter's work (which took place after the night of St. John as part of the June festival), I was lying in bed in the inn after having stripped off my sweat-sodden farda. Then, at some point, with my eyes closed, I was forcefully "pulled upward" within myself and then . . . although I am struggling here a bit, since whatever words I write will inevitably sound trite and banal compared to the profound Sacredness, the inherent Majesty of the experience itself. Nonetheless, I "awakened" in another world, an overtly heavenly world. And in this world I could clearly perceive God (yes, *the* God— that Knowledge was inherent to the experience itself) in the form of a strong, muscular, regal, simply adorned, indigenous King. He was wearing beautiful yet casual flowing clothes. Jeweled armbands were on His upper arms; He was holding an intricately carved staff. And He was sitting at His ease in a stark but beautiful room with walls of polished dark wood—almost as if it were the home of a native Hawaiian king.

And then I became aware of the Divine Mother who was seated by His left side. She had long dark brown hair and wore a flowing, simple yet elegant dress. Her Face (which like God's Face, was more felt than clearly seen) was extremely kind, beautiful, and gentle. They were both deeply, innately, noble, centered, radiant, and loving. Their Presences were so powerful, so overtly Sacred—they were continually radiating wave after wave of Divinity Itself.

And in this world, I was not Bill Barnard watching Them from a distance. Instead, I Knew that I had always lived there with Them. I belonged there; this was my home. I was (am) their beloved Son. I was tall, strong, healthy—a vital and muscular young man. I was completely at ease; my heart shone with love; and I just Knew: this is me in my truth, in my depths, as I am Now, always—fully connected to my divinity, empowered, complete, whole.

It might appear that this miração was a recipe for megalomania and over-the-top grandiosity. But fortunately, in that miração I also Knew that I was not the *only* Son (or Daughter) of God and the Divine Mother. (May we *all* Wake Up, more and more, to that sacred Knowledge.) And lying there on my bed in the inn, after I emerged from that literally heavenly world, feeling so filled with awe and thankfulness, I also knew that there was a *long* way to go between my glimpse of that Archetypal Reality and actually incorporating that Light, Love, and Presence fully into this world, because on other important levels of my being, I was/am just this professor guy, stumbling through life, doing his best, with the grace of all the divine Beings, to wake up. (I've noticed, for myself at least, that profound mirações often generate a concurrent deep feeling of humility and gratitude.)

And yet I also knew then, and I know now, that these types of mirações are profoundly True; that they are, in fact, spiritually crucial (at least to me, in that moment). I have been shown, time and time again, how the Daime, via these sorts of over-the-top mirações, has been working, gradually, to upgrade my subtle body; how it has been slowly, over time, "rewiring" my capacity to increasingly manifest those highly refined frequencies of Being within this everyday world. (And in this world of contraction, depression, fear, and anxiety, we need all the help we can get!)

But these sorts of profound visionary/mystical experiences are, at least arguably, not quite as high as yet another level of mirações (here's where the term itself becomes extremely, as it were, stretched), that is, the overtly unitive, "formless" experiences that can and do take place both within profound moments of inner stillness and in-and-as our moment-to-moment experience of the ordinary world.

Every now and then, during profound moments of meditation, the Daime will open up our inner sight and we'll be blessed with the utterly certain mystical Knowledge: I Am That. We are shown, without any doubts, the Truth. We will be shown that the deepest Source of our identity, our truest, highest Self, is in fact One with All. We will Know that there is only that One, and We are that One, taking the form of All that is. This quality of experience doesn't happen often, and as far as I can tell it doesn't happen to every daimista, but when those moments of unspeakable grace descend, the realization can be earth-shattering, given our deeply engrained attachment to our egoic sense of ourselves. (I still vividly remember talking to one long-term, highly dedicated daimista who had just undergone one of these profound mystical experiences during a work. He was rather shaken, and as he tried his best to share with me what had taken place, I'd periodically murmur, "How beautiful," or "I'm so happy for you," but every time he heard me say these words of comfort and support, he'd grimace, shake his head, and say: "I'm not quite there yet." The sheer Power of that level of realization can be a lot to assimilate.)

By the way, while I used to be a monist (someone who believes that sheer Oneness is the only Reality), at this point I'm not. For me, Oneness coexists, happily, with many-ness; unchanging Being and the ceaseless flux of becoming are both equally important qualities of divinity; God and the Goddess are always dancing together in each moment. Each one of us, in our precious, utterly unique, irreplaceable individuality is, to my way of thinking, a holographic incarnation of that One. It's not so much that the drop merges into the Ocean, as it is that the Ocean is fully present in each drop.

There are also those timeless and time-full moments in which our heart flowers and Love flows in-and-through us effortlessly. Or moments in which the pleasurable currents of life and joy surge in-and-through us, and we are given the opportunity to "marinate" in the energy of those divine Qualities (and countless others). Or moments in which our egoic boundaries dissolve and All That Is, simply Is—innately Perfect, inherently Sublime, intrinsically Divine. And paradoxically, just by being who we are, in the moment, we know that we are effortlessly and fully manifesting divinity.

In the face of this profusion of sacredness, the very notion of ineffability itself becomes almost laughable, in that simply saying that these levels of experience are "ineffable" so little encompasses the Immensity and Grandeur, to say nothing of the utterly natural quality, of that depth of mystical awareness, that the word is barely useful as a cognitive marker. What can labeling an experience as ineffable actually tell us that is even remotely helpful or relevant in the face of the Immediacy, the crystalline Brilliance, the boundless Joy, and the all-encompassing Love that shines forth from the Heart of these sorts of realizations. In these moments we're not so much having a vision as our vision of life and ourselves is being radically transformed. Here, each moment, as it is, in its luminous simplicity, *is* the vision.

THE QUESTION OF THE TRUTH AND/OR VALUE OF MIRAÇÕES

Just as with powerful visionary/mystical experiences in general, profound mirações catalyzed by the Daime can radically challenge and at times even transform our tacit, taken for granted, deeply engrained sense of ourselves and our understanding of the nature of life itself. It therefore seems important to ask ourselves: how do we know that the information that we are receiving from these experiences is trustworthy? Are there any criteria by which we could assess whether these visionary/mystical experiences, whether entheogenically inspired or not, are actually true and/or valuable? Once again, William James's perspective is extremely helpful.

In *The Varieties of Religious Experience*, James offers three criteria by which we can assess the validity and value of visionary/mystical experiences: "immediate luminosity," "philosophical reasonableness," and "moral helpfulness."[19] "Immediate luminosity" is the criterion that acknowledges the evidential value of the experiential component of a visionary/mystical state of mind—its immediate force; its raw voltage; its direct, tangible feeling. "Philosophical reasonableness" is the criterion by which we can assess whether these powerful nonordinary states of consciousness can be shown to be reasonable and coherent by virtue of their place within an articulate and rationally defensible system of beliefs. And finally, "moral helpfulness" is demonstrated if and when these nonordinary states of consciousness can be shown to initiate, on the whole and over the long run, positive consequences for the individual and/or the community.

The qualifiers "on the whole" and "over the long run" are important. There are many times in the spiritual life when we can for quite a while feel as if we've actually gotten worse—times when our stubbornly entrenched sense of who we are and what matters in life is being taken away from us, bit by bit, and nothing better has arrived; times when we can feel as raw and vulnerable as a lobster having molted its shell; times when all sorts of long-buried negativity and reactivity is rising to the surface to be healed, and we're just barely able to cope. Genuine spiritual growth takes time, and it is crucial that when assessing our own spiritual progress, hopefully with kindness, faith, and patience, we look more at the overall arc of our spiritual lives rather than who we are at our worst moments.

For James, these three criteria are not mutually exclusive, but rather, they interact with and depend upon one another. For example: how do we determine whether the changes we are perceiving within ourselves are positive without drawing upon philosophical reasonableness to say: here's what "positive" means, and why. Furthermore, assessing the truth and/or value of visionary/mystical experiences is not a matter of precisely weighing the percentage of each criterion's importance—it is instead a holistic, cumulative process. As James emphasizes, the final test for assessing states of consciousness is not the individual "score" of each of these criteria, but rather, their cumulative weight, the way they work as a whole and on the whole.[20]

Mirações are striking exemplars of the criterion of immediate luminosity, in that (at least for most of the daimistas that I have spoken with), in a way that is similar to visionaries and mystics throughout history, powerful mirações—at least those that are further up the ladder—can feel at least as real/true as sense experiences. Such experiences come into consciousness carrying with them, innately (again, just like sense experiences) the powerful sense that "this cannot be doubted." (We're returning, yet again, to knowledge-by-acquaintance.) When these types of experiences arise, the visionary/mystic just Knows. Therefore, not surprisingly, most visionaries/mystics have no doubts about what they experienced.

As usual, even here there are exceptions. For example, in the Christian mystical tradition, there are numerous examples of mystics who at times agonized whether a certain visionary experience or mystical revelation came to them, to put it crudely, from God or the devil. And certain streams of the Buddhist tradition often work hard to relativize, or even at times to disparage, the value/validity of the visionary/mystical experiences that might emerge within an intensive meditative practice.

And James fully understands, and in fact *appreciates*, this mystical sense of certainty. As he points out, "Mystical states, when well developed, usually are, and have the right to be, absolutely authoritative over the individuals to whom they come."[21] For James, these experiences are not, at least necessarily, solipsistic figments of the imagination; they are not necessarily irrational. They are, instead, powerful glimpses into the more-ness that, above our heads, surrounds and inter-penetrates our normal waking awareness. As he recognizes, there's a "there" there with visionary/mystical experiences. There is something substantive, something that can push back against our ideas and theories, a "given-ness" that is not, at least solely, the creation of the visionary/mystic. Therefore, according to James, visionaries and mystics can and should trust the truth of these profound alter-ations of consciousness *and* those who have not had powerful visionary/mystical experiences should, at least ideally, respect the right of these visionaries/mystics to say: "What I experienced was True."

Nonetheless, James goes on to emphasize that a visionary/mystic's certainty about the truth of what she or he experienced during a powerful visionary/mys-tical encounter simply does not apply to someone who has not had that same quality of illuminative insight. James therefore argues that these visionaries/ mystics, in turn, have no right to say to others: "What I experienced was and is universally True—not just for me, but for all people and for all times." James makes this point not only because different visionaries and mystics often endorse a wide range of at times contradictory religious beliefs based on their profound experiences, but also because the belief systems that these visionaries/mystics *do* endorse with such passion and certainty can, at least at times, be somewhat less than inspiring and lofty (for example, the self-righteous, bigoted, xenophobic, misogynistic, violence-inciting claims made throughout history by various aya-tollahs, prophets, and "inspired" leaders). As James notes, powerful visionary/ mystical experiences themselves, at least if/when they are used as "evidence" to make universal truth claims, do not come, as it were "preapproved," but rather, must themselves "be sifted and tested, and run the gauntlet of confrontation with the total context of experience."[22]

And yet, James also acknowledges that powerful visionary/mystical expe-riences "absolutely overthrow the pretension of non-mystical states to be the sole and ultimate dictators of what we may believe."[23] As he points out, based on his own mystical experience using nitrous oxide, these powerful experiences demonstrate:

> That our normal waking consciousness . . . is but one special type of conscious-ness, whilst all about it, parted from it by the filmiest of screens, there lie po-tential forms of consciousness entirely different. . . . No account of the universe

in its totality can be final which leaves these other forms of consciousness quite disregarded. How to regard them is the question,—for they are so discontinuous with ordinary consciousness. Yet they may determine attitudes though they cannot furnish formulas, and open a region though they fail to give a map. At any rate, they forbid a premature closing of our accounts with reality.[24]

James's discussion of the three criteria of immediate luminosity, philosophical reasonableness, and moral helpfulness is his attempt to consciously acknowledge the complexities that surround any attempt to assess the value and/or validity of the truth claims made by visionaries/mystics. His primary focus is on how non-mystics could/should evaluate mystical truth claims, but I would suggest that to the extent that we ourselves are visionaries/mystics (and I think many of us are), we could also benefit from these criteria. They are, at least potentially, helpful starting points for examining the truth and/or value of our own visionary/mystical experiences. Therefore, if (as rarely happens) we choose to become visionaries/mystics who are willing and able to closely examine the validity/value of what has been revealed to us by our own visionary/mystical experiences— and it's difficult to do so when they come to us with such a compelling sense of authoritative Truth—then we could do worse than to use James's three criteria as a starting point.

If we choose to embrace this level of reflexivity, then we can and should begin by acknowledging the primacy and central importance of the raw immediacy and the self-evident "suchness" of the visionary/mystical alterations of consciousness in which so much that is True about both ourselves and the underlying, and typically hidden, nature of reality is revealed to us, often in strikingly persuasive ways. We can and should underscore that Something Powerful and True was shown to us by the immediate luminosity of the experiences themselves.

But what exactly *is* that Something? It's at this point that it makes sense to draw upon philosophical reasonableness. This criterion encourages us to look carefully at the conclusions that we've drawn from these experiences; to examine the belief systems that often come wrapped around the experiences themselves; to investigate whether those belief systems actually are intrinsic to the experiences themselves or whether, as is often the case, we are covertly using the prestige and power of the experiences to "prop up" the truth status of our systems of belief. We don't have to come up with some systematized, completely logical, airtight conceptual system in order to be philosophically reasonable, but surely it's a good idea to clearly examine our own underlying assumptions about what we believe and what we don't—to ask ourselves, with courage and honesty: What should we accept from a given tradition, and why? What should we reject/seek to change, and why? What beliefs, attitudes, and practices make sense to us (and why) and what doesn't (and why)?

Based on my own decades long reading of mystical literature, it seems clear that many people who begin to have powerful visionary/mystical experiences will often simply adopt, wholesale, the belief system that undergirds the tradition in which these experiences emerged. That is, if we have had powerful experiences in a Buddhist context, we'll typically take on Buddhist beliefs, whereas if we have had powerful experiences in a fundamentalist Christian context, we'll typically endorse that set of beliefs.[25] Nonetheless, we can choose a different option. We don't have to endorse the dictates of any religious tradition; we don't have to unthinkingly follow any spiritual authority figure, whether master or guru, padrinho or madrinha. We can have deep respect for our spiritual elders, while also claiming the right to think for ourselves, the right, in this case, to come to our own conclusions about what our mirações have revealed to us.

And yet, at the same time, we need to apply that discerning attitude toward ourselves as well. If we're willing to question everyone and everything, then why not also question ourselves? Why not ask ourselves: "What have I been blind to within myself? Are there ways in which my own sense of myself and reality, and my own assumptions about what's true and valuable might in certain respects be either limited or mistaken? Is it possible that some of my attitudes toward my mirações (and visionary/mystical experiences more generally) and what they have revealed to me need to be questioned and/or revised?" Can we be willing to let go of what we might have previously taken-for-granted? Can we accept that, at least in certain moments and in certain ways, we might well be wrong? Or misguided?

Furthermore, is it possible that we might actually need to learn from the tradition itself—the very tradition that we're questioning? Perhaps *we* are the ones who need to have our preconceptions challenged, not the tradition—a tradition that is often a wellspring of genuine wisdom and powerfully transformative practices, a tradition (such as the Santo Daime) that is filled to the brim with profound insights and spiritual disciplines that have proven themselves, time and time again, over decades (and in the case of other traditions, for centuries or millennia).

As seekers *and* finders, we need to learn to trust our deepest Knowings, and yet we also need to engage in openhearted, thoughtful, and respectful dialogue with others (including learned elders or adepts) who might see things differently than we do. We can question authority *and* we can allow ourselves to be challenged by it as well. We can, as the Zen tradition emphasizes, possess both great Doubt *and* great Faith.[26] We can trust in what God has shown us *and* we can look closely at the conclusions we might have drawn from those powerful encounters with divinity. We can ask ourselves: If I'm going to believe something, based on my powerful visionary/mystical experiences, what exactly should that be? And why should I believe in this way and not in some other way?

We can also remember that our beliefs do not have to be set in stone, and they do not have to be explicitly delineated and impeccably defended with airtight logic. We can, and in fact must, have a set of beliefs, but we can learn, more and more, how to hold those beliefs lightly. We can create a "this is the best I've got for the moment" open-ended belief-system, rather than hunkering down behind the protective walls of dogmatic rigidity (and there are as many dogmatic atheists and nihilists as there are religious fundamentalists). We can rest, with an open and trusting heart, in what feels true and good to us, while at the same time working to let go of our (at times) anxious clinging to our beliefs and our egoic need to be right. We can learn to embrace not having all the answers; we can relax into uncertainty and not knowing—all of this while also remaining at ease within ourselves with the Truths that have been so graciously and beautifully revealed to us.

I know that, speaking personally, I could only remain a daimista over these years because the Santo Daime tradition "wears its doctrines lightly." A daimista is rarely, if ever, told: *This is what you should believe.* And certainly not: *You better believe everything that so and so (that is, some authority figure) tells you is true.* There's no pope or catechism in the Santo Daime; there are no formal sermons; no one is pressured to believe anything. There are beliefs, for sure, but Santo Daime beliefs are rarely explicitly articulated. Instead, it's more like there's an underlying assumption that as a daimista you'll just sort of "get it" through doing lots of works; and drinking lots of Daime; and singing lots of hymns. And the teaching moments that *are* there tend to emerge casually and informally, often in the context of interactions with friends who are also daimistas—for example, standing around a kitchen table after a work eating, chatting, sharing stories, proposing ideas, asking questions, and so on.

Nonetheless—and I wouldn't be writing this book if I didn't also think that our spiritual lives can deepen through a willingness to examine our own metaphysical conclusions in a thoughtful, sustained, and disciplined way—whether through prolonged contemplative study of the texts of various wisdom traditions and/or through engaging in spirited dialogue with others, we can and should let ourselves be challenged. We can and should learn when and how to stand up to the perhaps ill-founded challenges of others. We can and should take the enormous but crucially important responsibility to consciously create and continue to shape our knowledge-about assumptions and beliefs. We can and should be able to write our own stories, to sing our own songs—to be willing to grow up and own our divine heritage as mature, spiritually awakened beings who are empowered to create the type of world that we want to inhabit.

We also have the right and the responsibility to ask ourselves: "Have I truly grown from the experiences that I have had within the context of my tradition? Have the beliefs and practices of that tradition genuinely helped me—and others—to become better? And if so, in what ways?" (And perhaps more subtly, we can ask: "What are the assumptions that I am drawing upon in order to make that assessment itself?") Here we're moving into normative territory; here we're infusing our "is-ness" with some well-needed "ought-ness"; here we're entering into the land of moral helpfulness.

We don't have to become hard-core Jamesian pragmatists to find the criterion of moral helpfulness useful. Truth, even for a pragmatist, doesn't have to be reduced to simply "that which is useful." We can, for example, certainly claim (as James never seemed to recognize he was implicitly doing with the criterion of immediate luminosity) that truths can, in fact, possess a type of extra-worldly foundation. (I know that as a daimista I've become much, much more Platonic than I was before drinking Daime. Repeated voyages into Astral realms that simply ring with inherent Truth tend to do that to you.)

Nonetheless, even if we recognize that truths are, at least at times and to a certain extent, rooted in, or emerge from, some higher level of Truth itself, we can also acknowledge the multiple and important ways in which truths are as much created as they are discovered. (Think about constellations—the stars are really there, but it's we who create the meaningful patterns that turn them into constellations.) There can, indeed, be higher Truths, Truths that we can depend upon, Truths that we can trust. *And* we can realize how truths are inevitably intertwined with what "works" (for example, from the perspective of pragmatism, something is true when it helps us to move forward in our investigations, when it allows us to join together two previously irreconcilable positions). We can and should have faith in the Truths that we've experienced within ourselves, while we can and should also acknowledge that the vast majority of our truths emerge, then exist for a certain period of time, and then gradually or suddenly change into something else—all of this mutability taking place within a deeply human, highly interactive, and cultural/historical context in which almost everything is up for grabs and almost nothing is certain. Truths need to continue to prove themselves again and again and again—to prove that they "work," to prove that they remain valuable to us and our communities, on the whole, and over the long run.

It seems clear to me that daimistas continue to engage in the difficult and demanding path of the Santo Daime at least in part because they recognize the physical, moral, emotional, mental, and spiritual transformations that they perceive within themselves and others as a result of drinking the Daime. Speaking for myself, it seems undeniable that at least part of the reason why I remain a daimista is not only because of the immediate luminosity of powerfully and innately convincing mirações (although that certainly helps); and not only because the vast majority of the teachings of the tradition resonate deeply with me, and because I deeply respect the inherent open-mindedness, and openheartedness, of the tradition itself; but also because, in some fundamental way, the Santo Daime just "works" for me. It is often, quite simply, an unparalleled catalyst of healing and transformation on every level. I have seen over the years several seemingly miraculous physical cures that were clearly linked to the person's willingness to drink, and to continue to drink, Daime. I have also known numerous former "in the gutter" alcoholics and opioid addicts who are now shining exemplars of what it means to be genuinely good human beings, in large part because of their willingness to drink and to continue to drink Daime (and because of their willing to do the hard work within themselves that was catalyzed by that repeated immersion in that liquid Light.)

In *Gift of the Body*, Jonathan Goldman describes, very beautifully, the process through which one of his key mentors, José Rosa, was cured of advanced pancreatic cancer through drinking the Daime, as well as, crucially, from following the internal guidance he received from within during that prolonged and arduous process.[27] In addition, Titti Kristina Schmidt, a Swedish anthropologist who spent fifteen months in Céu do Mapiá, offers a story of the seemingly miraculous curative effects of the Daime, giving the example of Barbara, a woman diagnosed with an inoperable brain tumor:

> When Barbara started to drink the Daime she had what many members call a "spiritual surgery" . . . Under the influence of the Daime brew, she witnessed her own operation done by a group of doctors in spiritual form. After the operation, the spirits told her to rest and eat only certain prescribed food. Later when Barbara recovered, she returned to the hospital in Sao Paulo and asked them to [t]ake a new x-ray. To the surprise of the doctors, the tumor was gone. What amazed them even more was that Barbara (who has no Western medical training) could explain the whole operation, which corresponded to an ordinary brain surgery. She could even describe the instruments used by the spiritual doctors, instruments that, according to Barbara, the doctors in Sao Paulo confirmed were similar to the ones used during ordinary brain surgeries.[28]

Schmidt goes on to note that due to stories like this, "Céu do Mapiá has today a national reputation as a healing community. The villagers claim that they can treat a whole range of well-known diseases, for example, skin problems, respiratory diseases, contagious infections, hepatitis, diabetes, leprosy, malaria, worms, dysentery, digestive problems, anaemia, fevers, influenza, mental disorders" and so on.[29] According to Schmidt, "the community has also gained recognition outside Brazil, attracting people who hope to be cured from terminal diseases such as cancer and HIV/AIDS."[30]

It is important to emphasize, however, that within the Santo Daime tradition, healing is not necessarily equated with a physical cure. The Daime is said to do much more than cure physical or emotional ills. Equally importantly, daimistas believe that drinking the Daime engenders and supports healing at the deepest level, in that it ignites a powerful process of spiritual growth, that is, the movement from the darkness and suffering of ignorance and illusion toward the Light and Joy of divine Love and self-awareness. In this broadest sense, the entire thrust of the Santo Daime tradition can be seen as unifying the often separate tasks of healing and spiritual development.

Speaking for myself, I celebrate the fact that I have grown, profoundly, over the more than fifteen years that I have been immersed in this tradition. On the whole, I can honestly say (and importantly, my wife agrees) that my heart is more open; I'm increasingly able to remain calm and centered in the middle of external or internal upheavals; I am much less reactive and angry; I possess an expanded and increasingly refined ability to discern and work with subtle energies; and my mind has gained an increased ability to remain quiet and focused. (Again: this assessment is always "on the whole"—I'm as human as anyone, so I try not to judge myself, or others, by my less than perfect moments.)

And I can see these same positive transformations taking place in numerous other daimistas as well. Admittedly, nobody is perfect; we all occasionally stumble and fall; we make stupid mistakes and do things that we later regret. In addition, the Daime is not for everyone, and not every knot of inner distortion can be untangled just be going to lots of Santo Daime works. The Daime is not a panacea. You have to work *really* hard as a daimista, and not everyone is willing, or perhaps even able, to put in the sustained effort that is needed to heal old wounds and shift stubbornly embedded defense patterns. (And to be frank, sometimes we just need some good old-fashioned psychotherapy—hopefully with a therapist who is open to the healing potential of entheogens.) Nonetheless, I have to say that it seems clear to me that the overall arc of most daimistas is profoundly healing and transformative. I know several daimistas who, as far as I can tell, are genuinely saintly human beings, and the vast majority of my Santo

Daime brothers and sisters are clearly moving, with a lot of discipline, self-effort, and faith, in that direction as well. I know so many precious and highly lovable daimistas—people who are stepping up, again and again, to do the work that really matters: acknowledging and healing knotted and contracted energies, both within themselves and in the world around them; transforming darkness into Light, suffering into Joy, hatred into Love, bondage into Freedom. And, as far as I can tell, most of them (again, on the whole and in the long run) are succeeding in this difficult, yet innately rewarding, spiritual work.

There are, of course, not surprisingly, exceptions. Some daimistas seem to flower initially, only to wall off their hearts over time; some daimistas (amazingly) seem to become even more self-involved, inflated, rigid, and dogmatic than they were before; and some daimistas just seem to be spinning around in a hamster wheel of their own making—putting in seemingly enormous effort, but getting nowhere.

Nonetheless, assessing the spiritual progress of others is, at best, a perilous undertaking. (Assessing our own progress is difficult enough.) The depths of the pain and distortion that some people are working to overcome; the complex underpinnings of why people act as they do—what do we know, really, about any of this? How could we possibly be so arrogant as to judge, usually with a tacit air of superiority and close-hearted condemnation, another person's spiritual progress? Therefore, while I think that it is crucial to be able to see ourselves and others clearly—to not be blind to the hidden motivations, reactive patterns, and knee-jerk defensiveness of ourselves and others—it also seems important that we make sure that these clear-eyed assessments of what is happening, on multiple levels, within ourselves and within others, are increasingly, with divine grace, accompanied with a gentle-hearted, tender sense of compassion. We can and should learn to see ourselves and others with the "bifocals" of clarity and open-heartedness; we can and should both acknowledge what needs healing, while simultaneously seeing the innate Perfection that Shines within.

And, in a nod toward theoretical humility, let's just admit, openly, that it is not completely clear that the positive changes that we perceive in ourselves or in others are simply the result of drinking Daime. It could also be the case that for many daimistas these changes are due in large part to the hard work that they have done/are doing in other areas of their lives. That is, perhaps our deepening compassion, or our increased awareness of beauty, or the ease with which we respond to challenging situations actually emerges at least as much from our yoga practice, or our hours of meditation, or our often courageous willingness to acknowledge and heal the shadow sides of ourselves via prolonged psychotherapy, or the other inner work we are doing as it does from drinking the Daime. The difficulty of ascertaining any simple, corresponding cause of changes in our life is at least one reason why working with the criterion of moral helpfulness can be so complex and daunting. As human beings who are, I believe, profoundly interconnected with the entire cosmos, who are intertwined with countless vectors of influence coming to us from all directions, how can we possibly say, "This, and this alone, is what caused me to change"?

Nonetheless, I think it is clear that no one would *ever* continue to drink the Daime unless they were convinced, on some deep level, that it was benefiting them, often in profound and unexpected ways, *and* that drinking the Daime appeared to be creating and sustaining a community that was, for the most part, genuinely and sometimes spectacularly positive. And so, while the assessments that we make based on this third criterion will almost inevitably be imprecise and ad hoc and primarily rooted in an inchoate felt-sense of whether our participation in the Santo Daime is working for us, it is good to acknowledge that it is important to make the effort—that it is worth the time and energy to at least try to ascertain, with as much clarity, openheartedness, and humility as possible, what's working for us, and what's not, and why—to answer, for ourselves: *How am I getting better as a human being, and where am I still stuck? What do I value about our community, and what do I think needs to change, and why?*

And to me, even that willingness itself—that is, the willingness to ask difficult questions, questions that really matter—is itself one of the clearest indications of spiritual growth, both within individuals and within the larger community itself. It isn't easy to probe into some of these tender areas within ourselves, and it can be difficult, as a community, to be willing not only to tolerate but even to encourage tough and ideally humble and openhearted questions about our particular tradition. But if we can actually begin to do this level of spiritual work, what an amazing gift we are offering to ourselves and to our community. How beautiful it is to be willing to ask these sorts of truth-seeking (and hopefully kind) questions of ourselves and others; how beautiful it is to learn how to respond, fruitfully, with heart, to this type of rigorous, balanced, and compassionate self-inquiry.

For years I've been flirting with whether it made sense to add a fourth criterion to the list. I'd tell myself: "Surely when we're assessing the truth/value of our spiritual experiences, beliefs, and practices, beauty needs to enter into the picture as well." But at this point, I'm rather reluctant to say too much about why I think that beauty could/should be a fourth criterion. At best I'm willing to offer a few tentative initial observations—the barest beginnings of what could be said. First, it seems to me that mirações are quite often truly stunning. And the beauty that appears in mirações, in-and-of itself, qua beauty, seems, at least to me, to possess its own inherent value as well as its own sui generis quality (beauty is "its own thing"—it is neither cognitive nor normative; it is something distinctive, something irreplaceable, something that is not reducible to anything else). Second, so much of what I value about the Santo Daime as a tradition can be found in its beauty—the beauty of the hymns; the beauty of the salão; the beauty of the natural world from which the Santo Daime emerged and within which it thrives. Third, one of the most prominent and positive shifts within myself that emerged soon after I began to drink the Daime has been my deepening sensitivity to and appreciation of beauty in the world around me and within my own being. There's a lot more that could be said, but I'm going to stop here before my monkey mind begins to raise too many objections.

PADRINHOS AND MADRINHAS: ELDERS IN THE SANTO DAIME

I want to go on record: I am deeply grateful for all of the enormous physical and spiritual work that elders in the Santo Daime tradition have done, often at great cost to themselves, and with genuine sacrifice and tremendous courage, to share the Light and Love that they have received in-and-through the Santo Daime. I have such respect and reverence for these individuals who have spent decades drinking Daime, who have blazed the trail, and who are steeped in the Santo Daime path. Nonetheless, while I think that we always need to remain humbly open to the wisdom and guidance of elders, it also heartens me to see so many long-term North American daimistas who are calmly and naturally standing on their own two feet; daimistas who, without making a big deal about it, have acknowledged, in the conduct of their own lives, how important and valuable it is as daimistas to grow up, to claim our spiritual inheritance as (in the way that daimistas phrase it) Daughters and Sons of God. Of course, the madrinhas and padrinhos should be revered. They have labored to give birth to the Santo Daime and continue to work tirelessly to cultivate and strengthen this profound religious tradition. But at the same time, as these elders themselves would be the first to emphasize, on another and crucial level, all of us are equal; we are *all* Daughters and Sons of God and the Divine Mother. And I can say that North

American churches of the Santo Daime have worked extremely hard to embody just these attitudes. While the padrinhos and madrinhas are, for the most part, deeply revered, the ultimate decision-making power rests with the leaders of the North American churches themselves.

We're all, elders included, fallible human beings doing our best in this world of illusion. We're all working on our own cluster of buried psychological material; we're all having to deal with acknowledging and correcting our own distorted perspectives on others and other selves; we're all having to work to moderate our hair-trigger reactivity. And given that the Daime will often compassionately but forcefully bring so much of this material to the surface in the context of Santo Daime works, not surprisingly, dysfunctional issues around power, hierarchy, and submission to or rebellion against authorities can play themselves out in the context of Santo Daime works.

For example, it can sometimes be just so tempting to want to transfer all sorts of infantile psychological "stuff" onto Santo Daime padrinhos and madrinhas— especially if and when these madrinhas and padrinhos have become energetically linked in our memories with extremely powerful visionary/mystical openings and mediumistic encounters—moments of transcendent beauty and countless other spiritual unveilings that have forever altered our world. It's only natural that we would, often subconsciously, ascribe almost godlike powers to the individuals who were leading the works in which these transformative events took place; that we'd enjoy looking up to them; that we'd feel uplifted in their presence. And all of this is, at least to a certain extent, completely natural and to be expected. We just need to keep alert: the mostly well-deserved respect that most daimistas feel for our elders can at times become intertwined with "something else": the deeply human subconscious desire to remain a child and to have others make decisions for us; the childish belief that there is some wise, benevolent, superior, almost godlike being who is always, and in all ways, acting in our best interests. We often do this so we don't have to do the hard work of thinking for ourselves and making our own choices.

And even if we're consciously aware of the tendency to idealize or demonize padrinhos and madrinhas (or gurus, roshis, lamas, and so on) that type of transference can still be tremendously alluring. For example, I remember one evening when I was standing by the front door of a Santo Daime church that I was attending, and I watched in amazement at how quickly and easily I got swept up in the "glamor" of this one padrinho as he walked in: suddenly, even though I had rather recently become somewhat disenchanted with certain aspects of his behavior (another story all to itself), I found myself filled with fondness for him; and it wasn't hard to spot within myself the almost irresistible desire to do or say something that would please him. On some level, I could tell that I was swimming in the juicy goodness that everyone seemed to be hooking into as he walked in. I was relishing that feeling of joyfully connecting with everyone, as we were all energetically uplifted in his presence. And basking in all of this glowing energy of positivity, as everyone was offering folded-hand hyper-respect to this highly charismatic padrinho as he sat down, it was almost impossible to remain the grumpy negative "realist" who was crystal clear about certain less than positive personality features of this particular padrinho. (And in retrospect, my willingness to let go of my negativity was clearly a boon: I never want to close my heart to anyone, at any time. I can continue to see someone clearly, but I try to make sure that this seeing is infused with compassion.)

Still, I have to say that, almost to a person, the madrinhas and padrinhos in the Santo Daime tradition are very humble, simple, straightforward, down-to-earth, and openhearted people. They are individuals who are extraordinarily easy to be with. When I have had the opportunity to spend time with them, often in the home of someone they don't know well (that is, a family hosting them during that stop on a tour), they are almost always completely at ease, joking and sharing stories.

Yet I have also been struck time and time again by how unique each madrinha and padrinho is, each possessing a highly specific configuration of gifts. Some are firebrands, seeking to ignite the spiritual fires of others; some are gentle shining hearts of maternal Presence; some are embodiments of clarity, openness, and Light; some are centered dynamos that radiate love for God. Nonetheless, each one, in her or his own way, has labored for decades and with enormous selfless devotion to God to share the Santo Daime with others. Yes, these elders are human beings, just like all of us. They clearly struggle at times with their own psychological issues, just like all of us. But they make no claims of infallibility or final enlightenment. Instead, they simply work hard to share with others the Light that they have received from Mestre Irineu, and each Santo Daime church can, in its own way, testify to the gifts that they have received from these elders.

MORE IS NOT ALWAYS BETTER

Even given all of my admiration, and even love, for the Santo Daime as a religious tradition, I have to admit that there are occasionally aspects of the tradition that I think could use some nudges in a different direction. I'm thinking, in particular, of the "more is always better" mentality that some daimistas appear to have internalized.

The ideal for many daimistas is to become a disciplined soldier in the army of the Queen. And after all, we can't get anywhere in our spiritual lives without discipline. At times it's really valuable to prod ourselves to move past our laziness; to release the ego's ingrained tendency to whine and complain; and to simply keep moving forward, with commitment and faith, doing what we need to do to better support others in the salão who are sharing the work with us. And if practiced with a sense of balance and care, these attitudinal norms can be extremely helpful in our spiritual life. Given the fact that the Santo Daime path inherently and repeatedly asks a *lot* from us, there are definitely many times when, as daimistas (and more generally as human beings), we need to dig really deep within and find the capacity to keep going, even if we might be convinced that we simply cannot. During works we can at times feel stretched to the limits of our capacity (and then some), and so at times we simply have to be willing to push ourselves beyond those often self-imposed limits.

Nonetheless, if we're not careful, as we keep pushing and pushing and pushing, we can suddenly find that we've lost the innate joy that used to fuel our desire to do works. We can find that this joy has been replaced, almost without our noticing, with a dull and heavy sense of obligation.

Working with the more is always better tendency within ourselves, both as daimistas and simply as spiritual seekers and human beings, can at times be extremely perplexing. There's a delicate balance between the often admirable desire to plunge headlong into the Santo Daime path—going to as many works as possible and giving yourself completely to each and every work—and the less admirable tendency to go to work after work because the child within is hyper-vigilant, seeking to please various internalized versions of Santo Daime authority figures by doing those works in exactly the way that we imagine they think those works *should* be done (and perhaps projecting scowls of disapproval onto real Santo Daime authority figures when we fear that we didn't quite live up to their expectations).

However, with the help of the Daime itself, it is possible to gradually recognize and heal much of this highly dysfunctional psychological material. The Daime itself will often illuminate, for example, the ways in which, at least in part, we might go to work after work because on some level we believe that we need that "hit" of expanded consciousness to feel complete or know that we are worthy of love or overcome a nagging sense of "wrongness" within ourselves. With the help of the Daime itself, it is possible to gradually recognize how we might, on a subtle level, be attending works due to an inner voice of guilt and shame. With the help of the Daime itself, it is possible to begin to recognize the extent to which we have been taking Daime as a way to escape from the complexities and demands of daily life—as a way to avoid doing the hard, nitty-gritty work that is needed to nurture ongoing intimate relationships with our family and non-daimista loved ones, to create and sustain a thriving career, or to attend to the other important aspects of human life.

None of these insights, in-and-of-themselves, are reasons to stop drinking Daime—especially because it's often the Daime itself that has been bringing us those very realizations. It is the Daime itself that can help us to slowly and gradually learn to accept and love ourselves, fully, exactly as we are. It is the Daime itself that can show us that we don't need to do anything in order to be loved, unconditionally, by God and the Divine Mother. It is the Daime itself that can show us directly and forcefully that more is *not* always better.

And yet it's complicated, and I know this. Because there are numerous daimistas, many of them good friends of mine, for whom more *is* better. These daimistas not only take on the full Santo Daime liturgical calendar, but also frequently travel around the country, or go to Brazil for extended periods of time, in order to participate in works with various Santo Daime elders. And these friends of mine, who I deeply admire and respect, thrive in this rigorous, full-bore immersion into the depth and breadth of the Santo Daime tradition. It is crystal clear to me that, at least for these daimistas, at this time in their lives, it is deeply healing and powerfully transformative to plunge into the maelstrom of ongoing Santo Daime works. (I know the feeling well: I have done it many times myself.) It can feel inherently valuable to simply spend all of those hours marinating in the current, to become immersed fully in the ongoing liturgical calendar of the Santo Daime tradition.

Nonetheless, we're all different. We're all at different stages of our lives, and we all have different configurations of what we need spiritually. And it is clear, at least to me, that for some daimistas, that pedal to the metal ritual schedule can simply be too much.

I have seen several full-bore daimistas who gradually began to recognize that the immersion into the Santo Daime calendar that had previously worked wonderfully for them in their lives was no longer feeling appropriate. And this should not be surprising. It can be exceedingly difficult for daimistas to balance, at least for extended periods of time, doing the whole Santo Daime ritual calendar with other perhaps equally important aspects of their lives, such as spending time with their family; nurturing their careers; taking part in activities that are physically, creatively, and emotionally rejuvenating. And so, it is not uncommon to see long-term, deeply committed daimistas who will suddenly need to "take a break" from the ongoing round of works—a decision that the spiritual leaders within the Santo Daime basically accept and support. (Spiritual freedom is deeply valued in the Santo Daime tradition.) It's just that the break can all too often become a complete split with the tradition.

> The Santo Daime tradition might well benefit from a close examination of the ways in which the spiritually based more is always better mindset is perhaps, on a subtle level, an echo of the acquisitive, purely quantitative, more is always better mentality that leads many people within our capitalist culture to believe that they are only successful if they've earned more money or have more power than others. (See Andrew Dawson's contribution to this discussion in *Santo Daime: A New World Religion* [London: Bloomsbury, 2013], 153–192.) I think it is crucial for daimistas to acknowledge, both within ourselves and within the tradition itself, distorted "spiritual" versions of this compulsive, driven, "I've got to get ahead" mentality—our own versions of "spiritual materialism." (See Chögyam Trungpa, *Cutting Through Spiritual Materialism* (Boulder, CO: Shambhala Publications, 2002).

The more is always better mentality that many of us have internalized can also convince us that all we really have to do is to come to lots of works and drink lots of Daime and all of our problems will automatically disappear—no other inner work is needed. But this assumption is clearly, at best, only a partial truth. It is simply not the case that the more Daime you drink, the more automatically evolved you become. Spiritual evolution can never be quantified in this way. There are all too many daimistas who have drunk gallons of Daime and yet clearly, at least to my admittedly fallible vision, seem to have plenty more spiritual work to do within themselves. And conversely, there are people who are relatively new to the Santo Daime and yet, perhaps due to their prior spiritual work/good karma/the grace of God, appear to be natural shining examples of what a human being can become.

Clearly, we can and do gain a lot from drinking the Daime. As I have emphasized, our subtle body can gradually become realigned and upgraded; deep levels of subconscious material can arise for healing; we can become increasingly aware of and aligned with subtle flows of powerful energy; we can become more and more responsive to the guidance that is given to us from countless Beings of Light; we can deepen our capacity to be openhearted

Again, I'm keenly aware of the difficulties of making spiritual assessments of the relative spiritual "progress" of any other human being. We can never really know what a person is working on within themselves, or what spiritual tasks they have been called upon to accomplish in this lifetime. I would be the last person to claim that I know what is best for someone else—that assessment is completely between her/him and God/the Divine Mother.

and compassionate and to see life and ourselves with clarity and Light; and we can become increasingly able to remain firm within—grounded, centered, calm, and in our hearts—even in the middle of the whirling maelstrom of the Force. But equally clearly, drinking large amounts of Daime, both in works and over time, does not automatically produce these positive changes within us. Drinking Daime is *not* like taking a pill, where we can just lie back and, predictable as clockwork, a certain specific dosage of chemical ingredients will automatically produce the results that we expect (or perhaps demand). The Daime is a powerful and benevolent partner in our spiritual journey, but it is not a one-size-fits-all panacea. Drinking Daime by no means absolves us from taking full responsibility for our spiritual progress. We always bring all of who we are—our attitudes and assumptions, our goals and desires, our choices and decisions—into our spiritual lives. The Daime opens countless doors within us, and it is a genuine fountain of divine grace, but ultimately we are the ones who have to steer the boats of our spiritual lives.

Nonetheless, it is also true that we can benefit strongly from the good company of others who are strongly committed to their spiritual paths. I have often felt deep gratitude to certain key leaders of the Santo Daime tradition who have taken on the not always easy task of encouraging their fardados to overcome their inertia and attend works in a regular, committed way. And I am also keenly aware that these same Santo Daime leaders also emphasize the importance of balance and moderation; they let their fardados know, often with genuine kindness and patience, that the Santo Daime path is closer to a marathon than it is to a sprint; they communicate to their fardados that they can and should recognize that the spiritual life has a type of organic timing that it is important to honor—there's a time to plunge in, full-bore, without holding back, and there's a time to dial things back a bit, to rest and assimilate the riches that have been received. Many of these Santo Daime leaders (especially the elders) are highly skilled at this challenging balancing act: knowing when to "rally the troops" and when to ease up a bit, when to "crack the whip," and when to comfort and soothe those who need their heartfelt support.

I would reiterate, therefore, that we learn from these skilled elders and continue to examine, both within ourselves and within our respective communities, if in fact more is always better and, instead, have faith that everything is in God's hands. We can cultivate patience with our failings and flaws, relax, open, and surrender to what is, in the moment, with no need to go anywhere else or to become someone else.

In addition, I think that it is important to recognize that while the Daime can be a powerful catalyst in our spiritual lives, ideally taking the Daime can and should be integrated with other aspects of an ongoing spiritual life, such as regular periods of meditation, mantra repetition, yogic asana practice, bodywork, scriptural study, therapeutic work, and so on. My sense is that the best daimistas are meditators *and* the spiritual depth of even seasoned, well-practiced meditators often skyrockets with the help of the Daime.

All of the fruits of an ongoing, regular meditative life—increasing our capacity to focus on what's happening in the present and deepening our ability to still and quiet our minds, so that we can, more and more rest in that ever-present Silence and spacious Awareness that surrounds each and every thought and feeling—all of these abilities can help daimistas, little by little, to learn how to successfully navigate the Force during works. Seasoned meditators who drink the Daime have the capacity to recognize when their minds are running away from them and they can then gently come back to the present, to the breath, to the heart. Having worked over prolonged periods of time to learn how to quiet and focus their minds, long-term meditators are typically not thrown around quite as much as non-meditators by the often-turbulent waves of the Force and are often more skilled than non-meditators at cultivating a calm, mindful Presence during works.

And, again, it is also true that the spiritual life of long-term meditators can also be helped tremendously by drinking the Daime. As someone who meditated regularly for decades before drinking the Daime, I continue to be deeply grateful for the ways in which the Daime helped to rekindle my spiritual longing and deepened my faith as a direct result of the powerful visionary/mystical experiences that I have received through the Daime. Before drinking the Daime, I had been blessed with several powerful visionary/mystical experiences, but not to the degree or with the frequency that became possible with the Daime. Over and over again, the Daime has bestowed so many wondrous visionary/mystical experiences that my spiritual life has become utterly revolutionized. The Daime is an inner Fire that continues to encourage me to return to my mat, to my prayer life, to my contemplative study, to my practice of mantra repetition, with increased enthusiasm and joy, having Known, often repeatedly and in a multitude of ways, the previously unseen riches of the many dimensions of reality that are increasingly unveiling themselves within my inner sight.

8

Mediumship in the Santo Daime

Returning yet again to my time in Céu do Mapiá, I'd like to describe a powerful mediumship work: the *Mesa Branca* (the "White Table") work.[1] However, before I dive into my experience with the Mesa Branca in Mapiá, it might be helpful to present a brief outline of the decades-long development of mediumistic studies within the CEFLURIS line of the Santo Daime, since in certain respects, the Mesa Branca is the culmination of that development and synthesizes within itself the various streams of that ongoing evolution. (More detailed information about the evolution of healing/mediumship works is available in "The Historical Development of the Santo Daime: Section Two—The Life and Work of Padrinho Sebastião" at www.liquidlightbook.com/padrinho.)

Mediumistic works in the Santo Daime are often called "healing" works, since these works are held with a powerful healing intention, not just for members of the church, but also for disembodied beings. Furthermore, the healing that is the focus of these works is seen as happening on all levels (physically, emotionally, mentally, energetically, and spiritually). Mestre Irineu himself, from the beginnings of the Santo Daime in Rio Branco in the early 1930s, was a well-known and powerful healer. While he had previously (between 1916 and 1917) worked with ayahuasca within a mediumistic context as a high-ranking member of the Círculo de Regeneração e Fé (the Circle of Regeneration and Faith), the healing works he created within the context of the Santo Daime were not mediumistic. Instead, they were Concentration works in which, for example, a group of daimistas would gather around the bed of a sick person, drink Daime, and share a period of concentration, drawing upon the healing power not only of the Daime but also of the combined healing intentions of the participants.[2]

The movement toward explicitly mediumistic works within the Santo Daime took place primarily due to Padrinho Sebastião, a man who was born with strong mediumistic gifts. In 1955, when Sebastião Mota de Melo was living in the Juruá River valley, he met a Spiritist medium named Mestre Oswaldo and began training with him. Mestre Oswaldo helped Sebastião to develop the capacity to work with two spirit guides, Dr. Bezerra de Menezes and Professor Antonio Jorge, who manifested within him in order to heal those who were sick and suffering. Sebastião was also a *rezador*—a person who uses prayers in a focused, ritualistic way to heal various illnesses or wounds (Sebastião was said to be especially effective in curing the illnesses of young children.)[3] Sebastião became well known in the region for his healing abilities, but after a year or so of working together, Mestre Oswaldo prophesized that Sebastião would discover his spiritual destiny in Acre, a neighboring state in Brazil. Inspired, Sebastião loaded up his large family and all of his possessions into a wooden canoe that he had built, and after an arduous almost forty-day journey (with him and his older sons dragging the canoe upstream), he arrived in Rio Branco in 1957 and settled in the Colonia Cinco Mil (or the 5000 Colony) with his wife's extended family.

After his arrival in Colónia Cinco Mil, Sebastião continued his healing/mediumistic sessions. But in the late 1950s, Sebastião became very ill, and was only healed after going to his first Santo Daime work with Mestre Irineu in 1964. During that work he received a powerful healing from spirit doctors who removed the spiritual source of his illness. Not surprisingly, Sebastião became an ardent member of the Santo Daime and rather quickly, with Mestre Irineu's blessing, began to lead a Santo Daime community in Colónia Cinco Mil (although Padrinho Sebastião and his followers also regularly attended festival works in Mestre's community, walking several hours both ways).

During this time period, and for a few years following Mestre Irineu's death in 1971, Padrinho Sebastião had not been working mediumistically. His spirit guides had informed him that they were going to recede for around ten years, except for emergency cases, in order for him to have the space to immerse himself in the Santo Daime. Then, sometime in 1977, following a series of traumatic events that powerfully impacted the community of Colónia Cinco Mil, Padrinho Sebastião's mediumship opened up once again as a way for him to work to transform the negative entities/energies that he and his community were struggling with—work that continued when he relocated his community deep in the forest in a settlement that they created and called Rio do Ouro (River of Gold).

In Rio do Ouro, Padrinho Sebastião began to do powerful mediumistic works called the *trabalho da mata* (the "forest work") in order to spiritually transform these negative entities/energies, working especially with a being known as Tranca Rua. When these beings were finally "indoctrinated"—that is, when they shifted from being enemies of the Santo Daime to being its allies—they asked that the Santo Daime community build a small house for them so that charitable works could continue for the purpose of illuminating and transforming "suffering spirits," a request that led to the creation of the first "Star House." In the Star House works, the healing hymns of Padrinho Sebastião, and later the hymns of others as well, were sung to help suffering spirits who were seeking the Light of the Daime.

Meanwhile, around this same period of time, beginning in Colónia Cinco Mil, in the wake of the community challenges mentioned earlier, Padrinho Alfredo, Sebastião's son, also began a powerful series of mediumistic works that eventually became formalized as the St. Michael work—a work with similar goals to that of the Star House work—illuminating and transforming suffering/obsessing spirits.

The St. Michael work eventually ended up absorbing other healing/mediumistic modalities into itself, especially the work with spirits that had been developed within the Umbanda tradition—a powerful and widespread Brazilian mediumistic religion. When the Santo Daime first expanded outside the Amazon rainforest region in the early 1980s, people who had exposure to Umbanda discovered the Daime. This contact was deepened and "formalized" around 1985 when Baixinha, a Mãe de Santo, or long-term leader of an Umbanda community, began to participate in Santo Daime works in Padrinho Alex Polari's community in Mauá, a process that eventually led her spiritual guide, Tupinambá, to decide to take on the task of developing the mediumship of daimistas. Soon afterward, periodic Umbanda sessions, or *giras*, began to take place within different Santo Daime contexts, eventually leading to the development of Umbandaime rituals—a process that was deepened by the arrival in Céu do Mapiá of two other Umbandista-trained mediums: Maria Alice and Clara, who helped to usher in this fusion of Umbanda mediumship and the Santo Daime.[4]

Then, in the time leading up to Padrinho Sebastião's death in January 20, 1990, the community in Céu do Mapiá underwent another powerful and tumultuous process during which Padrinho Sebastião was not only physically in pain from an ongoing, debilitating illness but also suffering from numerous negative entities that were manifesting in-and-through him. During this time, Padrinho Alfredo led a series of special works to illuminate these beings—works that evolved and continued after Padrinho Sebastião's death: works in which "spirit doctors" would manifest through various members of the community and do spiritual "operations" on people who were suffering, both physically and mentally.

Soon after Padrinho Sebastião's death, Isabel Barsé, a daimista from the south of Brazil, began to receive messages from the Emmanuel line of spiritual beings—that is, from various disembodied ("ascended") Masters and cosmic Beings who, it is said, work to bring the Energy and Light of the Christ Consciousness to our plane of reality. The Mesa Branca works began when Padrinho Alfredo, Padrinho Corrente, Padrinho Alex, and Isabel Barsé decided to combine the Emmanuel line of esoteric study/spiritual development with Padrinho Sebastião's healing works, Padrinho Alfredo's St. Michael work, the works that invoked the spirit doctors, and works from the Umbanda lineage brought by Baixinha, Maria Alice, and Clara. The Mesa Branca was created in order that there could be an explicit format for the regular study of these various types of mediumship within the CEFLURIS line of the Santo Daime.

The Mesa Branca work also drew upon the occult eclecticism of the Esoteric Circle of the Communion of Thought—the spiritual group that Mestre Irineu and his community (including Padrinho Sebastião) were officially affiliated with from 1963 to 1970—with its emphasis on the Ascended Masters, yoga, developing self-knowledge, spiritual affirmations, and the search for spiritual perfection. The Mesa Branca work was explicitly understood to be the venue in which different "lines"— not only Umbanda and the Emmanuel line, but also (at least theoretically) other spiritual paths such as yoga, Sufism, and the Kabbalah—could be presented within the church. In addition, the choice to have the Mesa Branca work take place in Céu do Mapiá on the twenty-seventh of each month came, at least indirectly, from the Esoteric Circle of the Communion of Thought, in that this group also met on this date during Mestre Irineu's affiliation with this organization.

MESA BRANCA: CÉU DO MAPIÁ

On July 27, 2010, the Mesa Branca work began just a little after 7:00 p.m. and finished after 1:30 a.m. When the work started, the church was, as usual, almost empty. But it began to fill up after the Oracão, when Padrinho Alfredo arrived (the locals in Mapiá seemed to have a type of "padrinho radar"). He led us in some special prayers that only happen in this work (during one of them he was holding three lit taper candles in one hand, candles that were then set on the floor in front of his seat at the central altar, arranged in a triangular pattern). Padrinho Alfredo also read throughout the work at different moments from a collection of spontaneous talks given by Padrinho Sebastião and, equally episodically, offered off-the-cuff prayers of his own on behalf of all of us.

During this work I drank Daime three times: the first time the shot glass was full, the other two times it was only about half full. After about thirty minutes of heartfelt singing, I began to notice that the Force was becoming active within me. Not only could I feel this Force viscerally coursing through my body, but in response to that energetic pulsation, my head and torso began to softly, yet quite rapidly, oscillate around the central energetic pillar of my body, accompanied at times by extremely fast, albeit rather quiet inhalations and exhalations through my nose. Seen from the outside, it probably looked like I was rapidly shaking my head back and forth, but from within, it felt as if my body was being moved, without my instigation, by a Force that was simultaneously deep within me and yet also, in certain respects, "other" than me.

These initial sounds and movements, which were accompanied by the intuitive sense that both my subtle and physical body were being prepared and opened for the next stage of the ritual—full-bore mediumship—were almost identical to the spontaneous bodily movements and sounds (or *kriyas*) that I used to make, decades before, when I was a member of Siddha Yoga, a neo-Tantric Kundalini yoga and meditation tradition.[5] Similarly, the shapes that my hands were beginning to take and the movements that they were making (primarily elaborate circles and spirals, often while rotating at the wrist as the fingers subtly but decisively repositioned themselves, all without any conscious effort or decision on my part) looked a lot like the *mudras* that are commonly seen in yoga or the hand gestures of classical Indian dancers.[6]

I will admit that I am fascinated by the ways in which much of the spiritual work that I did before my exposure to the Santo Daime seems to have anticipated and/or prepared me for the experience of mediumship. I am convinced, at least in retrospect, that I was being prepared for mediumship during the decade in which I was a practitioner of Siddha Yoga, working explicitly with the energies of the awakened Kundalini. From that spiritual tradition, I gained a familiarity and ease with a sense of a benevolent spiritual power that could and would move my body in unexpected, yet intriguing, ways. During that time I developed within myself the capacity to open up to a Greater Power; I learned how to let go and trust that this Power would manifest itself within me in just the way that it should. I also learned how to watch from some calm, quiet place within me while something apparently greater than my ego would initiate movements and sounds within my body—movements and sounds that were the physical manifestations of a deeper, more subtle pulsation of spiritual energy, movements that I could never replicate by sheer force of will but could always stop if they became too intense or if I was in an inappropriate social setting.

I believe that I was also trained for my mediumship in the Santo Daime by what I learned, about a decade after I had left that meditation group, as both a student of and teacher in not one but two energy healing schools that both had, in part, a strong neo-Reichian orientation. I did transformational work there that involved helping myself and then others to free up the body and voice and learned (and then taught) how to most effectively release and free up bodily energies that, due to personal traumas or social pressure, had previously been locked down or held back.[7] For many years as a neo-Reichian practitioner and teacher within those two energy healing schools, I was offered a context in which I was not only trained to sense the ebb and flow of subtle energies, but I was also strongly encouraged to move my body in ways that dramatically went against my own internalizations (from early childhood) of social models of how a person should move, stand, and speak.

That hard-won visceral willingness to let my body freely follow the flux of subtle energies served me well during the development of my mediumship in the Santo Daime tradition, in large part because a crucial aspect of the development of my mediumship has been my attempts to overcome my fear of exhibitionism, as well as my perceived "too much-ness." I know those tendencies in myself, so at times I have had to fight against strong inner prohibitions and complex knots of psychological defenses that say: don't act like that; don't embarrass yourself; don't be too loud, too wild, too crazy.

Nonetheless, even though I have been intrigued by the similarities between the quality of energy work that I have learned in these strikingly different traditions, it is also clear to me that there is a unique energetic "note" to what I experience in-and-through the Daime, a note that became increasingly insistent as I took the next step forward in this ritual process, which was the collective singing of another group of hymns that have the explicit intention of invoking various "spirits of Light" (*espíritos da Luz*), in particular, hymns invoking the archangel St. Michael and his retinue. During the Mesa Branca, even before singing these hymns, I had already begun a process of inner opening and preparation—manifesting numerous bodily movements that at times felt similar to those of some sort of underwater plant, swaying and undulating in a river of Light and Force. (Rick, who also attended the work, later commented that I looked like a combination of a sweet autistic child and a daimista Stevie Wonder.) And so, when my consciousness finally returned to an awareness of the room and the people around me, it was not at all surprising that almost as soon as I started singing the St. Michael hymns, my mediumship began to strongly open up within me, and I began to incorporate various spirits of Light.

At this point, the women mediums in the church also began to "pop" left and right: the church was soon filled with young, middle-aged, and older women—some of them standing up, arms raised, sending blessings out to everyone; others spinning in circles; others dancing wildly in the aisles; others walking around from person to person, at times stopping to energetically heal people who were sitting down in their chairs, where they would place their hands on the person's chest, or brush the person down. Other female mediums were shouting out a rush of unintelligible phrases, while others were roaring away—alternately laughing and weeping and screaming—in the women's healing room. Another woman began to strongly sing out a personal hymn of her own in the salão just as one of the "formal" hymns ended and before another could begin. And yet another sat in her chair, arms extended out from her sides shaking unimaginably fast along with her head and torso.

During all of this wildness, I was not exactly Mr. Tame and Timid myself. The hymns invoking the presence of the archangel St. Michael seemed to stir the pot, mediumistically speaking. So much opened up, so fast, so strong, for so long—hours and hours of nonstop mediumship. The mediumship movements all came and went so quickly, in such a rush, with so little conscious intention, and I was carried along with the Current so strongly, that it was almost impossible to remember even a fraction of what occurred. But I do remember at one point my right hand, in what I call the "deer" mudra (my thumb and pinky and pointer fingers up, and my middle two fingers pointing down) began to rotate and revolve in front of my chest whipping around over the top of my head, as if I was lassoing and pulling down the Light, while at another moment my right and left hands took turns vibrating and shaking, very rapidly, over my head as if I was a type of hovercraft attempting to take off.

RUMINATIONS ON MEDIUMSHIP

It seems important to say a bit more about the dauntingly complex and endlessly fascinating topic of mediumship before continuing my description of the Mesa Branca work.

To begin with, to my mind, *every* Santo Daime ritual, at least to a certain extent, is mediumistic, in that the Daime embodies the Consciousness of a vastly intelligent and compassionate divine Being, a Being that, for Santo Daime practitioners, is equated with the transformative Light and redemptive Love of the Christ. Therefore, simply by drinking the Daime within the context of a work, daimistas consciously allow themselves to act as a conduit by which this Christ Consciousness can incarnate within human form in order, as Jonathan Goldman writes in the preface to *The Religion of Ayahausca*, "to provide teaching, comfort, healing, and spiritual evolution" to those who have gathered together to take this sacramental brew, as well as to compassionately transform the darkness, suffering, and negativity of the planet into Light and Love.[8] (By the way, the Daime, at least to my way of thinking, is a *genuine* sacrament: it is the physical manifestation/vehicle of a Divine Being. By drinking the Daime our physical bodies and the materiality of the Daime conjoin, they commune, until we are, physically and energetically permeated by and suffused with the Christ Consciousness.)

Yet even though just drinking the Daime is in this way a very exalted form of mediumship, there are several works of the Santo Daime tradition that are explicitly dedicated to the cultivation of mediumship, and the Mesa Branca work is one of the most powerful. Mediumship works are opportunities, at least for those daimistas who have this specific mission, to develop and utilize their mediumistic abilities for the sake of others. (Daimistas often say that all people are mediums, but not everyone chooses to unfold and cultivate this latent capacity, at least within this lifetime. I have been working to develop my mediumship for quite a few years now, but I am still learning. There are many daimistas whose mediumship is much, much more developed than mine will perhaps ever be.)

A medium is someone who willingly permits their aparelho (literally, "instrument," that is, the person's body, mind, and spirit) to incorporate a variety of spiritual beings. Numerous spiritual entities are frequently invoked within the context of Santo Daime rituals, entities who are connected to and emerge from Amerindian, Catholic, Spiritist, esoteric, and African traditions—Jesus, the Virgin Mary, John the Baptist, Orixás (the powerful spirits of nature that come from the Yoruba tradition of West Africa), spirit guides, angels and archangels, *caboclos* (in this context, understood to be the spirits of deceased Native Americans), and *preto velhos* (the spirits of deceased African slaves). And these are only the spirits of Light. There are also countless other spirits drawn from the Umbanda tradition, such as *exus*—spirits of men who in their prior lives had been very coarse and rough, perhaps addicted to alcohol and violence, and yet, having received divine grace, have become (still rather down-to-earth) protector spirits; or *pomba giras*—the spirits of "women of the street" who (again with the help of divine grace) have transformed themselves into emissaries of beauty and love. There are also countless nameless spirits that can appear within the context of a Santo Daime ritual that are difficult, if not impossible, to categorize, as well as those entities known as suffering spirits (*espíritos sofredores*), the spirits of human beings who have died and yet, because of their lack of spiritual development, continue to have a negative influence upon living human beings. (I will write much more about all of these entities later on.)

I have to say right up front that at times it can be hard, at least at my level of development, to be certain as to exactly who or what is manifesting within my aparelho during a mediumship work (whereas more developed mediums will often say that they receive highly detailed information about the specific characteristics of the beings that they are incorporating). All that I know for sure is that whoever or whatever arrives does so under the power and protection of the Daime. (I remember Jonathan Goldman saying that the most important thing to understand about mediumship in the Santo Daime tradition is that in-and-through the Daime, mediumship has been anointed with Light, so that mediumship in this tradition always functions for the greatest good of everyone, unlike in some other mediumship traditions, where mediumship can be used for less than positive purposes, such as for personal gain or to have power over others).

There are certain times during the process of my own mediumship in which I *will* have a clear visionary sense of who or what is arriving, especially (for some reason) when I am incorporating the spirits of Light, who I will at times perceive as living, vibrant, extremely powerful, and intricately geometric forms of crystalline Light, Beauty, and Presence. At other times, I have seen what might be called "doctors" of Light who gather around my often-prostrate physical body in order to clear and attune the various levels of my subtle body. But there frequently are also times in which the only knowledge that I have of who or what is manifesting within me is gained through watching, almost from above, the ways in which my physical body moves. And there can be a *lot* of variety in that movement, especially when I'm incorporating spirits of Light.

For instance, I might find myself standing up, my arms raised, my head and back arched up and back, singing the hymns full force, my eyes closed and forcefully drawn up and back within my skull, as I see golden Light raining down on me, and I'm feeling, again and again, waves of ecstasy. Later, I might find myself with my arms moving in front and to the sides of my body in overlapping circles, with my two middle fingers arching forward and my thumb, pointer, and pinky fingers pulled upward as if they are being stretched and elongated by the lines of energy coursing through them, and watching as my hands then respond to that coursing flux of energy by rotating rapidly at the wrist, as if manifesting some sort of three-dimensional, ever-shifting infinity sign that interlaces itself in harmony with the rhythms and melodies of the hymns that fill the hall. I can be doing all of this while calmly noticing the fact that I am deeply breathing in and out while my tongue flutters inside my mouth—producing, again without thought, rapid, high-pitched, whistling reverbs of sound.

It feels inherently right and good to have my body moving in these ways. I feel in tune and aligned with the pulsations of the Force as it surges through my aparelho and I want to give whoever is wanting to express themselves in-and-through me the permission to manifest themselves within the protected space of the salão in order that they can transmit their blessings in whatever way they see fit.

In many ways, therefore, my knowledge of who or what is manifesting within me is primarily a kind of bodily or kinesthetic knowing rather than intellectual understanding. Very early on in the development of my mediumship, for instance, during a mediumship work with Jonathan Goldman, I was prompted from within, rather insistently, to move into the center of the circle (this particular work was more informal than some other Santo Daime ritual contexts and everyone was gathered in a large circle, which offered plenty of space for the mediums to work). I quickly found myself hunched over, with my left arm rather insistently and forcefully bent behind my back, as if I was trying to scratch my spine, while my right hand was raised and shaking back and forth rapidly in front of my mouth, all while releasing a quick series of high-pitched whistles. After the work ended, I talked to some of the more experienced daimistas, asking them if they had any sense about who or what was moving my body in this rather unusual way, and they all said very casually, "Oh that? That was a caboclo." (A caboclo, by the way, as I mentioned earlier, is—at least in this context—understood to be a spirit of a Native American.) At that point I had never even heard of such an entity. I had never, at least consciously, seen anyone else manifesting in that particular way. And so how then did my body somehow know exactly how a caboclo moves? Perhaps the simplest explanation is because a caboclo was actually incorporating within me.

Nonetheless, the more that I participated in different mediumship works, the more that I began to see that mediums tended to manifest a cluster of fairly predictable movements and sounds. And the more that I paid attention to the typically off-the-cuff comments of people who were more experienced than myself, the more that I was able to learn which stereotypical movements and sounds were associated with which particular group of spiritual beings.

At this point, for instance, I think that I can say that I'm fairly familiar with what it looks and feels like to incorporate a caboclo during a mediumship work. In fact, I'm fairly familiar with a whole panoply of different beings who have incorporated within me. And I would like to hope that these beings were manifesting in this way without any forcing on my part. Because as a medium, I've made a promise to myself to stay seated and to keep singing the hymns until the inner tug comes so insistently that I simply have to respond. But when I feel that clear-cut, albeit often extremely subtle, inner prompting, I'll take off my glasses and then quietly go to a place in the salão where I can move more freely. Then, rather quickly, I'll (for example) find myself bent over, my eyes partially shut, one hand arched behind my back, the other hand vibrating extremely fast in front of my face like some sort of energetic antenna, and then I'm off: whirling around the room like an entranced martial artist, sinking my weight down in one leg while rapidly moving my arms in circles—moving in ways that echo my Tai Chi background, all while my tongue is making loud sharp clicking noises; or while forceful exhalations or inhalations of air move in and out of my body as my tongue moves back and forth in my mouth producing quick percussive surges of sound; or as I make loud whoops or cries while stomping my feet on the ground and/or rapidly clapping my hands together. All of that repertoire of movements/sounds is "caboclo-esque"; it's part of a repertoire of potential "caboclo-like" movements/sounds (movements/sounds that might well have differing purposes: some might, for example, be manifesting as a way to cleanse and purify my own energetic "knots," while other very similar sounds/movements might be pouring through me in order to bless the space or to help shift the knotted energy of another daimista.)

I think that it is safe to say that these sorts of dramatic physical manifestations of mediumship demonstrate very vividly not only to the mediums themselves, but also equally importantly to the others in the worship hall, that something intense, grippingly vivid, and clearly significant is taking place. It quickly becomes clear that through the power of the Daime, an awe-inspiring, multifaceted Otherness is entering into the community and manifesting itself. In a very tangible way, those daimistas who might not be mediums can watch, fascinated, albeit with perhaps just a touch of apprehension, as the various mediums, seemingly sparked by the energies and rhythms of particular hymns and/or riffing off of each other in what might be called the "contagion" of mediumship, begin to shake and rock and stomp and cry and whistle and howl, clearly demonstrating to everyone present in the hall that this Divine drink that everyone had taken is full of Power.

During the Mesa Branca work, throughout this influx of dramatic bodily manifestations, which believe me was happening quite powerfully to *lots* of people in the hall, those who were not mediums (at least at the time) continued to fulfill their role, which is equally, if not more valued than mediumship; that is, while singing the hymns, they remained firm, grounded, and centered, acting as deeply rooted conduits for the Force to descend from the Astral in order to radiate to the world, healing and blessing it.

In fact, I would go so far as to say that while mediumship is valued in the CEFLURIS line of the Santo Daime tradition, it is also looked upon, at least by some and at certain times, with a complicated mixture of admiration, anxiety, envy, concern, and perhaps even, at least to an extent, a hint of veiled contempt. (I have heard some daimistas wonder out loud about the level of egoic involvement that they perceive in the mediumistic manifestations of others.) In many ways, the Santo Daime tradition deeply values those who can and do control their bodily movements—those who remain calm and still and focused—and it is these more reliable, more dependable, daimistas who are typically seated up front, close to the altar, whereas those daimistas with mediumistic tendencies, while perhaps admired, are also often seen, especially at the beginning of the development of their mediumship, as unpredictable and potentially disruptive.

As a medium, I completely understand this need to pay close and careful attention to those who are developing their mediumship. I remember Jonathan Goldman saying that mediumship has three parts: inspiration, ego, and drama. It is important, therefore, for a medium, while acknowledging the inner inspiration that she or he is receiving, to also try to minimize ego and drama as much as possible, all the while knowing, with humility and self-acceptance, that these somewhat less than positive aspects of mediumship will always be present, at least to a certain extent. (In fact, I would suggest that the mediums to watch out for are those daimistas, usually rather new to the tradition, who can at times become rather puffed up, self-certain, and self-righteous about their mediumship; those daimistas who will at times rather loudly, assert that everything that they say or do is fully and perfectly guided by God or some other equally divine Being of Light.)

On the other hand, I am deeply sympathetic with the difficulties that those who are new to their mediumship often face. Each medium has to navigate a highly dynamic, interactive, extremely intimate, and ceaselessly shifting spectrum of "me" and "not me," and it's sometimes easy to get lost. Mediums discover that the universe is thronging with countless beings who do not have the same clear-cut physical boundaries that we normally use to mark out the delimitations of the material space that we tend to believe that we inhabit.

SUFFERING SPIRITS

Even given all of this complexity, I think that I can safely say that although incorporating spirits of Light and/or having encounters with other countless beings that seem to inhabit our multidimensional universe is at times a rather charged and challenging process, for the most part, this form of mediumship can often be quite pleasurable, even ecstatic. However, incorporating suffering spirits is a whole other story.

Within the Santo Daime tradition, it is understood that suffering spirits are the spirits of human beings who have died but have not moved on to a higher realm. They are, in essence, stuck here in this level of reality, often due to unfinished business (regret, longing for revenge, unfulfilled desires) as well as addictions of various kinds (to drugs, alcohol, sex, violence), but due to the lack of a physical body they are not able to fulfill that endless craving. And these spirits are genuinely suffering—they are filled with almost unimaginable anger, terror, despair, self-loathing, and negativity. And unfortunately, to whatever extent that we have not worked on ourselves spiritually, we can and do attract these spirits to ourselves through our own negative behaviors, emotions, or beliefs. Whether we are daimistas or not, these spirits want nothing more than to encourage us to deepen our negativity so that they can, in-and-through our body and mind, continue to experience and reenact the same quality of addictive behaviors, obsessive thoughts, and dark feelings that they evidenced in their previous existence. Most of us, however, are not aware of this symbiotic and parasitic relationship, and we will often, unfortunately, allow ourselves to become subconsciously influenced by these suffering spirits—an influence that, if not corrected, can lead to a flood of toxic and disturbing emotions and thoughts, which in turn can catalyze a wide range of debilitating and detrimental psychological and even physical illnesses.[9] (In fact, within the Santo Daime, it is often said that the only people who are actually ever possessed are those individuals who, without their knowledge, allow themselves to be negatively influenced by suffering spirits.)

It is therefore the task of daimistas to work at becoming conscious of the ways in which these suffering spirits negatively impact their day-to-day existence and, with the help of the Daime, to attempt to become free from this previously unconscious influence.

Daimistas, however, do not typically practice exorcism. (There is one exception: the Crosses work. I will say more about this work later.) Daimistas do not seek to expel suffering spirits from their aparelhos. Instead, they are taught how to transform these spirits.

During this particular Mesa Branca work, this transformative process with suffering spirits began, as is typically the case, after the spirits of the Light had manifested themselves for a long period of time in a wide variety of forms, so that the aparelhos of the mediums had already been cleansed, opened, and filled the energy of divine Light and Love. Suffering spirits, like all spirits, on some level of their being, are understood to want to spiritually evolve. Therefore, they are attracted to the Light and Love that the Daime brings, which means that they will often crowd into the hall when they are invited, even if, at the same time, many of them arrive resisting that Light every step of the way, often literally kicking and screaming.

These suffering spirits were invited, at least implicitly, when we began to sing another collection of hymns that almost invariably seems to open the door to these spirits—the hymns of Cura I, a collection of hymns that were received by different elders and were often used within some of the early, extensive, and intensive, work with suffering spirits that took place within the CEFLURIS line of the Santo Daime. Over and over again, I am struck by how the energy changes in the room when these hymns are sung. In this case, the work of mediumship continued, but at least for me, its quality shifted: it became less about invoking and channeling wildly powerful archangelic energies and more about getting down and dirty, either releasing stuck, old, dark energetic debris from my subconscious or providing an opportunity for the suffering spirits to manifest themselves within my aparelho for the sake of transformation.

The process of incorporating suffering spirits began almost immediately for me. During the next hour or two, I sat in my chair, singing the hymns, if it was possible, sometimes feeling a bit nauseous or bloated from the presence of the Daime as it actively worked within my body. I'd then suddenly feel an influx of ecstasy, joy, love, and light that let me know that a Being of Light had arrived. And throughout the process, this Being (or Beings) would remain, and I would feel myself centered in my heart, calmly watching and witnessing everything that was going on within me and around me. Then, at a certain point, my physical body would suddenly and forcefully contract and tighten up as I was flooded with a quality of suffering that manifested either as anguish, rage, terror, grief, or self-loathing, depending upon the specific nature of the suffering spirit who had arrived.

I primarily remained seated in my chair during this part of the Mesa Branca work. There have been other works in which I would need to get up from my chair, and perhaps even go outside, so that I could give a spirit sufficient free space in which to express itself. But in this case, it was almost as if there was some sort of prior agreement between me and these spirits. It was almost as if on some level of my being I had told them, *Listen, you can enter, but there can't be a lot of drama—there are a lot of beings in line after you, so just come in, show yourself, manifest as minimally and quickly as possible, and then keep moving so that you can let yourself be raised up and transmuted.* Therefore, when a suffering spirit would arrive, I would, for example, hunch over in my seat, grimacing, my hands perhaps bent at the wrists, my fingers coming together like lobster claws, my arms almost hugging my body, while I groaned and moaned with anxiety and fear; or

I'd snarl as I roughly wiped my face, sneering with contempt at everything that was taking place, as I would carelessly blow astral phlegm into my hand and then shake it off to the side in disgust and disdain; or my hands would cover my face as I breathed in and out heavily and through my nose and mouth, not wanting to see or to be seen, writhing in self-loathing. I'd be hunched over, my body twisted and contorted, forming itself to the energetic quality of the being that was manifesting within me, while at the same time, another part of me would be "sitting back" inside myself, very calm, very still, very loving, offering compassion to this suffering spirit. Then, often rather quickly, sometimes in a matter of seconds, my torso would rise, I'd breathe in deeply, relax, and open up to the Light, and this being would be released and hopefully transformed. It was, in other words, a very restrained and modulated work with suffering spirits.

Although it didn't happen in this work, at times, if the suffering spirit is manifesting in a particularly dramatic way—and there can be a lot of screaming and thrashing and weeping at certain points in these sorts of works—one of the leaders of the ceremony might stand next to me, quietly say a few words of welcome to the spirit who was temporarily present in my aparelho, and then offer that spirit a small extra serving of Daime to drink—in-and-through my aparelho— as a way for that spirit to be filled with the transformative divine Light of the Daime. At other times, advanced mediums might also work with a spirit within me to help it to calm down or to move on, perhaps brushing my aparelho energetically or snapping their fingers around my aura or smudging my aparelho with the smoke of a sage stick.

But in this particular work, I simply remained in my seat as each being would come in, carrying with it a very clear sense of individuality. I would give the spirit some time to express itself, then little by little, very gently and patiently, following inner guidance, I'd begin to sit up straighter and let my torso begin to move and sway from side to side, almost as if I was shrugging off some emotional or energetic heaviness, as I would feel, and at times even see within myself, the energetic body of that suffering spirit beginning to uncurl and untighten; as I would watch or simply feel the dark, knotted strands of its prior substance unfurling, opening up. And I would feel tremendous grace and compassion as this being, often to its amazement, was welcomed and assisted by the Beings of Light who accompanied and guided it during this process.

There have been many times in which I have been deeply moved by how these suffering spirits would at first resist this inner welcome, would fight against the unconditional forgiveness they were receiving from the Beings of Light, protesting that they were not worthy of this level of Love, and yet finally, amazingly, they would let go. They would take in that Compassion and Light. Then, with sight, I would watch in awe as they would transform into a swirling ـs of crystalline light and almost explosive joy that rose upward and then merged, literally in a flash, into the Light that surrounded and welcomed them. (Some daimistas even believe that the more *negative* energy that the suffering spirit brings with it into that transformative encounter, the more *positive* power that spirit will manifest when that process is completed.)

In this particular Mesa Branca work, as with many other mediumship works, the transformational work with suffering spirits just went on and on, lasting about two hours. Almost the moment that one spirit had moved on (signaled by me sitting up fully erect, often lightly brushing off my arms, chest, back, legs, and head while making low soft whistling sounds, and then centering and aligning myself, once again, with my higher Self and/or the spirit of the Christ within me), then another spirit would arrive, with almost no breaks in the process. It was as if I was a spiritual train who would stop, take on a passenger, move forward, let them off, and then take on someone new.

By the end of the work I was, not surprisingly, extremely tired. This sort of incorporation process can be exhausting work, but it is also tremendously rewarding. Not only is it said that mediums acquire enormous merit from taking on this often difficult and demanding task, but more importantly, mediums also vicariously experience within themselves the Love, Light, and Forgiveness with which the suffering spirit was showered during that transformational process. Simultaneously, as mediums increasingly come to identify with the power of the Higher Self, with the I Am (the *Eu Sou*), or the power and presence of the Christ that is working within them, that identification itself, as it deepens, allows mediums (to the extent that they have purified themselves of their egoism and negativity) to become increasingly translucent to the Christ, who is their true being and who is manifest in the Daime itself, so that this Light and Love and Power can work in and through them to take on the sufferings of the world in order to transform and redeem them.

Interestingly, however, mediums do not have to be completely pure in order to do extremely powerful work. One of the amazing things about mediumship in the Santo Daime tradition is that our own neuroses and psychological complexes actually provide opportunities for suffering spirits to manifest themselves. What happens is that these spirits, drawn to a corresponding energetic "stuckness" within us, are in a sense provided with a door through which they can enter into our aparelhos. Paradoxically, therefore, it is through our own fears, doubts, anxieties, anger, and envy that these spirits are given an opportunity to incorporate within us. And as they are redeemed and transformed, so are we. Their healing becomes our own. The goal of mediumship, therefore, is not so much to eradicate or exorcise these less than perfect aspects of ourselves, but rather to bring them forward into our awareness with compassion, patience, and faith and allow them to transform.

OTHER FORMS OF MEDIUMSHIP

In the Santo Daime tradition, the incorporation of spirits (whether spirits of Light or suffering spirits) is actually only one form of mediumship, even though it is the most obvious and/or dramatic. Many mediums are so willing to serve and are so open to the pain and suffering and darkness that they sense around them, that they will, often without a lot of fuss, take that negativity into themselves to clear and transform it with the help of the Daime and the spirits of Light. Some daimistas actually argue that often the most advanced forms of mediumship are actually the least dramatic and do not even have to take place within the setting of a Santo Daime ritual.

Similarly, highly refined forms of mediumship can and do occur outside the ritual context of a Santo Daime ritual and don't necessarily involve a clear-cut spirit entering your body and mind. For example, I think mediumship is operative when you're playing the piano and then, out of the blue, something More begins to play in-and-through you. Or you're playing tennis, or dancing, and something similar happens. That is, there are those moments when you can feel yourself swept up into a powerful flux of energy and expanded awareness (and/or that energy/awareness pours down into you—take your pick of spatial metaphors) and your normal egoic boundaries dissolve. And then those activities suddenly undergo a qualitative shift; they take on a heightened sense of significance; they begin to feel more fluid, more connected, easier, and more attuned to the depths within.

In addition, moments of intuition and inner attunement with the depths within you can also be seen as powerful forms of mediumship. I know that I experience this myself when I'm teaching or giving a talk and I simply let the words flow from some deep, quiet place within, with no premeditation. I'll simply enter fully into the interaction in that moment with that particular conjunction of people, feeling the ever-shifting configuration of energies in the room intermeshing, not knowing moment to moment what I'm going to say, just trusting my alignment with my depths, letting "Something" speak in-and-through me. That's also full-bore mediumship, and I want to honor it as such.

In fact, much of *Liquid Light* is, perhaps not surprisingly, itself a result of mediumship, even while, in a consciously Escher-esque level of narrative doubling back on itself, *Liquid Light* is also a text that frequently and explicitly—such as right now—attempts to describe and explore some of the many subtle and complex layers of the fascinating phenomenon of mediumship. During the process of writing this book, I have consciously and repeatedly, in an ongoing way (as much as possible) offered my body and mind as what I hope is a fairly well-tuned vehicle for something More to pour "Itself" out into this world, even in the often painfully limited form of written words. Or, said differently, as I write, moment to moment I seek to lean back into Vastness; I let myself sink deep within myself (another "direction," if you will, of mediumship) as my mind gradually drops into an Ocean of Silence. Then, if I'm fortunate, I will often simply watch as words flow out on the computer screen, as a result of this creative interplay between "me" (whatever that is) and the Divine (whatever that is).

This focused, ongoing attempt to align myself with my divine nature—a process that, to me, is the deepest/highest form of mediumship—has been there, actively, for decades now, so it would be odd if I suddenly put all of that spiritual practice (the true heart of my life) on the shelf, unused and unacknowledged, while I dutifully attempted to write the "right" way—completely in my head, drawing almost solely on my intellectual and cognitive skills, keeping my own personality and life experiences safely missing from what I write. It became clear to me that first-person, introspectively nuanced accounts of what it feels like, from within, to be a daimista were essential. Therefore, *Liquid Light* draws upon and expresses as many strata of my being as I know how to access—including the fact that I am a mystic (that is, someone whose central life task is to unite with a divine or supreme Source, and who has had frequent, powerful, transformative experiences of that communion or union). I am also a theurgist (that is, a mystically infused magician—someone who works consciously, and I would like to think increasingly skillfully, with subtle energies while in close alignment with divine Presences).[10] And I am a medium (that is, someone who consciously and cooperatively works to incorporate various strata of nonphysical beings or energies). No hiding my Light under a bushel for me!

I know that for some readers these claims might sound at best like hyperbole, and at worst, sheer megalomania and grandiosity. For me, however, they are simple truths, stated as clearly as possible. At the very least, I think that it is crucial, in the Flatland, dis-enchanted world that we live in, to reclaim these titles; to acknowledge them as what William James would call "live options," rather than seeing them as romanticized, idealized stories about others who lived in other times and in other places (usually far, far away). Again, we can *all* become mystics, theurgists, and mediums, given enough innate talent, enough grace, and enough self-effort, as well as at least a background penumbra of belief that such things are actually possible. And drinking Daime certainly doesn't hurt.

And the moment in which the tasks of a mystic, a theurgist, and a medium all blend together for me is this: when, as a daimista, I am increasingly able to remain calm, centered, and firm in the I Am or Christic presence during the moment-to-moment flow of daily life; when I have begun, in an ongoing way, to practice being a divine Being, right here, right now. In this way mediumship, in the end, transforms into a type of ongoing practice of Presence and Heart, the conscious practice of divinization, in which, having become increasingly translucent to the Light of God within, the medium increasingly comes to rest within the awareness similar to St. Paul when he said, "It is no longer I who live, but Christ who lives in me."[11]

Here, at least for me, is the real fruit of the Santo Daime and of spiritual practices in general: not in the "peak experiences" of mirações (although it is wonderful that so much Light can pour from these visionary/mystical experiences), but rather, in the profound grace to be able to reorient ourselves, in the present, to our divine selves; to remember and to draw ourselves back to the Center, to the heart of our Being, with ease, since doing so is the most natural thing in the world.

MORE RUMINATIONS ON MEDIUMSHIP

Mediumship never ceases to fascinate and delight me—both experientially and intellectually. Even using the term "mediumship" itself raises questions for me, since mediumship doesn't seem to be just one thing. Instead, mediumship appears to be an umbrella term for a complex of multifaceted and multilayered phenomena. I've often gone so far as to wonder if what we call "mediumship" is just a tiny fraction of a complex interplay of "self" and "other" that is continually taking place during our everyday lives under the radar of normal awareness, in-and-as our conscious experience. (For example, miraculously, during our experiences of the external world, somehow what is outside and other becomes, in-and-as our experiences themselves, intimately inside and self. And what is mediumship itself, if not that fascinating play between what is inside and self and what is outside and other?) At the very least, mediumship—if taken seriously—should radically challenge our typically atomistic, billiard ball–like vision of ourselves as solid, clearly bounded, beings and should prompt us instead to recognize the inherent fluid interrelationality of the cosmos and ourselves.

However, to make room for mediumship within our typically taken for granted sense of the way things work (that is, letting what is, at least for many, something that is outside their experience to be taken within themselves—itself a type of intellectual mediumship), it helps if we can release our typical, rarely examined, understanding that consciousness is nothing more than the aftereffect of neurochemical interactions in the brain. (Even though how consciousness is produced in this way remains profoundly mysterious to most academics and scientists, who typically work with the taken for granted assumption that everything reduces down to nonconscious material "stuff." And it doesn't matter how complex the interactions are among all of that stuff, because in the end, zero consciousness plus zero consciousness should not end up as our conscious experience.[12])

I would suggest that an understanding of consciousness in which mediumship has a friendly and welcoming place would, in one way or another, almost have to envision some form of cosmic Consciousness or universal Mind that is itself the stuff of which everything is made. If that were true (and I'm convinced it is), then mediumship, with all of its varied and interwoven layers of self and other would simply be one phase of a much larger spectrum of Consciousness that is "It-Self" manifesting in a variegated profusion of interpenetrating, overlapping, co-arising fields of distinct (but not separate) fields of consciousness. (And, by the way: "it" is not an "it"—if anything "it" is an "I"—*the* I.) In this vision, we are, beneath the surface, always being touched by and intimately intermeshed with the entire universe—a universe that is itself formed by and a form of the ever-changing flux of Consciousness. Within such a vision of Consciousness as the underlying fabric of it all, the coexistence of a few discrete (albeit overlapping) fields of consciousness (that is, mediumship) is really no big deal.

Here's another reason why mediumship is inherently intriguing to me. Mediumship is simultaneously quite visceral, and hence is filled with deeply felt, immediate sensations, *and* mediumship is extremely mysterious, in that what is actually going on in the process of mediumship is often hidden from view and is operating in ways that I can only haltingly guess at—much of it seeming to play out above my conscious awareness.

For me, the inherent physicality of mediumship is a beautiful way in which the spirituality of the Santo Daime is earthed. Mirações, as we have seen, tend to be "up and out" sorts of affairs—they are ways in which we daimistas can learn how to leave our socially inscribed normal sense of ourselves as confined within the limits of our physical bodies, and instead, we can begin to identify with wider/deeper realms of experience. Mediumship, however, moves in the opposite direction. Mediumship is "down and in"; it plunges us deeply into the body, but it does not encase us within its boundaries. Instead, over time, as we again and again experience ourselves filled with differing "vibratory frequencies" of nonphysical presences/consciousnesses that are coexisting within the field of our conscious awareness, we are able, little by little, to free ourselves from the iron jaws of our prior egoic identification. Over time, via mediumship and/or simply through drinking Daime with a sacred mindset, our enfleshed being becomes, as it were, "resurrected" or "spiritualized." Saturated with consciousnesses that are, on a deeper level, differing qualities of that one divine Source, the "wattage" of our subtle bodies gradually becomes elevated; our energy field shines brighter; and we become increasingly attuned to the flux of subtle energies moving in-and-through us, energies that over time begin to permeate our physicality.

Mediumship, when it is developed, also increasingly teaches us how to transition, more and more gracefully, through radically different permutations of coexisting consciousnesses, and in this way it helps us to become more responsive, more fluid, not only within the parameters of a Santo Daime work, but also while plunged into the flux of everyday life itself—a flux that, always, inherently, involves the cohesive integration of a multitude of different overlapping qualities of experience.

During certain forms of mediumship, the movements of the physical body appear to be, as it were, the tail end of the shockwave created on more subtle levels of reality—the rippling out emanation of the interweavings of more primary streams of subtle energy that are coursing in-and-through our physicality. This streaming opens up our physical structure so that it can become more vital, alive, and glowing with health; it upgrades it so that our being can increasingly open up to joy and tap into the sheer pleasure of being alive. In this way, mediumship, at its best, is when we allow these energies to pulse through us; when we feel from within the fluxes of Love flowing into and out of a heart that is increasingly able to tap into and radiate that Love. The bodily movements of mediumship at this level can be seen as a beautiful way to appreciate and celebrate our physicality, instead of running from it or rejecting it. Through mediumistic movements, the body learns the innate goodness and satisfaction of moving from within, as our bodies are moved in a way that is attuned to and guided by the pulsations of a cosmic energy that ebbs and flows in-and-through each moment of felt experience. The overall developmental arc of mediumship is incarnational: our physicality over time becomes so permeated with the dance of subtle energies and subtle beings that it begins to glow from within and it becomes, little by little, increasingly translucent to the Light of that divine Source.

The physicality of mediumship also guarantees that we take the phenomenon of mediumship itself seriously. It's hard to doubt the undeniable, in-your-face reality of having your body be moved from within, with no conscious volition on your part, spontaneously moving in ways that, later, in more "normal" states of consciousness, are either impossible to replicate or would feel awkward and forced, quite unlike the cohesive fluidity that emerges during mediumship. And all of those movements appear to be simply the responsive aftereffect of a more primary underlying power/energy that we can feel, immediately, viscerally, as it surges in-and-through our physical body.

Speaking for myself, in these sorts of mediumistic openings, my body just wants to move of its own volition, perhaps creating a rippling upward from the pelvis helix that spirals from the base of my spine up and out my head, all while my feet are firmly planted on the earth, and my legs alternately press into the earth like a kitten kneading her mother's belly—where all the movements are interconnected, one flowing into the other, each one changing effortlessly and seamlessly into another unanticipated, spontaneous configuration of movement.

However, where does all of this energy/power emerge from? And what is actually going on via mediumship? And what is the potential value of these movements? All of these questions are difficult, if not impossible, to answer with any certainty.

Although I have described various specific kinds of beings that I—and other daimistas—have experienced, there are still more philosophical questions that we can ask about mediumship. For instance, *Is the energy that I feel pouring in-and-through me as a medium simply the typically unnoticed but ever-present background thrum of cosmic energy that continually enlivens and sustains this cosmos, or is that energy that I feel coursing through me integrally connected to a somewhat hidden from view, participatory interaction between me and some other?* The bottom line is this: is all of this flurry of mediumistic manifestation best described as me sensing and responding to an "entity"? If so, how interwoven are these entities with me and to what degree are they ontologically separate beings? And if what I'm feeling and responding to isn't me interacting with some type of entity, then what *is* going on? Why is my body moving in this way? What exactly is that energy/power that I can feel moving so forcefully within?[13]

Let's get specific: when a visceral throb of energy makes my body move (and hiss, and breathe deeply and loudly, and whistle in a type of sonic semaphore, and so on) or when I am hunched over and semi-davening at my desk, my face all scrunched up, my body doing its always changing but increasingly familiar pulsating "dance" (radiating up from deep within and rippling out to physicality), is all of that the outward manifestation of some being possessing a specific energetic signature interacting with my own various layers of physical and subtle bodies? Or, despite how particular it can seem, is the energy that I'm responding to "nonpersonal"? Or is there some "in between-ness," or "both-and-ness," that needs to be acknowledged?[14]

Personally, I prefer to not land solidly and with utter certainty on what is *actually* happening underneath it all. I'm a big fan of ontological humility. Nonetheless, it also feels deeply worthwhile to dive into numerous, empirically grounded, and carefully thought through metaphysical envisionings of what might be playing itself out during mediumship.

I'm convinced that taking the time to craft a metaphysical vision that takes my experiences with these beings into account is crucially important—at least for me. How could I not? While I'm exceedingly aware of the limitations of language to accurately mirror these types of subtle (and not so subtle) experiences, I also want to honor and make sense of my own decades-long, ongoing, extremely powerful and convincing experiences of encounters with different forms of nonphysical beings and differing qualities or "felt textures" of subtle energy. These beings and energies aren't theories to me; they are viscerally real. They have come into my consciousness with the taken for granted immediacy of my sense experiences. They inherently feel real in the same way that I would never doubt the visceral reality of nausea. Why in the world would I doubt what I'm feeling so vividly—not just in-and-as the coursing of subtle energy through me but also in a way that gives mediumship some experiential "heft," in-and-as the weighty, enfleshed movements of my physical form in response to the pulsations of that subtle energy?

As James himself mentioned well over a century ago, there are few experiences in one's life that can convince you as quickly and fully of the reality of spiritual beings than to have your body moved by forces that feel as if they originate outside the parameters of your typical egoic awareness (a phenomenon that James called "automatisms").[15]

Nonetheless, I am also acutely aware (due in part to my background in James and Bergson) that all of these experiences come into consciousness at least partially shaped, preconsciously, by the penumbra of beliefs, assumptions, theories, and cultural norms that I have internalized within myself. I recognize, again, in a way that typically escapes my notice, that with no conscious intent to do so, I seamlessly overlay all of these tacit assumptions onto the "raw data" of the directly felt, nonverbal layers of experience. Therefore, all of my experiences with subtle energies and subtle beings are at least in part molded by, for example, my prior study of these phenomena in numerous religious traditions and by my ongoing assimilation of my culture's assessment of these phenomena (which for the most part relegates them to the very profitable realm of television, books, films, and video games, where they are seen as nothing more than fascinating fictions). They also have been molded by the gradual infusion within my worldview of cultural concepts originating from Brazil (caboclos, preto velhos, and all of the assumptions that come with those terms), as well as by countless other cultural/philosophical influences.

Nonetheless, my experiences as a medium don't always dovetail nicely with what I've been taught in the past. Mediumship has often surprised me—even startled and amazed me—arising within me so spontaneously and taking various forms within my consciousness and body that were often unanticipated, even if, on another level, my set of beliefs/theological-philosophical frameworks clearly not only helps me to put words to these experiences but almost certainly, at least subconsciously, even helps to shape them.

Nonetheless, and this is crucial, there is an inescapable objective "otherness" that is integral to the phenomenon of mediumship. There's always a "there" there. It's not just made up. Mediumship is clearly a wildly intricate participatory dance.

I will admit that for the sake of simplification, I'll often put to one side my own complex, interactive, processual model of these beings/energies and, instead, happily use, for example, the language of Umbanda/Daime (when these traditions speak about "caboclos" or "suffering spirits").[16] That is, I am (lightly, provisionally) willing to accept and/or to not question too closely the historically and culturally specific assumptions about the nature of those spirits. But really, in the back of my mind, I always return to an apophatic understanding of reality: that is, to the philosophical-theological understanding that what's really Real is always beyond any and all concepts and theoretical structures, no matter how subtle and sophisticated these understandings are (as well as beyond this understanding about apophasis itself).

I'm a scholar of comparative mysticism, so somewhere in the back of my mind, I'm silently roaring out the Mu of Zen—the negation that negates its own negation and then negates that negation of negation itself as well. I am swinging the sword of Manjushri, again and again cutting through all of my vain attempts to encase what Is within the tidy box of my concepts. (I actually prefer the Taoist image of an uncarved block of wood peacefully floating down the river, spinning in its currents.)

I am reminded of what William James taught me: when it comes to knowing what's actually going on around us and/or within us, it's quite likely that we're like a dog in a library. The dog's experience of a library is markedly different than the experience of a human being (at least a human who has been raised in a culture that has libraries). Putting aside for the moment the fact that the nose, eyes, and ears of a dog work quite differently than human noses, eyes, and ears, the dog—more importantly—has no sense of what a book actually is, what written words are, what it even means to "mean." And so, when it comes to mediumship (and mirações as well), I am all too aware that, at least on certain levels of my being, I am just like this dog when it comes to understanding what's really going on around and/or within me. Therefore, I walk in this territory with humility, with a keen awareness of the limitations of any of my attempts to put the wild, free openness of "what is" into some conceptual framework, no matter how logically convincing and coherent it might be. To me, who or what these spirits and/or energies actually are remains an open question—a question that I am always seeking to answer, with humility, through the refinement of my ongoing experiences in conversation with others.

Because of the extremely vivid spiritual encounters with countless beings and/or complex, intricate, and forceful streamings of energies that are made possible by the Daime, what happens, at least to many daimistas, is that the world suddenly opens up; magic, mystery, and wonder return—the iron cage of modernity no longer feels quite so inevitable.[17] We begin to see with great clarity how we had previously, unknowingly, been living in a Flatland, two-dimensional world, a world created by our limited assumptions and experiences[18]

As daimistas, we have the priceless opportunity to emerge from our self-imposed epistemological limitations. We become participants in an exuberant democracy of mysticism in which mysticism is no longer just for the elite. To become a daimista is also to become, knowingly or not, a member of an academy of mystically infused magic. And an essential part of the curriculum of that school of magic and mysticism is what we can learn from our encounters with nonphysical, other-dimensional beings. It is as if, as daimistas, we get to become scientists making new discoveries or explorers entering into previously unknown territory, in that the Daime offers us the opportunity to engage in ongoing, open-ended, data collection (or a type of spiritual ethnology) in which we get to learn and grow from multitudes of highly detailed interactions with countless strata of nonphysical beings and/or energies.

It's simply a fact, a fact that countless people within the Santo Daime have experienced directly, that through the phenomena of mediumship, as well as through visionary encounters and travels—mirações—we increasingly get to know these beings (and they get to know us better as well). With the help of the Daime, it is possible to have ongoing encounters with a profusion of nonphysical beings—encounters that matter of factly occur, over and over again, not in some solipsistic purely internal way, but while embedded in and emerging out of a profoundly communal setting.

And there's a *lot* to learn from those ongoing encounters—encounters with spiritual entities; encounters with the energies that emerge from and pour through everyone doing the work; encounters taking place on multiple levels of our being in repeated and dramatic ways—in ways that aren't arbitrary or whimsical but take shape within a social context that approves of them and on the whole applauds those who have them.

As daimistas, we have the opportunity, if we so choose, to be immersed in a genuine mystery school, a school not only for spiritual awakening but also for learning and growing in the deepest levels of our being. (There are times in which I simply shake my head in wonder, envisioning what these encounters with spiritual forces and beings might reveal to us in the future, if/when more and more people begin to use entheogens, especially when these entheogens are taken with an explicitly spiritual intention, within carefully crafted ceremonial contexts.)

In *Cleansing the Doors of Perception*, a collection of essays on the religious significance of entheogens, Huston Smith, a prominent and well-regarded religious studies "elder," claims that our culture has "an urgent need" to connect with "a convincing, inspiring view of the nature of things and life's place in it." He suggests that entheogens may well have an important role to play in catalyzing this "ennobling vision."[19] According to Smith, one possible solution to our cultural predicament would be "to devise something like the Eleusinian Mysteries to get us out of Plato's cave and into the light of day."[20] He stresses, however, that because "religion is more than a string of experiences," such entheogenically inspired visionary/mystical experiences would, like the Eleusinian Mysteries, ideally need to take place within a ritual structure that was part of a disciplined way of life and in a context where the goal was not so much to have the experiences for their own sake but to integrate the revelatory and transformative insights provided by these entheogens into the fabric of daily existence.[21]

I would suggest that Smith's desire to see the birth of a modern-day mystery school that revolves around the sacramental use of entheogens has in fact been fulfilled. As Jonathan Goldman so eloquently states: "The Holy Daime Path is an authentic mystery school. There are levels of knowledge, stages of initiation that one passes through in one's program of rapid evolution. . . . The job of the initiate is to show up, drink Daime, work on the earth to live the teachings . . . [to] love God, love the earth, love all beings in God's creation, including yourself, [to] love and respect your brothers and sisters, accept the truth of your own divinity and of your own faults, [to] learn to embody forgiveness and mercy, and [to] gain the hard won humility that comes from meeting a Divine force head on."[22] I think it is crucial that both within the "school" of the Santo Daime and within the broader world of open-minded, intelligent human beings, we begin to have some thoughtful conversations about what/who these energies/beings are, rather than doing what many academics do, which is to simply ignore the data or relegate it to what "other people" in "other places" and/or "other times" have believed. We don't have to silently acquiesce to the dominant cultural understanding that these beings aren't "really real." It's time for those of us who know differently to speak up, at least among ourselves.[23]

And we need to speak from our experience. Metaphysics shouldn't be just a play of words or theories that are divorced from something that is sturdy, dependable, real. I know that I want my own metaphysical vision to be rooted in and emerge out of the ongoing accumulation of my direct, immediate experiences with these energies/beings (and from my experiences of nonphysical worlds)—repeated, highly detailed, affectively engaging, visionary experiences that my ego could *never* have consciously created; experiences that have emerged powerfully and effortlessly into my consciousness.

Now clearly, I also want to make sense of those experiences. I want to interpret them, to learn from them. And to do this, I will happily draw upon my deeply valued, decades-long, immersion in the field of religious studies. I want to articulate the most sophisticated, intelligent, nuanced model of mediumship that I know how to create—a model that is rooted in a Jamesian radical empiricism; that is, an empiricism that takes the immediate data from personal nonordinary experiences seriously; a model of mediumship that is actually open to what the experiential data tells mediums, over and over again—directly, immediately—which is that spiritual energies and beings are *real*.

The shamanic cultures took that fact for granted; and mystics and visionaries have repeatedly written about these spiritual forces and beings.[24] And now we get the opportunity to rediscover these beings and these energies for ourselves—and in the process, to discover strata of our own being that have previously been hidden from our gaze.

A SPECTRUM OF BEINGS

My initial attempts to make some sense of who/what these spirits are leads me to think that the energies/beings that are contacted via the Daime (as well as in many other spiritual contexts) are part of a fluid spectrum of existence—a spectrum of energies/beings that overlaps with and plays within our own sense of self. Mediumistic encounters, one of my primary sources of knowledge about these energies/beings (along with mirações) are always a both/and participatory event. they are an intricate intermingling of self and "other"—subjective and objective. *And*—to add yet another layer of complexity—although these encounters themselves take place within my own consciousness, that consciousness, to my way of seeing things, is actually a manifestation of Consciousness Itself; my consciousness is itself the expression of an even broader field—a still, spacious Awareness, an ever-present Pure Consciousness, the universal I Am within.

But then, at least within my own metaphysics, *everything* is a form of that cosmic Consciousness; every moment is the dynamic, utterly divine interplay between Knower and Known; the ongoing flow of our own experience is nothing but the erotic dance of Shiva and Shakti, God and the Goddess—the One that is Two that is Many.

So to me, all the beings that I encounter (and that encounter me!) are varying forms of that One Consciousness—as is everyone and everything at all times and places. And, importantly, so am I. Consciousness itself, to me, is the underlying "stuff" that the spectrum of mediumistic beings rests in, the "stuff" that each being is formed by and emerges from; Consciousness is the background matrix which, although typically unseen, is the Source of it all—including mediumistic encounters.

Nonetheless, within that broadest field of Consciousness, there seems to be plenty of room for abundant ontological diversity. In fact, it appears to me that the nonphysical dimensions of this universe contain a host of ontologically distinct spiritual beings ("species" if you will). Some of these beings bring with them the sense that they are not only "other," but that they are even "hyper-other"— jarringly, weirdly different from me; whereas other beings (or Beings) feel as if they are "overtones" of my own being, higher octaves of selfhood, manifestations, to a certain degree, of dimensional levels of my own being that are going on, right now, above my normal, this-worldly, level of awareness.

Examples of these "weirdly alien beings" might include the *shimmering bejeweled-with-scales-of-living-Light rainbow lizard beings* or the *clicking, tall, spindly, mantis beings*—beings that just seem to come out of nowhere during a Santo Daime work and appear with striking clarity within my consciousness and are like nothing I've ever imagined—beings that come into my consciousness with a specific, very clear-cut sense of "otherness" to them. There is even, at times, a flat-out sense of alienness about them, and yet there they are, suffusing my energy field, overlaying it, interpenetrating it—appearing (just like my thoughts, feelings, or memories) as an object within the field of my consciousness.

And so, just for the fun of complicating the issue even further, let's take a second to examine what is going on when I'm perceiving some of these beings. Let's use my perception of the lizard being that I mentioned. When it appeared, and I remember the moment vividly, my body was writhing in response to the energy emanating from it. I was feeling a semi-startled delight, tinged with a patina of fascination and awe. I was seeing (with my inner eyes) the wondrous beauty of the shifting spectrum of pure colors rippling off its scales, or better yet, light itself was actually forming the colors of its scales. And I was receiving a type of knowledge emanating from that encounter—the inherent nobility of this being combined with a somewhat jarring sense of otherworldliness. Now, taking into consideration the total gestalt of that perception, I have to ask: Did I just have a mediumistic encounter with that being? Or did I have a miração of that being? Or did I have a mediumistic miração?

Because, as I mentioned earlier, it's clear to me that there is often, perhaps always, a complex interplay between these two rather mysterious phenomena. Mirações aren't just about going up and traveling in the Astral, (although, admittedly, they often are exactly that) and mediumship can't be reduced to a descent of beings into the medium, where these spirits then become encased in the body/mind (aparelho) of the medium. Instead, it seems to me that there is an interactive flux of spiritual "directionality," in which the influx of a divine being can flow down into you from above like a waterfall of grace, while you simultaneously feel yourself shooting upward into the Astral, as if riding a geyser of Power that can erupt from deep within. And sometimes there's a type of temporal timing to it all, as when, for example, a shining, iridescent green Lady descends into your field of consciousness and bestows Love and Grace upon you and lifts you up, so that you begin to soar through the Astral on Her wings of tender Love.

And sometimes during a Santo Daime work, Beings can pour into your conscious field and open up your inner sight, and They come suffused with streamings of color and fluxes of organic (albeit somehow also deeply geometric) unfoldings of Beauty—carrying with Them, as it were, a whole environment. It is as if they are bodhisattvas and buddhas manifesting their own sacred mandala of experience; it is as if these Beings are bringing into this world the energy of a Pure Land that is super-conducive to spiritual awakening, a Heavenly Realm that is experienced in-and-through you, manifesting as the moment-to-moment particularities of your experience.

And so, the question remains: Is this mediumship or mirações? Both? Beyond either? And as if all of that weren't enough, here's another question: Is it only really mediumship when the nonphysical being is "fully" within my body (whatever "fully" and "within" mean in this context)?

Some daimistas might claim, for example, that what I experienced when that lizard being manifested within my consciousness wasn't really mediumship. It was, instead, a form of "irradiation." These daimistas are willing to acknowledge that we live in a world that is populated by numerous nonphysical beings—that we can and do feel their presence—and that these beings can and do influence us.

But these daimistas either do not believe that incorporation mediumship actually takes place, or if it happens, they do not think that it is spiritually helpful. Therefore, someone who was a proponent of irradiation might say, for example that this lizard being was *not* really "in" me. It was real, but it was only "nearby," and my physicality was simply responding to the energy of that being, as that energy was radiated from it, to me (hence "irradiation").

For example, many daimistas who are aligned with the Alto Santo lineage condemn incorporation mediumship, but they're willing to endorse the validity and value of irradiation, because Mestre Irineu clearly and repeatedly referred to it, especially after having been exposed to this concept by reading literature published by the Esoteric Circle of the Communion of Thought and participating in its rituals. For more information on Mestre Irineu's participation in this group, see Paulo Moreira and Edward MacRae, *Eu Venho de Longe: Mestre Irineu e Seus Companheiros* (Salvador, Bahia: EDUFA-UFMA-ABESUP, 2011), 294–304.

My best guess is that irradiation and incorporation mediumship are not, in reality, completely different. My sense is that there is actually an overlapping continuum between these two phenomena. I've come to this conclusion after having frequently discussed this issue with many daimista mediums who I deeply respect. I remember, for example, one elder (himself a deeply advanced medium) sharing with me about a woman he had seen dancing in the center of the circle of participants during an Umbandaime ritual. The medium said that this woman talked to him after the ritual and was convinced that while she was dancing, she was incorporating a caboclo. The medium told me, however, that in reality, the caboclo had not, in fact, incorporated within this woman; instead, she was just being stroked on her face by the caboclo's feather—that is, the caboclo was "touching" the energy field of this woman with his own energy. And this irradiation from the caboclo was what had prompted that woman to move in ways that, to her, felt like a caboclo *had* entered her body.

Now this way of expressing things makes a lot of sense to me. I don't think that powerful nonphysical beings always completely manifest themselves within the aparelhos of mediums. I am convinced, therefore, that at least at times using the concept of irradiation to describe what is taking place during incorporation mediumship can actually be quite helpful. However, I will also admit that when I heard this medium sharing this perception with me, several questions arose within me. To begin with, it seemed that the medium that I spoke with was bringing a whole host of assumptions into that assessment itself. That is, it seemed to me that he was convinced that he had seen what was "really" going on; he was also, it seemed clear to me, assuming, albeit probably preconsciously, that he was more advanced in his mediumship/subtle perceptive ability than the woman was. Now his assessment of that situation might well have been true, but how is that assessment of higher/lower or more advanced/less advanced itself assessed? Is mediumistic development simply a matter of putting a certain number of years into the process? Do certain types of mediumistic knowledge come "certified" as to their truth/reliability? I'm not saying that these questions cannot be answered. Instead, I'm raising them as a way to demonstrate the complexities that underlie any oversimplified discussion of the subtle processes of mediumship.

And what was all of that about a feather? Was that way of phrasing things simply metaphorical? Or did he "spiritually see," in a fairly straightforward manner, pretty much what he had described to me? If so, it still seems pretty likely to me that all of that feather stroking by the caboclo was still coming through charged with inherent symbolic meaning. That is, what he saw carried with it a cluster of meanings that probably radiated from a multitude of ontological levels—most of which I probably couldn't even begin to comprehend. My best guess is that all sorts of wild and wonderful energy exchanges were happening in the in-between-ness of that caboclo and that woman, and so I'm a bit leery of saying, or hearing others say, with supreme certainty: *That's all that was happening there.*

I'm also a bit leery of claiming that I actually know, for sure, what it means to develop my mediumship. There are indeed numerous highly refined mediumistic lineages, with clear-cut signs of one's development. (I'm thinking here of Umbanda, with its varying initiations, symbolized by different colors and numbers of the bead necklaces that initiates receive as they work their way up the Umbanda spiritual hierarchy.) But that particular structure of mediumship, for better or worse, simply hasn't been part of my learning curve. In my world of mediumship, there doesn't seem to be any sort of mediumistic algorithm that we can infallibly plug into; any sort of predetermined, one-size-fits-all set of rules and formulas to follow; any inscribed in stone, universally accepted pronouncements as to what qualifies as advanced mediumship.

On the other hand, I'd like to hope that I've grown at least somewhat in my years of working as a medium. And in my own developmental arc, I'd say that the movement has been toward subtlety. In my first few years of mediumship, the beings/energies would typically come roaring into my aparelho. It was almost as if I needed to be shaken like a rag doll for me to be convinced that they were actually present. (All of the high intensity that went with being seized in this way may well have been partially self-created, in that in the beginning of the unfolding of my mediumship, I was very clear that I didn't want to force anything, so that if the beings wanted me to act as a medium, they were going to have to make sure that I was crystal clear that this was what needed to happen.) At this point in time, however, the inner nudge ("We're here!") is often very soft, almost imperceptible, even if it's still quite distinct. And how I respond to that inner tap on the shoulder is also less dramatic; it's smoother (and dare I say more beautiful?) than it might have been in earlier years. It's not like there aren't times in which things can still get a tad "out there." But even then, my baseline for mediumship remains constant: first and foremost, I link up with the Christ/the Divine Mother; I rest in that divine Source within my depths; and then and only then, from that place of calm, centered, grounded, open-hearted Presence, whatever needs to happen in terms of the manifestation of other levels of mediumship can happen—but only within that consecrated inner space.

In terms of the distinction between irradiation and incorporation styles of mediumship: if the distinction between these two phenomena rests on the question of whether the spirit was outside you or inside you, then I'd have to say that this distinction itself seems rather problematic, especially in light of the fact that it's again not at all clear what the terms "inside" and "outside" even mean in these sorts of contexts. Are these spatial metaphors even appropriate for this type of subtle phenomena? Does a nonphysical being even have spatial/physical boundaries? Can those boundaries be measured? If so, how? And if it doesn't have distinct spatial boundaries, and if it can't be measured, then how can we possibly say whether it was inside or outside our bodies? (This outside/inside conundrum even applies to our perceptions of the physical world. For example, at the risk of repeating myself, let's imagine that you're reading this book in your living room. Is your consciousness within the living room? Or is the living room within your consciousness?)

The notions of "subjectivity" and "objectivity" are similarly problematic. For example, let's return to the original example of my encounter with the lizard being. When I felt/sensed the presence of that being within my own consciousness, to that extent, the lizard being was subjective. Nonetheless, just like a physical lizard in the physical world, that lizard being appeared without any effort or expectation on my part and seemed to come with a whole, ready-made history. It appeared to act from its own self-contained center of initiative—and therefore, in these and numerous other ways, it seemed to have a sense of objectivity to it, in that it seemed to exist, as it were, *outside* me. But again, I was experiencing that lizard emerging within *my* consciousness—and so, in that way, it seemed that the lizard was actually subjective, that it was actually something that was happening *within* me. And don't even get me started down the rabbit hole of who this "me" actually is!

A SPECTRUM OF SAMENESS/OTHERNESS

Regardless of the complexities of overlapping subjectivity/objectivity that are found during encounters with nonphysical beings, I nonetheless think that it is valuable to maintain the tension between subjectivity/sameness and objectivity/otherness if we're going to appreciate the subtleties of what's going on during complex, multilayered mediumistic encounters (or encounters within mirações) with various beings. Therefore, after examining my mediumistic and "visionary" interactions as carefully as possible, I have placed these different types of beings on a continuum of "otherness" (different from self) and "sameness" (similarity to self) in order to begin to categorize these encounters in a loose-limbed, open to new data way.

Way down on the objective/other end of that continuum, we find those exotic, deeply other spirits (like the lizard being, the mantis being, and multitudes of other, wildly, at times almost jarringly, different entities), that is, the *alien* beings. Some of those beings seem like they're not that far on the ontological scale from us in that it feels as if they are basically aware of themselves as fairly bounded, discrete entities, even if, at least in certain cases, these entities are much more porous and energetically responsive than most human beings are.

But then there are those awe-inspiring times in which the Daime can take you up into other-dimensional realms in which there are *Huge Archetypal Presences and Cosmic Powers* that stride through these rarified, ringing with Presence levels of the cosmos with supreme self-possession and almost indifference—utterly absorbed in and utterly at home in worlds beyond imagining. Nonetheless, these are worlds that we can somehow still know, intimately, albeit not as a being who is separated from that world, but rather, only after we are given (via the grace of that dimension itself and the beings in it) the capacity to merge with that world itself—when the world becomes, as it were, an extension of our own being. In this case, we know that world by *being* it, since at that moment we are miraculously vibrating at the same ontological "frequency" as that world and the beings that "dwell" in it.

And yet, at the same time, right along with all of that merger and sameness, there's an enormous otherness about those worlds and those beings. They're about as nonhuman as it gets.

Slightly further in the direction toward sameness are *suffering spirits*. I experience these beings as *very* different than me. I have a clear sense that they're "over there" and I'm "here." In this way, and to that extent, there's a pronounced sense of otherness to them. Nonetheless, these spirits also feel, as it were, closer to me than the alien beings. What I mean by that is that suffering spirits are typically human in their configuration (although at times, a sort of highly contracted, twisted, and distorted, fun-house mirror form of human-ness). Suffering spirits, at least those that appear to me, are often rather compacted—that is, they feel really dense or heavy, as if they've been pressed down on all sides. They've also got a congealed "there-ness" about them that is very specific, very personal. They tend to come with rather clear-cut edges, almost like they've still got a physical body. They're a very bounded "package"—each one of them, like each one of us, seems to possess a highly specific emotional tone, usually some combination of fear, anger, despair, unclarity, confusion, or hurt.

And, as I mentioned earlier, suffering spirits often seem to enter into my consciousness through a doorway of my own doubt, resentment, hurt, fear, and so on. In that way, they are attuned to a very specific vibratory frequency within my own psyche, and they therefore appear to be reflections of certain aspects of me (albeit my less than uplifting, shadow aspects). And in this way, *their* healing is, at least vicariously, *my* healing: we are both bathing in the same Light and unconditional Love and Mercy that is radiating from the Beings of Light who are assisting in (who are essential to!) that redemptive work. We are both having knotted, locked-tight, segmented strata within us lovingly unraveled. We are both bathed and cleansed in a river of Forgiveness. We are both upgraded into a newer, higher, freer quality of energy. We are both given the gift of having the darkness within us transformed into Light, or even better, we're able to experience such a quality of transformation that even the memory of darkness no longer exists, because within the Light, there's just Light, there's always Light.

And an essential dimension of that process of illumination are the beings that appear next on the continuum of sameness/otherness: the *Beings of Light*.

For example, when the caboclos (a type of Light-filled spirit that, as I mentioned earlier, I have frequently incorporated during Santo Daime healing works) appear, they usually do so with an energetic whoosh, they surge into my consciousness with their own unique energetic "signature." They love to whirl and to spin like spiritual ninjas; or they will dance and stomp; or they will cry out and/or make loud whistling noises—doing all of this, it seems, to rouse the energy within a room, to stir things up, to free and enliven everything.

Working with caboclos is quite different from working with suffering spirits. With suffering spirits, I work hard to clearly distinguish "me" from "them," even while acknowledging our shared humanity, so that I do not mistakenly begin to identify with the typically low level of consciousness that they bring with them. (It took quite a while in the development of my mediumship for me to gradually begin to discern that crucial difference.) However, when caboclos manifest, I willingly open myself to them; I consciously and joyously let them/their energy fill me, to such an extent that, momentarily at least, I almost merge with them. I do this perhaps because they tend to feel inherently closer to my normal level of selfhood than suffering spirits—even while I also maintain, within myself, an ongoing awareness of the difference between myself and that caboclo.

Once again, there's a highly specific "there" there when a caboclo arrives, a there that is quite different than, let's say, when we sing the hymns that summon what I'm going to call another Being of Light: the *Archangelic Beings*. Then, often quite suddenly, Something (Something that is big and glorious) begins to shine in-and-through me. Whenever what I'm calling an archangel appears within me, my bodily movements alter: the movements become more hierophantic, more exalted. It is as if the movements themselves are intrinsically broadcasting sacrality. When these Beings manifest within me, I often find myself creating these large, open, sweeping circles with my arms; my hands might begin to weave an intricate dance of various mudras around my energy field as "I" (the Archangelic Being and I conjoined) radiate blessings and Light to everyone around me. At this point my head often begins to tilt back, while my eyes roll up and back into their sockets. Ecstasy surges up through my body, and scintillating points of blue (and sometimes gold) Light begin to fill my field of inner, and at times even outer, vision.

These Archangelic Beings feel much less bounded than caboclos and much less this-worldly. I can understand why caboclos are typically thought of (in the context of mediumship) as spirits of human beings (in particular, Native Americans) who have continued to evolve spiritually in the Astral world, in that they still carry with them the felt-sense of a continuing link to humanity. (However, I have to admit that they often also feel really birdlike as well; they often seem linked to eagles and hummingbirds). In contrast, the Beings that tend to appear during the hymns that invoke the archangelic Presences feel qualitatively different—they feel, at least at times, less like beings and more like complex patternings of highly refined, intrinsically divine, energies. They don't feel as if they've ever been human, per se—but at the same time, they feel as if they are a higher octave of the spectrum of human potentiality. They seem to be the shining Light and Power of divinity itself that "fits" easily within a human consciousness and that belongs there—albeit, at the deepest/highest levels of what it means to be human (as contrasted with, for example, the wildly, weirdly alien, utterly nonhuman energy of the lizard or mantis beings.)[b]

I am not certain what is it, exactly, about certain hymns that often links them to the mediumistic manifestation of specific beings. Yes, it makes sense that there is a deeply engrained social set of assumptions that "this hymn" will summon or invoke one particular type of being (let's say a suffering spirit), whereas another hymn will summon or invoke a completely different quality of being (let's say a caboclo). Given that set of assumptions, mediums in the salão will naturally tend to manifest what is expected. Nonetheless, I have to say that I'm convinced that there's more to it than that. In my experience, there's a highly specific vibratory quality of certain hymns that enables them to act as keys that unlock certain, rather specific, doors to the vibratory realm where those specific beings "live." And other hymns are different keys to different doors.

And then, at the far end of the continuum, in the direction of "sameness," there is the *Christ* and the *Divine Mother*. Here's where I am, simultaneously, the most unsure of myself and the most certain. Here the interplay between self/other deepens. I'm going to focus, for the moment, on the Christ. For myself, theologically, what I'm calling the Christ is not so much the human being Jesus of Nazareth, as it is, instead, the Christ Consciousness (which I have no problem believing that Jesus of Nazareth incarnated during his earthly existence). In my experience, this Christ Consciousness is a highly specific configuration of Light/Energy/Love/Power that descends into this plane of existence. It frees, redeems, and transforms any and all contracted energies; it enlightens and illuminates all darkness. It is supremely Powerful, compassionate, and utterly divine. These experiences of the Christ Energy have arisen within me frequently enough, and powerfully enough, that they have dramatically and convincingly overwhelmed any of my preconceived notions of what "the Christ" should look or act like. These experiences have instead brought with them the overwhelming certainty, the indubitable Knowing, of the Truth, the sheer majesty, glory, and divinity of the Christ, full stop. And yet that Truth isn't static or unchanging. Instead, it's very dynamic, very alive, very rich, very open-ended. And there's a specific patterning to all of that dynamism. The Christ Consciousness is not amorphous, it's not vague, it's not neutral. Instead, it is an energetic configuration that is not only filled with beauty, but actually is Beauty Itself.

And that specific form of divinity simultaneously *is* me and *is not* me. It's my deepest essence (and again: "It" is not an "it," it's an I, it's *the* I, the I Am), and it's the Christ—the supremely Holy One, the archetypal Son, the full flowering of divinity. It is a Being who is ontologically at the very summit of reality, a Being who is radically different from my normal egoic consciousness. The Christ is, therefore, most deeply my Self, and most fully Other. At the same time.

The *Divine Mother*, for me, comes with the same overwhelming sense of certainty that comes when I feel connected to the Christ. In both cases, I Know that this Being is utterly divine, pure Love, pure Power, pure Sacredness. However, in the case of the Divine Mother, my experiences come suffused with an inherent maternal quality to them—a quality of gentleness, of nurturing, of sweetness, of softness, of gentleness—archetypal configurations of the energy of motherhood that are, at best, only partially reflected in our this-worldly experiences with our human mothers. (And, by the way, my experiences of the Divine Mother in the Santo Daime are often strikingly different—qualitatively different—than my previous visionary/mystical experiences with Hindu Tantric Goddesses such as the Shakti or the Kundalini.)

As a daimista, I will often sing rapturous hymns to the Divine Mother, and while I am doing so, it's almost as though I willingly play at being dualistic, that I am creating in this way, for the sake of Love and by Her Grace, an interrelationship between a Lover and a Beloved, a type of temporary duality that offers an opportunity for my heart to pour out love and devotion toward this divine Other. But I'm always, even at the very height of devotional rapture, keenly aware that the Divine is *always more* and can never be captured within the confines of any particular way of conceptualizing. Therefore, I'm aware that my feelings of ardent devotion to Her are, to a certain extent, a bit like playing, or being in a play; for example, even while I am praying to her with heartfelt devotion, and even while I Know that She is, ontologically, actually much more Real than I am (at least in my normal egoic sense of identity), I am also keenly aware that, on another level, there is *much* more to the Divine Mother than I could even begin to imagine. Nonetheless, for the sake of joy, for the sake of pleasure, for the sake of Love, I celebrate the form of the Divine Mother, that Beauty that only comes from Her, that specific patterning of divinity. I let that love-saturated difference between us create a joyous focus for my feelings, so that I can give myself freely and fully to the immensity of that Love that pours into me and out from me—this powerful, uplifting, recursive infinity sign circulation of Love that flows from Her to me and back again to Her.

And yet, to reiterate: I am also convinced that both the Divine Mother and the Christ are manifestations of the deepest, truest, most divine level of my own being—a level of my being that I can consciously choose to deepen and nurture within my moment-to-moment existence. Then, whether it's during a Santo Daime work or just in my daily life (such as right now, writing this), my job is to simply rest back into that vastness, my mind serene and quiet, my heart open and expanded, feeling transparent and linked up to that Source within. My job is to let that fountain of maternal Compassion, and that I Am, that Christ within, radiate in-and-through-and-as me, in-and-as the present moment. During those deeply holy *and* deeply normal moments, that divine Presence is free to simply shine forth, relatively unobstructed. (But really, what could, in truth, ever obstruct That? "It" is always shining, "It" is always present—and as I said before, "It" isn't an "It"—"It's" an "I," it is *the* I, the only real I.) During those deeply blessed moments, I stay present; I love; I am Love; I follow my heart; I seek to serve; I choose, over and over again, freely, joyfully, to align myself with that Source within; I let joy and love and compassion and wisdom shine forth. And I do all of this while I remain deeply human.

Exploring the depths of this paradoxical conjunction between divinity and humanity is, at least for me, the beating heart of my spiritual life. A spiritual life that is profoundly, albeit not exclusively, fueled by the Daime.

THEOLOGICAL RUMINATIONS ON THE DAIME

The Daime itself is, of course, the central divine Being that daimistas contact during Santo Daime works. Nonetheless, when it comes to speaking about the Daime, I prefer to move slowly and carefully, with a profound sense of respect, not pretending to know more than I do. I do so because the Daime, in-and-of itself, is exceedingly mysterious and amazing to me. It doesn't easily fit into any of my neat metaphysical categorizations. It is a physical substance that can be weighed, measured, quantified, and chemically analyzed, yet it is also, inherently, much, much more. Again, to me, the Daime is a powerful, divine, working only for the highest good for all, crystalline matrix of Consciousness that is inherently transformative, a Consciousness that is intimately intertwined with the creative capacity of our own consciousness.

By "consciousness" I mean our daily, ongoing, unrepeatable, highly individualized, flow of conscious experience. Nonetheless, for me, all of these utterly unique and irreplaceable fluxes of consciousness are always rooted in and constantly emerging from an utterly Free, all-pervasive, ceaselessly Creative, divine Source—that is, Consciousness—a Consciousness that is, moment-to-moment, birthing the cosmos in-and-through each one of us. Each of us is the Center of the Whole; each drop fully contains and manifests the Ocean.

I think that these descriptions of the Daime more or less point in the right direction. But what the Daime *actually* is—well, that's something that has to be realized on a whole different ontological level, and I'm not sure that words are actually going to take us there. But fortunately, we have the opportunity to take the Daime for ourselves; we have the chance to engage in a deeply personal, extended over a prolonged period of time, experiential engagement with the Daime. We can come to know, within our own selves, in multiple ways, what (who?) this Being is—how It (She? He?) is manifesting within us. That is, we can, through Santo Daime works, begin to accumulate a rather extensive and intensive knowledge-by-acquaintance of the Daime.

We can also, if we study and if we think seriously about these issues, accumulate over time a fairly sizable and multifaceted knowledge-about the Daime. We can, for example, contemplate the teachings of various elders (especially Mestre Irineu and Padrinho Sebastião), particularly as those teachings are transmitted in-and-through their hymns, and if we're so inclined we can examine what various scholars of the Santo Daime and/or ayahuasca have written about the Daime and/or ayahuasca.[25] We can then weave all of this together within our own minds until we come to our own opinions. In this way, we have the chance to articulate our own good enough for the moment understanding of what/who the Daime is, for us. That is, we can consciously choose what knowledge-about we wish to have about the Daime. And the specifics of this knowledge-about can make all the difference. By consciously choosing how we wish to understand the Daime, we get the chance to draw to us a corresponding quality of experience within Santo Daime works (and more broadly in every moment of life). In this way, we have the opportunity to be genuine theurgists who are skillfully weaving a spell with words—words that have the literal magical power to invoke certain specific qualities of experience within us.

Because, let's face it: it matters, for example, if we think of ayahuasca (as many within the neoshamanic vegetalista tradition often do) as something that can be used by the ayahuasquero as a weapon against his/her enemies, or whether we conceive of ayahuasca in the way that most (all?) daimistas do; that is, as the Daime, as a genuine sacrament—a physical substance that fully incarnates a divine Being within an extremely intense and difficult to drink liquid.[26] There are also, I'm sure, numerous similarities between how vegetalistas understand ayahuasca and how daimistas understand the Daime—but this particular difference is, admittedly, rather striking. It makes a huge difference if we think of ayahuasca as a malleable (at best) ethically neutral tool, rather than as a divinely powerful and utterly benevolent catalyst of personal and cosmic transformation.

I for one cherish the opportunity to contemplate how to best understand what the Daime is, how to best express that Mystery for myself. It's wonderful to have the inherent freedom to ask difficult to answer questions such as: Should we think about the Daime as an It, or as a She, or as a He, or as a They, or as none of the above? And how would thinking about the Daime in these different ways change our experiences? Should we understand the Daime to be a manifestation of God the Father? Or a manifestation of the Divine Mother? Or the Christ? Or all three? Or something much more? (And by the way, what do we mean when we say, "God the Father," "the Divine Mother," or "the Christ"?) And how would we/could we ever know, for certain, that we have the utterly reliable and completely true answer to any of these questions? Furthermore, what is the relationship between my selfhood/Selfhood and the Daime? If the Daime is the Christ Consciousness, and the Christ Consciousness (Juramidam) is the divine I Am within each one of us—then is the Daime different from me or is it the same? Or both? Or something much more?

And then there is the question: what is the Daime actually doing? From a certain perspective it seems that the Daime, in-and-as the Christ Consciousness, descends into this level of reality to redeem and transform contracted levels of consciousness, hence spurring on the spiritual evolution of the cosmos. However, from another point of view, it seems that the Daime catalyzes a wondrous awakening within us to what is already there. It opens us to our own preexisting divine nature, to who we already are and always have been. My sense is that the Daime as a liquid form of divine Grace appears to act in both of these ways—it works to transform darkness into Light and it acts as a sacramental conduit of the mystical knowledge of our preexisting Oneness with the Source. And clearly, there is a *lot* more that the Daime is doing within us that we simply can't even begin to comprehend.

At times it can certainly seem as though the Daime, as a divine Being, as a divine Other, effortlessly manifests worlds within worlds within us. And yet those same worlds often rather convincingly feel like they've always been there. And in this way, it seems as though the Daime isn't so much creating sheer newness as it is tuning us into previously unseen, but preexisting, realms of experience. To complicate matters, those same worlds always appear within *us*, within our own consciousness, *as* forms of our own consciousness/Consciousness. These worlds are always, and inescapably, forms of our own most intimate experiences. And in this way, the Daime doesn't seem so much Other, as it appears to be a manifestation of the deepest levels of Selfhood itself.

Furthermore, I continue to be amazed by the dramatic overlap between my prior experiences within a yogic/meditative tradition that centered around the awakening of the Kundalini energy and my more recent experiences with the Daime. My experiences of the Kundalini and the Daime have led me to believe that these two manifestations of salvific divine Power are by no means identical. The energetic "signature" of the Daime is simply much too unique for any simple conflation of the two. And besides, the Daime has that stubbornly physical, overtly liquid quality to it. Nonetheless, I can't help noticing that both the Kundalini and the Daime appear to be serving almost identical ends (transforming and awakening), that they do this type of work in strikingly similar ways (yogic "kriyas" are at times almost indistinguishable from mediumistic movements), and that the end results are often strikingly similar (both the Kundalini and the Daime clearly and explicitly upgrade the subtle body and open various chakras, both can and do bring intuitive guidance, both can and do grant powerful visionary/mystical experiences).

And so, how should I best understand what's going on here with all of this similarity and difference? My initial attempt to answer that question is to say that there is only One divine Source and that the Kundalini and the Daime are both linked to/manifestations of that Source. And yet, they're also somehow, importantly, intrinsically different from each other—that is, we're not just using two different, culturally/historically bound names (Kundalini or Daime) to describe a single salvific divine Power. I realize that this type of both-and-ness is not especially congenial to many people. Nonetheless, I don't feel in any real hurry to reconcile my conceptual clunkiness.

And there is also this difficult to unravel question: is the Daime moral? The Santo Daime tradition itself tends to speak about the Daime in moral terms, seeing the Daime as coming from/a manifestation of divine Beings (God the Father, the Divine Mother, Christ the Redeemer) who are themselves understood as Pure Goodness. And I deeply value and to a great extent agree with that understanding, in that I think that these divine Beings, working in-and-through (and as?) the Daime are always actively working for my highest good. Nonetheless, at times I'm not comfortable with the lingering overlay of folk Catholic moral beliefs (for example, regarding sin and punishment) that is all too often overlaid upon the Daime. For example, many daimistas, from the earliest times, have often interpreted works that were filled with difficulty and suffering as ways in which they were undergoing *peia*, a well-deserved divine punishment for their prior wrongdoings.

I would be the first to admit that there do seem to be moments in works in which I will suffer deeply, and at times that suffering truly *does* seem to be intrinsically linked to moral/spiritual lapses on my part. That suffering, in some really basic way, seems to be connected with the fact that in those moments of moral/spiritual unclarity, I chose not to align myself with my divine nature; I chose to ignore the subtle intuitive knowledge of what was being asked of me, even though, somewhere within me, I knew better. I think it is quite possible, therefore, that the suffering that I have experienced during those types of works arose, at least in part, to underscore that sharp, often quite difficult to assimilate quality of self-awareness; it emerged to underscore the seriousness of my spiritual/moral lapses.

At times it also seems as if the suffering that I am undergoing during works is intimately interwoven with my remorse for the pain that I have caused others—the ache that I feel because I was simply too undisciplined to overcome whatever old pattern (of desire, of reactivity) prompted me to behave in ways that I later regretted. Perhaps in works such as these, the suffering that I was feeling provided the opportunity for me to keenly feel all of that remorse and to viscerally sense to some extent some of the pain that I had caused others to feel. Nonetheless, in-and-through all of that suffering and remorse, I have *never* experienced myself as a sinner being punished by a judgmental, wrathful God. Instead, it has always felt, at least to me, as if the peia that I was undergoing had arisen within my consciousness as a way to grant me increased clarity about the consequences of my choices, as a powerful opportunity to heal and transform the pain and suffering itself, and as an opportunity to genuinely receive, and therefore learn to give, divine Forgiveness and unconditional Love. (And, if I were to guess, I think it is quite likely that this way of thinking about suffering is closely aligned with how many daimistas think about it.)

I also think, at least in certain instances, in a way that is similar to the Mahayana Buddhist notion of the bodhisattva, that we can understand that the suffering that we are feeling in the context of a work is actually not directed toward us at all, but instead is an opportunity for us, within the Force of the Daime, to shoulder more of the Christic task of transforming the contracted energies of suffering of the world itself into Joy and Freedom.

Ultimately, while I think that there is, inherently and importantly, a profound way in which the Daime is inherently moral, I also work hard, at least within myself, to be clear about what I mean by "morality." I think that it is crucial to disentangle the glowing core of Truth, Goodness, and Justice that I believe forms the ontological substratum for genuine moral distinctions, from any of the (to my eyes) often highly problematic overlays of distorted and contracted understandings of what it means to be moral. Therefore, when I say that I think that the Daime is intrinsically moral in a crucially central way, I'm referring to this specific sense of morality that has been "purified" of centuries of antiquated and problematic notions of morality—a morality that often comes steeped in notions of inherent sinfulness and harsh punishments by a wrathful God.

I realize that this critique of the notion of sin and punishment in the Santo Daime tradition might well put me at odds with some daimistas, given the fact that the idea of sin and punishment is present in some of Mestre Irineu's and Padrinho Sebastião's hymns (to say nothing about the Hail Mary). Nonetheless, while terms such as "sin" or "sinners" are clearly present in the hymns and the prayers of the Santo Daime, I would suggest that we can certainly choose how we want to interpret these terms. For example, I think that it is helpful to realize that the Greek word *hamartia*, which was later translated into English as "sin" was originally a term derived from archery, and simply meant "to miss the mark." (The link between sin and the term "*hamartia*"—"missing the mark"—is underscored by the fact that the Christian philosophical theology of sin is called "hamartiology.") Originally this term did not come loaded down with the extremely heavy, negative connotations that the word "sin" has carried for centuries now—the understanding, which largely emerged from Augustine of Hippo's notion of "original sin," that each person is, inherently, from birth, guilty of rebelling against God's will and hence deserves God's wrath and punishment. (See Daniel Patte, ed., *The Cambridge Dictionary of Christianity* [New York: Cambridge University Press, 2010], 892.)

While this way of understanding sin is extremely prevalent in the Christian tradition, there are also certain Christian mystics who offer, at least to me, less onerous ways to understand our inevitable human tendency to go astray, to make unfortunate choices, to cut ourselves off from the Divine. For example, the medieval anchoress Julian of Norwich, in her mystical masterpiece, *The Showings*, acknowledges that we all repeatedly "sin" and that there is indeed wickedness in the world; nonetheless, she also insists that in the end "all will be well and all will be well and every kind of thing shall be well" and that this well-being (which God so powerfully revealed to her) would emerge not *in spite* of our moral lapses but *because* of them. (See Carol Lee Flinders, *Enduring Grace: Living Portraits of Seven Women Mystics* [New York: HarperSanFrancisco, 1993], 83.) As she puts it, "I saw no wrath except on man's side, and He forgives that in us." (See Francis Beer, *Julian of Norwich: Revelations of Divine Love* and *The Motherhood of God* [Cambridge: Boydell and Brewer, Ltd., 1998], 45.) Personally, if/when I think about sin, I prefer this mystical, love-centered way of understanding it.

The Daime to me is fundamentally moral in that I think that the Daime is fundamentally Good, and therefore I deeply trust the Daime. There's nothing, at least to me, ambiguous about the Daime. It feels utterly benevolent. I'm convinced that the Daime works only for the highest good of all, at all times, in all ways; that the Daime is continually catalyzing healing on the deepest levels; that it ceaselessly rains down blessings upon all; that it only wants to transform darkness into Light; and that it actively promotes and bestows the highest possible levels of awakening.

But if the Daime actually does act in this way within us (and I very much think that it does), then how should I understand what's going on when indigenous shamans use ayahuasca (the same physical substance as the Daime) to help them form "spirit darts" in order to curse, harm, or even kill their enemies?[27] That type of activity does, I'll admit, seem—at least from my own culturally shaped perspective—immoral (or amoral?). I don't honestly know what to make of the rather difficult to wrap my mind around historical and cultural fact that ayahuasca has been used and continues to be used for these sorts of harmful, destructive activities. I can't even begin to imagine the Daime in any way connected to those sorts of behaviors. But the fact that the Daime is the same physical substance as ayahuasca raises many difficult to answer questions for me: Should I understand that while ayahuasca and the Daime are physically the same, that they are energetically different? Is the Daime, perhaps as a result of the sacramental activity of the feitio, actually incarnating a different ontological level of Being than at least some forms of ayahuasca? Or is the same Being somehow, mysteriously, in a way that we can't even begin to fathom, working in-and-through both? I'll admit, I remain very unclear about the "correct" answer to all of these questions.

I often prefer to think of the Daime not so much as moral but as "transmoral." That is, I think that the Daime is "trans" (beyond) any and all man-made moral constructs. But, at the same time, I also think that the Daime is completely Good and inherently trustworthy. My best sense is that the Daime, like God, is simply much too free to be tamed by our social mores; it's simply not bound by our culturally/historically conscribed boxes of what's right or wrong, good or bad. Yet again, it seems to me that the Daime is also the embodiment of essential Goodness. It inherently wants us to grow spiritually; it wants to turn darkness into Light. It is, in this way, transmoral: beyond any social constriction of morality yet simultaneously the very Fountainhead of the Good.

The Daime is, therefore, at least to me, inherently both/and. And this both/and-ness extends into how I envision and relate to the Daime. On the one hand, the Daime, for most daimistas and for myself as well, is intrinsically intertwined with an overtly moral understanding of the Divine Mother as the Source of the

Daime—the Divine Mother understood (and experienced) as the perfect manifestation of Purity, Gentleness, Mercy, and so on. On the other hand, there have been many times in which I've experienced the Daime in-and-through other very different interpretive lenses. For example, at times the Daime will also manifest itself as the wild, free, and unbound divine Source of all, unfurling wave after wave of explicitly erotic mirações of the divine Feminine (divine vaginas unfolding, cosmic breasts dripping with milk, and so on). Here the Daime unfolds itself within me as the ongoing and deeply erotic divine interplay of Male and Female energies—a fecund, fertile aliveness making love within me; creating new life; unfurling beauty; dancing in infinite configurations; birthing newness; catalyzing ecstasy; generating pulsations of almost unbearable Pleasure that course in-and-through my body. Even if some of those images are simply subconscious material arising within me, it often feels much more profound than that, as if the Daime itself is revealing a crucial dimension of its very Being to my inner sight.

And yet, somehow, all of this multilayered difference works for me. Somehow, the internalized worldview that emerged, at least in part, from my prior years of yogic/tantric training seems to interweave, almost seamlessly within me, with my more Neoplatonic, mystical-tinged Christian vision of life. And both of these visionary perspectives come together within me as I continue to seek a way to better articulate and comprehend my own often wildly variant experiences of the Daime, a cognitive dissonance that I actually value.

JAMES AND BERGSON ON CO-CONSCIOUSNESS

At least intellectually, I find that one of the most wondrous aspects of mediumship is the experience of several beings coexisting, simultaneously, on different levels, within my own consciousness—beings that are both "me" and "not me" at the same time; consciousnesses that are interpenetrating but distinct. Our normal, culturally bestowed sense of what constitutes selfhood doesn't have a lot of room for this sort of internal configuration. We are more or less raised to think of "selfhood" as a one body/one consciousness sort of arrangement. (And anyone who describes anything different than this taken for granted cultural norm of what constitutes personal identity would, under certain circumstances, run the risk of being seen as mentally ill.) There are few psychological or philosophical models within the modern West that can help us to make sense of the experience of mediumship, except perhaps Carl Jung's notion of a collective unconscious in which a multitude of archetypes coexist; or object relations theory with its discussion of a psyche that is constituted, at least in part, by a jostling horde of internalized, semi-autonomous figures or objects. Nonetheless, it can be difficult to find models that take the *ontological* "otherness" of these consciousnesses seriously.[28]

Once again, however, James and Bergson come to our rescue. Both of these thinkers discuss with great clarity how our ordinary conscious experience is already, right here, right now, the simultaneous fusion of continuity and difference; how the ever-changing particularities of each moment of experience come to us in as seamless, smoothly flowing connectedness.

Both James and Bergson, for example, point out how our ongoing conscious experience is a blend of a variety of intrinsically different qualities of experience. As James notes in his discussion of the "compounding of consciousness," if we examine our own experience right now, those of us with functional senses are simultaneously having the radically distinct experiences of seeing, hearing, tasting, smelling, and touching—and yet, each of these highly distinct streams of experience are somehow combined within as one seamless unified continuity. For example, right now I'm seeing my computer screen; I'm hearing the taps of my fingers on the keyboard; I'm tasting the aftermath of my morning mouthwash; I'm smelling the lingering smoke of the stick of incense that I burned an hour ago; and I'm feeling the skin of my feet touching my flip-flops. Each of these separate streams of experience is qualitatively unique. For instance, my ears simply have no way to know what my eyes take for granted: the experience of sight. Conversely, my eyes can never know what it feels like to hear, in that their entire world of experience is made of sight itself, and there's no space for anything else. Nonetheless, right here, right now, on some deeper, more encompassing level, my sense experiences, radically distinct as they are, are experienced within me as a unified, interwoven, whole. All of my sense experiences overlap; they interpenetrate; although distinct, they are not separate from each other. Instead, they are "co-conscious" within the totality of the larger field of my ongoing conscious experience—a totality that is also, crucially, brought into being due to the combined interpretive overlay of the condensed memory of my entire past, in which each sensory experience is (preconsciously or subconsciously) given enormous depth and meaning in-and-through the seamless overlay of the totality of my memory.[29]

And these experiences of co-consciousness are inherently temporal. Each field of experience (*our* experiences, happening right now) streams forth, carrying with it the entirety of the past, moving ceaselessly into the next moment, into the new reality that has taken birth, that is continually taking birth, right here, right now—the changeless Present that is inherently made of change—both at the same time, manifesting in and as our conscious experience in time, in and as time itself.

It is helpful, therefore, to think of the coexistence of various beings within the consciousness of a Santo Daime medium in a similar way. Each one of us can experience the co-consciousness of each of our varied streams of experience (not only our sense experiences, but also other qualities of experience, such as recollections of specific memories, the uprising of feelings, the play of thoughts), all of which are dynamically present within our more over-arching, cohesive, and unified personal field of consciousness.

Bergson also offers us another helpful metaphor to begin to make sense of the coexistence of a multitude of different streams of consciousness: the "musicality" of consciousness.[30] He asks us to imagine our consciousness as a vast, ongoing musical creation. This "vision" ("audition"?) of the nature of consciousness gives us a metaphorical way in which to begin to understand that oneness can and does coexist with many-ness (for example, the many-ness of different sense experiences unified together in the cohesive flow of our awareness); and that change can and does coexist with continuity (what would be a better description of our own internally verifiable, directly experienced felt sense of the nature of consciousness—ceaseless experiential change fused with stable continuity; the unbroken flow of pure difference). "Hearing" our consciousness through the metaphor of music and melody, it becomes easier to grasp how our consciousness might well be structured such that particularity and difference can and do coexist with some sort of underlying, even if hidden, connection and continuity.

For instance, it is tempting to think of a melody as an aggregate of separate, clearly delineated tones. Yet if we look (or rather, listen) more carefully, what we discover is that each individual tone, while it maintains its uniqueness and distinctness, is not abruptly cut off from the other tones. Instead, each tone, during the time it physically sounds, infuses and overlaps with other tones that are concurrently sounding. What is more, even after each tone has physically faded, it continues to linger in memory; it continues to persist in the mind. In fact, it is this very persistence in the memory that creates a melodic phrase. Melody, in order to be melody, needs both—the individuality and distinctiveness of particular notes and the ongoing continuity and connectedness of many notes brought together, over time, in-and-as memory.

Understanding the world through the metaphor of music also underscores the fact that our consciousness is intrinsically temporal. A melody cannot, by its very nature, exist without time. A melody cannot just manifest itself in an instant, utterly complete and whole. Instead, it unfolds and appears over time, note by note, phrase by phrase. We might like to think that a melody can in fact exist, timelessly, in the form of a static collection of notes written on the paper of a score, in much the same way that we might prefer to believe that the physical universe is reducible, in theory, to a predetermined, highly complex series of mathematical formulae. But as Bergson points out, notes on a sheet of music are not the melody itself, any more than scribbled mathematical equations on a page are the thickness and density of real experience. Both are simply highly abstract symbolic attempts to freeze a dynamic temporal reality into a static collection of manageable, replicable formulations; both are simply expressions of our inherent human tendency to see reality as a collection of separate and unchanging objects.

In neither melody nor our conscious experience do we find stable, unchanging objects that have a specific, concrete location in space. Asking "where" the notes of a melody actually *are* can be an illuminating exercise in futility; unlike visually perceived objects in space, sonic realities seem to be nowhere and everywhere. During their time of sounding, are the tones that we hear "in" the body of the instruments or the singer's voice? Are they "in" the air? Are they "in" our ears? Are they all of the above?

This melodic metaphor becomes even more fruitful if we cease to think of melody as simply a single melodic phrase and instead begin to envision a multilevel polyphonic (and/or polyrhythmic) musical piece in which several relatively independent melodic movements unfold both successively and alongside one another. (Significantly, it does not matter whether the interaction between the movements creates a harmony or dissonance.) For example, let's imagine a piece of music in which a saxophone has one melodic movement, a bass has another, a guitar a third, and even add the drums as a fourth melodic/rhythmic movement. Even if these various instruments are playing simultaneously, each melodic/rhythmic movement is relatively independent, in that each proceeds parallel to the other melodic/rhythmic movements (for example, the guitar, the sax, the bass, and the drum each have their own parts, even while they are playing together). If we are trained listeners, it is possible to hear each movement separately and distinctly. Yet at the same time, it is also possible to hear the more inclusive overall musical creation. In this level of hearing, each movement is enriched and gains a greater significance through its interaction with the other melodic/rhythmic movements. Together, they create a more complex, interesting, dynamic whole, a whole that is composed of relatively independent melodic/rhythmic movements that are organically interconnected and held together in memory. In this world of "co-becoming" or "co-fluidity," ceaseless change and seamless continuity coexist, and sheer diversity lives happily with stable ongoing presence.

In much the same way that we can use this musical metaphor to help us to better understand our own day-to-day conscious experience, we can also use it to make sense of mediumistic experiences as well. During a mediumistic manifestation, each being or entity (for example, our own personal consciousness, a suffering spirit entering into our aparelho to be healed, and the Light of Christ shining from the depths) has its own unique, ever-changing, "melody" or vibratory expression through time, even while we can also recognize that, simultaneously, each of these melodic structures is not utterly separate from the other melodic structures (that is, the other beings). Instead, we can train ourselves to perceive the ways in which each of these various "songs of being" overlaps, interpenetrates, and affects each of the other songs, creating an almost unimaginably complex, dynamic intermingling of beings/energies within the matrix of a more expansive wholeness.

This metaphorical way of understanding reality works best (and here is where the metaphor, like all metaphors, stretches and perhaps breaks) if we can imagine that the music is not the end result of a stable group of performers but plays itself—as if the various clusters of melodic movements were each conscious of themselves and the other musical patterns. This type of metaphorical imagination allows us to rediscover a musical worldview of consciousness and mediumship in which each note/being, while having its own inherent integrity and individuality, also resonates outward, overlapping with and affecting/being affected by, all of the other notes/beings that are simultaneously resonating— and in-and-through this interactive resonance, creating countless overtones and harmonics.

And of course, Bergson's musical "hearing" of the way reality is structured (both as the external world and as our own conscious internal experience) reflects, almost perfectly, what it's like to sing hymns during a Santo Daime work. In many respects the ongoing, inherently temporal experience of everyone in the salão, singing together (each singer independent yet interconnected with everyone else in the salão) almost perfectly embodies and expresses this "sonic" understanding of the patterning of existence.

In a Santo Daime salão, sounds and consciousness are often inextricably interwoven: the hymns have the power to transform consciousness in that they carry with them the Power of the vibratory Source of those inspired ("received") words, melodies, and rhythms. And that Power, that Force, "rides" the waves of sound—and these empowered waves of sound (and meaning) in turn catalyze, or carry with them, an expanded state of consciousness. And that uplifted state of consciousness itself, at least to a certain extent, is a manifestation of the divine Source of the hymn within the consciousness (or is it "*as* the consciousness"?) of the person singing the hymns, in much the same way as the *icaros* of an ayahuasquero are—at least at times—understood as the "sound bodies" of the spirits who bestowed the icaro.[31]

In addition, that transfigured consciousness itself infuses the singing of hymns during a Santo Daime work. (The difference between singing hymns "in the Force" and singing hymns while not in the Force is somewhat similar to the difference between reading the lyrics of "My Sweet Lord," and then hearing, for the first time, George Harrison singing that song on his album *All Things Must Pass*.) The power of the Daime adds another dimension to the experience of singing and hearing music; it prompts meaning to unfurl within the words of the hymn; it opens up the inner valves of awareness so that an ongoing, dynamic connection to the More can flow in and can be directly experienced and can be deepened over time.

In a Santo Daime work, each person's consciousness is not only elevated via the Daime, but it also is opened concurrently via the melodies and rhythms of the hymns—hymns that are themselves differing qualities of music that overlap within a flowing, interpenetrating unity: the rasping insistence of the maracás; the stunning melodic intricacies of notes pouring forth from the guitars, filling the salão; the temporal progression of lyrics sung with love, joy, and gratitude by daimistas who are singing words that ride on the breath, words that ripple out from their depths, from their center (from the Center—the I Am), everyone in the Force, together. The hymns blend into the Current that is circulating in-and-through everyone in the salão, everyone singing and hearing at the same time from the heart, simultaneously giving and receiving these words that are saturated with Love—everyone's voice touching everyone in the room, and everyone being touched by the voices of everyone in the room, voices that overlap and yet are utterly distinct, utterly unique.

ETHICAL ISSUES IN MEDIUMSHIP

The practice of mediumship, especially incorporation mediumship, can and often does raise a whole host of ethical issues. For example, in a way that is sadly similar, if not identical, to a tendency within certain evangelical Christians to blame the devil for their own less than ideal ethical choices, there can be a tendency within some daimistas to blame suffering spirits for their own problematic ethical decisions, saying in essence, "The suffering spirits made me do it." Thus they are able to tell themselves and others, for example that it really wasn't their own desires and/or egoic infatuation with the thrill of manipulating others that made them seduce someone, but rather it was the malign influence of a suffering spirit that prompted them to act in this way. Or it wasn't actually they who yelled at a fellow daimista in the healing room—it was really this spirit that they've been indoctrinating that made them do it. Abdicating our ethical responsibility is bad enough; to spiritualize that abdication is just adding insult to injury.

At least to my way of thinking, it doesn't really even matter, at least ethically, if we are beset by purely internal, psychological temptations or obsessions; or if we are dealing with cut-off fragments of our own psyche; or if we are struggling with the negative thoughts/feelings brought into our consciousness by a cluster of ontologically different beings (in this case, suffering spirits), especially given the fact that the promptings of those beings typically correspond with our own unacknowledged, preexisting tendencies. In the end, our choices are still our own. We are still the final arbiters of what we do and think. We are free agents. We are not victims.

Padrinho Sebastião time and time again stressed that each one of us is ultimately responsible for his or her mind/body/spirit (aparelho). He repeatedly compared the aparelho to a "home," and he emphasized that a crucial component of our spiritual work is the at times difficult task of becoming the "masters" of our "homes."[32] In this mediumistic vision, we are ideally like a welcoming, but also clear and firm, owner of a home. Our home is (again, ideally) clean, well-maintained, and decorated with love, *and* it is filled with people we love. From the perspective of mediumship, we share our home with our "family," that is, with loved ones who belong there (for example, the Beings of Light who accompany us/support us on our spiritual journey). Our home can also be filled with "friends and neighbors" we have invited to spend time with us (for example, the ongoing currents of thoughts, feelings, and energies that continually pour in-and-through us through our participation in the dynamic flux of an interconnected universe). In this way, there is nothing inherently wrong with having numerous beings coexisting within one home; in fact, it can be a joy to have a home that is filled with the hustle and bustle of loving interactions.

In theory at least, *everyone* is welcome to spend time in our home, as long as they behave appropriately. Therefore, if suffering spirits come at our invitation during a healing work, and if, as mediums supported and empowered by the Beings of Light, we choose to help these beings to move on, then all is well, since even if these suffering spirits might temporarily act out/express their pain, that acting out itself takes place within the salão; that is, in a context in which such behaviors are expected and can be dealt with safely and appropriately.

Seen from the mediumistic perspective of the Santo Daime (at least in its CEFLURIS/ICEFLU line), however, many individuals are like absentee land-owners whose properties have been invaded by squatters. Sadly, all too many people choose to denigrate their bodies with various addictive behaviors; or they indulge in gossip; or they seek to blame others; or they deny their own faults; or they engage in obsessive thoughts; and so on and so forth. In certain respects, these people are barely present, either in their bodies or in their lives in general. In essence, they have vacated the premises, leaving their aparelhos open to a whole host of harmful entities/energies (and some of these energies are directly linked to a multitude of negative attitudes and assumptions that these individuals have already unknowingly internalized from their cultures.)

I think that as human beings, we are complicated: we struggle; we make mistakes; we occasionally do horrible things to other people; sometimes we regret our actions; sometimes we rationalize what we have done or blame it on others. And if you add influences from disincarnate beings and/or sensi-tivity to nonphysical energies to the mix, then things get even more compli-cated. For myself, therefore, while it is important to see ourselves and others as clearly as possible, our all too human failings are primarily an opportunity to feel/extend compassion.

I would argue that all of us, to various degrees, are much more porous and multidimensional than we realize. As such, we are almost continually, under the surface of awareness, affected by the energies, thoughts, and feelings of others, both incarnate and disincarnate. And so, sadly, many people take on an enor-mous amount of "energetic stuff" on a daily basis, much of it very toxic, heavy, and polluting, with little or no training on how to process and transform these dense and difficult energies. And most people don't have a clue that this uncon-scious mediumship is taking place. And so, in a vain attempt to cut themselves off from this energetic overload, they attempt to numb themselves through drugs, alcohol, sexual addictions, workaholism, consumerism, and so on. But these highly destructive strategies simply do not work.

From the perspective of daimista mediumship, therefore, it is not *mediums* who are possessed by spirits (since during periods of incorporation, spirits are only in the body/mind of the medium with her/his conscious permission). Rather, the real examples of negative possession—that is, the highly destructive process in which individuals, typically unconsciously, have opened themselves to the influence of unevolved spirits and pernicious energies and are letting their lives be ruined by these dark and contracted beings/energies—actually takes place in people who are spiritually blind, who are not able or willing to consciously take responsibility for being the "master/mistress" of their homes, their aparelhos.[33],

> Of course, as always, it's complicated. I think that "obsession" by spirits—to use the Kardicist/Spiritist language—can also happen in people whose psyches are not sufficiently integrated and firm enough to handle the "wide openness" that comes hand in glove with incorporation mediumship. The literature of Spiritism is vast, but for an introduction to this genre, see Allan Kardec, *The Book of Mediums: Guide for Mediums and Invocations* (New York: Cosimo Classics, 2007); Allan Kardec, *The Spirits' Book* (New York: Cosimo Classics, 2006); Allan Kardec, *Introduction to the Spiritist Philosophy* (Philadelphia: Allan Kardec Educational Society, 2004). For Spiritism in the Brazilian context, see Emma Bragdon. *Kardec's Spiritism: A Home for Healing and Spiritual Evolution* (Woodstock, VT: Lightening Up, 2004); David J. Hess, *Samba in the Night: Spiritism in Brazil* (New York: Columbia University Press, 1994.) There are also some mediums who appear to become fascinated with the high-level drama and exoticism of mediumship and whose ego seems to enjoy the "glamor" of those sorts of wildly charged spiritual interactions—leading to what appears to be a type of addiction to mediumship.

The good news is that if we become aware of the porous nature of our self-hood and work consciously to develop our mediumship and are willing to take full responsibility for our aparelhos, then genuine transformation, both of ourselves and of the suffering spirits/negative energies that have infiltrated our energetic fields, *is* possible. And given the possibility that we are always taking on "stuff" from others, it makes sense to learn, from within, in our own experience, how to open ourselves to loving and wise energies or Presences so that we can increasingly begin to shine that love and wisdom on those more toxic energies in order that they might be transformed. It makes sense to work hard, not to shield ourselves from all of that heavy energy flowing into us (good luck with that), but rather to learn how to clear ourselves energetically (hence the "passes" of Umbanda and Spiritism).g

Many years before I became involved with the Santo Daime I received a multiyear training in spiritual/energy healing. We were taught that our task *wasn't* to shield ourselves from dense, heavy energies—not only because the very desire to shield ourselves itself comes permeated with an undertone of fear, but also because the attempt to create shields against energetic incursions cuts us off from access to the more expanded energies. We learned that our job, instead, was simply to connect to the deepest/highest levels of our being and to radiate that energetic potentiality to our clients.

While mediumship works can indeed be powerful, beautiful, and often deeply healing, I also think that incorporation mediumship is certainly *not* for everyone or for every work, in that it can often be energetically quite intense and demanding, both personally and collectively. Therefore, much of the "learning curve" of mediumship often has to do with finding balance; it is about discerning if/when mediumship is supported and called for and when it is not. As daimistas, we are invited to develop within ourselves subtle levels of discernment. We are asked to take on the challenging task of opening ourselves to the intuitive knowledge of what is called for in the moment—that is, what is needed, right here and now, to best create healing, harmony, and balance in our own personal lives and in the wider community of our fellow daimistas. And amping up intense energies through incorporation mediumship is not always the best solution. Instead, at times it is important for us to work to remain centered and grounded; to channel the hymns and the Force; to channel the I Am Presence within; to work to remain in our hearts—keeping ourselves open, clear, and transparent to the Light that shines from within our depths.[34]

Nonetheless, if and when healing works for suffering beings *are* called for within a community, there are different visions within the Santo Daime as to how to accomplish this powerful and important task most effectively. For example, many daimistas would contend that healing can only take place when these energetic "squatters" are forcefully expelled from our energetic field—hence the numerous hymns and invocations to St. Michael, with his shield of light, his sword of fire, and his foot placed firmly on the neck of a (now safely subdued) demonic being.

And I have to say that, at least in certain respects, I completely understand this attitude. I honor and respect the purity and power that St. Michael manifests: in-and-as discipline; in-and-as the focused capacity to overcome any impediments; in-and-as divine protection. St. Michael has our back in any and all circumstances, no matter how challenging. And I think that we can and should align ourselves with that potency, with that searingly pure Light that pierces through all illusion, that effortlessly overcomes all obstacles. We can and should invoke discipline, power, and divine protection into our lives.

However, as human beings, we can also distort that energy. We can at times project our all too human tendency to fear "otherness" onto that archetypal figure and can thereby, perhaps unknowingly, transmogrify St. Michael into a being that is fighting on "our side" against the insidious forces of evil that we fearfully believe are besieging us.

I am not exactly a big fan of that sort of martial mentality, if and when it presents itself within the Santo Daime—especially to the extent that it manifests in the tendency of some daimistas (myself included) to become, at least at times, self-righteous and rigid. Nevertheless, there *are* highly positive ways to invoke the martial discipline and Force that St. Michael radiates. And I believe that *this* configuration of martial qualities is what the Santo Daime, at its best, tunes into. I am not opposed to martial energy per se. In fact, as a practitioner of aikido for over twenty years, I have a profound appreciation for the martial arts, at least in their more elevated forms. I have a deep and lasting respect for the clarity, focus, discipline, and commitment that the martial arts can embody and convey—and not all martial arts are about conquering and dominating an opponent. At least in the case of aikido, martial efficacy flows forth, with powerful grace, from *harmonizing* with one's partner, with oneself, and with the universe.

The Santo Daime tradition can and often does tap into the purity of *that* sense of "martial"—the erect, composed, courageous, vigilant, enduring, fully committed "warriors" who fill the salão; those daimista "soldiers of the Queen" who, overcoming laziness and stubbornness within themselves, return again and again to the conscious, intentional effort it takes to genuinely transform themselves; those daimistas who are deeply committed to their inner evolution, and who seek to learn how to truly forgive, how to genuinely love both themselves and others.

And really, we are all are spiritual "warriors," if not only in the context of Santo Daime works but also in the middle of our daily lives, we continue "fighting" the forces of inertia, fear, ignorance, and other negative tendencies within ourselves. And eventually, with the grace of God and the Divine Mother, we can "move up the ranks." That is, we can become increasingly empowered to help others; we can be granted the spiritual capacity to increasingly be able to selflessly and more and more effectively shine the transformative Light of Compassion on the heartbreaking suffering of humanity.

Now *that* way of understanding what it means to be martial in the Santo Daime I can understand and support; engaging in a "battle" in which we all extend ourselves to lift up and encourage our weary brothers and sisters; we all work in alignment with everyone else, in our places, in our own way, while also working as One, as a highly attuned and disciplined phalanx of Light and Love (and kindness, and patience), moving forward, even when it might seem impossible, to illuminate what had previously been hidden, to bring the shadows into the Light so that they can dissolve. This is an army that I can belong to: an army with no external enemies, with no feared (and often hated) Other anywhere in sight.

I will admit, however, that I have at times been troubled by the ways in which I have (thankfully not often) witnessed some guardians who seem to tap into the implicit martial mindset of the Santo Daime (and humanity in general), using those metaphors of battle and the struggle between good and evil to justify certain, to my mind at least, unnecessarily stringent ways of working with suffering spirits. For example, at times I have seen guardians sternly order a suffering spirit to leave, adding all sorts of commanding hand gestures and forceful phrases, almost as if they were participating in a type of quasi-exorcism. Or more generally, I have seen guardians who will at times attempt to energetically "dominate" the spirit, commanding it to be quiet or to behave.

In Portuguese, the word *dominar* isn't always understood as "to dominate"; that is, the word isn't necessarily about overcoming and mastering with force. Instead, another equally valid meaning is something closer to "to have dominion over" or "to be effective."[35] In that sense, I would suggest that to "dominate" a spirit is incorrectly understood as "mastering a spirit by force." Instead, dominating a spirit is more accurately and certainly more compassionately understood as being at ease and filled with divine Power so that I can capably assist this particular being to align with its highest good. Daimistas will also often speak about "indoctrinating" suffering spirits. But it is important to point out that *doutrinar* in Portuguese doesn't, at least always, have the negative connotations that are often associated with how that word is often translated in English: that is, "to indoctrinate." For English speakers, indoctrination is often (perhaps accurately) understood as an attempt to force one's own set of self-righteous and unexamined beliefs upon another, often unwilling, person. But in the Portuguese, "doutrinar" often has much more positive connotations: it means to teach, to illuminate. And so, to "indoctrinate" a spirit isn't about giving that spirit a set of one-size-fits-all beliefs; and it isn't about forcing anything on anyone. Rather, it's about shining the Light of the Daime on that suffering being. It's about linking that spirit up with the Doctrine—the energetic matrix of the Santo Daime. It's about working to help that spirit to see the forgiveness that is there for it. Indoctrination is the work of teaching, illumination, and transformation.

Fortunately, most daimista guardians that I have seen working with suffering spirits do so in a way that, while disciplined and firm, is also patient and compassionate. What I have seen, again and again, are guardians who, while resting in/trusting in the Daime, give that suffering spirit the much-needed space and time to express its pain; to feel seen; to be energetically held with mercy and forgiveness. Most of the guardians I know don't interfere, or fuss, or try to fix a medium who is going through a passage—to say nothing of inserting themselves forcefully into the medium's often raw and vulnerable energetic space. Instead, what they do is simply "hold the space": they work to stay grounded, calm, clear, and in their hearts; and they work to link up with the Beings of Light who are there to assist that spirit to move on.

And even if the interaction between the guardian and the medium at times becomes more active and engaged—and sometimes a guardian will receive very clear inner guidance that it is important for her/him to enter the medium's energetic matrix—still, at its best (and Santo Daime guardianship is typically enormously skilled and sophisticated) that more intentional interaction itself happens while radiating an underlying energy that is sensitive, fluid, and deeply loving. To my mind, that sort of tuned-in, spacious, heart-centered presence is the best gift that a guardian can offer.

In the context of our development as mediums, daimistas can slowly begin to recognize that at least some of the internal psychic turbulence that we feel in our day-to-day lives is not really our own, but instead comes to us from "outside" ourselves, either from beings who have perhaps been in our fields for quite some time or from the general energetic heaviness and density that permeates many of the places in which we live and work. Recognizing that our inner struggles are, at least in part, catalyzed by our energetic interweaving with other strands of consciousness does not deny that we have the responsibility to work with our sufferings and difficulties with as much clarity and love and skill as possible. Instead of blaming others or life or fate for our inner agitation and struggles, we can consciously choose to work with these negative, dense, contracted energies that we discover within our fields with as much compassion and wisdom as possible, so that they can finally become transformed into Light.

And the best way that I know of to work skillfully with these negative energies is to establish an ongoing, living, powerful connection to the deepest strata of our beings—that is, to link up, repeatedly, experientially with the true Master of our homes—our Higher Self; our truest Self; the I Am Presence; the Christ within.

And so, to my mind, if we are drinking Daime and are attempting to increasingly embody that Christ consciousness in our own body/mind as we develop spiritually, then *of course* we would, if called, want to share in that work. To me, therefore, the highest mediumship is incorporating the Christ Consciousness and learning how to work skillfully, powerfully, and lovingly with any and all energetic manifestations, including suffering.

It is crucial to develop our capacity to know how to skillfully work with dense and dark energies. Because just as there are humans who get a type of distorted pleasure from hurting others, in the same way, there can be nonphysical beings who want to do harm, who want to create chaos. And just as we would not knowingly invite a psychopath into our homes, it's probably not a good idea to blithely open ourselves to any/all negative energies. And yet, to my mind at least, even these ill-intentioned beings (at times given the name *zombateiros* or "mocking spirits" in the Santo Daime) should ideally not be attacked or battled with, but rather should be firmly (and yet, compassionately) disciplined; they should be dealt with clearly and directly, without fear, with the knowledge and faith that we are completely protected in the context of these interactions because we are energetically linked up with a huge phalanx of Beings of Light who are there to either powerfully expel that dense and dark energy from the salão or to (safely) transform even this level of negativity into Light.[36],

Mestre Irineu himself would at times hold the *trabalho de mesa* ("table work"; often referred to as the "crosses work" in the CEFLURIS lineage). The crosses work is an explicit de-obsession work, an overt exorcism, designed to forcefully expel demonic/evil spirits from someone who is acting in ways that others might view as symptoms of mental illness. And I have to say that I respect these works. If Mestre Irineu, who many in the Santo Daime feel had incarnated that Christ Consciousness in an extremely powerful way, felt that these sorts of charged, dramatic, "exorcism-like" ceremonies were truly what was necessary, were what best served the interests of that suffering individual, then I trust that these ceremonies were genuinely for the highest good of that individual. But I also have faith that if/when Mestre Irineu (or later, Padrinho Sebastião) was leading this particular ceremonial form, then God's Light and Love, as well as the Mercy of the Divine Mother, were also continually there, operative under the surface.

It feels important to reemphasize: we can *always* choose to respond to whatever comes our way with presence, with heart, with clarity: it's just that some moments are more challenging than others. It is, therefore, crucial, not only as daimistas but also simply as human beings, to learn how to take responsibility for how we respond to challenging experiences. And this attitude, this intentionality, is especially important when we are developing our mediumship.

Instead of seeing suffering spirits as alien from us, and then engaging in an "us versus them" battle, we can instead choose to see them as contracted manifestations of God who, on some level of their being, also long to be free. We can realize that even if outwardly they are saying *no* (at times literally) to the Light of Forgiveness that is continually being offered to them, on a deeper level, they are drawn to the Light of the holy Daime. We can choose to see them as beings who, like us, hurt, long for love, and deserve to be freed from suffering. We can let our hearts be touched; we can let our connection with these beings kindle perhaps previously unavailable resources of deep compassion within us. We can let those interactions themselves deepen our own longing to serve—purely, powerfully. And like a mother (like *the* Mother) with a child who is hurt and crying, we can hold those beings with tenderness, with gentleness, with Love. And ultimately it is that Love itself that heals and transforms.

In this way, we can embody, in our own lives, the perspective of the Tibetan Buddhist saint Milarepa who during meditation was attacked by a horde of "monstrous" spiritual beings and did not react with fear or repugnance, but instead sang to them with compassion and wisdom, welcoming them as manifestations of the *dharmakāya*, the universal body of the Buddha. And with this empowered attitude, he is said to have transformed these monstrous beings into enlightened Protectors of the Dharma.[37]

As daimistas, we are given the priceless opportunity to learn to see *every* experience (including challenging mediumistic interactions with other beings) as a manifestation of the divine.

Again, it doesn't matter if the darkness, suffering, or ignorance that we are experiencing is our own or is coming from "outside." The process is the same: we can, over time, with grace, learn to welcome every moment that comes our way—especially the challenging ones. We can choose to see each moment as an opportunity to grow spiritually; to let go of our reactivity; to come back to our hearts; to feel compassion for ourselves and others; to see the face of God shining in-and-as those who are treating us badly; to welcome God in-and-as the suffering we are feeling so deeply.

And let's be real: as daimistas, we often feel a *lot* of suffering. Some Santo Daime works are basically just hours and hours of suffering—knowing (intimately, profoundly) what it's like to be homeless with people stepping over you and ignoring you; or what it's like to be an orphan in a refugee camp who has to shut down and go numb to cope; or simply feeling wave after wave of brute suffering that doesn't seem to have any specific reason or source. Given that as daimistas we're sometimes just going to feel suffering, as always, our attitude toward this suffering is crucial. We don't have to simply hunker down and endure it. We can, instead, widen out into Vastness; and from that skylike transparency within, a transparency that is infused with shining Presence of the Beings of Light, we can send out an energetic "note" of calm, of compassion, letting that energy suffuse the suffering. The suffering itself may not immediately disappear, but our relationship *to* that suffering can be radically transformed, and that makes all the difference. We might still feel that suffering, but we do not have to be lost in it; we don't have to be beaten down by it.

This spiritual strategy of how to work with suffering is not some sort of "spiritual bypass"; we aren't frantically attempting to rise above suffering; we aren't trying to lift ourselves into some divine realm in which we feel no pain.[38] We also aren't ennobling suffering from some (perhaps subconscious) belief that we deserve to suffer or that we only grow spiritually through suffering. We're neither running away from the suffering nor wallowing in it. Instead, we are responding to suffering from a divinely empowered place of compassion and heart.

Here again I see numerous similarities with Tibetan Buddhism—in this case, their practice of tonglen. Tonglen happens at a certain stage of your spiritual practice in Tibetan Tantric Buddhism, when you are ready/called to do so and when you have established a living connection with the inner Teacher. (See Sogyal Rinpoche, *The Tibetan Book of Living and Dying* (New York: HarperSanFrancisco, 1993), 193–195, 202–208. See also Swami Girijananda, *Tonglen for Our Own Suffering: 7 Variations on an Ancient Practice* (Portland, OR: Rudra, 2015).) In the practice of tonglen, you are instructed to consciously take within yourself, with compassion, the darkness and suffering of others. You literally breathe that suffering and darkness into yourself, carrying all of that darkness and suffering into yourself with your breath. That darkness and suffering is then offered to the Heart (or the Ocean of Compassion) within so that it can be transformed. According to Tibetan Tantric teachings, doing tonglen tremendously accelerates your spiritual growth, in that you are no longer simply doing spiritual work just for yourself. Instead, you are beginning to cultivate and embody your longing to serve others—others who you recognize are deeply interconnected with you and indeed with the whole cosmos. Doing tonglen, or more broadly, the willingness to spiritually take on the sufferings of others offers the practitioner the opportunity to recognize and deepen into spiritual practice as a shared, mutual endeavor. Doing so allows each practitioner the opportunity to deepen her or his compassion and wisdom: two of the key qualities of enlightenment itself.

I have to say that for many years in my own spiritual journey, taking on the pain, suffering, and darkness of another person was the *last* thing I wanted to do, especially given my own exceedingly painful awareness of my own limitations and suffering. Nonetheless, to my surprise and delight, as a daimista medium I'm actually at times practicing a variety of *tonglen*—willingly, joyfully, frequently, in a matter of fact way. And whether we call it (as many daimistas do) giving charity to spirits or practicing tonglen, that joyful willingness to offer one's very sense of self to promote the spiritual growth of others feels deeply powerful and spiritually positive.

After all of this discussion about suffering, I thought that it might be the right moment to offer up a hearty and heartfelt cheer of gratitude for the spiritual efficacy—heck, the bare-bones necessity—of joy, love, and pleasure.

SINGING AND RECEIVING HYMNS AS FORMS OF MEDIUMSHIP

It is important to reemphasize that mediumship is not limited to the process of incorporating a specific spirit within your aparelho. For many daimistas, singing Santo Daime hymns is a powerful and beautiful form of mediumship. Many puxadoras (the highly skilled and dedicated women who sing with such vigor and clarity during works so that everyone else can follow their lead) often appear to mediumistically channel hymns during a work. I have been told that these women will often become so energetically linked up with the inner Source of each hymn that, as they are singing, they become living conduits for the spiritual energy that the hymns carry and transmit. In this way, they are "channeling" the energy of the hymns in-and-through them. And this form of hymn-singing mediumship, although rarely discussed within the Santo Daime, can also happen to any who immerse themselves with discipline and heart into the process of singing hymns.

As I have noted, singing hymns in unison, with heart and focus, is a central component of the Santo Daime tradition. Hymns are *received*; that is, they are hymns that are not consciously created/composed, but rather have emerged spontaneously from some mysterious Source deep within the person who receives them. Daimistas believe that Santo Daime hymns have been transmitted "from the Astral." That is, they have been received from some higher divine Source and carry with them the energy that radiates from that Source. In certain respects, the hymns act as lifelines of energy that can link you up to that Source. Or seen from a different angle, the hymns can open up "portals" or "valves" that allow the energetic frequency of that Source to pour through and vibrate within you and around you, in-and-as your temporal experience of the melody/rhythm of that particular hymn, as it is sung, with heart and clarity of mind, linking everyone in the salão together into a unified, extremely uplifting, vibratory current. (Even if, as I have mentioned, different hymns seem to link up to/emerge from numerous different "doorways" into that One Source.)

MY FIRST TIME RECEIVING A HYMN

For my first couple of years in the Santo Daime, I had no clue what it would be like to receive a hymn. Doing so seemed to be quite a bit above my pay grade. I'd try to envision Mestre Irineu, for example, receiving a hymn, and I simply didn't have any viable analogues from my prior experience that could help me to get a sense of what that process might feel like. But then, on June 16, 2008, I received my first hymn.

I'm going to describe what it was like to receive a hymn. But I realize that I'm stepping onto holy ground here. I'm making no claims about the ontological status of my hymns. These are not the hymns of Mestre Irineu or Padrinho Sebastião; I'm not a Santo Daime elder. In fact, some of my hymns are a bit unorthodox. Nonetheless, I do feel called to write, with as much heart, clarity, and humility as possible, about what the process of receiving a hymn has felt like to me (at this point I have received over 30 hymns, and I've been receiving them now for over ten years).

And I recognize that an almost contradictory configuration of personal qualities was necessary, at least in my case, in order to receive a hymn. On the one hand, selflessness/humility was crucial. Hymns never come via a conscious effort of will. You can be respectfully attentive and grateful when they do arrive, and yet it also feels important to be as non-attached as possible to whether they ever come again. On the other hand, at least in my case, it was also crucial to have a willingness to stand up and be counted; to announce publicly, even "proudly," that I've received a new hymn and would you like to listen to it or sing it with me? And so, at least for me, in order to receive a hymn I needed both genuine self-valuing (as opposed to a narcissistic emptiness that craves the attention/admiration of others) and a level of genuine humility (as opposed to a lack of self-worth masquerading as selflessness).

When I received that first hymn, I had been to a Santo Daime work, and I was staying at the house of a friend. For some reason, I began to pray to the Virgin Mother, expressing how even though I knew that She was a significant figure in the Santo Daime, I had not felt Her Presence within. I then went on to ask if it was possible to deepen my connection to Her. Sometime the next day, after having endured the hours of travel and stress needed to get back home to Dallas, I collapsed on my sofa and had a very much needed nap. After about an hour of lying there, almost paralyzed with fatigue (while also feeling the typical post-Daime work "anti-hangover"), I woke up humming this lovely melody. It just wouldn't leave my mind. And there were some words that seemed to want to accompany that melody: "Come down, Virgin Mother, come down, and be with me." And so it continued for the next hour or so: the stanzas of the hymn just poured down, and knowing how easily I could forget what was coming through, I'd periodically record the new words that were arriving into my tiny handheld recording device.

Receiving this hymn felt like I was simply taking dictation: the words would rise into my consciousness from some mysterious place, and it seemed that my primary job was to pay attention and sing whatever came into the recorder. The heartfelt words began as a plea to the Divine Mother, asking Her to come into my awareness. They then spoke about Her arrival. Then the lyrics asked for healing and blessings. And finally, the words of the hymn thanked Her for those gifts. The hymn had this lovely "developmental arc" to it. It began with me feeling estranged and expressing my longing for Her Presence; it grew into me singing out my joy at having received her blessings; and it culminated in a sense of contentment and fulfillment, with me feeling so deeply grateful to Her for everything that She had so gracefully given to me.

And once I received the hymn, my sense of thankfulness and awe continued to deepen, since the hymn itself demonstrated to me that my prior prayer had been answered, in that it appeared that below the surface of my conscious awareness, the Virgin Mother and I *did* have a very loving and intimate relationship. And She was letting me know this, in-and-through that hymn, as it poured from Her Heart to mine. While the overt words of the hymn were asking Her to come down to me, in reality, the hymn *was*, in fact, Her coming down, gracing me and all those who would later sing it with the energy and blessings of Her Presence.

The indigenous and vegetalista use of ayahuasca is consistently associated with a process that is almost identical to "receiving" a hymn within the Santo Daime. The icaros of the ayahuasquero are not consciously created; they come to him/her in altered states of consciousness; and as I mentioned earlier, they are often understood to be the "language of the spirits," so that singing an icaro is a way to manifest the presence and power of that particular spiritual being within the sacred space/time of the ceremony; see Stephan V. Beyer, *Singing to the Plants: A Guide to Mestizo Shamanism in the Upper Amazon* (Albuquerque: University of New Mexico Press, 2009), 63–76). Similarly, in a fascinating cross-cultural correspondence, the words and melodies of the ancient Vedic hymns in India were understood in an almost identical way. These hymns are said to have emerged from deep states of meditation experienced by *rishis* or "seers." And some of these hymns are said to have arisen after the seers had drunk the mysterious psychedelic substance *Soma*, and then, having felt themselves ecstatically raised to the heavenly worlds or having felt themselves filled with the divine Light of the gods, they rapturously "heard" the words and music for these Vedic hymns. (These ancient hymns—the foundational, most important, revelatory level of scriptures within Hinduism—are called *shruti*—in Sanskrit, "that which is heard.") In fact, the sounds of the hymns themselves were often understood to be the divinely empowered "sonic body" of the deity that they were "describing," so much so that it was crucially important, during rituals, to sing those divine syllables with a precisely correct intonation, rhythm, and pronunciation. See Guy L. Beck, *Sonic Theology: Hinduism and Sacred Sound* (Columbia: University of South Carolina Press, 1993), 23–49; Gordon Wasson, *Soma: The Divine Mushroom of Immortality* (New York: Harcourt Brace Jovanovich, 1969).

After receiving that first hymn, I was extremely hesitant to share it. I was a bit concerned about whether it was up to snuff. And yet I was eager to share it. And then, months later, I decided to record that first hymn, and the others that followed in its wake, in a polished and professional way, with the crucial help of a dear friend who is a master musician and who has a recording studio in his backyard, so that I could share them not only with fellow daimistas but also with non-daimista family and friends. And after having received seventeen hymns, I decided to create my own hinário/spiral-bound book that included a CD of the recordings. The cover art on the hinário (a mandala) was created by another dear friend, an artist who herself received a powerful visionary experience that was the basis for that beautiful mandala.

I'll admit that all of this felt like a whole other level of spiritual audacity on my part. And yet, even though the hymns had been received and hence weren't really "mine," those hymns were (and are) also the purest, most cherished, expression of the deepest and truest dimensions of who I am. So of course I wanted to share them with my loved ones.

You can find the lyrics and the music for all of my hymns (the hinário is called *Awakening Heart*) at www.liquidlightbook.com/awakeningheart.

MORE ON RECEIVING HYMNS

There are times when receiving a hymn is utterly straightforward. On March 21, 2009, for example, I woke up from an extremely vivid dream. In the dream, I was with numerous friends in a large, contemporary, open house with tall white walls and lots of light. A young man was sitting on the wooden steps leading down into the living room area, and he was playing a guitar—in a very "Spanish" style—and he was singing the words to "You Start by Loving Yourself," my second hymn. In this case, all that I had to do was to get up out of bed and immediately sing the words that I had just heard him singing within the dream into my small handheld recorder. (I also went through a short period of hemming and hawing within myself, because I recognized that the hymn was structured in a rather unorthodox way and I questioned whether it was really a hymn. In the end, because the energy that accompanied the hymn was so powerful, and because the inner *yes* felt so right, I was willing to say to myself and then to others that it was indeed a hymn.

WHEN IS A HYMN A "REAL" HYMN?

The question of what is or isn't a real hymn is fascinating. In the olden days in the Santo Daime, the process by which a "might be a hymn, I don't know" received the stamp of approval was fairly straightforward: people would bring their hymns to Mestre Irineu, and he, or often Dona Percília—a woman who was appointed by Mestre Irineu to this exact task—would let them know if the hymns passed muster, or if they needed a bit more work. At this point in time, however, for better or for worse (and I actually think it's for the better), there's no single authority within the Santo Daime who can/will infallibly state whether a specific group of words set to a specific melodic and rhythmic sequence actually is or is not a hymn. With the exception of the uncontested collections of hymns that have been received by revered elders (for example, Mestre Irineu's hinário— the Ur-template for all hinários that followed), the process by which certain hymns get the stamp of approval appears to be rather casual. Often what happens is something like this: Let's say that a woman who leads a Santo Daime church begins to receive hymns, hymns that she offers during the Santo Daime works that she directs, hymns that are sung by her sisters and brothers in the church, perhaps with a guitarist picking out the melody and accompanying her. As these hymns are sung again and again, and as everyone in the church begins to know them better and better, and as each person begins over time to overlay onto these hymns an increasingly deeper and more complex set of powerful experiences that emerged while these hymns were sung (since these hymns are sung in the Force of the Daime, which elevates everything)—at a certain point, the issue of whether they are real hymns becomes sort of a nonissue. Everyone in the church loves singing them, and so her hymns become, almost by default, real hymns—at least within that local church setting.

EVEN MORE ON RECEIVING HYMNS

I received another hymn within a dream on January 10, 2017. I was lying in bed in my house in Dallas. I had recently been struggling with a bout of pneumonia, so I was really fatigued. I lay there in bed, in the dark, listening to powerful gusts of wind that were rushing through the leaves of the trees. And torrents of rain would come and go in waves as well. I lay there on the bed, feeling all of that aliveness, and then, all of the sudden, I could feel the Force of a hymn welling up from within me. But I was so exhausted that I began to sink back into sleep, even as I continued to try to align myself with the Force of the hymn. The next thing I knew, I was in a dream world. I was in a noisy room, filled with people talking, and I was listening for the hymn, futilely attempting to hear it. In the dream, I left the noisy room and entered into a large, spacious and quiet commercial kitchen where I found one of my wife's students, who is also a dear friend of mine. Seeming to sense that I needed quiet, she asked, "Am I in your way?" I told her: "No, it's fine for you to be here." Almost immediately, I was finally able to hear the melody of the hymn. And right after hearing that melody, I woke up and began to repeat it to myself, letting my body rock softly while lying there in bed. And then, in a rush of inspiration, the words came pouring through to hymn 22, "My Iansa," the hymn I received that focuses on the Yoruba Orixá/Goddess of the Wind—yes, the Goddess of storms and tornados, but also the Goddess of soft warm breezes and the gentle rustling of the wind moving through the leaves at night. Iansa is also, by extension, the Goddess of Breath—the Goddess of Prana, of Qi, of the Cosmic Force of Life Itself—a particularly poignant and important connection for me to make, given my battles with pneumonia.[39],

You'll find a word in the "My Iansa" hymn that I think I can safely say you'll not find in any other Santo Daime hymn: "Lover." To me, divine Love comes in numerous forms. We can love God as Lord, as Father, as Mother, as Son, as Child, as Friend—but (at least according to Hindu devotional categories) the highest form of divine Love is to envision God/Goddess as our Lover—a Lover we long to merge with; a Lover we adore, with our entire heart, soul, and body, not caring what society's rules might. And so, this is a hymn that opens into and embraces that very specific, highly exalted, quality of Love—a Love that flows like an infinity sign between Lover and Beloved; a Love that is deeply intimate, pleasurable, free, alive, joyous, and passionate. The hymn, in essence, is singing about the eroticism of the breath.

Both of these hymns—that is, "You Start by Loving Yourself" and "My Iansa"—were just pure, utterly unedited downloads that emerged out of an altered state of consciousness. But hymns have also come to me during very mundane moments of my life—for example, while in the shower, doing the dishes, or driving. Another hymn came through me on May 13, 2018—Mother's Day. I was once again gripped by that very Force-filled feeling of a hymn wanting to emerge within my consciousness, with that "virtual hymn" saying, in essence:

"I'm coming through: pay attention!" I was at my sister Brenda's house and I had just woken up from a dream (the same dream that I mentioned earlier about a brass cauldron filled with dancing snakes that someone had "capped," with poisonous results, prompting all of us to begin to sing "Oh Mother God" to calm and heal the situation).

I woke up from the dream with the phrase "Oh Mother God" ringing in my head and with the melody insistently repeating itself in my mind. But I didn't really have time to record anything, since everyone was already hustling around in the house getting ready to leave for a family breakfast in honor of my mother. I had to quickly hop into the shower. And so, with the hot water pouring over me, the first verse arrived, and I managed to record at least that part of the hymn when I was getting dressed, but because everyone was already heading out the front door, I sent up a prayer to Whoever/Whatever was the Source of that hymn, agreeing that when I had a moment I would give it my full attention and inwardly asked if we could just put it on hold for a while. I'm not sure if that prayer was answered in quite the way that I had hoped, since during the drive to the restaurant, and during the breakfast itself, and during the drive back to my sister's house, the energy of the hymn just kept gripping me, for hours. What this meant was that at times I felt pulled within so strongly that it was hard to interact with everyone. (I'd occasionally have to work to keep my eyes from rolling back in my head.) Thankfully, I don't think too many people noticed. (My mother was the exception. At one point she even asked: "You've been really quiet—is everything OK?" I was able, truthfully, to say that everything was going really well and that my heart was filled with love for her.) However, as soon as I got back to my sister's house, I rushed to the bedroom to record the words to "Oh Mother God" that came pouring through me.

There are many similar stories that I would love to tell of how various hymns emerged, but except for what I write about hymn 30, the following little tidbit will have to suffice: On December 25, 2017, on Christmas morning, I received hymn 26, "Your Love." My family loves to hear my hymns, and so I sang the hymn for them a few days later at my brother's beach house in Florida. A married couple who were long-time friends of the family were there also, and after I finished, the woman, who is a musicologist, said, "That's almost exactly the same melody as the Coventry Carol." It ends up that the Coventry Carol (a *Christmas* carol) was a well-known carol in sixteenth-century England. It is a lullaby in the voice of the mothers of the slaughtered innocents, that is, the babies who were murdered by King Herod. Although my hymn is about divine Love, the theme is actually not so different, since when is the purity of a mother's love for her child not divine?

RECEIVING HYMN 30

On October 12, 2018, I received my thirtieth hymn, "Come Right Now and Set Me Free." I was in the kitchen of my house, and I had been humming this beautiful melody as I was cleaning dishes in the kitchen, and I was thinking to myself that it was such a "Daime-esque" melody. I wondered if it was a hymn that I had sung in some Santo Daime ritual in the past. (My melodic memory is so poor and the hymns can often sound *so* familiar.) But at some point I realized that it was probably a hymn coming through. So I shifted gears.

Over the years, I've noticed that there are times—becoming increasingly common—when the "inner signals" that alert me that a hymn is arriving are, as it were, turned down a notch, even if the Force of the hymn, as it is emerging, is if anything even more powerful. In the beginning, there was *no doubt* that a hymn was coming up within me/pouring down into me. At times I would almost feel as if I was being shaken in the jaws of some sort of benevolent lion. But in the past few years, in a way that echoes my incorporation mediumship, recognizing that Something wants to express Itself in-and-through me (in this case, a hymn) has become an increasingly subtle process—something that feels less like being shaken and more like savoring the smell of roses drifting past or feeling my cat softly rub up against my legs.

When I was receiving hymn 30, I soon found myself in my bedroom, letting myself twirl in the Force—almost like a combination of a whirling dervish and an early Hasidic rebbe, with my arms over my head, "lassoing in" the energetic fluxes that were pouring into me, my body moving and swaying and spinning in genuine ecstasy. I was singing the tune over and over again to myself, letting sounds just bubble up from within me, in a kind of loving babbling, my head swaying from side to side, my body undulating. I was feeling myself swept up by the currents of Life that were pulsating in me, as I was moved (on all levels) by the Force of the hymn itself as it was manifesting within me. I worked to just let myself lean back into the Light and Love that I was feeling so strongly, sinking softly back into an ongoing, subtly shifting state of responsiveness.

And then the words themselves started to come through—clusters of lyrics surging up as complete, self-contained "packages." And so I wrote them down right away on sheet after sheet of paper that I set down on the top of the two oak dressers in the bedroom. At times I'd take periodic breaks to just sway and dance, my hands raised, my head tilted back, feeling such gratitude, awe, and wonder at the grace of receiving a hymn in this way. I would watch from within as the words would almost stitch themselves onto the melody, or seen another way, as the words emerged organically from the melody and rhythm of the hymn itself. I also noticed, even in the moment it was happening, how the lyrics themselves at times reflected/expressed the states of consciousness and energetic pulsations that I was experiencing as I was receiving the hymn itself: "Crystal beams of Liquid Light, shining now for my delight. / Waves of grace are pouring through, my eyes are filled with You. / Embracing Love with every breath is what I want to do." I watched in wonder as the lyrics arose from some deep place within me and I would periodically think to myself: "Oh my—that's really beautiful" or "Oh my—where did that little word play come from?" And the melody and the rhythm of the hymn was just so hypnotic and gripping that I'd find myself swept away in it as those rhyming, often startlingly profound lyrics would bubble up.

And then, there was that clear yet subtle sense of: "OK, that's it—we're done."

AND STILL MORE ON RECEIVING HYMNS

After I had received a fairly decent number of hymns, I began to realize that the energetic emergence of a hymn did not necessarily mean that the words would immediately come with crystal clarity. To my mind, as long as the hymn energy is gripping my body, then any editing I do (for example, deciding that a certain word doesn't quite feel right and then opening up/waiting until a new word emerges that does feels right; or feeling that a stanza that emerged chronologically earlier actually feels better later in the hymn) is all part of the process of receiving the hymn. All that really matters is that I'm in the Force and that I stay aligned. Similarly, when I'm receiving a hymn in Portuguese, as long as the process itself continues to feel charged with the energy of the hymn wanting to emerge, I feel completely fine sharing what I have received with my Portuguese tutor, and then working with her to fine-tune it, to get the words just right. The hymn, to my mind, hasn't fully been received until I clearly feel, "Yes, you've got it."

I'll admit that I'm truly fascinated by that mysterious intersection between "me" and the Source of the hymn that I'm receiving. On the one hand, it's very clear to me that the hymns are received from some "Other-ness." They never arise within my consciousness with any planning or intentionality on my part. There's a very strong feeling of something arriving, something coming into me from some Source that is not me. Nonetheless, I'm definitely part of the equation. The words, the ideas, all draw upon my interests, my training, my vocabulary, and my Portuguese skills (or lack thereof). And more subtly, the process itself depends a lot upon my own spiritual level of development—for example, the simple fact that I am (usually) able to discern when a hymn is coming versus thinking that I'm just humming some random melody. And even more subtly, when a hymn is coming through me, I draw upon my years of meditation and spiritual practice to quiet my mind; to open my heart; to hold the intention that those words and that music carry with them only the highest transformational energy. And so, while I never consciously attempt to craft a hymn, I can still say that my hymns come straight from my heart—that mysterious intersection (that we all share) of "me" and "the Divine." (I'm putting scare quotes around those terms as a signal that I don't really have a complete understanding of what either of those terms means.) In that way, my hymns actually *are* an expression of me, as well something that comes from some Other within. Both. At the same time.

9
The Holy House in Céu do Mapiá—Rosary Works

I would now like to return to Céu do Mapiá to describe the "Rosary work"—a work that was arguably the high point of my time in Mapiá. Almost every day (except during the intensity of the festival works), I took part in a series of these invitation-only works that focused on invoking and manifesting the energy of the I Am presence. In many ways, these works seemed to happen in a higher dimensional place/time, even if, in physical reality, they took place in the Santa Casa, the Holy House—a glowing interdimensional portal if there ever was one (as well as an amazing resource for charity and healing for those who were suffering in the village).

The Santa Casa was made possible because of Clara, a medium from the Umbanda tradition who lived in Céu do Mapiá.[1] About twenty years ago, a Japanese woman who had a skin disease as a result of her exposure to atomic radiation came to Mapiá. She lived with Clara (and Maria Alice, another Umbanda-trained medium) and received many powerful healings. This woman, after receiving a dream in which Mestre Irineu told her to give money to Clara to create a place of healing for those who were sick, took out a loan from the bank and gave the money to Clara. Isabel Barsé had earlier been given by an Argentinian a tiny, somewhat rundown house in Mapiá; with the money that had been given to Clara, they were able to remodel the house. Over time the Santa Casa began to grow as more money arrived: they created a small outdoor kitchen (which was later expanded and moved to the backyard area of the house, where it was used to serve food to those in need, while the original kitchen area became an informal "pharmacy" for storing/dispensing medicines). Later on, they also built a spacious *terreiro* (a place in which to hold Umbandaime works, as well as community meetings).

FIGURE 9.1 Terreiro behind the Santa Casa

Umbandaime works are, as the name itself signifies, Daime-fueled Umbanda mediumship sessions, called "giras" (literally, "circles," referring both to the circular format of the ritual structure of the works and to the revolving motions of the body that many mediums manifest when incorporating the various spiritual beings that populate the Umbanda universe). At one point during my stay in Mapiá, I was told a story about Baixinha, the tiny "Mãe do Santo"—the head of an Umbanda fellowship—who helped to train Jonathan Goldman and who played a crucial role in the introduction of Umbanda into the Santo Daime. (The introduction of Umbanda into the Santo Daime tradition and the creation of Umbandaime as one option within the Santo Daime repertoire is an important, albeit complicated, story. I describe at least some of the highlights of this process in "The Historical Development of the Santo Daime: Section Two—The Life and Work of Padrinho Sebastião," www .liquidlightbook.com/padrinho. See also Antonio Alves Marques Jr. "The Incorporation of Umbanda by Santo Daime," English trans. Daniel Thornton, www.neip.info/novo/wp-content/uploads/2015/04/marques_daime

_umbanda_english.pdf. Apparently, when Baixinha first came to Mapiá in the 1980s, she led the first ever Umbanda gira in Mapiá. She was channeling Tupinimba, her caboclo—her Native American spirit guide—and at some point during the work she was challenged, forcefully, by a large and extremely aggressive man. Baixinha, less than five feet tall, promptly picked this guy up and threw him across the packed earth circle where they were doing the ritual; she then wrestled him and even played around with him some, finishing by putting her foot on his chest as he was lying on the ground on his back. She then threw her scarf down on him as a sign of victory over him.

THE ROSARY WORKS

When I lived in Céu do Mapiá, I attended Rosary works in the Santa Casa almost every morning at 6:00 A.M. I would get up a little before 5:00 a.m. (often after having participated in a Santo Daime work the day before) in order to arrive on time. The humble, low-ceilinged, squeaky-floored tiny house was located far from the center of the village. It was here that a small group of us (typically around six people, and never more than ten) would take part in Rosary works.

The first day that I went to the Santa Casa (accompanied by Rick) was utterly magical—walking to the work in the early morning, when darkness was slowly shifting to light; the stars shining brilliantly in the sky; the frogs croaking; the roosters crowing in the distance; the calls of unknown birds echoing in the night; and the insects buzzing and whirring. Rick and I carefully made our way down the hill where the inn was located, following the dirt road as it twisted and turned within the narrow cone of illumination created by our flashlights. We walked quietly and carefully under the canopy of stars, hardly saying a word to each other, breathing in the almost-dawn air scented with the smells of the surrounding forest, letting the quiet whir of nocturnal insects wash over us, until after crossing a long wooden bridge over the river that tumbled past far beneath us, we were greeted by an enormous bull with long sharp horns. The bull was just standing there, exactly as if it had been waiting for us. It then proceeded to walk ahead of us for the next twenty minutes, turning at each fork of the road (which eventually diminished into a rather narrow trail), plodding along, without stopping, without looking back. It led us across

FIGURE 9.2 Santa Casa

a little rickety bridge with no guardrail (the bridge was only about four feet wide and was basically just some planks nailed down on some poles set up about ten feet above a tributary of the river). Finally, after passing a barbed-wire enclosed field and trudging up another small hill, we arrived at the gate of the Santa Casa, whereupon that massive animal simply continued steadily moving forward, having (apparently) accomplished its task of guiding us to this humble house.

The Rosary works took place in the central room of the Santa Casa, with everyone, depending upon which phase of the ritual we were in, either standing or remaining seated in rough-hewn wooden chairs around a rather long rectangular table covered with a white lace tablecloth—a table that acted as the altar for the ritual, illuminated by a single lit white taper in a cut-glass candle holder. At the very center of the table there was a wooden cruzeiro, adorned with a large wooden rosary and surrounded by about nine or so pointed crystals or stones of various kinds arranged in such a way, consciously or not, as to resemble a miniature Stonehenge, with the crystals interspersed with numerous rosaries made of beads of different shapes and materials.

The only other feature of this main room (besides the framed paintings of Christ, Mary, and a handful of smiling "ascended Masters," as well as pictures of various Santo Daime elders) was a small collection of books in Portuguese on various esoteric subjects that filled a simple white bookshelf set off to one side, directly beside an unassuming oak desk and chair. On both sides of this central room there were two smaller rooms, each with beds for the patients who periodically came to receive spiritual/energetic healing. One of these smaller side rooms also had a rather sizable collection of drums—mostly congas, used (I found out later) for Umbandaime rituals that the Santa Casa occasionally sponsored. The small "pharmacy" out back (albeit a pharmacy with no pharmacist) was basically a rather spartan but crucial collection of medicines such as antibiotics and salves, as well as homeopathic and alternative remedies. Just across from the pharmacy were a couple of often essential, even if rather rough-and-ready bathrooms and showers. In the well-swept and tidy backyard of the Santa Casa there was another separate, albeit even smaller, house that was used as a kitchen and eating area, and even further back in the yard there was a tall, wide, and spacious pavilion (the terreiro) that was used for Umbandaime works. This rather impressive structure was built in a traditional style—that is, it had a well-packed dirt floor, no walls (so that it was open-air), and a high, steeply slanted roof, made by interweaving countless layers of straw in and around thin wooden slats.

A ROSARY WORK

The Rosary works were typically led by Juliana, a revered Brazilian elder. During that initial Rosary work, beginning around 6:00 A.M., six of us sat together outside, about thirty feet from the house, on a small circle of rough wooden benches. Juliana led us in three Hail Marys, and then, after several minutes of silence, while each of us reverently breathed in the blessings of the Divine Mother, Juliana made the sign of the Cross, and we slowly and quietly walked back into the small house. The simple act of walking in that sacred way, while receiving the blessings of the sacred trees and the sacred sun, catalyzed a distinct shift within me; I had the palpable feeling of shrugging off my prior egoic self and simply stepping into divinity. That inner shift just snapped into place; my consciousness seemed to viscerally "click" as it cinched into a different, higher level of awareness, in which I just Knew: This is where I belong. This is who I Am.

I walked to the Santa Casa feeling a delicious and rich energy coursing through my cells, lighting them up. I relished the feeling of the sandy soil under my feet; the buoyancy of walking on the living, responsive earth, while claiming and affirming my birthright as a Son of God with each step.

After we entered the small house, Juliana served us a small glass of vinegary Daime stored in an old wine bottle that she kept, along with a handful of shot glasses, on top of the bookshelf. We then gathered around the central table, and stood, each of us holding a rosary from the table, fingering the beads with each heartfelt recitation of the Our Father or Hail Mary prayers of the rosary. At the beginning of the rosary, my body started to make a shrugging motion that loosened up my back and shoulders, while at the same time rotating my head around my neck—giving my spine several chiropractic "cracks" in the process. It seemed as if the Force simply wanted to create more flexibility, more fluidity within my body for it to be able to work more freely. I then stood there, my rosary in my hands, moving the beads with each Hail Mary or Our Father, erect, grounded, immersed in each prayer. And increasingly, with each prayer, I seemed to open into infinity and then I'd come back to bodily awareness, back to the prayer, back to the beads. It was if I was being breathed, exhaled out into the universe, and then inhaled back into my physical form.

More and more, as I prayed, I began to feel as if I was standing under a waterfall of Light that was pouring down, in-and-through me. I felt almost literally pushed into the ground. I kept clutching the floor with my toes—I was barefoot—while simultaneously feeling uplifted, expanded, and shining. The Light kept pouring into me, and I worked hard to not clench, trying instead to breathe deeply, to receive that energy as fully as possible, while feeling my crown chakra lit up and wide open. I was rocking and swaying in the currents of Energy that were streaming through me, as I was, over and over again, buffeted by those waves of Light. Again and again I called myself back to my center, as with a subtle internal shift in my orientation I sank inward toward my heart—a process that was helped tremendously by the repetition of the Our Fathers and the Hail Marys. Those prayers served as my foundation stone during that part of the work.

As the rosary continued, I began to feel this thick, heavy, velvety-soft energy descending over the room, almost as if Mary's mantle were being draped over us. But at the same time, I felt extremely solid, grounded, like a strongly rooted tree, erect, open to the heavens, filled with divine energy that was pulsing up and down through the center of my body. I stood there, a pillar of Light, plunged into the depths of the rosary, when I began to see, with my inner sight, a glowing, living Cross—a Cross that I could feel emerging from the center of my body. My arms were folded in front of my chest, my hands were holding the rosary, working the beads with each prayer, directly in front of my heart.

My chest was full and open, my shoulders were back, and I began to feel as if the arms of my subtle body were extending out horizontally from my sides. Little by little it began to feel as if my body itself was the living expression of the Cross that I was seeing. Then, in an instant, the Cross fractalized itself, simultaneously multiplying itself up and down, front and back, and at every angle, creating what felt like a multidimensional Cross, a holographic Cross, each individual Cross somehow also fully the Whole, the Center, and each "separate" Cross emanating from, and ceaselessly and effortlessly created and recreated from, the One Cross. I then had the insight that the second bar of the cruzeiro (that signals the second coming of the Christ in the Santo Daime, the living Presence of the Christic Consciousness within each one of us when we drink the Holy Sacrament) was a static representation of this dynamic multiplication of the Cross, of the Christ Consciousness, of the divine I Am, radiating out into every direction of space, sanctifying every being and every moment, regardless of whether someone drinks the Daime or not.

While I was going through all of this, Manuel (a young man from Argentina) was standing to my right, and he was also getting rocked by the Force. Very early on in the rosary, he began to lean forward, with this low moan, and then, all of the sudden, he began to fall backward. I caught his arm and supported him (as did Juliana coming from the other side), and then gently helped him down to his chair. But he didn't stay there long: soon afterward he walked away from the table and went out of the building to the backyard, where not long afterward we heard him retching, violently and repeatedly. Juliana sent Karen, a longtime daimista from Chicago, outside to give him some Daime.

With Manuel attended to, Juliana's mediumship quickly opened up. Sharp exhalations of breath whistled out between her lips; her eyes were closed and her body was seized and quasi-contorted by this unseen presence within her. She sat down with a sudden forceful hissing of breath and her arms shot out and up from her sides. She then sat there, hunched over, growling, and making a series of low and guttural sounds, her face twisted and averted, but willing to accept and drink the tiny bit of Daime that she was offered by Karen (who had by this time returned from attending to Manuel), as a way to help that suffering spirit to transform, to move on.

Juliana's mediumship appeared to trigger mine as well, in that as she was going through all of this, my body quickly started to move—in ways that felt good, in ways that helped my body to open up more and more to the energy that was cascading through it so powerfully. I started shrugging my shoulders, pivoting my torso, my body undulating in wavelike motions from the top of my head, rippling down to the ground and back again.

> I am repeatedly struck by the contagion of mediumship. It is often like a symphony, with each one of us playing a part, each in the proper time. Or it can be somewhat similar to watching trees being blown in the wind, the same Force rippling through each one of us, each one of us responding to that breath of Life in unique ways.

As I stood there, praying the rosary, I felt poised, alert, centered in my Divine Being. Then, all of the sudden, it felt as if I was becoming a living *lingam* (the iconic phallic manifestation of Shiva); it felt like I was incarnating Shiva in the same way that, mythologically, the Column of Light in which Shiva manifested Himself eventually shrunk down into Arunachala (the small mountain in South India where Ramana Maharshi spent so much time, where his ashram and tomb are located). It was as if a version of that same process was happening within me, as a Column of Light shone forth from my tiny aparelho, my erect form having become a living, glowing, lingam.

At the same time, I had the sense that my feet were rooted in the divine Shakti (in Tantra, the female dimension of divinity), in the same way that the phallic part of the lingam is rooted in the *yoni*, the vulva of the lingam-as-a-whole. And in the same way that devotees in temples to Shiva pour liquid substances (honey, milk, and yogurt) over the lingam so that they then flow down into the yoni and from there continue to flow downward to eventually be caught in a brass pot and later drunk as sacraments by the devotees, I also felt rooted in that divine fecundity out of which and through which every experience flows.

I was then given a powerful miracão in which I saw that I was surrounded, on all sides, above and below, by the *guha*, the cave of the divine Heart (an important Tantric image/understanding).[2] The masculine, phallic, erect posture of my body was placed within and was surrounded by the empty, open, yet rich and full, darkness/emptiness of the sheer potentiality of the divine Shakti as the guha, the vulva, the mother of all worlds and all experiences. I then saw the cruzeiro superimposed on the lingam and was shown (not so subtly), the union of these two paths within me.

At some point I simply had to put the rosary beads down, because my hands needed the freedom to move. They quickly took the shape of a pivoting, interlocking, dynamic mudra in front of my heart. It was as if a spinning, living geometric Being was expressing itself, incarnating within the movements of

I am keenly aware that this miração, and others, was deeply impacted by my decades-long study of Tantric scriptures. Yet I continue to be struck by the structural similarities between the Santo Daime and certain aspects of Tantra (especially non-dual Śaiva Tantra). For a glimpse into some of the key understandings and practices of non-dual Śaiva Tantra, see, for example, Mark S. G. Dyczkowski, *The Doctrine of Vibration: An Analysis of the Doctrines and Practices of Kashmir Shaivism* (Albany: State University of New York Press, 1987); Swami Lakshman Jee, *Kashmir Shaivism: The Secret Supreme* (Delhi: Sri Satguru Publications, 1988); Jaideva Singh, *Pratyabhijñāhrdayam* (Delhi: Motilal Banarsidass, 1977). Both traditions see themselves as a new revelation and/or a rapid path for spiritual growth and awakening. Both affirm that divinity is simultaneously male and female (while also transcending these polarities). Both consciously work to bring these two polarities of energies into harmony within each individual: in the Santo Daime via drinking the Daime, itself understood as the sacred fusion of male and female principles, *and* within the ritual space in the Santo Daime, by creating an alchemical ceremonial "container" in which the energetic interaction between the women in one half of the salão and men in the other half generates the sacred "current" that circulates throughout the salão, creating a ritual oneness-in-twoness. Both the Santo Daime and non-dual Śaiva Tantra affirm the innate divinity of each individual, with both paths emphasizing awareness of the "I Am" within each person as a key to this self-recognition. Both spiritual paths offer meditation, as well as participation in complex and beautiful rituals, as a way to awaken individuals to their true nature and to embody various strata/frequencies of divine energies. Both paths help individuals to become increasingly aware of subtle beings/energies, as well as subtle dimensions of reality, and offer powerful opportunities for practitioners to consciously work to transform negative, contracted energies into Light, with the ultimate goal of helping all beings to awaken to a profound, ongoing awareness of their divine nature. While there are, of course, many ways in which these two spiritual traditions differ, nonetheless, the similarities are quite striking, enough so that I, for one, have become convinced that if the Santo Daime is not flat-out tantric, then it is at least profoundly congruent with Tantra. (Some of the congruence between the Santo Daime and Tantra may be rooted in the Santo Daime's crucial affiliation with the Esoteric Circle of the Communion of Thought from 1963 to 1970. I discuss this affiliation in some detail in "The Historical Development of the Santo Daime: Section One—The Life and Work of Mestre Irineu," www.liquidlightbook.com/mestre.) Nonetheless, I would argue that a profound, underlying energetic affinity is also present. For a helpful list of key features of Hindu Tantra, see Christopher D. Wallis, *Tantra Illuminated: The Philosophy, History, and Practice of a Timeless Tradition* (Boulder, CO: Mattamayūra, 2012), 33–34. And for a lucid exposition of Tibetan Buddhist Tantra, see Lama Yeshe, *Introduction to Tantra: The Transformation of Desire* (Somerville, MA: Wisdom, 2001).

my body—movements that were emerging out of a prior and higher energetic matrix that was swirling and forming itself in-and-through my physical body. The hand motions had their own life, their own beauty. Sometimes they were slow and stately, formulaic, measured, and precise, and sometimes they were dancing and spinning around my torso in rapid, crisp motions, the movements in each ongoing moment manifesting more Presence, more Sacredness, more Divine Remembrance.

I then had the insight that hand mudras were (are) the physical, dynamic imprint of the vibratory expression of the Beings that were playing in-and-through my body.[3] They were also "valves" and/or conduits for the energy, ways in which that energy was channeled, at times rather forcefully, into specific patterns of beauty and power, as that energy was shunted off in different directions and for different purposes. They were one way in which a beautiful sacred dance was taking place between my aparelho and those Beings who were seeking to express themselves in this highly specific way, in this level of reality.

More and more I began to sink into my depths, into my Center. I began to breathe deeply, consciously, filling myself with Life Force, and simply let myself be moved by that Light. My shoulders began to roll forward and back in circles, as if I was genuinely opening up and freeing my Wings of Light. As my body moved in this way, I just Knew that I truly was unfurling those Wings; that in-and-through these particular spontaneous movements, I was birthing into this world a highly rarified quality of Being. The rotation of my shoulders then began to slow down, becoming instead something that slowly began to resemble the gentle flapping of the wings of the dove of the Spirit, its wings my left and right arms, my hands coming together and separating, intertwining and fluttering in front of my heart, the dove's body the organic rhythmic beating of my heart. I could increasingly see this dove of Light; I could feel how with each beat of its wings it was expressing the Love of my Heart, for all beings, for that Light that was flowing through me, for that divine I Am. And I could sense the vast open inner space that the Dove of Light flew in, as it shimmered into existence, and winged its way forward, softly, gently, compassionately, into time, as time, as the fullness of the Present, the Fullness of Presence.

I remember years ago watching a Tom Stoppard play in which there is a wordplay with the letters "l" and "e" of "angel" and "angle." This verbal connection between "angel" and "angle" is fascinating to me, given the angularity of my two major hand mudras; the angularity of the "wings" appearing behind my back; the angularity of the crystal beings I have interacted with in my mirações; the angularity of the Cross opening up and out to all dimensions; the angularity of the various postures that I will often assume, as well as the motions that will express themselves through my body, when I'm in the Force.

At one point as all of this was taking place, an insight-fused image appeared within me, where I "saw" the Force working with my body as if it were some invisible yet highly attuned and trained physical therapist. I realized that this profoundly intelligent Force was welling up and out from my depths, and simultaneously, and rather oddly, it was as if it were flowing down, from somewhere outside and above me, coursing in-and-through my body. And this both/and Force was moving my body in just the way that it needed, moment by moment, in order to augment the capacity of my aparelho to open up into the spiritual dimensions, to incarnate more Light, to become more balanced, grounded, and aligned: whatever was called for in that moment.

From the outside, it might have looked like my torso was revolving, physically turning from side to side, but I could feel within myself how the movement actually emerged from the inside out, as my physical form aligned itself, again and again, with a slowly shifting, energetic, and shimmering "scaffolding" that I could see shining within, adorned with different iridescent crystalline beads of color at each of the intersections—a pre-physical matrix of subtle energy that was the underlying catalyst of my bodily movements. And soon, I watched as new movements were added to my "repertoire": very soft and rapid finger clicking that spiraled up and around my head, my torso, my pelvis, and down my legs. And an insight arose within me that those clickings corresponded to very quick openings and closings of tiny portals into other dimensions; they were the unlocking and relocking of the "valves" that existed at each of the conduits of energy that were positioned at different points of my energetic field—each one winking on and off, shining and shimmering like brilliant jewels.

It is fascinating to me that while I can feel a strong sense of "otherness" moving my body during moments of powerful mediumship, there is never any sense of forcing, of invasion. Instead, it always feels like a cooperative venture—a mutual, cocreated experience. By "cocreated," I mean that when my mediumship is operative, it is because, from my heart, I have chosen to say *yes* to what is happening; I have chosen to remain receptive and responsive to that More. However, from another perspective, it is also true that as a medium, there is typically very little, if any, conscious choice involved as to how my body is moved from within. When I'm in the Force, I am moved (in both senses of the word). Everything emerges from a deeper level of knowing than my conscious awareness.

During the Rosary work, I realized that all that I had to do was to let myself be led from within, to let my body move in exactly the ways that it needed to move, very much like my body was receiving a type of subtle-energy Rolfing session that was impeccably guided from within by the pulsations of the Force.[4] I simply had to open up to, and allow, this spiral serpentine energy (almost identical to my decades earlier experience with the Kundalini) to rise up from within, all the while reveling in the joyful skill of the Master rope handler who was guiding my body's lariat-like movements from the inside out.[5],

During almost all of my mediumistic manifestations in the Santa Casa, a "tautness" was present—especially with the hand mudras. They were never loose. I'm tempted to say that they were tense, but that would give the wrong impression. It was not rigid tightness, as much as the fingers, while in the mudras, were locked into place, dynamically charged, strongly held by the Force in numerous different positions.

While all of this was going on with my hands and arms, I continued to pray the rosary. Frequently, my voice would sink deeper into my chest, lowering and deepening its tone. When it did this (and this often happened as well while I was singing hymns during more formal church works), it felt as though I was literally and metaphorically praying from my heart, as if the words themselves had become energized with the vibrations of Love—that they were resonating and reverberating with the words of the others in the room, aligning with the Presence that was making itself known in-and-through each one of us in that place, in that moment.

Throughout this section of the Rosary work, I was also being taught, on very subtle levels, about what was happening within me and for what purpose. For example, I had several mystically infused insights. I suddenly "saw" how Mary is the open, receptive, ever-fecund, Divine Source within, ceaselessly generating the Divine Son, our own Christ Consciousness, moment by moment, to the extent that we, like Her, are open, responsive, and surrendered to God's will. (This insight, by the way, corresponds point for point with how Meister Eckhart—a key Christian mystic and theologian—speaks about Mary).[6]

I was also shown—directly, powerfully—how Juramidam is all of us; how we are, together, forming the body of the Christ; how the Daime is lighting up each of us who drinks that sacrament; and how all of us, all together, actually *are* that second coming. I was also shown how this second coming of the Christ Consciousness (a Consciousness that, paradoxically, has always been the very heart of who we are) is linked to the Buddhist Bodhisattva vow to reincarnate, over and over again, even when that bodhisattva is not karmically compelled to do so, in order to help all beings to become enlightened, having realized directly, powerfully, from within that all of us are interconnected, that we all rise or fall together.

Later, after the recitation of the rosary was complete, we sat down and began to sing some of the hymns of Juliana's late husband. As we began to sing, it was as if an inner bell went off, and it was time for a Divine Being to be born. I began to have a miração of a seedling, its head emerging from the soil, then descending back under the earth again, then up once more, then back: like a film, winding, rewinding, or like the movie *Groundhog Day*—knowing that I had been given the grace to emerge again and again until I finally got it right. These images corresponded during the work with a level of spiritual awareness in which my divine nature asserted itself, and I felt held in the Light, swaying in ecstasy within that Light; and then, inevitably, I would return to a lower level of awareness, of forgetfulness, only to then spring back up again, waking up again to my true nature. This whole inner process was also very much embodied, with a quasi-bouncing motion in the knees that was (I suddenly "saw") my visceral response to the impact of the Light descending—letting myself be pushed into the Earth, only to then spring back up, reborn as a divine being.

Toward the end of the Rosary work, we began a group recitation of selections from the "Prayers, Appeals, and Invocations of Emmanuel," a collection of invocations and affirmations that was received by Isabel Barsé. These invocatory, prayerful, heartfelt words are powerful and pure transmissions of the I Am Presence—the Presence of the Christ Consciousness that shines within, and that can be manifested in-and-through the Daime. (My fourth hymn, "I Am Here," is offered to Isabel Barsé.)

The crucial importance of the I Am presence in the Santo Daime tradition began with the affirmations of the Esoteric Circle of the Communion of Thought, but its importance was deepened by Padrinho Sebastião's love of the book *I Am* by Jorge Adoum, aka Mago Jefa, which contains 365 affirmations that, according to Madrinha Sonia, can not only be read and repeated each day but can also be used as a focus during Concentration works. For example, we might repeat "I am the Great All that Is, so I Am God in me" over and over again while in the Force.

Not only during this Rosary work, but whenever I did these works, as we would recite these words together, I would experience directly, in a way that was overwhelmingly persuasive, the various Forces and Beings that were invoked through these prayers, appeals, and invocations: the Universal Flowing Light, the angelic court, the crystal Elohim, the Great Central Sun of the Cosmic Heart of the Universe, the Cosmic Christ, and so on.

On this day Juliana chose a particularly strong invocation of the Emmanuel spiritual lineage. Juliana first read the Portuguese, then I read the English translation. As often happened during the Rosary works, every word felt as if my voice itself was announcing and cocreating the Reality of what I was intoning: invoking the angels and the archangels, affirming the ever-new descent of the Divine Light, Light that had come to awaken all beings to their Divine Nature. As I was reciting those words, I noticed my voice deepening and spontaneously sinking into my heart as I simply got out of the way and let the Spirit speak, with Power and Presence, in-and-as those words.

To me, the words that I read were not just words. Instead, they were lifelines to other dimensions; they were doorways into the Astral; they were coded messages that linked me up to the Beings who transmitted the invocations in the first place. There was nothing abstract, or simply intellectual or philosophical about the process of reciting these invocations and affirmations out loud in that context. Rather, that process itself opened the floodgates; the words themselves established a living connection with the specific vibratory Reality that the invocations and affirmations sought to manifest.

Throughout the invocations and affirmations, I Knew that I was connecting with specific Beings, each with a specific quality of Presence. At a certain point, however, the sense of the Otherness of these Beings dissolved, and I was given the grace to become a conduit of the Christ Consciousness as it manifested within me, and I was able to express that Consciousness, and even transmit it, through the beautiful, ritually potent movements of my body and through the words that poured from my mouth.

I thought to myself that this work was like a form of Tantric Christianity, in that in the Tantric tradition one of the highest levels of spiritual practice is to simply remember and to practice being Divine, being a Buddha.[7] There's also a powerful *collective* dimension to this process, in that all of us, whether participating at that moment in the ritual or not, are awakening to our True nature as divine beings, as part of the Cosmic Body of the Christ, as the true Second Coming of Christ, on the earth, now, in this instant, simply by saying *yes* over and over again to what is most deeply True: our own Consciousness taking the form of each crystalline moment of experience. Throughout the invocations, I affirmed within myself the very real possibility, given divine Omnipotence and Mercy, that everyone could and would wake up, that *all* beings would remember their true nature. Again and again during the appeals/invocations, I would call this Reality forth for everyone.

During these invocations and affirmations, it felt like I was being initiated in different ways into this lineage and, as with other initiations, after this nothing would ever truly be the same—something firm and stable had been transmitted and received and that something that was structurally basic within me had been irrevocably altered for the better.

I also was given a powerful insight into the nature of resurrection: how, if it is understood mystically, it is very similar to the Tantric notion of the spiritualization of the physical. How, through resurrection, the physical form remained but was now filled with Light, Love, and Power. How, through resurrection, what was previously "dead" became truly alive. How the Incarnation of the Divine in-and-through Jesus was just the first step of the Second Coming, in which each of us will be resurrected—each of us will be incarnating divine Light, Love, and Power here on Earth; each of us will be an integral part of the Cosmic Body of the Christ; each of us, in our irreplaceable uniqueness, fully manifesting that divine Wholeness.

10

Final Days in Céu do Mapiá

LEAVING CÉU DO MAPIÁ

It was August 9, 2010, the day before I was supposed to finally leave Céu do Mapiá. I began the day packing and giving away a lot of my things to the people in the inn: Solange got a pillow, Damião got a lot of clothes, Raimundo got my thongs, and Soraya helped me to figure out which residents of the village were most in need of the other gifts. (I had already, a few days earlier, given some other gifts to different elders in the community.) I then went down to the internet café, and after Skyping with my wife, I went over to Antonieta's house (she had invited me over for a farewell lunch). I got there a little after 1:00 p.m. and stayed almost all afternoon. I was really charged up and anxious, since I still wasn't completely sure whether the transportation logistics would work out for me to be able to leave Mapiá the next day—and that was the absolutely last day possible for me to leave in order to make my flight. And so, when I arrived at Antonieta's, I was not exactly in an uplifted state of mind. She was extremely welcoming, however, and immediately gave me a towel and a bar of soap and sent me off to the igarapé behind her house. I went down there, stripped naked, and immersed myself headfirst into the current: it felt *so* cleansing, as though all of my worries and anxieties just flowed away in the reddish-brown water.

Later that evening, I went down to Vô Nel's home for the final Oração of my trip. About a month into our stay, Rick, Ron, and I had been invited to join Vô Nel and his extended family to sing the Oração on the veranda of his home, a practice that I continued almost every day for the rest of my time in Mapiá. On this final day, as I was singing the Oração, the people on the veranda subtly morphed—they shifted from welcoming strangers who had been extremely kind to a foreigner and became people who I was beginning to really know and care for; people who had really touched my heart. Each moment with them felt so sweet, so poignant. During that night, I could feel how important it was, for both me and them, that we had shared so many intimate moments together with each other (such as the times when Vô Nel would have trouble breathing, and one of the women there would thump his back, repeatedly, with so much tenderness and love).

The next day, August 10, the morning of my trip to Boca do Acre, I still didn't have a clue as to whether I was going to be leaving by car or by boat. By car, I would go to Fazenda São Sebastião, a little community where the Igarapé Mapiá met the River Purus. From there I would take a boat to Boca do Acre. Or I could take a really slow boat down the Igarapé Mapiá (which was extra shallow after months with no rains, making boat travel quite challenging) and then proceed up the River Purus until Boca do Acre.

I finally decided to go by car, since I had been informed that the road was indeed open (it had been closed the day before). I was, however, still somewhat less than calm, since I had been watching a bunch of guys hanging around a beat-up, tiny old VW station wagon that was beginning to look like it was going to be our taxi. They were looking under the hood and fussing with the engine, and the car wasn't exactly starting on the first try, and when it finally did start, it wasn't exactly purring like a kitten. Not only that, but the guy that I was assuming was going to be our driver kept adding air to the front right tire with a bicycle pump. And I didn't have a clue how all of our luggage and all of us (three women, a child, and me) plus the driver were going to fit into that tiny car. And I remembered Soraya saying that only a really tough and rugged car would be able to make it.

However, at some point, something shifted in me, and I was able to drop most of my anxiety. With some inner prompting, my mind was able to grow still and quiet as I sat there and watched the drama unfold.

Finally, after loading my luggage into the back of the car, I went over to the Big House (where Padrinho Alfredo lived with his family) with Tereza. I waited on the veranda for about twenty minutes while she fussed around the house, talking with Padrinho Alfredo. I then had a sweet, easy interaction with Padrinho. He asked me how my stay had been, and I laughed, telling him about this image that had come up for me: how my experience of Mapiá was like the story of Plato's cave, where some people had been fortunate enough to emerge from out of the darkness, and yet, when they finally left the cave, the sun was so relentlessly bright that it was a really difficult adjustment, but they also occasionally saw through their fingers (which were partially covering their eyes) these astonishingly beautiful glimpses of a world that they hadn't even imagined was possible before. Padrinho really loved that analogy, and we both laughed together for a while and then hugged goodbye.

And then, at long last, the three other passengers all piled into the back, and most of their luggage was tied to the roof, while I sat up front with the driver, and off we went, down the narrow little dirt road, into the forest.

I have to say that calling it a road is actually very generous. It was really more like a path. I soon learned that the road was kept open, as much as possible, by a group of saintly individuals who, when the road would get too muddy and become impassable, would simply hack out a passage around the obstacle; they would cut down small trees and lay the trunks down over the mud; or they would chainsaw a space through the huge trees that would frequently fall over the road. At one point, our car passed through one of those mini-tunnels with less than half an inch to spare on either side (and the tree trunk itself was at least six feet in diameter). It was a couple of hours into our trip when we drove forward through that chainsawed gap in the massive trunk. I wondered, what would we have done if they had made the cut an inch closer? The road was so narrow that it would have been impossible to turn around. Would we have gone back the whole way in reverse?

FIGURE 10.1 Leaving Mapiá

For most of the three-hour trip, the car was either in first or second gear. That tiny VW was basically a packhorse for our stuff. And believe me, there was a lot of praying out loud by all of us as it chugged its way up various hills and through various mini-ponds in the road. (Each hour that passed without the car breaking down or getting stuck was a cause for inner celebration.) But we finally made it to Fazenda São Sebastião. I was *so* thankful to have arrived. And it ended up that the whole trip cost less than I had been told: only 125 reais (along with five reais extra to pay for someone to carry our luggage from the fazenda down to the boat).

When we unloaded our luggage at the tiny little village, our ankles and calves were instantly attacked by swarms of nearly invisible bugs that were like blood-drawing gnats with piranha teeth. The insecticide that we all quickly slathered on any exposed portion of skin barely slowed them down, as we sat around for about half an hour waiting for people to carry our luggage down to the boat (which was driven by one of Padrinho Alfredo's sons). The boat was much larger than the boat that I had arrived in, and the motor was stronger, so when we finally got going (around 2:30 P.M.), the journey to Boca do Acre was a lot quicker and easier than the incoming trip had been.

We finally arrived in Boca do Acre around 5:30 p.m. And I was so happy to have made it that it didn't matter at all to me that the Hotel da Floresta where I had planned to stay was full and that I had to pay 20 reais for someone to carry my luggage to the Hotel São Pedro a few blocks away. It didn't matter that at first they tried to put Soraya and me into the same room. (I was very clear that I needed my own room.) It didn't matter that the bathroom wasn't working and that I had to go down the hall to take a shower. It didn't matter that the top sheet that they gave me for my double bed was meant for a single and that it was decorated with race cars. It didn't matter that the pillows were filled with what felt like scrunchies meant for lathering up liquid shower gel. I felt so happy when I sat down at the restaurant that evening with Soraya and Padrinho's son and ate a wonderful plate of fried fish and downed two liters of ice-cold Coke. The breakfast the next morning at the hotel was pretty good as well. And the room actually had a rotating floor fan!

CONCLUDING ODDS AND ENDS

I had several more "grumpy and anxious North American meets Brazilian bureaucracy" adventures that I won't detail (for example, the main branch of Banco Brazil in Rio Branco, the capital of the state of Acre, initially refused to cash my traveler's checks, and if they hadn't finally agreed to do so, I would have been forced to hawk my watch to pay for the taxi to the airport). When I finally arrived in Rio de Janeiro, I spent the next few days recuperating in the lovely home of some friends of mine, just reveling in gratitude. My heart just felt so open, and my mind was so calm and clear. And after that, everything just flowed, everything was on time, everything happened just as it should, and I finally arrived back in Dallas—fifteen pounds lighter than when I had left.

Several years after I left, I heard to my dismay that the church in Céu do Mapiá had to be torn down due to a termite infestation. The community had to erect a tentlike structure to serve as a temporary place in which to have works. They are now in the process of building a much larger, architecturally designed, gorgeous church—a process that was not exactly speeded up by the pandemic.

HEALTH ISSUES

A couple of weeks before I left Céu do Mapiá, I developed a rather bad case of bronchitis. And it stayed with me throughout my trip home. And in Dallas it got even worse, turning into pneumonia with a high fever. With the help of modern medicine I was finally able to shake off the pneumonia, but a chronic cough remained. Every day after that, especially in the afternoon and evening, I repeatedly coughed up yellow or green phlegm. Not surprisingly, I rather quickly began to visit medical specialists, as well as alternative health practitioners. And none of them were able to make a conclusive diagnosis. And the coughing continued, unabated, for over six years, interspersed with periodic pneumonias. (In one particularly intense round of pneumonias, I had eight back-to-back in one year.)

Finally, in February of 2017, while taking part in a *Yemanjá* (the Orixá of the Sea) healing work at a Santo Daime church that I frequently attended in the United States, I called out from within, with as much humility and fervor as I could, to the Divine Mother, asking her to heal—to *really* heal—my cough. And there was an immediate response to my prayer. It felt as though the heavens themselves had opened up within me and a stream of Beings of Light began to descend—washing me with waves of their Radiance and Love. That beautiful moment didn't last long, but I had faith that something substantial and signif-icant had shifted within me. And when the work was over, and I was lounging around in the salão with my friends, Lee, the sister of the man who ran the church, came over to me, and she was just glowing. (She was a skilled herbalist and I had reached out to her previously to ask if she'd be willing to work with me.) She sat down, took my hand, and began to talk to me. It felt as if the Queen of the Sea Herself was speaking right through Lee (which might well have been the truth). She agreed to work with me but said that I first had to change my diet. I knew what she was talking about, because we had discussed this issue before. I knew that she thought that I should go off dairy, gluten, and sugar, which I had thought was just too extreme. But at that moment, everything was lit up, and it suddenly became crystal clear that I needed to make those shifts in my diet. And when I did, my chronic cough almost immediately went away. (The pneumonias and a diagnosis of MAC—microbacterial avium complex, a noncontagious kissing cousin of tuberculosis—took a bit longer.)

11

Post-Mapiá Ponderings

Divinization

During the process of writing this book, I often pondered how it should end. And what kept coming back to me was that I wanted the book to conclude on the highest note possible. Therefore, I would like to offer a brief discussion of the spiritual goals of the Santo Daime path—goals that are perhaps not often explicitly stated but nonetheless can and often do serve as a type of implicit guiding star for the spiritual lives of daimistas.

When I was in Céu do Mapiá, I had the honor of interviewing both Isabel Barsé and Padrinho Alex Polari. And reading back over these interviews, I was fascinated to discover that both of these elders stressed that the main objective of the Santo Daime is for each person to become increasingly aware of the Higher Self—that is, the I Am or Christic Presence—within the Force of the Daime. They both stressed that other forms of mediumship are valuable ways to develop spiritually if and/or when we are called to work with those specific beings or energies, as long as we do so in a harmonious and integrated way and within the appropriate ritual context. Nonetheless, the highest goal of a daimista, according to these elders, is to awaken to our divine heritage as Daughters and Sons of God and the Divine Mother and then to increasingly embody that divine Light and Love and Power within us, as much as possible, moment to moment, in our ordinary lives.

I have also become fascinated with how this ongoing spiritual process of incarnating various divine qualities (such as Harmony, Love, Truth, and Justice—the "motto" of the Santo Daime, drawn from the Esoteric Circle of the Communion of Thought) is beautifully invoked and enacted within the affirmation that is read out loud at a certain point during every Concentration work: that is, the "Consecration of the Space" (another gift of the Esoteric Circle). The words of that affirmation state that "there is only one presence here," underscoring the divine Unity that is our common Source. Nonetheless, immediately following each of these affirmations of Unity, the words of the "Consecration of the Space" point out how that One Presence is revealed in a multitude of ways (similar to how light can and does manifest as a beautiful spectrum of colors).

This affirmation then culminates with the beautiful and powerful proclamation in which the person speaking recognizes the communion between her/his lower self and her/his Higher Self, "which is God in me," and realizes that by speaking these words in a heartfelt way she/he is calling forth the consecration of the salāo. This consecration of the salāo takes place in order that the salāo itself, as well as all of those within it, can become, as the affirmation states, "The perfect expression of all divine qualities, which are in me and in all beings." The person who recites this affirmation then emphasizes that she/he is consciously radiating these powerful intentions to all beings. She or he ends the recitation with a prayer of thankfulness for all that has been received from God in-and-through the words of the "Consecration of the Space" itself.

To me, the affirmations of the "Consecration of the Space" underscore the fundamental underlying transformative intentionality of the Santo Daime: to awaken to our Oneness with our divine nature and then to work to increasingly manifest divine qualities within our life for the good of all beings. In Santo Daime works, we are given the profound honor of having the opportunity to repeatedly dive into a vortex of high-level, inherently sacred, and deeply transformative energies. We are given the grace of having structured times and spaces in which we can, slowly, organically learn how to resonate, in our cells, in our subtle bodies, with these vibratory frequencies of divinity and then, with the grace of God and the Divine Mother, carry these energies out into the world, offering them in-and-through our own precious, unique, individuality to the world in which we live.

This process of embodying various divine qualities is what early Christianity called *theosis*, or divinization. The "church fathers,"—the central, most important theologians of early Christianity—didn't mince words. For instance, Clement of Alexandria (ca. 150–215) says, "The Word of God became man so that you could learn from a man how a man can become God."[1] Or Athanasius, bishop of Alexandria (ca. 296–373), says, "For he was made man so that we might be made God."[2] Drawing frequently upon the biblical verse that says, "Let us make [human beings] in our image, after our likeness" (Genesis 1:26, RSV), these church fathers claimed that the image of God shines within as the basic structure of each person's humanity.[3] According to these theologians, the image of God is always present within, but we have forgotten this immanent presence of God due to the Fall. However, through the incarnation of the Word and through experientially linking ourselves with the Son through baptism, we can gradually purify ourselves via the sacraments, as well as through the spiritual life more generally, thereby more and more accurately reflecting the *image* of God within, ultimately leading to the restoration of the *likeness* with God that was lost during the Fall. These church fathers did not think that human beings could ever become one with God's transcendent and ultimately unknowable Essence. Nonetheless, they insisted that through grace, we *could* increasingly learn how to "participate" in the divine qualities or energies of God, qualities that have been communicated to us by the Son and are mediated by the Holy Spirit in a process that ultimately leads to theosis. For these theologians, divinization was not only possible, but it was the completion of our humanity; it was the restoration of what was natural to human beings; and it was the accomplishment of God's plan for us.[4],

As I mentioned earlier, within the Santo Daime, theological/metaphysical understandings are rarely explicit and fleshed out. Nonetheless, I would suggest that the notion of divinization is implicitly present in many of the central hymns of the tradition. I would also argue that this spiritual goal is neither orthodox nor traditional. Divinization in the Santo Daime is, if anything, even more radical than the early Christian understandings of divinization, in that it relies upon the innate divinity of the human soul/ Self, unlike the more orthodox Christian emphasis on the necessity of the ontological death of the old self/rebirth of the new self, that takes place in-and-through Christ, in-and-through the sacrament of baptism. Within the Santo Daime, divinization implies the gradual spiritual transformation of our being—the ever-increasing incarnation of divine Energies—in-and-through the paradoxical realization of who we already are, who we always have been, under the surface of our day-to-day awareness.

As a way to express and invoke these energies of divinization, I would like to share a series of mediumistically received insights into divinization that poured into me when I was about four months into the process of writing this book, insights that arrived in one highly compressed download—the words simply flowed into my consciousness and were typed by my fingers without any break or editing. Because this type of language is really not meant to be read silently,

I would like to suggest that if you feel inspired to do so, you should read the words out loud. The words to "Divinization" (as well as to another received text, "Invocations and Affirmations") are reflections, from my particular vantage point, of the "Emmanuel" energy and teachings. "Divinization" can be found (either for you to read or for you to listen to me reciting it) at www.liquidlightbook.com/divinization. "Invocations and Affirmations" can be found at www.liquidlightbook.com/invocations.

Here is just a taste of "Divinization" (its first and last paragraphs):

"Divinization" (9/27/18)

What is divinization? For myself, as it was for early Christian mystics, divinization is the ongoing and ever-deepening incarnation, within my body and mind, of the Energies and Qualities of divinity—a process made possible only by divine grace. Divinization means sinking ever deeper into a calm, ongoing, softly blooming awareness of my rootedness, below the surface, in a divine Source. It is a process during which I increasingly discover, within myself, that sacred touchstone, the resounding and transformative mystical knowledge: I AM THAT. Divinization means that, over and over again, I lean back into that vastness—consciously, intentionally, aligning myself, again and again, with that profound silent spaciousness that surrounds and compassionately holds each thought, each memory, each feeling. Divinization means remembering God and the Goddess with each breath, linking up with that Presence that permeates each moment, that divine Source that is my True Nature, the divine Self that shines from within, illuminating everything. Divinization means affirming, consciously, intentionally, my divine Sonship; it is the heartfelt decision, freely reaffirmed at each moment, to step into my inheritance as a fully mature Son (or Daughter) of God and the Goddess.

I attempt (with the grace of God and the Goddess) to do all of this, even while (like Christ, who is fully human, and fully divine, at the same time), at times I fumble, and fall, and pick myself up; hopefully learning from every mistake; gradually, over time, releasing any harsh self-condemnation and judgments; and in their place, offering myself the same unconditional love and compassion that God and the Goddess offer to everyone, always.

May any and all obstacles to this awakening dissolve in the transformative recognition that these obstacles are themselves the fuel that catalyzes our transformation, they are themselves shining icons of divinity. May all illusion, all suffering, be healed and transformed in the Light of that Recognition. May we

all increasingly recognize our Oneness with that Love, with that Light. May we all come to know the hidden divine depths of our own Self, as we awaken, with wonder, with stunned and joyous gratitude, to the new facets of our divinity that are shining forth in every moment.

May it be so, now and forever, amen.

Notes

INTRODUCTION

1. See, for example, Rachel Harris, *Listening to Ayahuasca: New Hope for Depression, Addiction, PTSD, and Anxiety* (Novato, CA: New World Library, 2017); Neal M. Goldsmith, *Psychedelic Healing: The Promise of Entheogens for Psychotherapy and Spiritual Development* (Rochester, VT: Healing Arts, 2011); Erika Dyck, *Psychedelic Psychiatry: LSD from Clinic to Campus* (Baltimore: Johns Hopkins University Press, 2008); Joseph Tafur, *The Fellowship of the River: A Medical Doctor's Exploration into Traditional Amazonian Plant Medicine* (Phoenix, AZ: Espiritu, 2017).

2. Definitions of italicized terms can be found in the glossary, located at www.liquidlightbook.com /glossary, as part of the website dedicated to the book.

3. One notable recent exception is Marc G. Blainey, *Christ Returns from the Jungle: Ayahuasca Religion as Mystical Healing* (Albany: State University of New York Press, 2021).

4. There are, of course, exceptions to this admonition to not speak of your own experiences, especially within the discipline of cultural anthropology. See, for example, Paul Stoller, *In Sorcery's Shadow: A Memoir of Apprenticeship Among the Songhay of Niger* (Chicago: University of Chicago Press, 1987); Barbara G. Myerhoff, *Peyote Hunt: The Sacred Journey of the Huichol Indians* (Ithaca, NY: Cornell University Press, 1974); Edith Turner, *The Hands Feel It: Healing and Spirit Possession Among a Northern Alaskan People* (DeKalb: Northern Illinois University Press, 1996); David E. Young and Jean-Guy Goulet, *Being Changed by Cross-Cultural Encounters: The Anthropology of Extraordinary Experiences* (Peterborough, ONT, Canada: Broadview, 1994).

5. See, for example, R. R. Griffiths, W. A. Richards, U. McCann, and R. Jesse, "Psilocybin Can Occasion Mystical-Type Experiences Having Substantial and Sustained Personal Meaning and Spiritual Significance," *Psychopharmacology* 187, no. 3 (2006): 268–283; Michael P. Bogenschutz et al., "Psilocybin-assisted Treatment for Alcohol Dependence: A Proof-of-Concept Study," *Journal of Psychopharmacology* 29, no. 3 (2015): 289–299; Peter Gasser, Katharina Kirchner, and Torsten Passie, "LSD-assisted Psychotherapy for Anxiety Associated with a Life-threatening Disease: A Qualitative Study of Acute and Sustained Subjective Effects," *Journal of Psychopharmacology* 29, no.1 (2015): 57–68; Robin L. Carhart-Harris et al., "Psilocybin with Psychological Support for Treatment-resistant Depression: An Open-Label Feasibility Study," *Lancet Psychiatry* 3, no. 7 (2016): 619–627.

6. See Michael Pollan, *How to Change Your Mind: What the New Science of Psychedelics Teaches Us About Consciousness, Dying, Addiction, Depression, and Transcendence* (New York: Penguin, 2018);

William A. Richards, *Sacred Knowledge: Psychedelics and Religious Experiences* (New York: Columbia University Press, 2016).

7. See G. William Barnard, *Exploring Unseen Worlds: William James and the Philosophy of Mysticism* (Albany: State University of New York Press, 1997). For an earlier work that attempts a type of loosely Jamesian analysis of psychedelics, see Robert E. L. Masters and Jean Houston, *The Varieties of Psychedelic Experience* (New York: Dell, 1966).

8. My favorite translation of this scripture is Eaknath Easwaran, trans., *The Bhagavad Gita* (Tomales, CA: Nilgiri, 1985).

9. I am keenly aware that the issue of whether or not to vet your research with those you have studied is dauntingly complex. Clearly, in many cases doing so would result in censorship, or worse. The intersection between preserving academic freedom and the desire to treat the self-understandings of those being investigated with dignity and respect is at times difficult to navigate.

10. See Andrew Dawson, *Santo Daime: A New World Religion* (London: Bloomsbury, 2013).

1. FIRST ENCOUNTER WITH THE DAIME

1. For more about the Full Spectrum Center for Spiritual Awakening, see their website, Fullspectrumctr.org.

2. Alex Polari De Alverga, *The Religion of Ayahuasca: The Teachings of the Church of Santo Daime* (Rochester, VT: Park Street, 2010).

3. See Stephan V. Beyer, *Singing to the Plants: A Guide to Mestizo Shamanism in the Upper Amazon* (Albuquerque: University of New Mexico Press, 2009).

4. For a discussion of some of the daily details of what it's like to be part of a Santo Daime church in North America, see "Santo Daime Churches in North America" (www.liquidlightbook.com /northamerica).

5. See Douglas R. Brooks, Swami Durgananda, Paul E. Muller-Ortega, William K. Mahony, Constantina Rhodes Bailly, and S. P. Sabharathnam, *Meditation Revolution: A History and Theology of the Siddha Yoga Lineage* (New Delhi: Muktabodha Indological Research Institute, 1997).

6. See Wilhelm Reich, *Character Analysis* (New York: Noonday Press, 1945); Alexander Lowen, *Bioenergetics: The Revolutionary Therapy That Uses the Language of the Body to Heal the Problems of the Mind* (New York: Penguin, 1975).

7. See Roman Gonzalvo, ed., *Holotropic Breathwork and Other Hyperventilation Procedures*, special issue, *Journal of Transpersonal Research* 6, no. 2 (2014).

2. INITIAL PHILOSOPHICAL REFLECTIONS

1. See William James, *The Varieties of Religious Experience* (Cambridge, MA: Harvard University Press, 1985), 302.

2. See David Chalmers, "The Puzzle of Conscious Experience," *Scientific American*, December 1995, 63.

3. See Paul M. Churchland, *Scientific Realism and the Plasticity of Mind* (Cambridge: Cambridge University Press, 1979).

4. Stanislav Grof, *LSD Psychotherapy* (Pomona, CA: Hunter House, 1980), 69.

5. For more detailed information on the perspective in this chapter, see G. William Barnard, *Exploring Unseen Worlds: William James and the Philosophy of Mysticism* (Albany: State University of New York Press, 1997), 163–170.

6. William James, "Human Immortality: Two Supposed Objections to the Doctrine," in *Essays in Religion and Morality* (Cambridge, MA: Harvard University Press, 1982), 77–101.

7. James, "Human Immortality," 86.

8. James, "Human Immortality," 89.

9. James, "Human Immortality," 89.

10. James, "Human Immortality," 92.

11. William James, "Confidences of a 'Psychical Researcher,' " in *Essays in Psychical Research* (Cambridge, MA: Harvard University Press, 1986), 374.

12. James, "Confidences of a 'Psychical Researcher,' " 374.

13. See G. William Barnard, *Living Consciousness: The Metaphysical Vision of Henri Bergson* (Albany: State University of New York Press, 2011).

14. Henri Bergson, *Matter and Memory* (New York: Zone, 1988), 208.

15. Bergson, *Matter and Memory*, 235.

16. Bergson, *Matter and Memory*, 36

17. Henri Bergson, *Mind-Energy: Lectures and Essays* (New York: Henry Holt, 1920), 46.

18. George Wald, "Consciousness and Cosmology," in *Bergson and Modern Thought*, Andrew C. Papanicolau and Pete A. Y. Gunter, eds (New York: Harwood Academic, 1987), 349–350.

19. Wald, "Consciousness and Cosmology," 350.

20. Henri Bergson, *The Creative Mind* (New York: Philosophical Library, 1946), 69.

21. Bergson, *The Creative Mind*, 69–70.

22. Bergson, *The Creative Mind*, 93.

23. Aldous Huxley, *The Doors of Perception and Heaven and Hell* (New York: HarperCollins, 2004).

24. Bergson, *The Creative Mind*, 93.

25. For a detailed discussion of these issues, see Barnard, *Exploring Unseen Worlds*, 111–121.

26. William James, *The Principles of Psychology* (Cambridge, MA: Harvard University Press, 1981), 656.

27. For an insightful discussion of the inevitably participatory nature of spiritual experiences, see Jorge N. Ferrer, *Revisioning Transpersonal Theory: A Participatory Vision of Human Spirituality* (Albany: State University of New York Press, 2002); Jorge N. Ferrer and Jacob H. Sherman, eds., *The Participatory Turn: Spirituality, Mysticism, Religious Studies* (Albany: State University of New York Press, 2009).

28. For more on this theme in James's thought, see the essay "Great Men and Their Environments," in *The Will to Believe and Other Essays in Popular Philosophy* (Cambridge, MA: Harvard University Press, 1979), 163–189.

29. Stanislav Grof, who worked therapeutically with thousands of patients in high-dose LSD sessions, records several of these instances. See, for example, Stanislav Grof, *The Cosmic Game: Explorations of the Frontiers of Human Consciousness* (Albany: State University of New York, 1998). See also Stanislav Grof, *When the Impossible Happens: Adventures in Non-ordinary Realities* (Boulder, CO: Sounds True, 2006).

3. NEXT STEPS ON THE PATH

1. To daimistas: This is the version of a St. Michael work that used to be promoted/run by Padrinho Paulo Roberto, not the St. Michael work originated by Padrinho Alfredo.

2. The term "Archetypal" in this context does not refer to Jungian archetypes, but rather, refers to a type of quasi-Platonic preexistence, in higher, spiritual levels of reality, of cosmic energies that give form and structure to this "earthly" level of existence. For a thoughtful discussion of this understanding

of archetypes, see Christopher M. Bache, *LSD and the Mind of the Universe: Diamonds from Heaven* (Rochester, VT: Park Street Press, 2019), 169–170.

3. See David H. Brown, *Santería Enthroned: Art, Ritual, and Innovation in an Afro-Cuban Religion* (Chicago: University of Chicago Press, 2003); Jim Wafer, *The Taste of Blood: Spirit Possession in Brazilian Candomblé* (Philadelphia: University of Pennsylvania Press, 1991).

4. See John W. Cooper, *Panentheism: The Other God of the Philosophers, from Plato to the Present* (Grand Rapids, MI: Baker Academic, 2006); Philip Clayton and Arthur Peacocke, *In Whom We Live and Move and Have Our Being: Panetheistic Reflections on God's Being in a Scientific World* (Grand Rapids, MI: Eerdmans, 2004); Loriliai Biernacki and Philip Clayton, eds., *Panentheism Across the World's Traditions* (New York: Oxford University Press, 2013).

5. For an illuminating discussion of hierophanies, see Mircea Eliade, *The Myth of the Eternal Return: Cosmos and History* (Princeton, NJ: Princeton University Press, 2018); Mircea Eliade, *The Sacred and the Profane: The Nature of Religion* (New York: Harcourt Brace Jovanovich, 1987).

6. Marc Blainey, in a private communication, told me that in his research he has met some daimistas who saw the Daime as "just a drink" that doesn't contain Spirit itself, but rather is more of a practical key to opening a portal to the spiritual realms. He also noted, insightfully, the similarity between this issue and the transubstantiation disagreement between Catholics and Protestants about the meaning of the Eucharist.

7. For a fascinating discussion of the possibility that the early Christian Eucharist was, in fact, psychedelic, see Brian C. Muraresku, *The Immortality Key: The Secret History of the Religion with No Name* (New York: St. Martin's, 2020).

8. The notion of the divine "I Am" has a long history in the history of the Theosophical tradition, and the associated "I Am" movements. These movements themselves, not surprisingly, focus on the "I am who I am" self-denomination of God in Exodus 3:14, as well as the I am (*ego eimi*) sayings of Jesus in the gospel of John. The centrality of the divine "I Am" is also strikingly present in nondualistic Śaiva tantra. The Santo Daime inherited this focus on the divine "I Am" through Mestre Irineu and his community's several years of affiliation with the Esoteric Circle of the Communion of Thought, an esoteric/syncretistic movement in Brazil.

9. As Padinho Sebastião says in hymn 18 of *Nova Jerusalem*, "My Father's name is Jura and all of us are Midam."

10. Cyril of Alexandria, *On the Unity of Christ* (Crestwood, NY: St. Vladimir's Seminary Press, 1995), 63.

11. This chapter is an extensively revised version of an earlier publication: Barnard, G. William, "Entheogens in a Religious Context: The Case of the Santo Daime Religious Tradition," *Zygon* 49, no. 3 (2014): 666–684.

12. My heartfelt thanks to "C.C." the Santo Daime brother who, having read an earlier version of this chapter, offered many helpful insights—insights that are now woven into my discussion of the topics focused on in this chapter.

13. Paulo Moreira and Edward MacRae, *Eu Venho de Longe: Mestre Irineu e Seus Companheiros* (Salvador, Bahia: EDUFA-UFMA-ABESUP, 2011), 131.

14. For more about Mestre's link with the Esoteric Circle, see Moreira and MacRae *Eu Venho de Longe*, 294–304. For those who want to know more about the organization and its connection to the Santo Daime, see "The Historical Development of the Santo Daime: Section One—The Life and Work of Mestre Irineu" (www.liquidlightbook.com/mestre.)

15. For an insightful discussion of how the CEFLURIS line of the Santo Daime has incorporated a variety of religious and esoteric influences within itself, see Andrew Dawson, *Santo Daime: A New World Religion* (London: Bloomsbury, 2013), 77–152.

4. CÉU DO MAPIÁ—BEGINNINGS

1. Myer's dissertation is an invaluable contribution. Matthew Myer, " 'In the Master's House': History, Discourse, and Ritual in Acre, Brazil" (Ph.D. diss, University of Virginia, 2014), http://libra.virginia .edu/catalog/libra-oa:6576.
2. "Orange Tree," hymn 60 in *O Cruzeiro*.
3. The term "caboclo" also refers to the spirits of Native Americans believed to incorporate during mediumistic works in the Santo Daime.

5. FEITIO—THE RITUAL OF MAKING THE DAIME

1. Hymn 84 of *Cruzeirinho*.

6. EARLY WORKS IN CÉU DO MAPIÁ

1. Hymn 97 of *O Justiceiro*.
2. See Luis Eduardo Luna and Steven F. White, eds., *Ayahuasca Reader: Encounters with the Amazon's Sacred Vine* (Santa Fe, NM: Synergetic Press, 2000).
3. For a lucid scholarly examination of the role of music in the Santo Daime (and in the União do Vegetal—another Brazilian ayahuasca religion), see Beatriz Caiuby Labate and Gustavo Pacheco, eds. *Opening the Portals of Heaven: Brazilian Ayahuasca Music* (New Brunswick, NJ: Transaction, 2009).
4. I think that it is important to remember that hymns, while they are received from some Astral Source, are also always received by a particular human being, who is situated within a particular cultural and historical context. As such, the hymns inevitably carry two interacting strata within them, strata that at times (at least for me) need to be clearly distinguished from each other. As such, I can acknowledge that the lyrics of certain hymns simply do not speak to my own historical/cultural context, even as I can appreciate the underlying Force that they carry.
5. Indra's Net is an image that in the Hua-Yen school of Chinese Buddhism is used to depict the holographic interconnectedness of the universe. Indra (a Hindu deity) has an infinitely expansive net hanging in his home in heaven. At each juncture point in the net is a jewel, and each jewel reflects the infinite other jewels. See Francis Cook, *Hua-Yen Buddhism: The Jewel Net of Indra* (University Park: Penn State Press, 1977).

7. MIRAÇÕES—VISIONARY/MYSTICAL EXPERIENCES IN THE SANTO DAIME

1. This emphasis on the importance of relaxation in the Force of the Daime is beautifully expressed in the hymn 16 of Lúcio Mortimer (a prominent elder in the Santo Daime tradition): "*Se Afrouxar*"/"If You Loosen Up." The hymn says, in part, "If you loosen up, the Daime cures. / If you loosen up, the Daime helps. / If you loosen up, the Daime saves."

2. "Eu sou o daime e o Daime sou eu." Paulo Moreira and Edward MacRae, *Eu Venho de Longe: Mestre Irineu e Seus Companheiros* (Salvador, Bahia: EDUFA-UFMA-ABESUP, 2011), 302.

3. Wilber's oeuvre is vast, but for an early text that is representative of his understanding see: Ken Wilber, *The Spectrum of Consciousness* (Wheaton, IL: Quest, 1993).

4. For an in-depth exploration of the phenomenology of ayahuasca experiences, see Benny Shanon, *The Antipodes of the Mind: Charting the Phenomenology of the Ayahuasca Experience* (New York: Oxford University Press, 2002).

5. See, for example, Jeffrey J. Kripal, *Mutants and Mystics: Science Fiction, Superhero Comics, and the Paranormal* (Chicago: University of Chicago Press, 2011).

6. These metaphors of vibration and energy are not simply artifacts of my own cultural background. They are also endemic to the Santo Daime itself, in part due to the tradition's several-year affiliation with the Esoteric Circle of the Communion of Thought, a quasi-theosophical organization whose metaphysical perspectives were adopted (and adapted) by the Santo Daime. I would also argue, however, that these metaphors are quite appropriate—the experiences they point toward actually are, on some deep level, energetic and vibratory in nature.

7. Salutations to Christopher Bache for his brilliant and courageous writings, based on his twenty-year-long extensive work with high-dose LSD, in which he discusses, eloquently and thoughtfully, the creation and cultivation of energetic bodies that correspond to the "vibratory frequency" of differing spiritual worlds. See Christopher M. Bache, *Dark Night, Early Dawn: Steps to a Deep Ecology of Mind* (Albany: State University of New York Press, 2000); and Christopher M. Bache, *LSD and the Mind of the Universe: Diamonds from Heaven* (Rochester, VT: Park Street, 2019).

8. According to a friend in the know, the cane/hammer transformation occurs in the first appearance of Thor, in August of 1962, in *Journey into Mystery*, no. 83.

9. See, for example, William James, *Essays in Philosophy* (Cambridge, MA: Harvard University Press, 1978), 133.

10. As the well-known King James Version of 1 Corinthians 13:12 says: "For now we see through a glass, darkly, but then face to face: now I know in part; but then shall I know even as also I am known."

11. See, for example, Philip Kapleau Roshi, *The Three Pillars of Zen: Teaching, Practice, and Enlightenment* (New York: Anchor, 1989). Nonetheless, after a recent conversation with a roshi friend of mine, it appears that, at least from this roshi's point of view, an advanced Zen practitioner could (should?) be able to discern between insubstantial/ unimportant visionary manifestations, and those that are valuable manifestations of "higher" levels of consciousness.

12. Both Wilber and Grof are often either ignored or dismissed by academics, who tend to relegate them to the condescending category of "New Age authors." These thinkers, however, have articulated thoughtful and creative theories about phenomena that mainstream academics often refuse to acknowledge. Both authors, in essence, did not allow themselves to be "disciplined" by the academic disciplines. See, for example, Ken Wilber, *Sex, Ecology, Spirituality: The Spirit of Evolution* (Boulder, CO: Shambhala Publications, 2001); Stanislav Grof, *The Cosmic Game: Explorations of the Frontiers of Human Consciousness* (Albany: State University of New York, 1998).

13. William James, *The Varieties of Religious Experience* (Cambridge, MA: Harvard University Press, 1985), 24.

14. James, *Varieties*, 303.

15. James, *Varieties*, 337.

16. See William A. Richards, *Sacred Knowledge: Psychedelics and Religious Experiences* (New York: Columbia University Press, 2016).

17. As Chris Kilham says so well: "One simple rule to go by is to beware of any visions that impel you to make broad, sweeping, or dramatic life changes very quickly." Chris Kilham, *The Ayahuasca Test Pilots Handbook: The Essential Guide to Ayahuasca Journeying* (Berkeley, CA: Evolver Editions, 2014), 298.

18. For insightful discussions of the empowered imagination and imaginal worlds, see Henry Corbin, *Spiritual Body and Celestial Earth: From Mazdean Iran to Shi'ite Iran* (Princeton, NJ: Princeton University Press, 1989); Henry Corbin, *Creative Imagination in the Sufism of Ibn Arabi* (Princeton, NJ: Princeton University Press, 2014); Tom Cheetham, *Imaginal Love: The Meanings of Imagination in Henry Corbin and James Hillman* (Thompson, CT: Spring, 2020).

19. For the sake of readability, I have changed James's Victorian "luminousness" to "luminosity." See James, *Varieties*, 23.

20. James, *Varieties*, 24.

21. James, *Varieties*, 335.

22. James, *Varieties*, 338.

23. James, *Varieties*, 338.

24. James, *Varieties*, 308.

25. See Steven T. Katz, ed., *Mysticism and Philosophical Analysis* (New York: Oxford University Press, 1978); Steven T. Katz, ed., *Mysticism and Religious Traditions* (New York: Oxford University Press, 1984); Robert K. C. Forman, *The Problem of Pure Consciousness: Mysticism and Philosophy* (New York: Oxford University Press, 1997).

26. See Boshan, *Great Doubt: Practicing Zen in the World*, trans. Jeff Shore (Boston: Wisdom Publications, 2016).

27. Jonathan M. Goldman, *Gift of the Body: A Multi-dimensional Guide to Energy Anatomy, Grounded Spirituality and Living Through the Heart* (Bend, OR: Essential Light Institute), 383–389.

28. Titti Kristina Schmidt, *Morality as Practice: The Santo Daime, an Eco-Religious Movement in the Amazonian Rainforest* (Uppsala, Sweden: Department of Cultural Anthropology and Ethnology, Uppsala Universitet), 128.

29. Schmidt, *Morality*, 65.

30. Schmidt, *Morality*, 65.

8. MEDIUMSHIP IN THE SANTO DAIME

1. This account of the Mesa Branca is actually a fusion of a Mesa Branca work that I attended in Mapiá and a St. Michael's work that I attended several years later in the United States—a work that I previously described in the Reality Sandwich website. See G. William Barnard, "Multiple (and Subtle) Bodies: Entheogenic Incorporation in the Santo Daime Tradition: Part 1," Reality Sandwich, October 15, 2018, http://realitysandwich.com/323341/multiple-and-subtle-bodies -entheogenic-incorporation-in-the-santo-daime-tradition-part-1; G. William Barnard, "Multiple (and Subtle) Bodies: Entheogenic Incorporation in the Santo Daime Tradition: Part 2," Reality Sandwich, October 20, 2018, http://realitysandwich.com/323360/multiple-and-subtle-bodies -entheogenic-incorporation-in-the-santo-daime-tradition-part-2. I decided to combine these two descriptions in order to give the fullest, most detailed description possible of this quality of mediumistic work, even though these two works have different historical origins and subtly different purposes.

2. Paulo Moreira and Edward MacRae, *Eu Venho de Longe: Mestre Irineu e Seus Companheiros* (Salvador, Bahia: EDUFA-UFMA-ABESUP, 2011), 131.

3. Lúcio Mortimer, *Bençã Padrinho* (São Paulo, Brazil: Céu de Maria, 2000), 28.

4. The introduction of Umbanda into the Santo Daime tradition and the creation of Umbandaime as one option within the Santo Daime repertoire is an important, albeit complicated, story. I describe at least some of the highlights of this process in "The Historical Development of the Santo Daime: Section Two—The Life and Work of Padrinho Sebastião," www.liquidlightbook.com/padrinho.

See also Antonio Alves Marques Jr., "The Incorporation of Umbanda by Santo Daime," English trans. Daniel Thornton, www.neip.info/novo/wpcontent/uploads/2015/04/marques_daime _umbanda_english.pdf.

5. See Douglas R. Brooks et al., *Meditation Revolution: A History and Theology of the Siddha Yoga Lineage* (New Delhi: Muktabodha Indological Research Institute, 1997).

6. Mudras have a long history not only in classical Indian dance, but also in yoga and Hindu and Buddhist tantric traditions, where the gestures are thought to affect the flow of prana, the life-force, through the body/mind of the practitioner. See Cain Carroll and Revital Carroll, *Mudras of India: A Comprehensive Guide to the Hand Gestures of Yoga and Indian Dance* (London: Jessica Kingsley /Singing Dragon, 2013).

7. See for instance Wilhelm Reich, *Character Analysis* (New York: Noonday Press, 1945); Alexander Lowen, *Bioenergetics: The Revolutionary Therapy That Uses the Language of the Body to Heal the Problems of the Mind* (New York: Penguin, 1975).

8. Alex Polari De Alverga, *The Religion of Ayahuasca: The Teachings of the Church of Santo Daime* (Rochester, VT: Park Street, 2010), xxiii.

9. See Titti Kristina Schmidt, *Morality as Practice: The Santo Daime, an Eco-Religious Movement in the Amazonian Rainforest* (Uppsala, Sweden: Department of Cultural Anthropology and Ethnology, Uppsala Universitet, 2007), 131–141.

10. See Gregory Shaw, *Theurgy and the Soul: The Neoplatonism of Iamblichus* (New York: Angelico/ Sophia Perennis, 2014).

11. Galatians 2:20, RSV.

12. For a detailed examination of the issues pertaining to the nature of consciousness, see Edward F. Kelly et al., *Irreducible Mind: Toward a Psychology for the 21st Century* (Lanham, MD: Rowman and Littlefield, 2009); Edward F. Kelly, Adam Crabtree, and Paul Marshall, eds., *Beyond Physicalism: Toward a Reconciliation of Science and Spirituality* (Lanham, MD: Rowman and Littlefield, 2015); Edward F. Kelly and Paul Marshall, eds., *Consciousness Unbound: Liberating Mind from the Tyranny of Materialism* (Lanham, MD: Rowman and Littlefield, 2021); David Ray Griffin, *Unsnarling the World-Knot: Consciousness, Freedom, and the Mind-Body Problem* (Eugene, OR: Wipf and Stock, 2008).

13. For an illuminating discussion of some of the issues surrounding mediumship in a variety of religious contexts, including the Santo Daime, see Andrew Dawson, ed., *Summoning the Spirits: Possession and Invocation in Contemporary Religion* (London: Tauris/Bloomsbury, 2010).

14. For an insightful theoretical discussion of spirit possession, see I. M. Lewis, *Ecstatic Religion: An Anthropological Study of Spirit Possession and Shamanism* (London: Penguin Books, 1971). See also Mary Keller, *The Hammer and the Flute: Women, Power, and Spirit Possession* (Baltimore: Johns Hopkins University Press, 1974). For a helpful discussion of spirit possession in a contemporary Western context, see Michael F. Brown, *The Channeling Zone: American Spirituality in an Anxious Age* (Cambridge, MA: Harvard University Press, 1997).

15. Referring to these "automatisms," James notes that "incursions from beyond the transmarginal region have a peculiar power to increase conviction . . . Saints who actually see or hear their Saviour reach the acme of assurance. Motor automatisms, though rarer, are, if possible, even more convincing than sensations. The subjects here actually feel themselves played upon by powers beyond their will. The evidence is dynamic; the God or spirit moves the very organs of their body." William James, *The Varieties of Religious Experience* (Cambridge, MA: Harvard University Press, 1985), 377.

16. For more information on the various spirits of Umbanda, see Diana DeG. Brown, *Umbanda: Religion and Politics in Urban Brazil* (New York: Columbia University Press, 1994).

17. See Max Weber, *The Sociology of Religion* (Boston: Beacon, 1993).

18. See Edwin A. Abbott, *Flatland: A Romance of Many Dimensions* (New York: Warbler Classics, 2019).

19. Huston Smith, *Cleansing the Doors of Perception: The Religious Significance of Entheogenic Plants and Chemicals* (Boulder, CO: Sentient Publications, 2009), 115.

20. Smith, *Cleansing*, 115.

21. Smith, *Cleansing*, 30.

22. Polari De Alverga, *The Religion of Ayahuasca*, xxx.

23. There have been a few notable exceptions. For example, in his early groundbreaking study of DMT, Rick Strassman suggests that we "must begin by assuming that these types of experiences [i.e., encounters with seemingly autonomous nonmaterial entities] are 'possibly real.' In other words, they may indicate 'what it's like' in alternate realities. The earliest attempts at systematically investigating these contacts should determine the consistency and stability of the beings. With lessening shock at their presence, is it possible to prolong, expand, and deepen our interactions with them?" Rick Strassman, *DMT The Spirit Molecule: A Doctor's Revolutionary Research into the Biology of Near-Death and Mystical Experiences* (Rochester, VT: Park Street, 2001), 341–342. For further cutting-edge conversations regarding the possible existence of nonphysical beings contacted via psychedelics, see also David Luke and Rory Spowers, eds., *DMT Dialogues: Encounters with the Spirit Molecule* (Rochester, VT: Park Street, 2018). Luke has been at the vanguard of this discussion. See, for example David Luke, "Anomalous Psychedelic Experiences: At the Neurochemical Juncture of the Humanistic and the Parapsychological," *Journal of Humanistic Psychology* (2020), https://doi.org/10.1177/0022167820917767; David Luke, "So Long as You've Got Your Elf: Death, DMT and Disincarnate Entities," in *Daimonic Imagination: Uncanny Intelligence*, ed. A. Voss and W. Rowlandson (Cambridge: Cambridge Scholars, 2013), 282–291; David Luke, "Disincarnate Entities and Dimethyltryptamine (DMT): Psychopharmacology, Phenomenology and Ontology," *Journal of the Society for Psychical Research*, 75 (2011): 26–42; David Luke, "Disembodied Eyes Revisited: An Investigation into the Ontology of Entheogenic Entity Encounters," *Entheogen Review: The Journal of Unauthorized Research on Visionary Plants and Drugs*, 17 (2008): 1–9, 38–40.

24. See Felicitas D. Goodman, *Where the Spirits Ride the Wind: Trance Journeys and Other Ecstatic Experiences* (Bloomington: Indiana University Press, 1990); Michael Harner, *Cave and Cosmos: Shamanic Encounters with Another Reality* (Berkeley, CA: North Atlantic, 2013).

25. The scholarly literature on ayahuasca is vast, even in English. Beatriz Labate has been one of the key figures, having published many recent edited volumes on the subject. See, for example, Beatriz Caiuby Labate and Edward MacRae, eds., *Ayahuasca, Ritual and Religion in Brazil* (London: Equinox, 2010); Beatriz Caiuby Labate and Henrik Jungaberle, eds., *The Internationalization of Ayahuasca* (Berlin: Lit Verlag, 2011); Beatriz Caiuby Labate and Clancey Cavnar, eds., *Ayahuasca Shamanism in the Amazon and Beyond* (New York: Oxford University Press, 2014); Beatriz Caiuby Labate, Clancy Cavnar, and Alex K. Gearin, eds., *The World Ayahusaca Diaspora: Reinventions and Controversies* (New York: Routledge, 2017).

26. To my mind, the single best text on the subject of the use of ayahuasca as a weapon against one's enemies is Stephan V. Beyer, *Singing to the Plants: A Guide to Mestizo Shamanism in the Upper Amazon* (Albuquerque: University of New Mexico Press, 2009). See also Philipe Descola, *The Spears of Twilight: Life and Death in the Amazon Jungle* (New York: New Press, 1993); John Perkins and Shakaim Mariano Shakai Ijisam Chumpi, *Spirit of the Shuar: Wisdom from the Last Unconquered People of the Amazon* (Rochester, VT: Destiny, 2001); Michael J. Harner, ed., *Hallucinogens and Shamanism* (New York: Oxford University Press, 1973).

27. See Michael T. Taussig, *Shamanism, Colonialism, and the Wild Man: A Study in Terror and Healing* (Chicago: University of Chicago Press, 1987); Luis Eduardo Luna, *Vegetalismo: Shamanism Among the Mestizo Population of the Peruvian Amazon* (Stockholm: Almqvist and Wiksell International, 1986).

28. See, for example, C. G. Jung, *The Archetypes and the Collective Unconscious* (Princeton, NJ: Princeton University Press, 1959); Peter Homans, *Jung in Context: Modernity and the Making of a Psychology* (Chicago: University of Chicago Press, 1979); Jay R. Greenberg and Stephen A. Mitchell, *Object Relations in Psychoanalytic Theory* (Cambridge, MA: Harvard University Press, 1983); James W. Jones, *Contemporary Psychoanalysis and Religion: Transference and Transcendence* (New Haven, CT: Yale University Press, 1991).

29. For a discussion of James's exploration of the "compounding of consciousness," see G. William Barnard, *Exploring Unseen Worlds: William James and the Philosophy of Mysticism* (Albany: State University of New York Press, 1997), 196–203; as well as James's own ruminations on the subject in William James, *A Pluralistic Universe* (Cambridge, MA: Harvard University Press, 1977), 83–135.

30. For a detailed discussion of the "musicality" of consciousness, see G. William Barnard, *Living Consciousness: The Metaphysical Vision of Henri Bergson* (Albany: State University of New York Press, 2011), 88–101.

31. For a discussion of icaros and their link to spirits, see Beyer, *Singing to the Plants*, 63–76. See also Christina Callicot, "Interspecies Communication in the Western Amazon: Music as a Form of Conversation Between Plants and People," *European Journal of Ecopsychology*, 4 (2013): 32–43.

32. For a clear and helpful discussion of Padrinho Sebastião's notion of the need to become the "master of the house" during mediumship, see Titti Kristina Schmidt, *Morality as Practice: The Santo Daime, an Eco-Religious Movement in the Amazonian Rainforest* (Uppsala, Sweden: Department of Cultural Anthropology and Ethnology, Uppsala Universitet, 2007), 137–138.

33. Schmidt, *Morality as Practice*, 140.

34. Many thanks to José Sulla for sharing his thoughts with me on the complex and challenging issues regarding incorporation mediumship in the Santo Daime. For a lucid discussion of healing and mediumship in the Santo Daime religious tradition, see P. Joseph Sulla III, "The System of Healing Used in the Santo Daime Community of Céu do Mapiá" (Master's thesis, Saybrook Graduate School and Research Center, 2005, http://www.neip.info).

35. Regarding the Portuguese translation of "dominar," I wouldn't be surprised if many English-speaking daimistas have been puzzled when they read the translation of Padrinho Alfredo's thirteenth hymn in *Nova Dimensão*, which says, "Gazing at the moon, at the moonlight, dominating in harmony." A better translation, in my opinion, would be "ruling in harmony."

36. Many thanks to "C.C" and "T.R.," two Santo Daime brothers for sharing their thoughts with me on how to deal with contracted, negative energies most effectively in the context of a mediumistic work in the Santo Daime.

37. See Garma C. C. Chang, trans., *The Hundred Thousand Songs of Milarepa*, vol. 1 (Boulder, CO: Shambhala, 1962). I am also struck by how similar Padrinho Sebastião's work with Tranca Rua was to the way in which Milarepa worked with demons. For a more detailed discussion of this issue, see "The Historical Development of the Santo Daime: Section Two—The Life and Work of Padrinho Sebastião," www.liquidlightbook.com/padrinho.

38. The term "spiritual bypass" refers to the commonly found tendency of individuals who are practicing various spiritual disciplines such as yoga or meditation to attempt to "rise above" their "lower" unresolved psychological tendencies, believing on some level that these often quite problematic tendencies within them will be automatically transformed simply by more spiritual practice, instead of consciously addressing and integrating this material within themselves with clarity and compassion. See, for example, Robert Augustus Master, *Spiritual Bypassing: When Spirituality Disconnects Us from What Really Matters* (Berkeley, CA: North Atlantic, 2010).

39. See Baba Ifa Karade, *The Handbook of Yoruba Religious Concepts* (York Beach, NY: Weiser, 1994).

9. THE HOLY HOUSE IN CÉU DO MAPIÁ— ROSARY WORKS

1. For a vivid and accessible depiction of the beliefs and practices of Umbanda, see Lindsay Hale, *Hearing the Mermaid's Song: The Umbanda Religion in Rio de Janeiro* (Albuquerque: University of New Mexico Press, 2009).

2. For a description of the union of Shiva and Shakti in the divine Heart of each person, see Paul Eduardo Muller-Ortega, *The Triadic Heart of Śiva: Kaula Tantricism of Abhinavagupta in the Non-dual Shaivism of Kashmir* (Albany: State University of New York Press, 1989).

3. As Christopher Wallis points out, "mudra means not just 'hand gesture' but any posture of the hands, body, or awareness that arises spontaneously in profound meditation or mystical experience . . . a mudra is a sign of awakened consciousness." Christopher D. Wallis, *Tantra Illuminated: The Philosophy, History, and Practice of a Timeless Tradition* (Boulder, CO: Mattamayūra, 2012), 404.

4. See Ida P. Rolf, *Rolfing and Physical Reality* (Rochester, VT: Inner Traditions, 1990).

5. For a detailed description of the Kundalini, see Swami Muktananda, *Play of Consciousness: A Spiritual Autobiography* (Chicago: IPG/Siddha Yoga, 2000).

6. See, for example, Bernard McGinn, ed., *Meister Eckhart: Teacher and Preacher* (New York: Paulist Press, 1986.)

7. See, for example, Lama Yeshe, *Introduction to Tantra: The Transformation of Desire* (Somerville, MA: Wisdom, 2001), 117–130.

11. POST-MAPIÁ PONDERINGS: DIVINIZATION

1. Clement of Alexandria, Sir James Donaldson et al, eds., *Exhortation to the Heathen* (Scotts Valley, CA: Create Space Publishing Platform, 2015), chap. 1.

2. Athanasius, Saint, V. Rev. Dr. John Behr, ed., *On the Incarnation* (Yonkers, NY: St. Vladimirs Seminary Press, 2012), sect. 54.

3. Another biblical verse that is also cited in support of the doctrine of divinization is Psalm 82:6: "You are gods, sons of the Most High" (RSV).

4. For more on divinization within a Christian framework, see Michael J. Christensen, *Partakers of the Divine Nature: The History and Development of Deification in the Christian Traditions* (Ada, MI: Baker Academic, 2008).

Bibliography

Abbott, Edwin A. *Flatland: A Romance of Many Dimensions*. New York: Warbler Classics, 2019.

Athanasius, Saint. V. Rev. Dr. John Behr, ed. *On the Incarnation*. Yonkers, NY: St. Vladimirs Seminary Press, 2012.

Bache, Christopher M. *Dark Night, Early Dawn: Steps to a Deep Ecology of Mind*. Albany: State University of New York Press, 2000.

——. *LSD and the Mind of the Universe: Diamonds from Heaven*. Rochester, VT: Park Street, 2019.

Barnard, G. William. "Entheogen-based Religions and Spirituality." In *Religion: Mental Religions*, ed. Niki Kasumi Clements, 339–354. Farmington Hills, MI: MacMillan Reference USA, 2016.

——. "Entheogens in a Religious Context: The Case of the Santo Daime Religious Tradition." *Zygon* 49, no. 3 (2014): 666–684.

——. *Exploring Unseen Worlds: William James and the Philosophy of Mysticism*. Albany: State University of New York Press, 1997.

——. *Living Consciousness: The Metaphysical Vision of Henri Bergson*. Albany: State University of New York Press, 2011.

——. "Multiple (and Subtle) Bodies: Entheogenic Incorporation in the Santo Daime Tradition: Part 1." Reality Sandwich, October 15, 2018. http://realitysandwich.com/323341/multiple-and-subtle-bodies -entheogenic-incorporation-in-the-santo-daime-tradition-part-1.

——. "Multiple (and Subtle) Bodies: Entheogenic Incorporation in the Santo Daime Tradition: Part 2." Reality Sandwich, October 20, 2018. http://realitysandwich.com/323360/multiple-and-subtle-bodies -entheogenic-incorporation-in-the-santo-daime-tradition-part-2.

Beck, Guy L. *Sonic Theology: Hinduism and Sacred Sound*. Columbia: University of South Carolina Press, 1993.

Beer, Francis. *Julian of Norwich—Revelations—Motherhood of God*. Cambridge: Boydell and Brewer, 1998.

Bergson, Henri. *The Creative Mind*. New York: Philosophical Library, 1946.

——. *Matter and Memory*. New York: Zone, 1988.

——. *Mind-Energy: Lectures and Essays*. New York: Henry Holt, 1920.

Beyer, Stephan V. *Singing to the Plants: A Guide to Mestizo Shamanism in the Upper Amazon*. Albuquerque: University of New Mexico Press, 2009.

Biernacki, Loriliai and Philip Clayton. *Panentheism Across the World's Traditions*. New York: Oxford University Press, 2013.

Blainey, Marc G. *Christ Returns from the Jungle: Ayahuasca Religion as Mystical Healing*. Albany: State University of New York Press, 2021.

Bogenschutz, Michael P., Alyssa A. Forcehimes, Jessica A. Pommy, Claire E. Wilcox, P. C. R. Barbosa, and Rick J. Strassman. "Psilocybin-assisted Treatment for Alcohol Dependence: A Proof-of-Concept Study." *Journal of Psychopharmacology* 29, no. 3, (2015): 289–299.

Boshan. *Great Doubt: Practicing Zen in the World*, trans. Jeff Shore. Boston: Wisdom, 2016.

Bragdon, Emma. *Kardec's Spiritism: A Home for Healing and Spiritual Evolution*. Woodstock, VT: Lightening Up, 2004.

Bronfman, Jeffrey. "The Legal Case of the União do Vegetal vs The Government of the United States." In *The Internationalization of Ayahuasca*, eds. Beatriz Caiuby Labate and Henrik Jungaberle, 287–300. Berlin: Lit Verlag, 2011.

Brooks, Douglas R., Swami Durgananda, Paul E. Muller-Ortega, William K. Mahony, Constantina Rhodes Bailly, and S. P. Sabharathnam. *Meditation Revolution: A History and Theology of the Siddha Yoga Lineage*. New Delhi: Muktabodha Indological Research Institute, 1997.

Brown, David H. *Santería Enthroned: Art, Ritual, and Innovation in an Afro-Cuban Religion*. Chicago: University of Chicago Press, 2003.

Brown, Diana DeG. *Umbanda: Religion and Politics in Urban Brazil*. New York: Columbia University Press, 1994.

Brown, Michael F. *The Channeling Zone: American Spirituality in an Anxious Age*. Cambridge, MA: Harvard University Press, 1997.

Callicot, Christina. "Interspecies Communication in the Western Amazon: Music as a Form of Conversation Between Plants and People." *European Journal of Ecopsychology*, 4 (2013): 32–43.

Carhart-Harris, Robin L., Mark Bolstridge, James Rucker, et al. "Psilocybin with Psychological Support for Treatment-resistant Depression: An Open-Label Feasibility Study." *Lancet Psychiatry* 3, no. 7 (2016): 619–627.

Carroll, Cain, and Revital Carroll. *Mudras of India: A Comprehensive Guide to the Hand Gestures of Yoga and Indian Dance*. London: Jessica Kingsley/Singing Dragon, 2013.

Cemin, Arneide. "The Rituals of Santo Daime: 'Systems of Symbolic Constructions.'" In *Fieldwork in Religion*, ed. Beatriz Caiuby Labate and Edward MacRae, 256–285. London: Equinox, 2006.

Chalmers, David. "The Puzzle of Conscious Experience." *Scientific American*, December 1995, 63.

Chang, Garma C. C., trans. *The Hundred Thousand Songs of Milarepa*. Vol. 1. Boulder, CO: Shambhala, 1962.

Cheetham, Tom. *Imaginal Love: The Meanings of Imagination in Henry Corbin and James Hillman*. Thompson, CT: Spring, 2020.

Christensen, Michael J. *Partakers of the Divine Nature: The History and Development of Deification in the Christian Traditions*. Ada, MI: Baker Academic, 2008.

Churchland, Paul M. *Scientific Realism and the Plasticity of Mind*. Cambridge: Cambridge University Press, 1979.

Clayton, Philip, and Arthur Peacocke. *In Whom We Live and Move and Have Our Being: Panentheistic Reflections on God's Being in a Scientific World*. Grand Rapids, MI: Eerdmans, 2004.

Clement of Alexandria. Sir James Donaldson, Arthur Cleveland Coxe, eds. *Exhortation to the Heathen*. Scotts Valley, CA: Create Space Publishing Platform, 2015.

Cook, Francis. *Hua-Yen Buddhism: The Jewel Net of Indra*. University Park: Penn State Press, 1977.

Cooper, John W. *Panentheism: The Other God of the Philosophers, from Plato to the Present*. Grand Rapids, MI: Baker Academic, 2006.

Corbin, Henry. *Creative Imagination in the Sufism of Ibn Arabi*. Princeton, NJ: Princeton University Press, 2014.

——. *Spiritual Body and Celestial Earth: From Mazdean Iran to Shi'ite Iran*. Princeton, NJ: Princeton University Press, 1989.

Couto, Fernando da La Rocque. "*Santos e Xamãs*." Dissertation, Universidade de Brasília, 1989.

Cyril of Alexandria. *On the Unity of Christ*. Crestwood, NY: St. Vladimir's Seminary Press, 1995.

Dawson, Andrew. *New Era—New Religions: Religious Transformation in Contemporary Brazil.* Burlington, VT: Ashgate, 2007.

——. "Positionality and Role-Identity in a New Religious Context: Participant Observation at Céu do Mapiá." *Religion,* 40, no. 3, (2010): 173–181.

——. *Santo Daime: A New World Religion.* London: Bloomsbury, 2013.

——, ed. *Summoning the Spirits: Possession and Invocation in Contemporary Religion.* London: Tauris/Bloomsbury, 2010.

Descola, Philipe. *The Spears of Twilight: Life and Death in the Amazon Jungle.* New York: New Press, 1993.

Dyck, Erika. *Psychedelic Psychiatry: LSD from Clinic to Campus.* Baltimore: Johns Hopkins University Press, 2008.

Dyczkowski, Mark S. G. *The Doctrine of Vibration: An Analysis of the Doctrines and Practices of Kashmir Shaivism.* Albany: State University of New York Press, 1987.

Easwaran, Eknath, trans. *The Bhagavad Gita.* Tomales, CA: Nilgiri, 1985.

Eliade, Mircea. *Shamanism: Archaic Techniques of Ecstasy.* Princeton, NJ: Princeton University Press, 2004.

——. *The Myth of the Eternal Return: Cosmos and History.* Princeton, NJ: Princeton University Press, 2018.

——. *The Sacred and the Profane: The Nature of Religion.* New York: Harcourt Brace Jovanovich, 1987.

Ferrer, Jorge N. *Revisioning Transpersonal Theory: A Participatory Vision of Human Spirituality.* Albany: State University of New York Press, 2002.

Ferrer, Jorge N., and Jacob H. Sherman, eds. *The Participatory Turn: Spirituality, Mysticism, Religious Studies.* Albany: State University of New York Press, 2009.

Flinders, Carol Lee. *Enduring Grace: Living Portraits of Seven Women Mystics.* New York: HarperSanFrancisco, 1993.

Forman, Robert K. C. *The Problem of Pure Consciousness: Mysticism and Philosophy.* New York: Oxford University Press, 1997.

Franklin, George. *Some Segments of a River: On Poetry, Mysticism, and the Imagination.* Sebastopol, CA: Nicasio, 2019.

Fróes, Vera. *Santo Daime Cultura Amazônica: História do Povo Juramidam.* Manaus, Brazil: Suframa, 1986.

Fuller, Robert C. *Stairways to Heaven: Drugs in American Religious History.* Boulder, CO: Westview, 2000.

Gasser, Peter, Katharina Kirchner, and Torsten Passie. "LSD-assisted Psychotherapy for Anxiety Associated with a Life-threatening Disease: A Qualitative Study of Acute and Sustained Subjective Effects." *Journal of Psychopharmacology* 29, no. 1 (2015): 57–68.

Girijananda, Swami. *Tonglen for Our Own Suffering: 7 Variations on an Ancient Practice.* Portland, OR: Rudra, 2015.

Goldman, Jonathan M. *Gift of the Body: A Multi-dimensional Guide to Energy Anatomy, Grounded Spirituality and Living Through the Heart.* Bend, OR: Essential Light Institute.

Goldsmith, Neal M. *Psychedelic Healing: The Promise of Entheogens for Psychotherapy and Spiritual Development.* Rochester, VT: Healing Arts Press, 2011.

Gonzalvo, Roman, ed. "Holotropic Breathwork and Other Hyperventilation Procedures." Special issue, *Journal of Transpersonal Research* 6, no. 2 (2014).

Goodman, Felicitas D. *Where the Spirits Ride the Wind: Trance Journeys and Other Ecstatic Experiences.* Bloomington: Indiana University Press, 1990.

Greenberg, Jay R., and Stephen A. Mitchell, *Object Relations in Psychoanalytic Theory.* Cambridge, MA: Harvard University Press, 1983.

Griffin, David Ray. *Unsnarling the World-Knot: Consciousness, Freedom, and the Mind-Body Problem.* Eugene, OR: Wifp and Stock, 2008.

Griffiths, R. R., W. A. Richards, U. McCann, and R. Jesse. "Psilocybin Can Occasion Mystical-type Experiences Having Substantial and Sustained Personal Meaning and Spiritual Significance." *Psychopharmacology* 187, no. 3 (2006): 268–283.

Grob, Charles S., and Gary Bravo. "The High Road: History and Hysteria." In *Higher Wisdom: Eminent Elders Explore the Continuing Impact of Psychedelics*, ed. Roger Walsh and Charles S. Grob, 7–18. Albany: State University of New York Press, 2005.

Grof, Stanislav. *The Cosmic Game: Explorations of the Frontiers of Human Consciousness*. Albany: State University of New York, 1998.

——. *LSD Psychotherapy*. Pomona, CA: Hunter House, 1980.

——. *When the Impossible Happens: Adventures in Non-ordinary Realities*. Boulder, CO: Sounds True, 2006.

Hale, Lindsay. *Hearing the Mermaid's Song: The Umbanda Religion in Rio de Janeiro*. Albuquerque: University of New Mexico Press, 2009.

Harner, Michael. *Cave and Cosmos: Shamanic Encounters with Another Reality*. Berkeley, CA: North Atlantic, 2013.

Harner, Michael J., ed. *Hallucinogens and Shamanism*. New York: Oxford University Press, 1973.

Harris, Rachel. *Listening to Ayahuasca: New Hope for Depression, Addiction, PTSD, and Anxiety*. Novato, CA: New World Library, 2017.

Hess, David J. *Samba in the Night: Spiritism in Brazil*. New York: Columbia University Press, 1994.

Highpine, Gayle. "Unraveling the Mystery of the Origin of Ayahuasca," NEIP, 2012. http://www.neip.info/html/objects/_downloadblob.php?cod_blob=1184.

Homans, Peter. *Jung in Context: Modernity and the Making of a Psychology*. Chicago: University of Chicago Press, 1979.

Huxley, Aldous. *The Doors of Perception and Heaven and Hell*. New York: HarperCollins, 2004.

——. *The Perennial Philosophy*. New York: Harper Perennial, 1990.

James, William. *Essays in Philosophy*. Cambridge, MA: Harvard University Press, 1978.

——. *Essays in Psychical Research*. Cambridge, MA: Harvard University Press, 1986.

——. *Essays in Religion and Morality*. Cambridge, MA: Harvard University Press, 1982.

——. "Great Men and Their Environments." In *The Will to Believe and Other Essays in Popular Philosophy*, 163–89. Cambridge, MA: Harvard University Press, 1979.

——. *A Pluralistic Universe*. Cambridge, MA: Harvard University Press, 1977.

——. *The Principles of Psychology*. 3 vols. Cambridge, MA: Harvard University Press, 1981.

——. *The Varieties of Religious Experience*. Cambridge, MA: Harvard University Press, 1985.

Jones, James W. *Contemporary Psychoanalysis and Religion: Transference and Transcendence*. New Haven, CT: Yale University Press, 1991.

Jung, C. G. *The Archetypes and the Collective Unconscious*. Princeton, NJ: Princeton University Press, 1959.

Kapleau Roshi, Philip. *The Three Pillars of Zen: Teaching, Practice, and Enlightenment*. New York: Anchor, 1989.

Karade, Baba Ifa. *The Handbook of Yoruba Religious Concepts*. York Beach, NY: Weiser, 1994.

Kardec, Allan. *The Book of Mediums: Guide for Mediums and Invocations*. New York: Cosimo Classics, 2007.

——. *Introduction to the Spiritist Philosophy*. Philadelphia: Allan Kardec Educational Society, 2004.

——. *The Spirits' Book*. New York: Cosimo Classics, 2006.

Katz, Steven T., ed. *Mysticism and Philosophical Analysis*. New York: Oxford University Press, 1978.

——, ed. *Mysticism and Religious Traditions*. New York: Oxford University Press, 1984.

Keller, Mary. *The Hammer and the Flute: Women, Power, and Spirit Possession*. Baltimore: Johns Hopkins University Press, 1974.

Kelly, Edward F., Adam Crabtree, and Paul Marshall, eds. *Beyond Physicalism: Toward a Reconciliation of Science and Spirituality*. Lanham, MD: Rowman and Littlefield, 2015.

Kelly, Edward F., and Paul Marshall, eds. *Consciousness Unbound: Liberating Mind from the Tyranny of Materialism*. Lanham, MD: Rowman and Littlefield, 2021.

Kelly, Edward F., Emily Williams Kelly, Adam Crabtree, Alan Gauld, Michael Grosso, and Bruce Greyson. *Irreducible Mind: Toward a Psychology for the 21st Century*. Lanham, MD: Rowman and Littlefield, 2009.

Kilham, Chris. *The Ayahuasca Test Pilots Handbook: The Essential Guide to Ayahuasca Journeying*. Berkeley, CA: Evolver Editions, 2014.

Kripal, Jeffrey J. *Authors of the Impossible: The Paranormal and the Sacred*. Chicago: University of Chicago Press, 2011.

——. "The Future of the Human(ities): Mystical Literature, Paranormal Phenomena, and the Contemporary Politics of Knowledge." In *Consciousness Unbound: Liberating Mind from the Tyranny of Materialism*, ed. Edward F. Kelly and Paul Marshall, 359–405. Lanham, MD: Rowman and Littlefield, 2021.

——. *Mutants and Mystics: Science Fiction, Superhero Comics, and the Paranormal*. Chicago: University of Chicago Press, 2011.

Labate, Beatriz Caiuby, and Clancey Cavnar, eds. *Ayahuasca Shamanism in the Amazon and Beyond*. New York: Oxford University Press, 2014.

Labate, Beatriz Caiuby, Clancy Cavnar, and Alex K. Gearin, eds. *The World Ayahusaca Diaspora: Reinventions and Controversies*. New York: Routledge, 2017.

Labate, Beatriz Caiuby, and Henrik Jungaberle, eds. *The Internationalization of Ayahuasca*. Berlin: Lit Verlag, 2011.

Labate, Beatriz Caiuby, and Edward MacRae, eds. *Ayahuasca, Ritual and Religion in Brazil*. London: Equinox, 2010.

Labate, Beatriz Caiuby, Edward MacRae, and Sandra Lucia Goulart. "Brazilian Ayahuasca Religions in Perspective." In *Ayahuasca, Ritual and Religion in Brazil*, ed. Beatriz Caiuby Labate and Edward MacRae, 1–20. London: Equinox, 2010.

Labate, Beatriz Caiuby, and Gustavo Pacheco. "The Historical Origins of the Santo Daime: Academics, Adepts, and Ideology." In *The Internationalization of Ayahuasca*, ed. Beatriz Caiuby Labate and Henrik Jungaberle, 71–84. Berlin: Lit Verlag, 2011.

——, eds. *Opening the Portals of Heaven: Brazilian Ayahuasca Music*. New Brunswick, NJ: Transaction, 2009.

Lakshman Jee, Swami. *Kashmir Shaivism: The Secret Supreme*. Delhi: Sri Satguru, 1988.

Lewis, I. M. *Ecstatic Religion: An Anthropological Study of Spirit Possession and Shamanism*. London: Penguin, 1971.

Lings, Martin, and Clinton Minnaar. *The Underlying Religion: An Introduction to the Perennial Philosophy*. Bloomington, IN: World Wisdom, 2007.

Lowen, Alexander. *Bioenergetics: The Revolutionary Therapy That Uses the Language of the Body to Heal the Problems of the Mind*. New York: Penguin, 1975.

Luke, David. "Anomalous Psychedelic Experiences: At the Neurochemical Juncture of the Humanistic and the Parapsychological." *Journal of Humanistic Psychology* (2020), https://doi.org/10.1177/0022167820917767.

——. "Disembodied Eyes Revisited: An Investigation Into the Ontology of Entheogenic Entity Encounters." *Entheogen Review: The Journal of Unauthorized Research on Visionary Plants and Drugs*, 17 (2008): 1–9, 38–40.

——. "Disincarnate Entities and Dimethyltryptamine (DMT): Psychopharmacology, Phenomenology and Ontology." *Journal of the Society for Psychical Research*, 75 (2011): 26–42.

——. *Otherworlds: Psychedelics and Exceptional Human Experience*. London: Muswell Hill, 2017.

——. "So Long as You've Got Your Elf: Death, DMT and Disincarnate Entities." In *Daimonic Imagination: Uncanny Intelligence*, ed. Angela Voss and William Rowlandson, 282–291. Cambridge: Cambridge Scholars Publishing, 2013.

Luke, David, and Rory Spowers, eds. *DMT Dialogues: Encounters with the Spirit Molecule*. Rochester, VT: Park Street, 2018.

Luna, Luis Eduardo. *Vegetalismo: Shamanism Among the Mestizo Population of the Peruvian Amazon*. Stockholm: Almqvist and Wiksell International, 1986.

Luna, Luis Eduardo, and Steven F. White, eds. *Ayahuasca Reader: Encounters with the Amazon's Sacred Vine.* Santa Fe, NM: Synergetic Press, 2000.

MacRae, Edward. *Guided by the Moon: Shamanism and the Ritual Use of Ayahuasca in the Santo Daime Religion in Brazil.* NEIP, 1992. http://www.neip.info/downloads/t_edw2.pdf.

Marques Jr., Antonio Alves. "The Incorporation of Umbanda by Santo Daime," English trans. Daniel Thornton. www.neip.info/novo/wp-content/uploads/2015/04/marques_daime_umbanda_english.pdf.

Master, Robert Augustus. *Spiritual Bypassing: When Spirituality Disconnects Us from What Really Matters.* Berkeley, CA: North Atlantic, 2010.

Masters, Robert E. L., and Jean Houston. *The Varieties of Psychedelic Experience.* New York: Dell, 1966.

McGinn, Bernard., ed. *Meister Eckhart: Teacher and Preacher.* New York: Paulist Press, 1986.

McKenna, Dennis J. "Ayahuasca: An Ethnopharmacologic History." In *Ayahuasca: Sacred Vine of Spirits,* ed. Ralph Metzner, 40–62. Rochester, VT: Park Street, 1999.

Metzner, Ralph, ed. *Ayahuasca: Sacred Vine of Spirits.* Rochester, VT: Park Street, 1999.

Moreira, Paulo, and Edward MacRae. *Eu Venho de Longe: Mestre Irineu e Seus Companheiros.* Salvador, Bahia: EDUFA-UFMA-ABESUP, 2011.

Mortimer, Lúcio. *Bençã Padrinho.* São Paulo, Brazil: Céu de Maria, 2000.

——. *Nosso Senhor Aparecido Na Floresta.* São Paulo, Brazil: Céu de Maria, 2001.

Muktananda, Swami. *Play of Consciousness: A Spiritual Autobiography.* Chicago: IPG/Siddha Yoga, 2000.

Muller-Ortega, Paul Eduardo. *The Triadic Heart of Śiva: Kaula Tantricism of Abhinavagupta in the Non-dual Shaivism of Kashmir.* Albany: State University of New York Press, 1989.

Muraresku, Brian C. *The Immortality Key: The Secret History of the Religion with No Name.* New York: St. Martin's, 2020.

Myer, Matthew. " 'In the Master's House': History, Discourse, and Ritual in Acre, Brazil." Ph.D. diss, University of Virginia, 2014. http://libra.virginia.edu/catalog/libra-oa:6576

Myerhoff, Barbara G. *Peyote Hunt: The Sacred Journey of the Huichol Indians.* Ithaca, NY: Cornell University Press, 1974.

Patte, Daniel, ed. *The Cambridge Dictionary of Christianity.* New York: Cambridge University Press, 2010.

Perkins, John, and Shakaim Mariano Shakai Ijisam Chumpi. *Spirit of the Shuar: Wisdom from the Last Unconquered People of the Amazon.* Rochester, VT: Destiny, 2001.

Pinchbeck, Daniel. *Breaking Open the Head: A Psychedelic Journey Into the Heart of Contemporary Shamanism.* New York: Broadway, 2003.

Polari De Alverga, Alex. *The Religion of Ayahuasca: The Teachings of the Church of Santo Daime.* Rochester, VT: Park Street, 2010.

Pollan, Michael. *How to Change Your Mind: What the New Science of Psychedelics Teaches Us About Consciousness, Dying, Addiction, Depression, and Transcendence.* New York: Penguin, 2018.

Reich, Wilhelm. *Character Analysis.* New York: Noonday, 1945.

Richards, William A. *Sacred Knowledge: Psychedelics and Religious Experiences.* New York: Columbia University Press, 2016.

Rinpoche, Sogyal. *The Tibetan Book of Living and Dying.* New York: HarperSanFrancisco, 1993.

——. *The Tibetan Book of Living and Dying.* San Francisco: HarperSanFrancisco, 2020.

Rolf, Ida P. *Rolfing and Physical Reality.* Rochester, VT: Inner Traditions, 1990.

Schmidt, Titti Kristina. *Morality as Practice: The Santo Daime, an Eco-Religious Movement in the Amazonian Rainforest.* Uppsala, Sweden: Department of Cultural Anthropology and Ethnology, Uppsala Universitet, 2007.

Shanon, Benny. *The Antipodes of the Mind: Charting the Phenomenology of the Ayahuasca Experience.* New York: Oxford University Press, 2002.

Shaw, Gregory. *Theurgy and the Soul: The Neoplatonism of Iamblichus.* New York: Angelico/Sophia Perennis, 2014.

Shroder, Tom. *Acid Test: LSD, Ecstasy, and the Power to Heal.* New York: Blue Rider, 2014.

Singh, Jaideva. *Pratyabhijñāhrdayam*. Delhi: Motilal Banarsidass, 1977.

Smith, Huston. *Cleansing the Doors of Perception: The Religious Significance of Entheogenic Plants and Chemicals*. Boulder, CO: Sentient, 2009.

Stevens, Jay. *Storming Heaven: LSD and the American Dream*. New York: Grove, 1987.

Stoller, Paul. *In Sorcery's Shadow: A Memoir of Apprenticeship Among the Songhay of Niger*. Chicago: University of Chicago Press, 1987.

Strassman, Rick. *DMT The Spirit Molecule: A Doctor's Revolutionary Research into the Biology of Near-Death and Mystical Experiences*. Rochester, VT: Park Street, 2001.

Sulla III, P. Joseph. "The System of Healing Used in the Santo Daime Community of Céu do Mapiá." Master's thesis, Saybrook Graduate School and Research Center, 2005. http://www.neip.info.

Tafur, Joseph. *The Fellowship of the River: A Medical Doctor's Exploration Into Traditional Amazonian Plant Medicine*. Phoenix, AZ: Espiritu, 2017.

Taussig, Michael T. *Shamanism, Colonialism, and the Wild Man: A Study in Terror and Healing*. Chicago: University of Chicago Press, 1987.

Trungpa, Chögyam. *Cutting Through Spiritual Materialism*. Boulder, CO: Shambhala, 2002.

Turner, Edith. *The Hands Feel It: Healing and Spirit Possession Among a Northern Alaskan People*. DeKalb: Northern Illinois University Press, 1996.

Wafer, Jim. *The Taste of Blood: Spirit Possession in Brazilian Candomblé*. Philadelphia: University of Pennsylvania Press, 1991.

Wald, George. "Consciousness and Cosmology." In *Bergson and Modern Thought*, Andrew C. Papanicolau and Pete A. Y. Gunter. New York: Harwood Academic, 1987.

Wallis, Christopher D. *Tantra Illuminated: The Philosophy, History, and Practice of a Timeless Tradition*. Boulder, CO: Mattamayūra, 2012.

Walsh, Roger, and Charles S. Grob, eds. *Higher Wisdom: Eminent Elders Explore the Continuing Impact of Psychedelics*. Albany: State University of New York Press, 2005.

Wasson, Gordon. *Soma: The Divine Mushroom of Immortality*. New York: Harcourt Brace Jovanovich, 1969.

Weber, Max. *The Sociology of Religion*. Boston: Beacon, 1993.

Wilber, Ken. *Sex, Ecology, Spirituality: The Spirit of Evolution*. Boulder, CO: Shambhala, 2001.

——. *The Spectrum of Consciousness*. Wheaton, IL: Quest, 1993.

Yeshe, Lama. *Introduction to Tantra: The Transformation of Desire*. Somerville, MA: Wisdom, 2001.

Young, David E., and Jean-Guy Goulet. *Being Changed by Cross-Cultural Encounters: The Anthropology of Extraordinary Experiences*. Peterborough, ONT, Canada: Broadview, 1994.

Index

Page numbers in *italics* indicate illustrations.